T0335082

John Goldingay was an Anglican priest and professor in Nottingham, England, and Pasadena, California. He now lives in Oxford, where he goes to Morning Prayer in Christ Church Cathedral, writes Old Testament commentaries, eats pastries, goes for walks by the Thames and watches music videos on YouTube.
johngold@fuller.edu
www.johngoldingay.com

Tom Wright is Research Professor Emeritus of New Testament and Early Christianity at the University of St Andrews and Senior Research Fellow at Wycliffe Hall, Oxford. He is the author of more than eighty influential books, including *The New Testament for Everyone, Simply Christian, Surprised by Hope, The Day the Revolution Began, Paul: A Biography, Jesus and the Powers* (with Michael F. Bird) and *Into the Heart of Romans* (all published by SPCK).

DAILY BIBLE MEDITATIONS FOR EVERYONE

365 reflections and prayers
from Genesis to Revelation

John Goldingay and Tom Wright

First published in Great Britain in 2024

SPCK
SPCK Group
Studio 101
The Record Hall
16–16A Baldwin's Gardens
London EC1N 7RJ
www.spckpublishing.co.uk

Copyright © John Goldingay and Tom Wright 2024

John Goldingay and Tom Wright have asserted their rights under the Copyright, Designs and Patents Act, 1988, to be identified as Authors of this work.

All rights reserved. No part of this book may be reproduced or transmitted in any form or by any means, electronic or mechanical, including photocopying, recording, or by any information storage and retrieval system, without permission in writing from the publisher.

SPCK does not necessarily endorse the individual views contained in its publications.

Unless otherwise noted, Scripture quotations from the Old Testament are the author's own translation.

Quotations marked KJV are taken from the Authorized Version of the Bible (The King James Bible), the rights in which are vested in the Crown, and are reproduced by permission of the Crown's Patentee, Cambridge University Press.

Scripture quotations from the New Testament are taken from Tom Wright, *The New Testament for Everyone*, 3rd edn (London: SPCK, 2023).

British Library Cataloguing-in-Publication Data
A catalogue record for this book is available from the British Library

ISBN 978–0–281–09030–3
eBook ISBN 978–0–281–09031–0

1 3 5 7 9 10 8 6 4 2

Typeset by Manila Typesetting Company
First printed in Great Britain by TJ International

eBook by Manila Typesetting Company

Produced on paper from sustainable sources

Contents

Part 1

THE OLD TESTAMENT FOR EVERYONE

JOHN GOLDINGAY

February: From slavery to the promised land

March: The birth of Israel

April: Prophets and kings

Part 2

THE NEW TESTAMENT FOR EVERYONE
TOM WRIGHT

August: Scenes from the life of Jesus

Note to the reader

The quote on 23 March, 'All power corrupts; absolute power corrupts absolutely,' is attributed to Lord Acton, a British historian of the late nineteenth and early twentieth centuries.

The Jewish scholar mentioned on 25 May is Michael Fox, *Character and Ideology in the Book of Esther* (second edition; Grand Rapids: Eerdmans, 2001), p. 12.

Part I

THE OLD TESTAMENT FOR EVERYONE

JOHN GOLDINGAY

January

BEGINNINGS

1 In the beginning
Genesis 1

If you were God, how would you tell people about the origin of the world?

God inspired the author of Genesis to paint a picture that is a kind of parable. It says, picture God creating the world as someone doing a week's work, working for six days and then having a day off. This craftsman makes a plan for the execution of the work, spending three days over the project's framework and three days filling in the detail. So on Sunday he introduces light into the natural darkness and on Wednesday he puts the sun, moon and stars in the sky to mediate the light to the world. On Monday he separates the waters into two by means of the air, and on Thursday he creates the creatures that inhabit the (lower) waters and the air. On Tuesday he separates the land from the sea and creates things that grow there, and on Friday he creates the land creatures that will eat this produce, including the human beings who will rule the world.

God did not design Genesis 1 to tell us what a camera would have caught if it had been present to film creation. Faulting it for failing to do so misses the point, and defending it to show that it does do so also misses the point. We have no need to try to show that science is wrong and that actually the world was created in six days just a few thousand years ago. Equally, we have no need to try to conform the 'facts' of Genesis to those of science. That simply means focusing on concerns other than the ones God had in inspiring this story. Genesis 1 is a portrait, a dramatisation, a parabolic story. This fact does not imply it is not true; it means its truth is expressed in the manner of a parable.

Creation meant that God took things from formlessness to order, from gloom to brightness. God did that by speaking, and sometimes God separated things, such as light from dark and the waters above from the waters below. That meant God had introduced order into the world that people's later experience of disorder could not undo.

God, our creator, we marvel at your world and at everything in it that gives you pleasure and glory.

2 To put it another way...

Genesis 2

Genesis 1 had the broadest of horizons. It was concerned with the whole cosmos. Genesis 2 is more down to earth, and even more obviously 'just a story', but one with a further enlightening understanding of God, humanity and the world.

It begins with a bare landscape. Nothing is growing. But eventually, a farmer will be needed. The point about having human beings is revealingly expressed. Humanity is made to serve the ground, to help it grow things. Humanity and creation live in a relationship of mutual dependence.

The point is also hinted at by the way God makes the human being, scrabbling up dirt from the ground and shaping it into a body. In Genesis 1 God is the transcendent creator, often acting simply by speaking. In Genesis 2 God is more like a potter. But he doesn't stop at moulding. He bends down again and does mouth-to-mouth on the body, breathing breath into it to turn it into a living being.

In the garden there is now an orchard full of fruit trees for humanity to look after and enjoy, but also two other trees. If the human beings eat the fruit of the life tree, they will live for ever. Although they had God's breath breathed into them, this does not mean they would not die, but eating the tree's fruit would have that effect. This creation story presupposes the regular human wistfulness about death, and it suggests that death was never intended to be the end.

The other tree can convey good and bad knowledge, which is another way of describing wisdom. Like the life tree, the good-and-bad-knowledge tree is a sacramental means of God's conveying something that human beings will need. But strangely, they may not eat from it. Perhaps initially God just wants to find out whether they will do as he says.

The first human being is on his own, but Genesis doesn't say he is lonely. It does mean he couldn't fulfil the task for which he was made. Humanity is designed to share in caring for the garden. The man needs help. Until he has a partner, creation will not be 'good'. The idea of creation's 'goodness' is a motif shared with Genesis 1, but it is used in a different, complementary way.

Lord, thank you for giving us all things richly to enjoy.

3 Creation asserts itself
Genesis 3

We may see Satan behind the snake, but Genesis emphasises that the tempter is – a snake, the sharpest creature in the garden. Evidently the creatures God made were not necessarily inclined to live the kind of life God wanted. They needed humanity to exercise beneficent control over them. The snake successfully reversed the relationship of leadership between humanity and creation.

But the Old Testament often describes God as harnessing wayward acts to the fulfilment of a good purpose. This could have been the first instance: the ban on the good-and-bad-knowledge tree is a test for Adam and Eve, and the snake becomes part of the test. 'I can resist everything except temptation,' Oscar Wilde has someone saying in *Lady Windermere's Fan*. Adam and Eve don't wait to discover whether that is true of them. Genesis leaps straight from their creation to their failure. It rather implies there was no honeymoon period.

The snake makes God more restrictive and less generous than God is. Approaching Eve rather than Adam might be another expression of its shrewdness, not because of some weakness in Eve and thus in womanhood that makes her a pushover, but because Eve was not there when God told Adam about the freedom and the constraint. Perhaps the snake can con her?

So they didn't fall. They were pushed and they jumped. Their eyes do then open, but not with the result the snake promised. They don't gain anything like true wisdom. They start off as naive, simple people, but when they decline to live by the one constraint God placed on them, they become not mature and wise people but stupid fools.

'Where are you?' God asks. Perhaps he knows but wants to give them a chance to come out of hiding voluntarily. Or perhaps God wills not to know and would let them stay hidden if they chose.

The account of the consequences that follow portrays life as we experience it. There is conflict between the human world and the animate world. Eve will find motherhood so painful: she will watch one son kill her other son, so that unique vocation will be a source of pain. The co-equal relationship between the man and the woman becomes one characterised by patriarchy. Work becomes a frustration. Death becomes humanity's destiny.

God who seeks us, enable us to hear you when you ask where we are.

4 The first family
Genesis 4 – 5

Adam and Eve begin to fulfil the commission to fill the earth. Eve's first son is called 'Cain', which sounds like a verb meaning 'get'. Eve 'got Cain', got him 'with God'. God was involved in the process of conception and birth. So the disobedience that brought cataclysm on her and Adam has not cut them off from God. They are outside God's garden now, but God is active outside as well as inside.

Eve has a second son, Abel. As they grow up, Cain and Abel assume two key roles in the life of a homestead, which needs someone to look after the animals and someone to focus on the crops. As the boys grow up, instinctively they want to worship; it's a natural human thing to do. So they bring gifts to God. In the Old Testament, sacrifice can have various meanings. While it can express penitence, more often it expresses worship, commitment or gratitude. Each young man offers something from the fruit of his work. And God looks with favour on Abel's offering, but not on Cain's. We don't know how they know. And to judge from what follows, God doesn't indicate what was wrong with Cain's offering or what was good about Abel's. That is what raises questions for Cain and for us, who have similar experiences of not being able to see why God blesses other people and not us. What interests God is how Cain will cope when his little brother is blessed and he is not blessed. The horrific answer is that he kills him.

But Abel's blood cries out to God. It is a terrible fact, but a great fact. The blood of the slain cries out to God, and sometimes God listens. Admittedly, in this story things go further downhill until they reach a grim low point, but then Genesis backtracks to sound the positive note of the birth of a new baby, Seth, to Adam and Eve. In due course Seth, too, has a son, and a bigger sign of hope is that in this period people begin to call out in the name of the Lord, in the name of Yahweh, the God of Israel. The creation story is on its way to the story of Israel.

Lord, have mercy on us when we are resentful of the blessing enjoyed by other people.

8

5 Filled with violence

Genesis 6 – 7

Eventually, 'the earth was filled with violence', which generates four astonishing reactions in God. The first is regret at having created humanity. God's capacity to foresee things doesn't stop him having unpleasant surprises, like parents in relation to their children. And it doesn't stop him wondering whether it was a good idea to create humanity. Second, God sees how things are, and feels pain. Here's another emotion one might have thought was distinctively human, but it's felt by God, a further indication of our being made in God's image.

Third, God decides to wipe out humanity. The Scriptures can be tough-minded about attributing catastrophes to God's action. Stuff happens; and sometimes God not merely lets it happen but makes it happen. Fourth, nevertheless 'Noah found favour in Yahweh's eyes', found 'grace' with Yahweh. If that seems illogical, illogic is the nature of grace. But you could also say it's totally logical. God isn't actually very good at being tough-minded or at giving up on his projects. That's why Noah found grace, or grace found Noah.

After telling us that Noah found grace with God, Genesis tells us that Noah was a person of integrity, the great exception to the Genesis statement about everyone being corrupt. Noah's being a person of integrity somehow follows from God's grace rather than being its cause. Messing with the order in this story messes up the theology.

Then Genesis tells us about God giving Noah instructions for surviving the coming destruction, and it introduces another significant theological term, 'covenant', which is closely related to grace. It suggests a solemn commitment that one person or group makes to another.

Like the creation story, the flood story is more parabolic than historical. The Israelites could perhaps tell that they weren't to take too literally a story about a floating three-level box 150 yards long, full of animals. And there are lots of Middle Eastern stories about floods. Genesis takes that experience of floods and that kind of story and turns them into a way of portraying something about the world and humanity and God. In one of these Middle Eastern stories, the Noah figure shuts the boat door. In Genesis, God shuts the family in, like the steward on an aircraft making sure the door is secure.

God who grieves, have mercy on the world filled with violence.

6 But God remembered Noah

Genesis 8 – 9

After six months(!) God remembers Noah. This doesn't mean he has forgotten him. When the Scriptures say God remembers, they mean he is mindful and takes action. God remembers Noah because of the reason for enabling him to survive the flood. He is intent on setting his creation project going again. He has made sure that samples of every species have survived, and now the remnant of the original animate world can leave the box and set about being fruitful and numerous.

Noah's first instinct is to worship, like Cain and Abel. He offers the proper sacrifices, from those 'clean' animals of which he saved seven pairs. And God likes the smell of the sacrifices. Other peoples in Israel's world could imagine deities so humanlike they ate the sacrifices, in between being born, procreating and dying. Yahweh is at least humanlike enough to like the smell of barbecue, partly because of what it signifies about Noah.

When humanity had gone totally wayward and the world was to be flooded, that looked like the end, but it was not. There can be new life when one would have thought there could not. Almost destroying the earth made a point, though it gets no one anywhere. But God is going to have to work with humanity as it is. Only when you have acknowledged the situation can you start to do something about it. We learn nothing about what God will eventually do. Until we get to the Abraham story, God is involved only in a holding operation, 'because the inclination of the human heart is evil from its youth' (Genesis 6:5). God is again wondrously illogical as only God can be. God's grace will have to operate, not *despite* human sin but *because of* human sin.

God announced a covenant with Noah before the flood. Now God says in the present tense, 'I am establishing my covenant', one that looks beyond the family that benefited from God's commitment to preserving Noah and looks beyond the human beneficiaries of God's commitment to the rest of the animal creation. And God's covenant commitment applies to the whole animate world. The creation purpose that gave positive significance to the whole of creation is reaffirmed. Perhaps God won't even let humanity destroy the world, though Genesis doesn't say so.

Covenantal God, be mindful of your people.

7 Babylon becomes Babble-on
Genesis 11

Things have been developing in a promising fashion, on a national scale as well as an individual and family scale. A people is travelling in fulfilment of humanity's destiny to fill the earth. They find somewhere where they want to settle down, and they decide on a building project. It requires some ingenuity. If Israelites wanted to build something strong or impressive, they built it of stone. These poor guys have no stone, so they have to make do with mudbrick for the entire edifice. And they have no proper cement, so they have to make do with tar. They get high marks for innovation and ingenuity, and they bake the brick thoroughly, but please...

God comes down to have a personal look, rather than relying on omniscience or hearsay or distance learning. He brings his aides along ('Come on; let's go down'). He's uneasy about the building project because it suggests an assertion of independence. The issues parallel those in the Eden story, but this story considers them at the level of a people, not just an individual or a married couple. The Scriptures assume that peoples and nations banding together is bound to lead to self-assertion against God, not the furtherance of God's purpose. In human history, one does not need to hypothesise divine intervention to explain the failure of such institutions; human self-will can make them fail without God's needing to do anything. But Genesis here portrays God as recognising a need to take some action.

As if by magic, God makes the members of the community unable to communicate with each other. With typical paradox, Genesis sees it as both a divine judgement and a divine mercy. Nations could do terrible things if they could work together unhindered by differences in language. It's a neat coincidence that the name Babylon and the verb *babble* are so close to each other, like the equivalent Hebrew words (*Babel* is simply the Hebrew form of the name of the city we refer to as Babylon). Another effect of God's making the people babble on is to push them into scattering from Babylon and thus to accepting their role of serving the world on God's behalf by spreading over the whole world.

God who comes down, have mercy on us when we resist engaging in the fulfilment of your purpose.

8 Get yourself out of here
Genesis 12

A man called Terah takes his family on a journey northward from southern Mesopotamia. Then God bids Terah's son Abram move to another new home, in Canaan, a crossing point of east and west, north and south. Here God intends to make Abram a great nation. It seems implausible, given that his wife cannot have children, but God is not inclined to do things the obvious, sensible or easy way.

The people who wanted to settle down in Shinar made a name for themselves, but not in the sense they intended. God promises to bless Abram and make his name great. God will ensure that he has a legacy. God has surely done so, because there are few people better known in world history than Abram.

In making Abram a great nation and making his name great, God will 'bless' Abram. Blessing has been an important theme since Genesis 1. Simply blessing Abram's family does not mean God has given up on humanity as a whole. God will not only bless Abram but will also make Abram into a blessing. Genesis has told us nothing about Abram to suggest he deserves to be singled out to receive God's blessing, any more than Noah deserved to survive the flood. Abram is not being blessed because he has deserved it. That point is fundamental to an argument Paul formulates in Romans 4. God made promises to Abram *before* Abram did anything to merit God's approval.

There are two possible ways God wants to make Abram a blessing. With hindsight, one can see that Abram becomes a means of blessing other people, people like us. He is also to become the kind of person that other people can see as an embodiment of blessing, an example of the blessing they seek for themselves.

Abram and Sarai make their move and, like Noah, Abram builds an altar, in Canaan, as a sign that this land belongs to Yahweh. They continue on a preliminary tour of the land which is also a symbolic entering into possession of it. Everything is going brilliantly until they run out of food during a famine. So they continue south out of the promised land into Egypt. What else were they to do? Stuff happens.

Blessing God, make us a blessing in what we bring to other people, and in the prayers your blessing of us inspires.

9 The implausible promise
Genesis 13 – 15

So Abram and Sarai and their family 'went down' to Egypt and then 'went up' from there (as later their descendants will 'go down' to Egypt and then 'go up' again). The story is back on track. Except that it isn't, because another issue arises. Abram's family business is doing well, but there are just too many sheep and cattle, not to say donkeys and camels, to be able to stay together in the same tract of countryside. They need to split, and Abram lets his nephew Lot exercise the choice about which part of the land he will make his area. He looks east and sees regions like the Jericho oasis where natural springs turn desert into garden. It recalls the garden of Eden or the country of Egypt. That's the way he wants to go. It will turn out to be a fateful and unfortunate choice.

From where they are, Abram can look north, south, east and west, and God invites him to do so, not in order to choose a particular area to live but to see himself as heir to the whole country as far as the eye can see. He is heir, but not possessor. Some poignancy will attach to his survey of the land. He will look around but will do so as someone who will always be an alien. Possession lies in the future, and not for him personally. He illustrates a consistent feature of the life of the people of God. We live in the present and in the future.

Abram is part of a project God is undertaking. It will not come to fruition in his day, but he is part of it. His tour of the land will remind him of that. As stage one of this exploration, he returns a way he has been before, which might not seem very adventurous, but it is still a kind of enacted declaration of faith in God's promise. He began this symbolic action before his ill-fated Egyptian adventure; he completes it afterward. That misadventure did not derail God's purpose. Only at this point does Abram build an altar at Mamre (Hebron) to complement the ones at Shechem and Bethel. The whole country belongs to Yahweh, and Yahweh can be worshipped all over the country.

God of implausible promises, fulfil your promises to your people.

10 Hagar names God
Genesis 16

Sarai can't have children, the biological clock has surely stopped, and this matters not only because their personal fulfilment or security is at stake, but because of God's purpose. 'Yahweh has stopped me from bearing children,' Sarai says, with chilling boldness. Is she right? Genesis doesn't comment. Sarai's proposed solution to the problem and Abram's acceptance of it often shock Western readers, but it's a traditional version of surrogacy. It means Hagar moves from being a servant to being Abram's second wife. But surrogacy can issue in problems, and this one does. Hagar may be the number two wife, but she has the functioning womb.

And poor old Abram gets the blame for the tension between his two wives. Caught between the two women in his life, he throws up his hands and points out that Sarai is Hagar's boss; it's her problem, and she has the authority to deal with it. So Sarai effectively drives Hagar out. And Hagar sets off in the direction of Egypt, her home country.

But God's aide finds her there. And if one of God's aides comes to see you, it's quite like God in person coming to see you, though less scary. But he tells her, 'You have to go back and accept the ill treatment.' Maybe the assumption is that it's better to be with the people who are on the receiving end of God's promise and the place where that promise is going to see fulfilment and where God's purpose for the world is at work, even if it's grim. And as Abram's wife, she is to be the mother of countless offspring.

The aide gives her unborn son his name, 'Ishmael', which means 'God listens'. Really? The aide's words to Hagar draw from her a different response from the one we might have expected. God has pursued her, and this leads her to name God. She has thus been called the Bible's first theologian. He is *El-roi*, she says, 'God of my seeing/looking'. It could imply 'the God who sees me/looks at me/looks out for me' or 'the God whom I have seen/looked out for'. Both are true. She did not dream she would find God in the wilderness, but she did, because God found her.

You are the God who sees me.

11 A promise for Ishmael
Genesis 17

In this chapter about covenants, God first gives Abraham two significant biddings attached to his covenant with him. He is to live his life before God, with God watching him and watching over him. It's both an encouragement and a challenge. And he is to be a person 'of integrity'. The word is usually translated 'blameless', but that sounds impossibly demanding. God's word suggests a broader, positive quality. And God spells out some implications of his covenant promise. Abraham's descendants will have Canaan as a possession. It will be a long time before this happens, because there's no basis at the moment for throwing the Canaanites out of the country. But when God can justifiably do so, it can become Israel's holding.

Further, there is now a covenant sign, the circumcision of baby boys. Only the boys get the sign, but the girls are just as much part of the covenant. And everyone associated with Abraham gets the sign, not just the family. The covenant is not ethnically confined. Given that many peoples practise circumcision, making this the sign of the covenant is an example of God taking a practice from the culture and adapting it. But applying the circumcision to babies is a significant adaptation. The sign has the advantage of applying to the organ that often gets men into trouble. It hints at cutting men's sexuality down to size.

Yet further, God reaffirms that Sarah is going to be the mother of nations. He changes her name from Sarai to Sarah to mark the occasion, as he changes Abram's name to Abraham. 'Mother of nations?' Abraham falls down laughing, which might suggest both worshipful submission and a sense that God's promise is too good to be true.

But Abraham and Sarah don't actually need a miracle to fulfil the promise to them. They have Ishmael. Won't he do as the means of bringing about this fulfilment? Apparently not. But that doesn't mean God is not committed to Ishmael. While Isaac will be the son who counts for the fulfilment of the promise, God also loves Ishmael and promises blessing and fruitfulness to him too. The vast numbers of Arab peoples tracing their ancestry back to Ishmael witness to God's fulfilment of this promise. The covenant embraces Ishmael, too.

Lord, keep your covenant with the descendants of Abraham, via Isaac and via Ishmael.

12 Entertaining angels unawares
Genesis 18

Angels or aides are humanlike. When three humanlike figures arrive at Abraham's encampment, there's nothing to suggest that they are anything other than three men. 'Where's Sarah?' they ask. The message that follows is directed to her as much as to Abraham. What she hears again about having a baby makes her laugh, as Abraham laughed in Genesis 17. In response to that, God speaks (so that's who one of the three is). Sarah has to break out of her framework of expectations regarding what is possible – though the miracle birth will happen whether she believes it or not.

It then transpires that the three are actually on their way to Sodom, down in the Rift Valley. But God has been thinking. Given Abraham's significance in his purpose, he will tell Abraham what he intends to do. Abraham has some responsibility for what English translations call righteousness and justice, for the exercise of authority in a faithful way. God has heard that things are not like that in Sodom and intends to check things out and do something about it. Abraham knows what that will mean, and it drives him into talking to God about his intentions. It's less a prayer than a series of questions, but they imply a challenge.

God has to choose between two courses of action, neither of which is very good – act against Sodom and thus act against people there who are themselves faithful people, or not act at all. Abraham urges God to 'carry' Sodom in its waywardness. Translations use the word 'forgive', but Abraham uses the ordinary verb for 'carry'. It provides a vivid image for what we do when we forgive people. Instead of making them carry their wrongdoing and its consequences, we carry them. Paradoxically and boldly, Abraham suggests that this is how God must exercise authority in the world, carrying the people who misuse authority and will not live his way. Abraham cunningly turns back on God his description of Abraham as a person who is to act faithfully and rightly, in exercising authority. He does it with due deference, several times referring to the fact that God is his Lord. The story closes by noting that God has been speaking with Abraham. His 'prayer' takes place within God's purpose, not against it.

Lord, carry your world, though we don't deserve it.

13 Don't look back
Genesis 19 – 20

Lot is sitting in the gate area in Sodom, a natural place to watch the world go by, and his welcome of the two aides (without knowing who they are) resembles Abraham's welcome. But the story somersaults into a nightmare. The city's people want to rape these strangers. Yet what does Lot think he is doing in offering them his daughters? Perhaps he knows they will not accept them. Having sex with them wouldn't meet their desire to subjugate the two visitors. But at best, it's a high-risk policy.

The scene establishes the point God and the two aides have come to establish. No wonder the outcry against Sodom has reached God's ears. Lot needs to get out of there. Yet Lot is torn. He has to be dragged out of Sodom. His wife is also torn. Her look back is another expression of hesitation, an awareness of what she will lose by leaving Sodom, and she becomes frozen in her gaze. 'Remember Lot's wife,' Jesus bids his disciples (Luke 17:32).

In all this, God is mindful of Abraham's questions. By implication, Abraham was trying to persuade God not to destroy Sodom. He didn't mention the idea of rescuing Lot's family from there. But apparently this happened because of Abraham's prayer. The prayer made a difference to what God did, even though it was a different difference from the one Abraham had in mind.

It has been assumed that the condemnation of the homosexual act that the men in Sodom want to commit indicates the Scriptures' stance in relation to same-sex relations in general, but the story doesn't concern a form of same-sex relationship that anyone seeks to defend. Actually, God is taking action against Sodom because of the 'outcry' that has made itself heard in heaven, and when the Old Testament talks about an outcry, it relates to the violent way weak people are being treated by powerful people. If God can't find even ten faithful people in Sodom, maybe the cry is one like that of Abel's blood, one uttered by the blood of people who have been slain in the city. In its entirety the story is horrible, but it is a story about the real world – where God is involved, angels are involved and the people of God are involved.

Lord, have mercy on our Sodoms.

14 Do we ever learn?
Genesis 21

In a competition for designation as the world's most welcome baby, Isaac would be in the running. His name stands for laughter, a laughter in which Sarah rejoices. But then Ishmael laughs, and to Sarah it's as if he is pretending to be Isaac, trying to replace Isaac. So she makes a plan to rule that out. Abraham and God agree with her plan, though God also affirms his original plan for Ishmael.

If Hagar knew about God's renewed undertaking, one can imagine it wouldn't count for much when you have run out of water, know your child is dehydrated and know this is how people die in the wilderness. But God intervenes, not because of seeing Hagar's tears, but because of listening to Ishmael's cry. Either way would be fine with Hagar. She knows that God is one who sees and also one who listens. God lives up to the boy's name.

Hagar sees a well. Her story and Ishmael's story get a fresh start there. God is with Ishmael. He is the first person about whom that is said, even though he is the boy who doesn't count in terms of the great purpose that God is set on accomplishing.

After the pathos of that story, the story of Abraham and Abimelech is down to earth. Beersheba is a spectacular archaeological site, with a well outside the city's gate. You can stand there and imagine the scene in this chapter (there's no indication that this well existed in Abraham's day, but you can still use your imagination). *Beer* is the word for a well, and *sheba* is the word for 'seven', while *sheba* is also similar to the word for swearing an oath; Genesis works with both these links.

Abimelech makes quite a confession: 'God is with you in everything you do.' He can see it in the way things work out for Abraham. It implies God has fulfilled the promise to be Abraham's God. Abimelech is wise enough to want to be associated with that, rather than trying to work against it. Another aspect of God's promise is being fulfilled. Abimelech wants to have a positive relationship with the people where God is at work.

Lord, do not make me look on the death of the child.
(Maybe there is someone to pray that for.)

15 The test
Genesis 22

You might think the story of Abraham and Sarah is nearing its end. But now there is a bombshell. God decides on this test for Abraham. God has promised to turn Abraham into a great nation, Sarah has the son whose existence opens up the way to God fulfilling this promise. Yet God's test imperils the promise. 'Kill him, then, will you?' Isaac is not merely any son but the son through whom God will keep that promise. It is significant that God bids Abraham sacrifice his son and also that in the end God doesn't want him to do so. God wants to test Abraham's obedience and trust, and Abraham passes the test. When Abraham makes inescapably clear that he would do the terrible deed, then God stops him. The point of the test has been achieved.

The Old Testament condemns the sacrifice of children. Israelites, like other Middle Eastern peoples, did sometimes sacrifice their children, as we do in sending them off to war. Perhaps Isaac would know and accept this. Whether or not we would, one significance of the story for people hearing it would be the implication that God does not ask for that sacrifice. God has looked the idea in the face and turned away from it.

Then, at Jesus' baptism, God says to him, 'You are my Son, whom I love, with whom I am well pleased' (Mark 1:11). The words echo the commission of Abraham. They offer Jesus an understanding of his significance that is both affirming and solemn. God is prepared to do what he asked of Abraham.

Why did God need to test Abraham? The story again makes us ask whether God does not know how a person like Abraham would react to a command of this kind. While sometimes tests happen for the benefit of the person being tested, this story is explicit that the test happens so that God can discover something. 'Now I know that you revere God.' Perhaps God could know how Abraham will react, but God does not relate to us and to the world by mind games played inside God's head. It's one thing to know that someone who loves you would do anything for you; it's another kind of knowing when that person actually makes a monumental sacrifice for you.

Here I am, Lord.

16 Where to find Isaac's wife
Genesis 23 – 24

It must be worrying, odd and grievous to have to arrange a marriage for your son or daughter when your spouse has already died. In a traditional society, it's customary to marry someone from outside your household but inside your extended family or clan. So Abraham needs to send 'back home' for a wife for Isaac. But not marrying Isaac to a nice Canaanite girl is not only a cultural and ethnic principle. It is also a religious one. Making sure Isaac marries the right kind of girl is Abraham's last significant act. He can be confident about God's ensuring that his aide's search will be successful. God's own plan depends on it. The servant goes about his commission in light of that. Isaac's special place in God's purpose means that not everyone can expect to pray the servant's kind of prayer and have confidence it will be answered, though we can pray it and hope it might be answered.

Given that the commission is such an important one, it is striking that Abraham entrusts it to a mere 'servant', and it shows what a responsible and honoured position a 'servant' or 'slave' (the same word) can occupy. The way the servant goes about his task shows how well founded was Abraham's trust in him. He knows how to pray, and he knows how to be silent and watch and wait. He knows how to worship and give honour to the God who has answered his crazy prayer, and he knows how to keep his mission in mind even when social custom would oblige him to accept hospitality and hold back from anything that looks like business until much later.

Like Sarah, Rebekah knows how to find her way in a patriarchal world and knows that the men cannot take for granted her cooperation with men's projects. But, 'I'll go,' she says. So they marry and fall in love. The order seems odd to Western thinking, but it corresponds to the testimony of some people whose marriage was arranged.

Isaac and his family become a new family for Rebekah, and Rebekah becomes the person who brings healing to the grief following Isaac's mother's death, when he is himself presumably no more than a teenager.

Lord, lead me in the right way, so that I may see the fulfilment of your promises.

17 The birthright
Genesis 25 – 26

It's neat to picture Ishmael and Isaac together. Death in the family is one of those occasions when the tensions all come out. But Ishmael is a big man. There he is, joining Isaac in burying their father. Ishmael is a survivor. No one knocks him over. If he falls, he falls on his feet.

Like Isaac's parents, Isaac and Rebekah have trouble starting a family, and getting pregnant is then only the beginning of their problems. What's noteworthy about them is the way they react. It makes both of them pray. Isaac prays for Rebekah. And when she has got pregnant and has a tough time, Rebekah prays. Like other women in these stories, such as Sarah and Rachel, Rebekah is not the kind of person who just sits at home demurely submitting to her husband and accepting her lot. She takes action. At this point she does so by assuming that she too can talk to God about what the heck is going on. She doesn't have to leave prayer to her husband or go to God via him as if she has no relationship of her own with God. She has the freedom the Psalms illustrate to go straight to God with the issues in her life. The story makes clear the simple possibility of taking things to God and getting a response, though her succeeding in doing that doesn't establish that one will get a response every time.

Within humanity in general, there are people who want to be number one and people who couldn't care less. Jacob is the first and Esau is the second. They embody the two types. Esau is the older twin, just by a few seconds, but as they left Rebekah's womb, it was as if Jacob was already reaching out to catch up with his big brother. When they are grown up, Jacob is the chef and Esau is the hunter. Esau wants some of Jacob's stew. Jacob says the price is the position of number one son. Who cares, when what you need is something to eat? Jacob cares. When you need to be number one and you are not number one, you care deeply. You will do anything to get there.

Lord, if it is to be this way, why am I alive?
(Maybe there is someone to pray like that for.)

18 The trick
Genesis 27

We have different ways of being foolish from Isaac and Rebekah's way. Maybe as parents we don't have time or energy to favour one child over another. That is their foolishness: Isaac's favouring Esau, Rebekah's favouring Jacob. It leads to deceit, blasphemy, distress and fury. As the head of the family, Isaac has the responsibility to see things go well after his death, and to see that his eldest son gets the resources he needs to become the new head of the family. Blessing his eldest son is the way he goes about that. His word, solemnly uttered in the context of a meal, makes it rather like a covenant, and it has that effect. So for Esau and Jacob, the implications of what happens here are decisive. Esau loses his position, his responsibility and his security. Jacob gains all those. He gains the blessing. All his life, even before he was born, he has been seeking to grab it. That's what being Jacob, 'grabber', means. It makes all the difference. Except that it doesn't.

It's worthwhile to imagine being the Israelites (Jacob-ites) listening to this story. They would likely feel negative about Esau's descendants, the Edomites, with whom they were often in conflict. But the story puts them in their place. While Jacob is their guy, he is the one who cheats Esau out of his blessing. It is hard to imagine them reckoning that the story approves of the action of Jacob the deceiver. Maybe the audience shuffled their feet somewhat at the picture of Jacob grasping after Esau on his way out of Rebekah's womb – or maybe they were quite proud. Maybe they shuffled their feet somewhat at Jacob's driving a hard bargain with Esau about a helping of stew – or maybe they felt Jacob was vindicated by Esau's attaching such little value to his position as firstborn, with its privileges and responsibilities. Maybe they felt the more vindicated on hearing about Esau marrying a pair of Hittite girls. The Hittites, the people who lived around Hebron, were good neighbours to Esau's grandfather, but the listeners wouldn't be surprised that his marrying local people made Isaac and Rebekah bitter. Abraham had made sure Isaac himself didn't do that, which was what had led to Rebekah's coming all that way to marry Isaac.

Lord, protect me from the desire to be number one.

19 The stairway to heaven
Genesis 28

The fracas gives Rebekah reason to manoeuvre Isaac into sending Jacob off to do what Abraham's servant did for Isaac in getting him a wife from 'back east'. On the way, Jacob has a dream. In our dreams we are often processing questions, problems and upcoming tasks. No doubt Jacob is doing this. But in the Scriptures, dreams can be a way God speaks to people, sometimes in relation to issues that they are needing to process.

Jacob sees a ramp or a staircase joining the heavens and the earth. It constitutes a way for God's aides to move between the two. God thus opens Jacob's eyes to something that is happening all the time as God is involved in the world and sending aides on missions. They are still at work, not because Jacob deserves to have God active in his life, but because God will not be put off from acting by Rebekah and Jacob's stupidity.

God personally shows up in the dream, to give Jacob a message of encouragement. It begins, 'I am Yahweh,' which is a shorthand expression. Israelites know that Yahweh is the only God, so saying, 'I am Yahweh,' is like saying, 'I am God.' Yet it also reminds people that it is their own God, Yahweh, who simply is God. The self-introduction means, 'I remind you who I am. It is the basis for what I say when I declare my intentions or make promises.' All God's power and authority lie behind his promises. Adding 'the God of your father Abraham and the God of Isaac' underlines the point. Historically, that is more likely what God would have actually said to Jacob (given that the name 'Yahweh' itself was first revealed later, to Moses). In a way, all God says is, 'You know those promises to Abraham and Isaac? They apply to you, too, even though you are fleeing the country. They mean I will be with you on this journey that is both shameful (because you are on the run) and auspicious (because you are going to find a wife from your own people).' God will be with Jacob not merely to make him *feel* OK but also to ensure he *is* OK, kept safe until he is able to return.

Of all that you give me, I will definitely give one-tenth to you.

20 I want to know what love is
Genesis 29 – 30

Like most societies, Middle Eastern culture assumes there are some economic arrangements associated with marriage, a significance of which is to seal good relationships between families and to provide a framework for handling the consequences of the marriage breaking down or of one of the partners dying. And Jacob is here doing what Genesis 2 literally says: he has left his father and mother and he is uniting with his wife in the context of her family. If seven years seems a long time to wait, we may need to bear in mind that Rachel is likely just a young teenager and not ready for marriage when Jacob and Laban undertake their negotiation.

There are further patriarchal assumptions written into the ongoing way things work. A woman's self-esteem and significance are tied to her capacity to have children, so not being able to is a monumental deprivation. Rachel has the love, so God sees to it that Leah has the babies. God gets involved with Leah in her sadness. Further, God is committed to making the offspring of Abraham, Isaac and Jacob into a numerous people. These two women and their maidservants (who all count as Jacob's wives) are going to produce the ancestors of Israel's twelve clans.

Jacob's own involvement with his women differs from that which would seem natural to Western readers. In what sense does Jacob love Rachel, and why? Does he 'love' Rachel more than he 'loves' Leah? Or does he 'like' her more than Leah because she has nicer eyes and a sexy figure? Or is this a context where 'love' is more a commitment than an emotion – is he more committed to Rachel than to Leah? Yet although he especially 'loves' Rachel, he is happy to sleep with three other women.

Leah, at least, assumes she is unloved in all those senses. For Leah, Rachel means everything to Jacob and she herself means nothing. But God sees it. Her fourth son is Judah, whose name makes one think of the word meaning 'thanksgiving' or 'confession', and intriguingly she declares, 'This time I will "confess" Yahweh.' Has she determined to praise God anyway? Or is this her last forlorn hope, that God is about to give her reason for such testimony?

Lord, stay with us in the messiness of our marriages and relationships.

21 The secret leaving
Genesis 31

Most biblical heroes of faith are people with clay feet. Jacob is such a man, with clay hands, heart and mind, too. He continues to be the great deceiver. He decides it's time to get back to Canaan, and Laban tries to make sure he doesn't take too many sheep back with him, but Jacob knows how to defeat his plan. The shrewd Laban has met his match in the even shrewder Jacob.

Laban's sons are understandably resentful at Jacob's having prospered at their father's expense, and thus at theirs. Jacob himself is afraid of what Laban may do. Leah and Rachel know they have nothing to gain from Laban because Laban has nothing to gain from them now that they belong to Jacob.

Pasturing large flocks means spreading them out over a wide area. Thus the family business makes it easy for Jacob and his entourage to make a run for it when Laban is some distance away, sheep shearing. By the time Laban and his posse catch up with Jacob, he has gone three hundred miles and reached Gilead. He is nearly home.

It was God who told Jacob it was time to go home. Ironically, Jacob is then the victim of Rachel's deception when Laban accuses Jacob of stealing his effigies (figurines that Laban would use in seeking guidance), when actually Rachel has stolen them. No one can afford to trust anyone in this family. Given that it was Laban who suffered through the departure of his daughters and their offspring, it is neat that despite the failure to resolve the question about the effigies, the two families become reconciled and finally part happily.

Jacob has a complex relationship with fear. He speaks of God as the 'Fear of Isaac', the 'Reverence of Isaac'. A positive fear expresses itself in reverence, awe and commitment. A negative fear means being scared. Knowing reverence and awe toward God should mean you increase in your confidence in life in general. But the nearer Jacob gets to home, the more scared he gets.

God is again involved in this messiness. He doesn't make a priority of seeing that people who deserve to do well prosper, and that people who do not deserve it fail to prosper (that would mean waiting for ever).

I am not worthy of your love. But rescue me. Because I'm scared.

22 God struggles
Genesis 32

Jacob thinks that his wealth should enable him to buy his way back into a peaceful relationship with his brother, but he now hears that another posse seems to be coming to meet him. He assumes that they may just appropriate the flocks, thank you, and kill him. He is scared.

People refer to what happens next as Jacob wrestling with God. But Jacob doesn't start this fight. God is wrestling with Jacob. Actually, it says 'a man' wrestles with Jacob, though it eventually does speak of Jacob struggling with God. This is another of those occasions when God appears as a human being and only afterward does someone realise he was more than a human person.

Really, God has been wrestling with Jacob all Jacob's life. Here God tries again, but succeeds only by cheating. Jacob doesn't want to yield, and he never does. Yet God does bless him, and he gives him a new name that says something about him. As is often the case, the comment about the name has some subtleties about it. It links Jacob's new name with the fact that he is the great fighter. Yes, Jacob is someone who keeps fighting with God in order to stay the man he is. In the end, God lets him do that because even God cannot force people to change. God can only make them limp.

Yet the new name *Isra-el* doesn't actually mean 'he fights/persists/exerts himself with God'. It's a statement of which God is the subject. If anything, *Isra-el* would mean 'God fights/persists/exerts himself'. God strives to get a person like Jacob to become the kind of person he could be and should be and that God wants him to be, and he keeps at it in this struggle with Jacob. Once more the story presupposes that its audience *is* Jacob, *is* Israel. The people of God are a people whose nature is to struggle with God to avoid becoming the people we could be, and a people with whom God continues to struggle to try to take us there. The listeners might also be inclined to assume that actually the verb in this name looks more like a different one and that the name means 'God rules', which also encourages some reflection.

I will not let you go, unless you bless me.

23 An amicable parting
Genesis 33 – 35

Whereas Jacob assumes that Esau still cares about the blessing, and probably wants to kill him, Esau is interested only in meeting his brother again. Jacob is then all prostration, and Esau just wants a hug. They both weep, with the tears meaning something different for Jacob from what they mean for Esau.

Thus Jacob continues on his journey into Canaan, to Shechem, where a doubly grim story follows. There is something like date rape. The two fathers think they have found a way of handling the situation that will suit everybody. But, again with irony, Jacob falls for his sons' deceit, as Hamor and his sons do. The grim story continues to be told with dark humour. The darkest element is that the descendants of Jacob-Israel are supposed to be a means of bringing blessing to the nations. But they turn the sign of the covenant, the sign of life, into a sign of death.

Did that meeting with God at the river Jabbok change Jacob? The way he approached Esau afterward doesn't make it look like it. Here, Genesis 35 tells us again about Jacob being renamed Israel. But the change of name still doesn't seem to imply a change of personality. This doesn't mean God has given up on him, nor on his sons. With God, hope springs eternal. Even though we do not change, and we carry on making the same mistakes, this does not make God throw up his hands in despair and abandon us.

Jacob's next move, from Shechem to Bethel, takes him only a short distance down the mountain chain, but it brings him to a place associated with God rather than with the shameful events at Shechem. Giving up 'alien gods' fits with that (they are likely something like Rachel's effigies). Although Jacob is not transformed, then, his action does suggest a renunciation.

After a while the family sets off again for the south, where Isaac still lives. On the way, Rachel bears the family's twelfth son, but she dies in childbirth. She gives her life for her child, as women often do in traditional societies. Her grave sits there as a place of weeping when Judahites go off into exile (Jeremiah 31:15) and when Jesus' birth leads to great grief (Matthew 2:16–18).

We promise, Lord, that we will put away the foreign gods from among us.

24 The dreamer
Genesis 36 – 37

Genesis tells us about Esau's descendants before telling us about Jacob's, on whom the story is to focus. Edom is part of God's story, even if less central than Israel. Now Genesis turns to Jacob's line and notes Jacob's favouritism toward his young son Joseph, which does not thrill his big brothers.

This young son has a dream. There is no hint here that it is a God-given dream, and our modern instinct is to read it psychologically. Young Joseph dreams of being top dog, just as his father wanted to be. And he is so naive, he tells everyone his silly dreams. It almost costs him his life. It gives his brothers a chance to show they have their father's genes: they are as good at deceit as he is. Once again deceitfulness thus catches up with Jacob, who was sometimes beaten at his own game by his cousin and by his wife, and in his dotage is now beaten at it by his sons.

Yet the irony is that Joseph's dreams will come true. The dreams will hang over all that we read in the coming chapters. The question is *how* will they come true, especially when events are such as surely to take Joseph's destiny in quite other directions? But having a hunch that we know where the story must go helps us see the significance of events as they unfold. Not untypically, human waywardness and fortunate coincidence play a part in its development. While one cannot blame the older brothers for regarding Joseph as more than a little tiresome, understanding that does not extend to tolerating the cynical ruthlessness of their action.

The Middle Eastern climate meant people needed ways of conserving water for the dry season, so they collected it in large cisterns. There is something mafia-like about the way the brothers throw Joseph into the empty cistern to die, then coolly settle down for dinner. It then seems strange that Judah's recognition that 'he is our flesh and blood' doesn't extend to hesitation about selling him into slavery. And it seems strange that this recognition doesn't extend to hesitation over putting Jacob through his terrible grief. Perhaps the brothers were glad to get back at their father for making Joseph his favourite.

Lord, fulfil your dream for your people.

25 The false allegation
Genesis 38 – 39

Deceit again plays a key role in the story of Judah and Tamar. After the death of two of his sons, Judah declines to follow the expectation that when a man dies without children, something needs to be done to keep the man's memory alive, to keep his family going, to provide a destiny for his inheritance and to produce offspring who will look after his widow as she grows older. So Tamar pretends to be a prostitute, manipulates Judah himself into getting her pregnant, and makes a public fool of him into the bargain.

With the subsequent story of the mess with sex that Joseph manages to avoid, we may wonder about the woman's version of what happened. Would she say that this hot guy was flaunting his muscles around the house, asking for it? We get hints that her husband is clueless. All he cares about is his work and what's for dinner. The story is a melodramatic tale about a handsome young man, a stupid husband and a lonely wife.

But another element in it is God's involvement, and linking these two aspects of it is wisdom. Stereotypical characters such as these people are the staple of the teaching in Proverbs. Proverbs wants to help young men avoid getting entangled with the 'strange woman', the 'other woman', the woman who doesn't mind having an affair, the woman from outside the community who may have different mores or religion and may lead one astray. Potiphar's wife fits the category, but Joseph deals with sexual temptation or sexual instincts in a different way from Judah.

And God is with Joseph. This doesn't just mean he has a feeling that God is with him. It means God makes things work out well for him. As William Tyndale's old translation put it, 'The Lord was with Joseph and he was a lucky fellow.' It does look as if this idea of God being with him collapses when Joseph ends up in jail, yet Genesis then takes up that idea again. Joseph is the guy who keeps bouncing back, not because he has an inherent resilience but because God is with him. He ends up in the same position of responsibility in the jail as the one he held with Potiphar.

Lord, inspire us to stay by you, and will you stay by us.

26 Interpretations belong to God
Genesis 40

Like people in the modern West, the people of ancient Egypt believed in research and sought to base their lives and their policies on the best resources of information. In their case, an equivalent to scientific research was dream research. We have Egyptian examples of dream books listing motifs that recur in dreams and what they 'mean'. If you dream about a well, or about weaving, or about looking at yourself in a mirror, or about thousands of other things, these could portend something good or bad that was going to happen. While such guidance might be general, it could point to some specific future event. But dreams reveal the future only in an oblique way. You need to know how to interpret them. In Egypt there were unofficial and officially recognised dream experts who could help ordinary people interpret their dreams.

Whereas Joseph is in prison despite the fact that he has resisted the temptation to 'offend against God', Pharaoh's chief cupbearer and chief baker have 'offended' their boss. We don't know how they did so. The perils of life in a Middle Eastern court may mean only that the fish pie was not spicy enough. In their troubled situation in prison and their anxiety about what the future may hold, they assume there should be something to learn from their dreams, but they don't have a dream book or a dream expert handy; at least, so they assume. But Joseph asks them the rhetorical question that both undermines their natural assumption about dreams and promises that they might be able to find a way forward: 'Don't interpretations belong to God?'

Our own expertise in research has to have set alongside it the limitations in what empirical research can discover. Its findings are always provisional, and they themselves need interpretation. We cannot sell our souls to research or think we can save ourselves through research. It may be even more dangerous that we see research as the key to politics. We spend millions on 'intelligence' yet continually make decisions about involvement in other nations' affairs that turn out to have been misguided. We had lots of information, but we lacked a big picture and we lacked wisdom.

Lord, interpretations belong to you. Give us the humility to face our limitations.

27 Joseph as Prime Minister
Genesis 41

Pharaoh in turn dreams, and he has all those resources, but his experts are baffled by his dreams. This is where Joseph comes in again.

It's tempting to live by the motto, 'Spend first, save later.' Joseph's interpretation of Pharaoh's dreams makes it possible to save first and then manage through the crisis when it comes. Joseph surely doesn't have to be a genius to formulate a plan to handle what will unfold over the periods of surplus and shortage. Yet with hindsight one could say that likewise our world doesn't have to get into the economic messes it gets into from time to time. One big factor that generates the messes is a combination of greed and stupidity. More specifically, greed makes people throw wisdom to the winds. The years of prosperity could make Egypt do that. Joseph shows them how to stay cool and take the longer view.

We might reckon it is not surprising that someone who lives by God's promises and by trust in God would have the insight to see the wise basis on which to run the country's economic policies in years of plenty and in years of lack. On the other hand, there will in time be a downside to the 'big government' that Joseph suggests.

The actual factor that makes Pharaoh put Joseph in charge of implementing his economic policies is not so much the innovative nature of his proposals but the supernatural insight indicated by his ability to interpret dreams. It leads Pharaoh to identify Joseph as the first person in the Scriptures in whom the spirit of God is at work. Wisdom is a gift of God's spirit, to be desired in any ruler.

But Joseph misses his family, and he expresses the point indirectly in naming his sons. For people listening to the story, the account of the two boys' births will have a further significance. Manasseh and Ephraim became two of the most significant Israelite clans, dominating the northern part of the country. Yes, God made Joseph fruitful. Ephraim's own name could remind people of this because of its overlap with the word for 'be fruitful'. For one of Jacob's youngest sons to be the forefather of these two significant clans is typical of God's working in Genesis.

Lord, you have made me forget. You have made me fruitful.

28 What game is Joseph playing?
Genesis 42 – 43

Joseph is a mystery throughout this story. For several chapters he seems to be playing games with his brothers. Is it because he needs to draw them to genuine repentance for the wrong they have done, and because they need to be pushed lower and lower into remorse and shame before it will be wise to let them rise from it? 'What is this that God has done to us?' they ask. Are they serious enough yet about the question?

Or is Joseph playing games with his brothers because he has some understandable resentment in his heart for what his brothers did to him as a teenager in selling him into servitude, exiling him from his family and his homeland and (indirectly) causing him to end up in prison through no fault of his own?

If we were able to ask him which of these motivations impels him, perhaps he would not know. If he deserves his reputation as a person of insight, he might be wise to acknowledge the possibility that both motivations drive him and that he is not sure which is dominant. And if we could ask God's opinion about what is going on, perhaps God would reckon that the brothers do need to be brought to a deep and genuine repentance, that the way Joseph is treating them does have the capacity to bring this about, and that even if Joseph's resentment is driving him more than it should – well, God works through human weakness and sin as well as through human strength and righteousness (as Joseph himself will eventually point out).

Not only may Joseph be playing games with his brothers, but the author of Genesis may also be playing games with the people listening to the story. In the end, we cannot be sure of the answer to the questions about Joseph's motivation. The effect of the story's lack of clarity is to put the ball into the readers' court and make them examine themselves. If they were Joseph, what would be their motivation? What do they learn from the way they read the story? Paradoxically, the Scriptures can work on readers by leaving things unclear, making them fill in the gaps and then asking why they fill them in the way they do.

God Almighty, grant us compassion before the people who could be tough with us.

29 Not you but God
Genesis 44 – 45

If Joseph is not simply trying to exact revenge from his brothers; he may also be trying to combine willingness to forgive with rigour in seeking to get his brothers to face the facts about what they have done. The story would have challenging implications for many of its readers. After Israel (that is, Jacob's descendants) divided into two nations dominated by the Judah and Joseph clans, relations between them were often adversarial. This story about the relationship between their forebears points them toward a realism that doesn't hide from issues, but also toward an openness to and desire for family reconciliation.

For the third time, the brothers prostrate themselves before Joseph, fulfilling his annoying dream. This doesn't alter the fact that it was an expression of his brashness. Nor does it quite establish that the dream was God-given. Once again, Genesis doesn't connect the dots. It leaves the audience with the questions. But they can think about them with the conviction that Joseph expresses, even if he does not mean it literally when he says it was not his brothers but God who sent him to Egypt. The Scriptures assume that events can sometimes be described at more than one level.

Joseph refers to God using the brothers' action to keep alive 'a body of survivors'. It is a term that will be of significance for many people hearing the story. The expression is usually translated 'a remnant'. It denotes people who go through some catastrophe but live to tell the tale. Specifically, it comes to denote those who survive the destruction of the people by Babylon centuries later. It is an expression that initially conveys bad news; the people who survive are only leftovers. But it can imply good news; at least some people survive who can be the nucleus of a renewed and restored people. God promises that this restoration will indeed come about, even in a foreign country such as Egypt (or Babylon).

God knows about the human weaknesses manifested by Joseph and his brothers, and he makes these the means of providing the whole family with a way of surviving the famine and thus of keeping in existence the family through whom God has promised to bless the world.

Lord, you make all things work together for good, and we thank you.

30 Call no one happy until they are dead
Genesis 46 – 48

An ancient Greek saying urged people to call no one happy until they are dead. It's not the gloomy statement it at first sounds; it means that only at the end of someone's life is it possible to make a judgement, when you can look at the life as a whole. Looking at the stories of Abraham and Isaac shows God involved in the individual incidents in their lives, but also in the whole. The Joseph story shows God involved in the long haul of a life. It shows how experiences and events are interconnected, with God involved in the interconnections. Only at the end can you make a judgement on Joseph's story, or Jacob's.

Jacob now goes down to Egypt. So the entire family goes, which will be the means whereby it will not only survive but flourish, and whereby God's purpose will not only stay on track but also advance. Jacob seems to hesitate for a moment at Beersheba, the southern boundary of Canaan. So there God appears to him again, once more telling him that things will be OK. God will be with him in going and in coming back (for his burial in Canaan). Jacob knows Egypt is not the land of promise. He wants to be buried back in Canaan with his family, not in this foreign country, and he gets Joseph to swear a solemn oath in this connection.

Joseph is the Scriptures' great nationaliser. He exercises power in Egypt at a moment of great crisis, a crisis he knew was coming, and one with which he knows how to cope. Presumably he is able to store the surplus grain from the good years because he buys it from the people. Then, when they need to buy it back from Joseph, it will not be surprising if they find the price has gone up. It feels as if there is something wrong with a process whereby everybody ends up as Pharaoh's servants or serfs, something like sharecroppers, but it is what happens. The deepest irony is that the serfdom Joseph introduces naturally embraces his own family and dependants. It means that eventually they will need to be rescued from a 'household of serfs'.

Lord, help us see what we can of the big picture of our lives, and live accordingly.

31 Am I in the place of God?
Genesis 49 – 50

When you know you are going to die soon, it may concentrate the mind. Jacob is the first of a line of Old Testament figures who deliver significant discourses when they are about to die. Jacob's is distinctive for the way it speaks to his sons and to their descendants, the clans bearing his sons' names. Sometimes it speaks in the future because these are events that are yet to happen; sometimes in the present or past because they are already actual in Jacob's mind's eye and in the experience of the clans. Once again we can imagine the clans listening and finding that Jacob's words answer questions they might ask about themselves. The importance of the blessing theme throughout Genesis makes it appropriate that this should be prominent as the book ends, and the motif's importance to Jacob makes it an appropriate one for Jacob himself to emphasise.

When you have been wronged, you want justice. Joseph's brothers knew it would be natural for Joseph to want justice, though the plan they hatch to avoid his having his justice is laughably pathetic. Joseph does not even point out how patent are their lies. It is as well for his brothers that he has a different framework for looking at events. He's willing to 'carry' his brothers' wrongdoing; that is the literal meaning of the word for 'forgive', the word Abraham uses in Genesis 18 in urging God to 'carry' Sodom's wrongdoing. When we forgive someone, we take responsibility for the effect of their wrongdoing and its consequences, even though the responsibility really belongs to them. We refuse to let it have the effect that it logically should have.

There is not much indication that the brothers feel contrite about the wrong they did. Their dominant feeling is fear for their own future. What if Joseph relates to them in the way they related to him? Notwithstanding how he may have been trying to drive them to repentance earlier, he does not ask himself questions about whether contrition is a necessary condition for forgiveness. He knows he must carry their wrongdoing, as he has been doing for most of his life. If there is some ambiguity about the way he treated them earlier, there is none here.

Lord, we acknowledge that we are not in your place.

February

FROM SLAVERY TO THE PROMISED LAND

1 How to resist the authorities
Exodus 1

Like a TV flashback, the first paragraph in Exodus takes up from Genesis. The Israelites are fruitful, teeming and numerous, as God commissioned the creation to be, and this worries the new Egyptian administration. A change in the Egyptian dynasty means the previous staff lose their positions. And the new administration wants to cut down these Israelites.

The Ten Commandments require people to give true witness in court, but the Old Testament sees truth telling as part of a broader truthful relationship. Where there is a truthful relationship between people, telling the truth is part of that relationship. Where there is no truthful relationship, the Old Testament doesn't isolate truth telling as an obligation. Where powerful people are oppressing powerless people, the powerless are not obliged to tell the truth to their oppressors. Revering authorities should be a way of revering God, but when the authorities are requiring murder, all bets are off. You give God what belongs to God as well as giving Caesar what belongs to Caesar. Whereas people can pay with their lives for revering God rather than the authorities, on this occasion God honours that stance, an encouragement to other people faced with their choice.

Specifically, women who are expected to kill their own babies or someone else's babies are not expected to cooperate. Like the women in Genesis, these women show that they are not people you can assert headship over. Telling us the midwives' names makes them real people; they are not just anonymous functionaries. They are people who revere God. Exodus knows them by name; we know them by name; God knows them by name. It is less important for the representatives of the Egyptian court to be named.

Letting the baby girls live also hints at Pharaoh's incompetence. Killing the baby boys reduces the size of any potential Israelite fighting force but also reduces the size of the potential Israelite workforce; letting the girls live means they can bear many more offspring. Pharaoh recognises that wisdom is important in managing his empire and anticipating its problems, but he does not manifest such wisdom. At the moment of crisis, the people with insight are the women who have no trouble pulling the wool over Pharaoh's eyes.

We pray, Lord, for people who are threatened by the powers or bidden to do wrong.

2 From guerrilla to fugitive
Exodus 2

Some more women devise another simple plan, this time to pull the wool over Pharaoh's daughter's eyes (though maybe she is a willing accomplice). She also turns out to be the means of frustrating Pharaoh's strategy. The womanly instincts that prompt the midwives, the mother and the sister also prompt the princess. The midwives revere God; implicitly, the mother and the sister trust God. Revering and trust are part of wisdom.

The first stories about Moses make clear that he was decisive, hasty and impetuous. His heart was in the right place, but that can be a mixed blessing. His adoption did not mean he was unaware of his ethnic identity, nor did he come to share the official Egyptian attitude to Hebrew or Israelite serfs. He takes decisive action, which he intends to be circumspect, but in that respect he fails, as he discovers when acting the same way the next day. Subsequently he likewise doesn't sit by when shepherds appropriate the water some girls have drawn for their flock. Exodus doesn't comment on the right or wrong of any of his actions.

He ends up as an alien in a foreign country. Reuel's daughters describe him as an Egyptian, presumably reflecting the way he dresses and/or speaks. Actually, he lives his whole life as an alien. Maybe that helps him fulfil the calling God gave him.

Meanwhile, the Israelites are groaning, crying out, crying for help and lamenting. It isn't explicit that they are crying out to God. They are just crying out in pain. But God can have a hard time resisting a cry of protest, whether or not it's addressed to him.

Alongside four words for pain, Exodus uses four verbs for God's response. First, God listened. It is great to have someone listen when you are in pain, but most people who listen to us can do nothing about it. In this case the listener could. Thus, second, God 'was mindful of his covenant'. He 'remembered' it in a way that meant taking action, Third, he looked, which matches listening. And fourth, he knew, or rather acknowledged, recognised what was going on, which matches being mindful. The vignettes about Moses and this statement about God leave us in suspense. What will happen next?

Lord, listen to the oppressed, be mindful of them, look at them, take notice of them.

3 It was an ordinary working day
Exodus 3

Moses is engaged in the family business, but he is out on his own and he won't get home for dinner, or even bedtime. There in the wilderness he sees a strange sight. The bush in question would be something like the spiky acacia. One can then hypothesise natural ways in which a bush might catch fire, but that would miss the point. Whatever is happening to the bush, it attracts Moses' attention. He turns aside and finds himself meeting God. God has turned this place into a portal where movement between heaven and earth can take place.

Like other Old Testament stories, Exodus is ambiguous about the identity of the figure appearing to Moses. It is initially called a divine aide, a heavenly being acting as God's representative, but then the figure speaks as if it actually is God. Suggesting it is a divine aide makes the experience less scary. Suggesting that God in person speaks underlines the event's significance; God's actual words necessarily convey a mixed message: Come near, but be careful about coming near.

What does Moses know of God? God first speaks as 'the God of your father', so God has been involved with Moses' family. God adds, 'the God of Abraham, Isaac and Jacob'. There is a straight line from God's involvement with the ancestors to God's involvement with Moses' family. Being involved with Israel's ancestors means God has now taken note of their descendants' suffering. He was unwise enough to make promises to them, and being God means you cannot get out of keeping your promises.

As Moses listens to God, I like to imagine him saying to himself, 'This is great, but why is God telling me all this? Where is it leading?' I wonder whether he guesses the answer before God gets to the outrageous point. 'What, me?' Moses first asks. But what then counts is God's 'I will be with you.'

As well as being the God of Abraham, Isaac and Jacob, God's actual name is 'Yahweh', a name that could remind people of the verb 'to be', so Yahweh adds, 'I will be what I will be.' I will be with you. So get on with leading your people out of Egypt.

Lord, you are the one who can be whatever you will be, for our sake.

4 Get back

Exodus 4

Moses has more questions and objections. 'What if they won't believe me?' Yahweh gives him another kind of sign. 'What about the fact that I am no speaker?' This is as irrelevant as Moses' earlier 'Who am I?' Finally, he asks, 'Oh, couldn't you just send someone else?' The person who is to lead has to be dragged into a position of leadership. God is long-tempered with Moses, but not infinitely tempered, yet that doesn't mean he has a change of mind. For some reason, he is set on using Moses.

The exodus story is the first great conflict in the Scriptures between God and an imperial power. Pharaoh thinks he is king, virtually thinks he is god. But this is the moment when the real King wants to act and do something that the human king will oppose. Israel has a position in relation to God a little like that of a firstborn son. It is due to receive the firstborn's inheritance or blessing, the gift of a country that belongs to its Father.

Moses has a family in Midian and a family in Egypt, so returning home means facing some questions about family and some questions about his own identity. Returning involves him in a near-death experience. God knows that the old Moses has to die if he is to fulfil his vocation. Inevitably this affects his family. It pulls Moses' wife and son into a new relationship with him and his vocation. It also involves Moses facing the question of his relationship to the covenant, whose sign he has neglected. Once again, the exodus story would have derailed had it not been for a woman's action.

We are not told how long Moses has been in Midian. Who knows what his family would make of his return with his Midianite wife after all this time? It's easy to imagine that the return of this migrant claiming that God has commissioned him to lead the Israelites out of Egypt would provoke a sceptical reaction. It is as well that God has also anticipated this, both in appearing to Aaron and in giving Moses (and now Aaron) the signs to perform. So the people 'believed'. Exodus is not directly talking about their believing in God, but they bow low in prostration.

Lord, give us grace to go when you send us.

5 'Let my people go, so that they may serve me'

Exodus 5 – 7

Service is a major theme in the exodus story, though English translations use a variety of words such as worship, bondage and slavery as well as service to translate related Hebrew words. Pharaoh makes the Israelites serve with harsh service. They cry out because of their service and they speak of themselves as Pharaoh's servants, but their cry by reason of their service reaches God, and he intends to bring them out from their service. Their escape will mean being brought out of a country of servants. They are going to be free of service to the Egyptians. Yet this is not in order simply to be free but in order to become Yahweh's servants.

Another key theme in these chapters is the toughness of Pharaoh's will. As Israel's Father, Yahweh's objective could be fulfilled simply by getting the Israelites out of Egypt. As King, however, God wants to make a point to the pretend king, his subjects and the world as a whole that hears about this event.

Translations then traditionally speak of the 'hardening of Pharaoh's heart'. But in English, the heart suggests feelings, whereas in the Scriptures it more often suggests thinking, taking up attitudes and making decisions. It's closer to what English refers to as the mind. So strengthening or stiffening the heart suggests making up the mind firmly. Moses is going to put pressure on Pharaoh to let the Israelites go, but God is also going to put pressure on Pharaoh not to. A quick and easy victory would do that, but prolonging the conflict will do it another way. It will suit God if Pharaoh resists the idea of letting God's son go. It will give God more chance to show who is king around here.

How will God go about stiffening or strengthening Pharaoh's resolve? Moses seeks to stiffen Israel's resolve by reminding Israel of what God has done for them. I imagine Yahweh does it by reminding Pharaoh how useful it would be to keep the Israelites as his serfs. The Israelites then have to decide what they will do, and so will Pharaoh. God won't be forcing him, though. Exodus often makes the point that he hardens his own heart.

Thank you, Lord, that your service is perfect freedom.

6 (Un)natural disasters
Exodus 8 – 10

If you are inclined to 'natural' explanations of things, you can see these stories as magnified accounts of 'natural' events. But Exodus has bigger things to say by means of these stories. God is intervening in the political, military and social affairs of Egypt, confronting the way it handles an immigrant community. Exodus is showing that nature, like humanity, is subordinate to God's purpose and that God is prepared to be as ruthless in relating to the natural world as in relating to the human world.

Moses' vocation draws him into being Pharaoh's prayer partner, prophet and adviser. Praying for him is a way of turning the other cheek. But Moses knows that Pharaoh's professions of repentance are false, and the prayers and their answers also demonstrate Moses' power. They function as part of what leaves Pharaoh without excuse. One of God's aims in bringing this series of disasters on Pharaoh is that he 'may acknowledge that there is no one like God in all the earth'. Forget the gods of Egypt.

But Pharaoh is the Scriptures' great flip-flopper, always changing his mind. 'This time,' he eventually says, speaking as if he has indeed come to a new position, 'I have sinned. Yahweh is in the right and I and my people are in the wrong.' With hindsight, we know where this flip-flop will end. But every time God acts in mercy toward Pharaoh it gives him a real chance to change.

Pharaoh models the way for a king to speak with a prophet when he knows he has done wrong, and it reminds the Israelites and their king not to flip-flop in these circumstances. Pharaoh wants Moses to plead with God to 'remove this death from me', to remove the epidemic bringing death to him and his people because the locusts have eaten everything that grows. But when God does that, he again changes. Whereas Pharaoh keeps seeking a compromise, both Moses and Yahweh are less and less inclined to compromise. This is a contest for the highest stakes, a contest to the death. An irresistible force is meeting an immoveable object. But the object will have to move in the end. Moses will express his anger, and so will God.

Lord, have mercy on the pharaohs, the people they lead and the people they oppress.

7 The angel of death passes by
Exodus 11 – 12

It's not only Pharaoh that Yahweh wants to draw into acknowledging Yahweh. These signs are designed also to draw Israel into that acknowledgement. The deaths of the firstborn happen 'so that you may acknowledge that Yahweh makes a distinction between Egypt and Israel'. Israel is God's firstborn: that is, the one God intends to privilege with a special responsibility and role to fulfil for its Father. Pharaoh is trying to hold on to this firstborn for his own purposes. It's not going to happen.

One strange aspect of the event is the daubing of blood on people's doors. It will mark the door as a home God can 'pass over'. Does God not know which are Israelite homes? Once again God prefers to look and see rather than rely on omniscience. In calling this a sign 'for you', however, Exodus also hints at the significance of daubing the blood for the people. It is their proclamation of who they are; they mark themselves as Israelites and not Egyptians.

Oddly, in the order of events in Exodus, the rules about how to observe Passover are detailed before the Passover event actually happens. It's an anticipatory festival, celebrated by faith. Then the actual Passover happens. Once again, the Egyptians are the victims of their leadership's stupidity. On the other hand, the Israelites are not the only beneficiaries of the event. There is also a mixed crowd of non-Israelites – Egyptians who had become convinced that Yahweh was God, and/or who saw no future for themselves in Egypt for one reason or another, and/or who had fallen in love with Israelite girls, and/or who were members of other ethnic groups.

Can they take part in Passover? Are they more like foreigners or Israelites? How does God relate to them? The answer is that they have to choose. If they want to become part of this covenant people, they can be circumcised and then take part. They and other people may always be aware that they belong to another ethnic group, but Israel is totally open to people from other ethnic groups joining the covenant community. You do not have to be born an Israelite in order to be part of God's people.

Lord, we celebrate your redeeming us from servitude and your making us your servants.

8 One kind of fear turns to another
Exodus 13 – 14

The obvious route from Egypt to Canaan goes up the coast, but Canaan was part of the Egyptian empire; there was much traffic along the coast, and going that way would mean trouble. God took them by an inland route, which involved crossing the Red Sea, the 'sea of rushes'. We can't locate any of the places Exodus mentions, but it is clear that God guides the Israelites into a cul de sac. One can hardly blame them for reacting as they did, and it doesn't mean God abandons them.

As usual, God has a bigger picture in mind. The Israelites' escape from Egypt didn't mean the exodus story was over. Pharaoh flip-flops once again. Each time there is a disaster, things look different when it's over. It's not clear that Pharaoh has really acknowledged who is God. Once again events demonstrate that Yahweh is God. But the Israelites go from hands held high in praise and confidence and triumph to abject fear. They cry out to God, which is the right thing to do, but their words to Moses indicate how terrified they are.

Like the disasters in Egypt, the parting of the sea has been explained as a natural event; a strong wind blew at just the right moment to let the Israelites through and then abated and caught the Egyptians as they followed. The story's conviction is that the event proved that Yahweh is God and that Pharaoh is much less powerful than he thinks. 'When Israel saw the great power Yahweh exercised on the Egyptians, the people feared Yahweh and trusted in Yahweh and in his servant Moses.' At the beginning of the story the midwives feared God in a good sense, rather than fearing Pharaoh and doing what he said. At the end of the story Israel gives up fearing the future and fearing Pharaoh in a bad sense because it has seen the reason for fearing God in a good sense. That it is a good fear is indicated by the fact that it goes along with trust. The Israelites have caught up with the midwives, who feared in the good sense.

We revere you, Lord, and we trust you.

9 Dancing by the sea
Exodus 15 – 16

As the women started off the exodus story, they round it off. When God acts to bring judgement, to show who is really God, or to put down oppressors, there is reason for grief and sadness and for joy and praise. You could call Exodus 15 the first psalm in the Bible. It emphasises a note running through the exodus story. The great power's leader thought he was god, but God has shown who is God. In addition, Israel sees the far-reaching significance of what God has done. It provides a basis for declaring that 'Yahweh will reign for ever and ever.'

Christians may be ambivalent about the church, and the Scriptures are ambivalent about the Israelites. After their deliverance at the Red Sea I imagine their hands were high again, but they soon discover that God's defeat of Pharaoh by no means solves all their problems. The Psalms make clear that it is fine to complain against God about things that happen to us. But the Israelites complain against Moses and Aaron, which requires less courage. Fortunately, Moses knows what to do. He cries out to God, who tells him to throw a tree branch into the pool of bitter water they have found. This seems a silly suggestion, but Moses has considerable experience of God doing exotic tricks.

The way the people then complain about their food supply suggests they have learned nothing ('Sin' is just the Hebrew name of the wilderness – it's not the Hebrew word for 'sin'). Indeed, things have got worse, and time has given a rosy glow to their life in Egypt compared with the reality Exodus has described. 'It's God you're complaining about, not us. God will act so spectacularly, it will show it was God who brought you out, not me,' Moses and Aaron reply.

The concrete way the provision of food will test them is that it will come every day, except that they will get two days' supply on Friday so they don't have to do anything to make sure they have enough to eat on the Sabbath. This puts them into daily reliance on God. It's another crazy divine expectation. But sense lies in trusting that things will work out if they do what God says.

I will sing to the Lord, because he has triumphed gloriously!

10 The first enemy and the first convert
Exodus 17 – 18

The Amalekites and the Midianite Jethro represent two attitudes to Israel and to the Jewish people over the millennia. Both were descendants of Abraham, so Israel's relationship with them is not like its relationship with Egypt. It is a relationship within the family. Exodus gives no reason for the Amalekites attacking the Israelites. Perhaps they think they can appropriate their flocks and herds. Perhaps they feel threatened by the Israelites advancing their way. Greed, resentment and fear have often fuelled antisemitism.

What do you do when Amalek attacks you? Moses and Joshua assume control of the power God gave to them at the Red Sea and direct the forces of heaven in the battle that follows. The battle is not merely a this-worldly one but one where God's forces are active in ensuring that Israel is not defeated. It resembles the conflict with Pharaoh, except that here for the first time the Israelites are involved in fighting; they do not just watch while God acts. Joshua wins a vital victory, though it doesn't involve annihilating Amalek; indeed, it's not explicit that the Israelites killed anyone (maybe the Amalekites ran for it). The promises with which the story closes are important for the future.

The story of the Midianite Jethro offers a contrast. Moses has the chance to tell his father-in-law what God has done for Israel in rescuing them from Pharaoh and then from the troubles they have had on their journey through Sinai. Jethro bursts out in praise, and brings his offerings to show he means it. It's quite a reaction from a Midianite priest. One should perhaps not call him the first convert; maybe that was Hagar in Genesis, and then there are all those people who accompanied the Israelites when they left Egypt. But he is the first person whose detailed conversion story we are told.

He also stands as a reminder of a better promise than the one concerning the destruction of Amalek, a promise that God will bring about a drawing of the world to acknowledge Israel's God. After offering Moses some fatherly advice, Jethro doesn't stay with Israel; he goes back home to resume his life. Yet he can never be the same.

Now I know that the Lord is greater than all gods.

11 Preparation for meeting God
Exodus 19

The Israelites' arrival at Sinai brings a new stage in the covenant relationship between God and Israel. God is already in a covenant relationship with them. What happens at Sinai is a kind of renegotiation of the terms of this covenant. When God made a covenant with Israel's ancestors, it was 99 per cent a commitment purely on God's part, a promise about something God was going to do. God has now initiated the process whereby the covenant promise is being fulfilled, the people are on their way to the country God promised them, so now God can reasonably think that the commitment between God and Israel should become more mutual.

'Kingdom of priests' and 'holy nation' is a twofold way of describing the same thing. They are a nation like any other nation, but they are a holy nation, a nation sacred to Yahweh. Being sacred and being a priesthood then reminds them (and reminds the monarch and their priests) that they all have a priestly relationship with God.

'All that Yahweh spoke, we will do.' Ah, if only! As well as putting a relational and moral challenge before the people, God's appearance at Sinai puts before them a spiritual and emotional one. For some people, God is a rather frightening person, and such people may be more comfortable with Jesus; the description of God in Exodus 19 confirms their worst fears. For others, God is a loving Father, and they are put off by the description. Exodus offers both sorts of people something to learn.

In the New Testament, Hebrews 12 takes up the Sinai story, notes how terrifying was God's appearance at Sinai and draws a contrast with the position of Christians. But it doesn't imply that they don't have to think in terms of fear. The contrast it notes is that the Israelites were merely listening to God on earth. If we turn away, God's speaking to us will also be terrifying. The Sinai audiovisual phenomena and God's warnings to Moses are designed to get Israel to take God's God-ness really seriously, though they need not be afraid of God, because they have already seen how God cares for them. So (says Hebrews 12:28–9, like Exodus 19), 'Let's worship God acceptably, with reverence and awe, because our God is a consuming fire.'

All that you have spoken, Lord, we will do.

12 A rule of life
Exodus 20

The Ten Commandments are the beginning of Israel's rule of life, especially addressing the heads of families. They begin from Yahweh's having brought Israel out of its serfdom in Egypt. The Israelites are now to be exclusively committed to him. They will live alongside people in Canaan who turn to other gods for what they need. Israelites are to rely on Yahweh for all these needs. And they are not to make statues to help them worship. A statue can never truly represent the real God. In effect, worshipping with the help of a statue means worshipping a different god.

They must not associate Yahweh with things that have nothing to do with him and actually have no reality, maybe by waging their own wars and calling them Yahweh's, or building a sanctuary to suit them and saying this is Yahweh's will, or making their own decisions and calling them Yahweh's, or appointing the government they want and calling it Yahweh's. They are to see to the observance of the Sabbath. A householder is to make sure that everyone can observe it, including the servants and even the animals.

The householder is to honour his parents as they grow old and may be more of a nuisance. The family is basic to the way Israel is to work, and failing to honour parents imperils the fundamental structure of the society. No one is to murder anyone. The KJV has 'Thou shalt not kill', but the command uses not the ordinary word for kill but a word for slaying someone without warrant. It does not preclude execution or war. It does presuppose that relationships can get so fraught in the community that one person might want to kill another. People are not to have affairs, another reality of life that imperils the family and thus the society. They are not to steal: their neighbour's animals and crops are the family's livelihood. They are not to testify that their neighbours have done something that they have not. That can be a 'legal' way of achieving the same ends as murder or stealing.

They are to look to the inner attitude that lies behind such outward acts. Be content with and do your best with what you have, says the command. Trust that things will be OK.

We will have no other gods but you, Lord.

13 Seeing God
Exodus 24

In Exodus 20 – 23, Yahweh has laid down some more detailed expectations in connection with his covenant relationship with Israel, and said some things about how they are going to get to Canaan and what will happen there. In light of that, now he sets up a procedure for them properly to affirm their covenant commitment.

I'm not sure what kind of 'seeing' God Exodus 24 then refers to. It tells its story in a confusing way. Who goes up the mountain? Moses? Moses and Aaron with Nadab and Abihu? Hur? Seventy elders? Some 'pillars' of the community? Joshua? And who sees what? Part of the genius of this way of telling a story is to make some realities clear yet leave you with an appropriate sense of mystery.

People reading this story can know it is making a series of vital affirmations. God really met with Israel at Sinai. The average Israelite was protected from the scary aspect of that meeting; the people's leaders met with God on the people's behalf. Key to God's meeting with them was sealing the new version of the covenant relationship, so the people who hear this story can have assurance about God's relationship with them. Key to the covenant sealing being effective is Israel's making its own commitment to God; so the people who hear this story need to affirm that commitment for themselves. God did make sure that Israel knew how it was expected to live in the future; so the people who hear this story can be sure that they know God's expectations.

The actions with the animals' blood are not regular sacrifices but a special ceremony that can be associated with the making of a covenant. We know of an ancient document recording a treaty between Syria and Assyria that involves dismembering a lamb and the Syrian king praying that he may be treated the same way if he breaks the treaty. Thus when Exodus speaks of 'sealing' the covenant, it more literally refers to it as 'cutting' the covenant. The ceremony involved dismembering the animals and spattering the blood on the people, and also on the altar, which stands for God. God and people are thereby saying, 'May I be dismembered and my blood be spattered if I break this covenant.'

On my life, I really will keep the covenant, Lord.

14 How to pray for rebels
Exodus 32

One sympathises with Aaron. Against the background of an idyllic scene on top of the mountain, with Moses memorising Yahweh's instructions for the sanctuary that the people are to construct so that God can come to dwell among them, at the bottom of the mountain the people are engaged in something close to the opposite of what God has in mind. With Moses seeming to have got lost, they turn to the leader's apparent next-in-command and urge him to do something.

God has to be incensed, and so is Moses. He encourages anyone on God's side to exact terrible punishment on the people involved in the apostasy. But first he confronts God. God's inclination is simply to abandon the people and start again with Moses. Cleverly, Moses says, 'You can't do that. What will the Egyptians say? What about the promises you have bound yourself by?' How is God to respond to the rebelliousness and failure of the people of God? God is torn between the obligation to cast off and the obligation to be merciful. He relents.

In prayer we are like children begging our parents to do what we want. Significantly, when he challenges God, Moses is not praying for himself but for the people, and praying about God's own honour. Is prayer about conforming our will to God's will? Moses thinks prayer is about conforming God's will to our will; or rather, Moses knows that God's will is not always inexorably fixed, that God has to wrestle with conflicting obligations, and that it can be only on a fifty-one to forty-nine basis that God makes a decision about which of the obligations that press on him has priority. It might be easy to push the figures the other way.

Moses speaks again later like someone brash and audacious, totally committed to Israel: 'If you won't have them, you can't have me.' God's 'book' might be simply God's list of the people belonging to Israel or God's plans about how to fulfil the purpose to take Israel to its destiny and bring blessing to the world. This time God resists Moses' argument, to make another point that needs making. There is such a thing as individual human responsibility. Moses has to let his people accept theirs.

Lord, when you are tempted to act in wrath, remember that we are your people.

15 The magnificent presence
Exodus 33 – 34

The meeting tent for which Moses has received specifications has not yet been built, but a meeting tent evidently already exists where people could go to talk to God, and where Moses goes to talk to God about this journey to Canaan. In that connection, Moses says, I need you to show me your way, to show me the kind of God you are. God's response is, 'My presence [more literally, my face] will come and I will give you rest.' That's not enough for Moses; he wants to see God's splendour. That's unrealistic; it would be like looking at the sun. But God takes Moses as close as possible to this, yet protects him from its mortal danger. God will proclaim the goodness, grace and compassion associated with the name Yahweh in their wide-ranging reach ('whomever').

The implications are worked out in God's self-description, a succinct summary of systematic theology, of a doctrine of God that is often referred to in the Psalms and the Prophets. What is God like? What is God's way? God is compassionate: the word is similar to the Hebrew word for the womb. God is gracious: grace means showing favour to someone in a way unrelated to whether they merit it. God is long-tempered: the readers of Exodus can look back over Israel's story and see how God's not casting off the people shows how long-tempered he is. God is big in commitment, staying faithful though people forfeit any right to expect that he would. God is big in truthfulness: when God makes promises, they come true. God keeps commitment to thousands of generations. God carries waywardness rather than making people carry it. God does not acquit: he may eventually say, 'That's it.' Indeed, God can pay people a visit as a result of their waywardness, the way the mafia do. The good news is that you can take God for granted. The bad news is that you cannot take God for granted.

When Moses comes down the mountain, his face emanates, apparently radiating something horn-like and frightening. Yes, God's splendour is something that in a sense people need protection from. But for Moses to reflect God's splendour means he really has been in God's presence and really can mediate God's message to people.

Go with us, Lord, even though we are a stiff-necked people.

16 Be holy as I am holy
Leviticus 19

The last part of Exodus relates how the Israelites duly constructed a sanctuary for Yahweh, and the first part of Leviticus describes how sacrifices were to be offered there and how some of the priests who were to offer them got in calamitous trouble through the way they did so. It details some rules about taboo and cleansing, including one that Mary observed after Jesus was born, and some others that Jesus told a man to observe. Leviticus then puts together a wide variety of imperatives that need to shape the community's life.

One aspect is a concern for things to be fair for the powerless, the alien and the ordinary worker. The Torah is aware of the temptation for the community to ignore such people's needs and for the community court to ignore such people's rights. Further, if someone treats you wrongly, or you discover that someone has committed a wrong, your job is to talk straight and confront the person. It's not to share in the guilt because you've been complicit, or hold on to grievances and look for a chance to take matters into your own hands. You are to care for your neighbour even when your neighbour does wrong. You can't 'hate your enemy'; it is your enemy that you are bidden to love or care for. Jesus' exhortation to love your enemy brings out the Torah's implications.

Leviticus offers two considerations to motivate you in your relationships, especially when there is conflict. The community are your neighbours, your kin, your brothers and sisters. You are to make the family your model for relationships in the community. The other consideration lies in God. You are to be holy because God is holy. In itself, God's holiness lies in God's deity, God's distinctiveness, God's extraordinariness. Israel is to be distinctive over against other people in some ways that may seem random, as they are listed in the rest of the chapter and the rest of Leviticus.

Yahweh's distinctiveness also lies in qualities such as integrity and love, and Israel is expected to mirror those, too. That expectation finds expression in biddings that cover clothes, sex, food, honesty, mediums, festivals, fights, debt…: the whole of life.

Lord, we commit ourselves to being holy as you are holy.

17 Missing garlic
Numbers 11

The first part of Numbers relates how the Israelites get ready to leave Sinai. Then within five minutes there's trouble because all they have to eat is this 'stuff', the 'manna'. This word simply transliterates a Hebrew word that looks as if it would mean 'What?' It is apparently a resin-like substance, present in the morning on certain trees in Sinai. But why does everyone get so worked up?

Here are some of the points from the two opening stories in this chapter.

1 Disappointments often come to the people of God.
2 These often affect basic physical needs, such as health or food.
3 Taking too much notice of people on the edge of the community can lead the community astray.
4 Disappointments test the people of God, bringing to the surface who they really are.
5 They can make us look wistfully to the past and make us wish God had never taken hold of us.
6 The people of God are then inclined to complain rather than talk to God about their troubles.
7 The disillusion can be contagious, hard to dissociate oneself from.
8 God overhears, finds it annoying and reacts by sending more trouble.
9 The job of leaders is to plead with God on the people's behalf.
10 The complaints often get the leaders down as they feel responsible for the people.
11 It's OK for leaders to bring their complaints to God in the most confrontational terms.
12 God responds to such prayers and cries.

God then gives seventy senior Israelites some of the spirit on Moses, and they 'prophesy', which means something like speaking in tongues. This even affects two men who hadn't come to the meeting where God gave this gift, which worries Joshua. The story reminds Israel's later leaders not to feel the need to control everything that God's spirit may do.

Then a supernatural wind deposits quail three feet deep all over the camp, which seems like an answer to prayer but turns out to be something more complicated, because God subsequently strikes down some of the people. Perhaps they ate bad quail, though Numbers comments that nevertheless it is God who strikes down the victims. It's the kind of story that Paul thinks churches need to learn from (see 1 Corinthians 10:1–13).

Lord, would that all your people were prophets!

18 Dealing with ambition
Numbers 16

Moses continually has to deal with the pressures of leadership. Among the later Israelites there may have been tensions over who should have the role of priests. Is it everyone who can claim to be descended from Levi? The Torah declared that only Aaron's descendants are priests, the other Levites being their support staff. The Old Testament then bids Israel be charitable to Levites, as it must be to widows and orphans; this suggests they were in a vulnerable position. And what about the relative positions of Aaron's sons and their descendants? What about the relative status of different clans? The chapter is convoluted and looks as if it combines more than one story and more than one version of a story. Evidently the questions are important.

The chapter will support the special position of Aaron's descendants. But the context either side of this chapter includes critique of Aaron, so it will be unwise for his descendants to make too much of this story. The next chapter will also provide some solemn things to think about and will underline how ordinary people are wise to rejoice in being ordinary people.

The story is another one that urges the later community to continue taking Moses seriously. But Moses has no successors. Taking Moses seriously means paying heed to his teaching rather than to teaching that seeks to displace him. Aaron's descendants also have to remember that Korah and his friends are right; the leadership always has to remember that the whole community is holy and God is in its midst.

Yet the story presupposes that their arguing for this point is self-serving. They are not seeking to introduce democracy, to give power to the people. Their claim is that they have as much right to be leaders as Moses and Aaron. People who seek leadership claiming they do it for the people's sake when really it is because they want to exercise power have to remember the story of Korah and his friends. Moses' and Aaron's vocation is to continue serving the people and praying for them. They are to do nothing to prove that they are in the right. It is God's job to vindicate them, not theirs.

Lord, will one person sin and you become angry with the whole congregation?
(Numbers 16:22)

19 One fatal mistake
Numbers 20

Miriam, Aaron and Moses should have led Israel into the promised land, but they all died before they got there. Indeed, a whole generation of Israel has died. Their children are now the people who have arrived at the staging post for entering Canaan.

So it is decades since Miriam made the mistake that was related in Numbers 12. A few months previously, Aaron had made his first mistake, with the gold calf. He is now implicated in Moses' fatal mistake. The Bible story can be depressing; nobody ever learns anything. Or perhaps it is encouraging, because we have the same experience in the church.

There is again no water. Again the community is in a panic about themselves and their animals. Again they look back to Egypt with rose-tinted spectacles. Again they blame their leaders rather than God. Again Moses and Aaron turn to God. Are they distraught, or at a loss, or scared for themselves or for the people? Again God tells them what to do and declares that there will be miraculous provision. Again they do it, and there is.

Yet everything goes wrong. How do the two of them fail to trust God and make God holy in the Israelites' eyes? God instructed them to tell the crag to produce water. What they do is upbraid the people as rebels, and Moses twice hits the crag with his staff. There is some contrast with the story in Exodus 17 where God gave Moses instructions and Moses simply 'did so'. It doesn't seem a huge contrast, but God sees it as implying a double failure, upbraiding the people and striking the rock. When God accuses them of a failure of trust, it likely means they are trusting in themselves to solve the problem. It would link with Moses' hitting the rock rather than merely addressing it. In turn it would imply failing to make God holy, to recognise and honour God's God-ness. Their action does not involve the precise obedience Moses shows on many occasions, which maybe indicates that something has gone wrong with their attitude. But one would never have guessed this was happening if Numbers had not told us. Moses and Aaron make a tiny mistake that has shattering consequences for them both.

We promise to trust you, Lord, and not to ascribe too much responsibility to ourselves.

20 A snake epidemic, and an attempt to be peaceable
Numbers 21

Snakes as a means of chastisement are a new feature in the story. The copper snake is then an example of God working through a physical, sacramental sign. God could heal people without such means but he chooses to use physical means, perhaps because we are physical people. But the Israelites can turn a physical sign into a superstition. They eventually burn incense to the copper snake as if it were a kind of idol, so King Hezekiah breaks it up (2 Kings 18:4). (In John 3:14, Jesus turns the lifting up of the snake into an illustration: he will be lifted up, on a cross, and people will look to him and find healing.)

The snake story sits between several war stories. The Israelites needed to pass through the Edomites' territory and they asked for a transit visa, but the Edomites got ready to attack instead of granting it. So the Israelites went another way. Don't fight if you can help it. The Aradites attacked them and the Israelites had the frightening idea of promising Yahweh that they would kill them all and offer them up as a kind of gift to Yahweh if he made it possible to defeat them, and God agreed. It is a horrifying moment, because it's the first time that the idea arises of killing everyone like that.

Marching north, they come next to the territory of Og, the king of Bashan, which extends into the modern Golan Heights. This time there is no reference to negotiation. Og simply attacks, and God bids the Israelites not be afraid: 'I hereby give him into your hand.' So by accident Israel enters into possession of substantial land east of the Jordan. Another such victory follows as the Israelites reach Amorite territory, when again they declare no interest in this land, but the people come out to attack and find themselves defeated, slaughtered and dispossessed.

Israel is learning to live as a nation in the world as it is, and God is going with Israel through that process. The modern world has at least four attitudes to war: just war, pacifism, crusade and pragmatism. None is distinctively biblical and the stories in Numbers give us raw material for our thinking.

Help us to see straight as we have to live in the world, Lord.

21 A story about several asses
Numbers 22 – 24

The Old Testament recognises that prophecy, like priesthood and sacrifice, was known among other Middle Eastern peoples. Indeed, a prophet called Balaam appears in an inscription dating from Old Testament times, from a place near Jericho. Numbers assumes that God can work through foreign prophets as well as through Israelite ones, and Israel does not need to be afraid of their power. Even if they have the power to curse, God can make sure Israel is not imperilled by that power.

When the second embassy arrives offering more impressive rewards than the first embassy, to entice Balaam to come and do his stuff, Balaam is dismissive of them. His prophetic power cannot be bought. Yet evidently God reckons he should have simply accepted God's original 'No' rather than attempting to reopen the question of whether he might agree. So God's permission to go with the embassy doesn't indicate this is what God really wants; God is adapting to Balaam.

There turn out to be three donkeys in this story. The first is Balak, who thinks you can buy your way into frustrating God's will for Israel. The second is Balaam, who thinks God may be willing to have a change of mind about blessing Israel. The third is the donkey that Balaam hits, the character with the most spiritual insight in the story. The joke is that the donkey can see what Balaam cannot see. She can see when God sends an aide to stand in Balaam's way like a highwayman, and God can enable her to tell Balaam so. It will be stupid for Balaam even to think about opposing God's purpose by attempting to curse Israel.

But Balaam sees Israel not merely as it is at the moment but as it will be. The further joke is that the Israelites know nothing about the drama unfolding in the mountains. It's also apposite that this Gentile blessing comes near the end of the story that takes Abraham's people from the initial promise that they will possess land in Canaan to the fulfilment of this promise in their entering into that land. Over the centuries God has not stopped Gentiles from cursing Israel and the Jewish people, yet they have continued in existence.

Lord, you are not a human being to lie. You have promised, and will you not do it?

22 Moses' last sermon

Deuteronomy 6

The challenge, 'Listen, Israel: Yahweh our God Yahweh one', is the central expectation that Jewish faith lays on people. As a sentence, 'Yahweh our God Yahweh one' works in Hebrew, as it doesn't in English, since in Hebrew you can have a sentence without a verb.

We could describe this commitment to Yahweh by Israel as monotheistic, but that risks missing the point, which is not merely that there is only one God. It declares who this God is and affirms that people acknowledge this God and repudiate others. The Old Testament does not dispute that there are many supernatural beings (gods with a small g, we might say), but it knows that Yahweh belongs to a unique class of heavenly being, a class with only one member. Yahweh is the creator of all these other beings and the one with sovereignty over them all. They are Yahweh's underlings and aides, though often not very faithful ones.

In his exhortation, Moses uses a sequence of words that we have noticed occur in the Scriptures with different association from the associations that attach to the English equivalents. In the traditional translation, his affirmation goes on to urge Israel to 'love' Yahweh, but in English the word *love* suggests primarily emotions. The way Moses qualifies the word presupposes it has a wider significance. People are to 'love' or dedicate themselves or give themselves to God with their whole mind, their whole person, all their might. The word for 'mind' is literally 'heart', but in the Scriptures it suggests the inner person as a whole, the person thinking things through and deciding things. The word for 'person' itself is often translated 'soul', but it denotes the whole person with all its life. The commitment Moses is looking for is a self-giving that involves all people's energy and focus.

Moses wants Israel to fear Yahweh in the sense of revering him. And as with love (and hate), it's then not merely a matter of feeling but of action. To revere motivates and implies obedience. 'Forget' and 'remember' also suggest action and imply something deliberate, not accidental. Deuteronomy encourages Israelites to have ways of encouraging themselves to remember and to talk about God's involvement with them all the time.

You, Lord, are our God, you alone.

23 Moses dies on the mountains
Deuteronomy 34

Moses dies on the mountain heights east of the Jordan; he will not lead Israel into the promised land. His work is done, and he dies when he has lived a full life, three whole generations. There's a saying: Moses spent forty years learning to be somebody, forty years learning to be nobody and forty years showing what God could do with somebody who had learned to be nobody.

Yet he dies unnaturally, without setting foot in the promised land. But Deuteronomy doesn't seem to fret about that on his behalf. God invites Moses to savour the sight of the length of the land from where he is. Deuteronomy rather implies that being able simply to view the whole land is enough.

God has an excuse for not allowing Moses to enter the land, but God's instinct to be merciful would surely make it natural to overlook the rebellion that sealed Moses' and Aaron's fate. Moses' fate ironically parallels that of the Canaanites themselves. Although they were an immoral society and couldn't claim they did not deserve judgement, they were no more immoral than average, but they were in the wrong place at the wrong time. Maybe something else is going on. Moses belongs to the age that is passing; there is an appropriateness about having a new leader to take Israel into the land.

Either way, God is prepared to be tough. When God commissioned Moses, it was not for Moses' benefit, and when God decommissions Moses, it is not essentially for reasons to do with Moses but with God's purpose and Israel's destiny. The point is summed up in the title Deuteronomy gives to Moses. He is not a leader but a servant – not the people's servant but God's servant. It's easy to attach too much importance to a leader, and God wants Israel to attach importance to Moses in the right way. The mystery about Moses' death is that he simply disappears. He climbs the mountain and never comes back. Apparently God buries him. That means they could never turn his grave into a pilgrimage site. The location of his body was not what mattered. The way to remember Moses wasn't to put flowers on his grave but to follow his teaching.

Lord, stay with us until our time comes, and then continue to stay with us.

24 Meanwhile, in the saloon
Joshua 1 – 2

Joshua and Israel have one more river to cross. In literal terms it's not a very impressive river. For much of the year it's a shallow, muddy affair. But symbolically, it's a big deal. On the other side are all those Canaanites, whose large size struck the Israelite spies a generation ago. Historically, they are indeed a stronger and more sophisticated people than the Israelites.

But God has promises for Israel's new leader, though he also has exhortations for him. The promise 'I will be with you' sounds routine, but it is not to be skipped over. It means God will make sure things work out. Joshua will succeed in the task set before him. This is what can enable him to be strong and stand firm.

The exhortations also relate to that possibility. The key to successful leadership is sticking close to the teaching Moses has bequeathed to him. But what then follows is odd: Joshua sends two men to reconnoitre Jericho, as if he is going to attack it. Actually, all Israel is going to do is undertake a religious procession, blow their horns and watch the city's walls fall down.

Jericho is a stunning oasis in a barren landscape, a thousand feet below sea level, too hot in the summer but pleasant in the winter, a Wild West town, with the saloon doubling as a lodging house and the manageress doubling as madam. Evidently the sheriff knows about the Israelites hovering the other side of the Jordan. Rahab shares the sheriff's assessment of the situation but reacts differently. Rahab the Canaanite reacts the same way as Jethro the Midianite when hearing about the miracle at the Red Sea, recognising that Yahweh is more than merely Israel's tribal god.

The Torah gave no indication that Yahweh would make any exceptions when driving the Canaanites out of the country, but the two men take for granted that there is no reason to drive out or kill anyone who submits to Yahweh. Like Jonah's declaration that all Nineveh is to be destroyed, whenever God threatens destruction, the threat always presupposes 'unless you repent'. Rahab models the sensible way to respond to God's threats of punishment. She will appear in Jesus' genealogy in Matthew 1.

You, Lord, are God in the heavens above and in the earth beneath.
(Joshua 2:11)

25 On getting your feet wet
Joshua 3 – 4

I think the image of 'getting your feet wet' derives from this story. Often you can't achieve something or learn something without making a commitment that may seem risky.

When the Israelites came out of Egypt, Psalm 114:3 recalls, 'the sea saw and fled, the Jordan turned back'. Things have moved on now. Israel has with them the covenant chest, the 'ark', a more concrete symbol than the column of cloud and fire. But the book of Joshua tells this story in a way that shows how it pairs with the Red Sea story. God again does 'wonders', waters stand up in a 'heap', the people pass through on 'dry ground' and the waters then return to their usual place. And the event demonstrates Yahweh's power to the world as a whole, so that kings dissolve in fear, to confirm Rahab's words and indicate that Joshua's words are finding fulfilment.

The Israelites cross the river and make their camp at Gilgal on the day that signifies the beginning of the observance of Passover, with its broader commemoration of the exodus. Locating the twelve stones there and portraying the crossing as a repetition of the Red Sea crossing means that a pilgrimage to Gilgal could become a remembering of the Red Sea deliverance as well as the people's arrival in Canaan. One can imagine how priests might re-enact the event and bring it to life before the people.

Gilgal will thus be an important place for festival-type celebration. One can imagine Joshua's scenario being realised as families make pilgrimage here and children point to the twelve stones and ask what they signify; and if they don't, because they are too busy running to the river to wade and swim, their parents will tell them anyway over dinner.

Crossing the river didn't require a miracle. The Jordan miracle is an extravagance on God's part, a sign of Yahweh's power and commitment designed to embolden the Israelites for all that is to follow. Like the Red Sea miracle, it's open to being 'explained' as a natural event (a fortuitous earthquake upriver), though that either destroys the point of the story or makes even more miraculous the way it happened at precisely that moment.

You, Lord, are the living God who dried up the waters of the Jordan and took your people across.

26 Joshua fit the battle of Jericho
Joshua 6

Actually, there was no battle at Jericho, or if anyone fought at Jericho, it was not the Israelites but God. The Israelites simply processed, blew horns and shouted loud. The essential involvement of the priests made it more like the procession around the parish bounds that churches sometimes do. The presence of the covenant chest, the 'ark', as the symbol of their relationship with God was an effective sign of God's presence.

Then the Israelites 'devoted' the things and the people there. Devoting things means giving them over to God. This sometimes implies giving them over for God's service, but it sometimes implies executing them, and both significances apply in this story. The plunder from Jericho is to be put in the sanctuary treasury; the living things are executed (though God never commissioned that action).

Like other ancient cities, Jericho comprises a huge mound made of the remains of a sequence of cities that accumulated over the centuries, like the layers of a cake. When you visit Jericho, you stand on top of the remains of the mound and look down into excavated areas that are much older than the place where you are standing.

Once when I visited Jericho, a tour guide there humorously but also somewhat seriously assured his party that if they climbed down into the hole and looked by the walls, they might find Joshua's trumpet. The walls to which he was pointing are actually a thousand years older than Joshua's day. There are no remains at Jericho from Joshua's day. It seems that no one lived in Jericho at that time. The story of his conquest of Jericho is just a story, which might both cause us anxiety and offer us relief. It is a basically fictional story, but one that God was happy to have in his book. He apparently liked the story with its account of how the Canaanites deserved judgement and how he used Joshua in bringing it about. Even as a more-or-less fictional story, it vividly symbolises the fact that God gave Israel its land. It reminded Israel that it did not gain control of the land by its own efforts.

Lord, we thank you for fulfilling your promise to our ancestors and giving them the land you promised.

27 The ambush and the celebration

Joshua 8

At first things went wrong at Ai, for reasons Joshua 7 explains, but the story then shows that if you sort things out with God, you can have a new start. Once more God gives Joshua a game plan, quite different from the Jericho one, yet one that also means that it is not by military power that Israel is going to take Canaan. But the Ai plan involves no divine intervention. If you had been there and things happened as the story relates them, you would be admiring Joshua's stratagem and feeling a bit sorry for Ai because the people were so gullible. Sometimes God acts by miracles, sometimes God acts through human means.

It's even clearer than is the case with Jericho that in Joshua's day no one lived in Ai. The name gives the game away: 'Ai' means 'ruin'. It had been a ruin for a thousand years in Joshua's day. But one can imagine Israelites going down to Gilgal to celebrate the way God gave them the country and passing these ruins and making them the subject of stories that expressed in vivid terms the fact that God gave them the country.

According to these stories, all Israel has done so far is cross the Jordan and defeat two city-states, and thus only made a beginning to occupying the land. Yet here Joshua builds an altar at the centre of the country as if it's all over. Israel's initial victories symbolise and guarantee the fulfilment of God's intentions for them.

The ceremony also places a challenge before them. They have been given the country in fulfilment of God's word; they have to be committed to living by God's word. Making a copy of Moses' teaching symbolises this commitment. Because the covenant chest contains the stone tablets inscribed with the basic covenant requirements, to stand by the covenant chest for the reading of the covenant blessings and curses adds to the symbolising of this commitment.

The story emphasises the involvement of men and women, young and old, native-born Israelites and aliens who have chosen to associate themselves with Israel. Your sex, age or ethnic background make no difference. All have benefited from what God has done; all must accept the obligations that follow.

We too, Lord, commit ourselves to heeding your biddings as you have fulfilled your promises to us.

28 How to get taken in
Joshua 9

'Mum, if we were supposed to kill the Canaanites, how come there are all those Gibeonites working in the Temple?' Children's questions can be embarrassing. 'Well, Joshua was a great guy, but…' Joshua was gullible, and the Hivites were clever. The story is both funny and serious. Joshua should surely have seen that there was something fishy about the Hivites' story and should have asked God what to do instead of just sampling their stale bread and believing their vague story. He knows consulting God is what Moses used to do; he was in charge of the tent where Moses went to ask God things. Ignoring that possibility, he makes peace and makes a treaty.

'But Mum, you didn't explain how those Hivites come to be working in the Temple every day now.' The Hivite cities are all near Jerusalem, but at this time Jerusalem is just an obscure little town off the main road. It will eventually be the site of the Temple, which will need considerable support staff. That's where the local people come in. There's no suggestion that being Temple servants means ill-treatment or oppression, and it's preferable to being dead.

But there's more to it than that. The Hivites are like Rahab and her family, who were due to die as part of God's judgement on the Canaanite peoples as a whole. Rahab knew how to react when she heard about what Yahweh had been doing with the Israelites, and she became part of the Israelite community without losing the awareness that ethnically she was a foreigner. The Hivites, too, have heard what Yahweh has been doing with the Israelites but they haven't responded either with Rahab's straightness or with the other kings' hostility. So they end up in a support role in the Temple. We don't get told whether they ever come to identify with Israel's commitment to Yahweh in the way Rahab, and Moses' Midianite father-in-law Jethro, and Ruth did, but at least they had the chance to.

'You see, son, when you've promised something, you have to keep your word, even if the other people deceived you, and even if you should never have let yourself be deceived. Who knows, God may bring good out of it.'

Give us wisdom, Lord, and give us grace to keep our word.

29 'You can't serve Yahweh!' 'Yes, we can!'

Joshua 24

Joshua has spoken much of God's reliability in fulfilling promises. Here he speaks tough. The people need to recognise that God is holy: different, special, extraordinary, and someone you can't mess with. God is passionate: he feels things really strongly. It's hard for God to dismiss people's unfaithfulness with a shrug of the shoulders. God does do that quite a lot, but parents can reach a point with their (grown-up) children, and teachers can reach a point with their (grown-up) students, when they must say, 'That's it!' God is also like that. Joshua needs the people to recognise those dynamics to a relationship with God. There's a sense in which it's safer not to make a commitment to God at all.

Joshua's reference to their putting away foreign gods is a surprise. Surely we should have heard about their possessing foreign gods somewhat earlier? In Joshua's own context, it may carry an interesting implication. The scene is Shechem, where Israel erected the altar and made the commitment a little while ago. What was odd there is that they had not fought the people of Shechem or attacked the city. So, to connect a few dots into a big picture, maybe this is an occasion when people like the Shechemites made their commitment to Yahweh, with the whole community doing what Rahab did? That would explain the toughness of Joshua's argument and their need to put away other gods, and it would fit in with other indications that the Israelites becoming a settled and united people in Canaan was not just a matter of killing off or chasing off the previous inhabitants.

Historically, that question of local people making a commitment to Yahweh will more likely have arisen much later than Joshua's day. The Old Testament story will be telescoping events, as it does in describing all God's promises as being fulfilled already. In later centuries, there will be an ongoing need that people who come to see themselves as belonging to Israel truly recognise what belonging to Israel implies. One thing joining Israel in this way implies is that Israel's story becomes their story. But it also means they have to live with the implications and become the exodus people and the covenant people.

As for me and my household, we will serve you, Yahweh.

March

THE BIRTH
OF ISRAEL

1 The power of forgetting
Judges 2

The chapter begins with a recap – Joshua hasn't died yet. But his death marks a significant transition in the people's life. So far, Yahweh has focused on involvement in political events and war, on getting the people out of Egypt and into Canaan, and less on the natural world and the cosmos. Now the Israelites are settled in Canaan, they need a deity who knows how to make the crops grow.

And the Canaanites said their gods knew about that. They also knew about making contact with family members after they died, and, as generations passed, the Israelites, too, would no doubt like to be able to keep in touch with their family members after they die, and maybe learn from them. Further, the lively nature of the dysfunctional family life of the Canaanite gods and goddesses, with their fighting and sex and drinking and procreating and dying and coming back to life, may have intrigued the Israelites, even if they also professed to be appalled.

Involvement with the Canaanite gods will now characterise Israel's life for centuries. Judges portrays the period it covers as a series of stories of forgetting, apostasy, chastisement, mercy and restoration. The Israelites do what is 'bad'; God makes 'bad' things happen to them. Israel knew that life didn't always work out with that logic, but sometimes it did. Judges will portray these events as involving 'Israel', though now that Israel is spread over Canaan, more literally they involve individual clans or combinations of clans in different parts of the country.

The Old Testament refers to Canaanite deities as Baals, but Baal is an ordinary word for Lord or Master, so they are more literally the Masters. Judges also mentions the Ashtoreths; there are various ways of spelling that word, and this may be an insulting Israelite way of spelling it, because it combines the consonants of the name as the Canaanites would spell it with the vowels of a Hebrew word for 'shame'. The effect is that even naming this deity suggests it is something shameful. Ashtoreth was a particular goddess, but this name also came to be used as a general term, in this case for a goddess. So the Masters and the Ashtoreths denote Canaanite deities in general.

Lord, you are the God of politics and history and nature and harvest, and we acknowledge you.

2 The left-handed assassin
Judges 3

God isn't bound by eldest-ism. As elder brother, Othniel had the Caleb whom Joshua 14 – 15 showed to be a star, but that doesn't make God unwilling to use his little brother, and it doesn't make Othniel bashful about finding himself as God's agent. His emergence is God's response when the people cry out, even though they are paying the penalty for their waywardness. The extraordinary nature of Othniel's achievement is an indication that God's dynamic and forceful spirit is at work.

God isn't bound by able-ism. Leviticus requires a priest to be a 'complete' person. There was some symbolism about that wholeness. But it didn't mean that in other connections God wasn't prepared to use someone who was handicapped. There was also some symbolism in this. Ehud couldn't use his right hand, but his disability becomes God's means of making him Israel's deliverer. More than any other chapter in Judges (maybe any other chapter in the Scriptures), the scatological Ehud story turns upside down our assumptions about what a holy book ought to be. One can imagine Israelite teenagers enjoying it. God uses a disabled man, and uses a gruesome story about a disabled man.

God isn't bound by ethnocentrism. God makes Shamgar son of Anat someone who delivered Israel. The name Shamgar is not Israelite, and Anat is the name of a Canaanite deity, so it's not too adventurous to infer that Shamgar was a Canaanite. The unfortunate Canaanites were being pressed from the west by the Philistines and Shamgar evidently won a victory over some of them. And any victory over the Philistines could be seen as a means of God delivering Israel. Thus, presumably without realising it, Shamgar was God's servant in this respect.

Our modern inclination is to explain events in empirical and natural cause–effect terms. We see the effect of economic and social factors in the way history unfolds. We don't instinctively bring God into the picture. The Old Testament likewise from time to time shows that it's aware that history works out in cause–effect terms and reflects the ambitions and needs of nations and individuals, but it doesn't confine itself to that level of explanation. Judges thus invites us to look at history from this other perspective.

We acknowledge with gratitude, Lord, that you have so many ways of delivering your people.

3 Deborah the judge
Judges 4

Deborah is the Hebrew word for a bee, and there was a sting in her words. An irony lies in the description of her as 'the wife of Lappidoth'. Translations take it as her husband's name, but it's an odd name, and it may actually be a description of Deborah herself as 'a fiery woman'. She is the first prophet since Miriam and Moses, and maybe there wouldn't be much room for another powerful person in their marriage.

Institutional ministry in the Old Testament belongs to men. But when God wants to break in, prophecy is one way he does so, sometimes through women prophets. Deborah is also another example of an unlikely saviour. God is again working against human expectations and categories. It looks as if people come from a distance to consult Deborah, because her office is in the middle of the country, whereas Hazor lies in the far north, and the battle takes place in between.

Jael is another tough woman, in the mode of Ehud. Her husband, too, is missing from the story. Sisera had reason to think he would be safe in Heber's encampment, but Heber and Jael were related to Moses and thus to Israel. In Heber's absence, Jael does not feel bound to give priority to politics over family, and she knows how to use her femininity on Sisera. She welcomes the exhausted warrior into her tent, feeds him, lulls him to sleep, then hammers a tent peg through his skull. The result is that the glory for Israel's victory goes to a woman rather than to Barak. Again, there's an irony about his name, which means Lightning, but Barak hasn't lived up to his name. He loses the glory in two senses as it goes first to Deborah and then to Jael.

Sensitive Western readers are troubled by the violence of people such as Deborah and Jael, but apparently God wasn't. Here, they are part of the way 'God subdued King Jabin of Canaan before the Israelites'. The New Testament includes this event among the achievements of the people who acted by faith in conquering kingdoms, becoming powerful in battle and routing foreign armies, though with a final reverse irony it is Lightning whom it actually names (Hebrews 11:32–4).

Thank you, Lord, that you will use all means to work through people who act in faith.

4 More about strong women

Judges 5

Many aspects of Deborah's poem are hard to interpret. Maybe it would have puzzled Israelite readers, too. It might be like us reading Shakespeare. But it's no coincidence that as a prophet Deborah speaks in poetry, like Miriam and most of the later prophets. Prophecy uses human words to express profound divine truth, and poetry is the natural form for expressing profound truths. Like the Psalms, this poem addresses human beings (specifically kings) whom the poet challenges to join in recognising the greatness of God that has been manifested in the events it celebrates.

Talk of earth trembling and heaven pouring rain may indicate that Israel's victory involved rain clogging the enemies' chariots. The battle takes place in the plain between the Ephraim mountains and the Galilee mountains, near the big Canaanite cities of Megiddo and Taanach. The Kishon Wash or Wadi runs there; it's usually just a stream but it could become a torrent after sudden rain. On the other hand, the talk of the stars also fighting reminds us not to be too prosaic in interpreting poetic images.

The poem also testifies to the importance of the human beings' actions. This victory was not like that at the Red Sea or Jericho, when people just watched God act. Paradoxically, despite the fact that the situation seemed hopeless and there seemed no way the Israelites could do anything about their oppression, Deborah summoned them to take action, because God was going to give them an impossible victory. The victory depended on the clans offering themselves and on God working through and with them to do something supernaturally extraordinary. Thus the poem is scathing about clans that held back. Most of all, it lauds the achievement of Jael in doing away with the enemy general. That is how God's enemies deserve to be dealt with, Deborah finally notes.

The closing lines offer a further contrast. There in Sisera's home town is Sisera's mother, evidently an important person in her own right, with her body of servants. They are looking forward to the return of the victorious general, imagining their men raping the women who belong to their victims and plundering their possessions, bringing some nice things back for their women at home. They are due for disappointment.

Yes, the earth trembles, the clouds pour water, the mountains quake, before you, Lord!

5 The mixed-up hero

Judges 6 – 7

Gideon is beating out wheat inside the family winepress. This makes the story's audience snigger. Everybody knows you beat out wheat in the most open place possible, preferably on top of a hill, so you can then hurl the beaten wheat into the air, the wind can carry away the chaff and you're left with a nice stack of pure wheat. In contrast, a winepress is a small structure, built in some sheltered place, where you can tread the grapes and let the pure juice flow down into the collecting basin. Beat wheat in a wine press?! It shows how beaten down and humiliated the Israelites themselves are.

There is a good reason, the usual one that runs through Judges. The beating down has happened because the Israelites have behaved in a way that offends Yahweh. But it looks as if they don't realise, and neither does Gideon. He's no more spiritually bright than they are. Yet for some reason God chooses him to conscript in connection with delivering Israel. Gideon shows as little enthusiasm and insight as Moses did, but this doesn't make any difference. Neither does his requesting a sign, a further indication that he lacks spiritual insight.

Having been granted the sign, Gideon does as Yahweh says, though he makes a point of doing it when no one is looking. But he gets discovered. His dad now plays an impressive cameo part in this drama, challenging the village to join in the stand for Yahweh. Then, in the crisis that follows, God's spirit 'clothes itself in Gideon', and Gideon behaves like someone who has new power and dynamic, transformed from someone who was overwhelmingly scared into someone who will take on Midian, Amalek and the easterners.

God's reducing Gideon's army to three hundred means it will take something like a miracle for them to dispose of the Midianite army, though God involves them in bringing the victory about. Yet they carry no weapons, only the means of performing a silly trick. There is no indication that God tells Gideon what to do with the horns, jars and torches. It looks as if he works it out for himself, as he worked out which was the safest place to beat out wheat.

How can I play a part in your delivering your people? Only if you are with me.

6 Yahweh is the one to rule over you
Judges 8

It was a fantastic victory with an impressive aftermath of a chase (though it may seem to raise a moral question or two), and it issues in the Israelites inviting Gideon to become their ruler. No, Gideon says, God is the one to rule over you. Having a human ruler doesn't fit with the fact of God ruling. Gideon's refusal is arguably the high point of his story. Eventually he retires and dies in a good old age and joins his family in the family tomb. It's the way a hero's story should end.

Other aspects of the story compromise that refusal and leave us with a thoroughly ambiguous impression of mixed-up Gideon. He has numerous wives and seventy sons. That's a king's lifestyle. There is the ephod that he makes. An ephod is usually a type of priestly garment, but the use of fifty pounds of gold suggests something more substantial, so here the term perhaps implies a statue clothed in an ephod, and this fits its becoming something that leads people astray in their worship. More literally, it leads to their acting immorally; the word is one that literally refers to sexual immorality, and this is an image the Old Testament often uses in speaking of people being unfaithful to Yahweh. What was Gideon thinking?

The story doesn't explicitly blame him for Israel's going astray after his death. Explicitly, it draws attention to their having failed to keep commitment with Gideon himself in response to all he had achieved for them. Yet their 'acting immorally' is an example of the pattern running through Judges. The phrase to describe their going astray is the one that describes their 'acting immorally' in relation to the ephod. Gideon has some responsibility for what happened.

The ambiguity running through Gideon's story is summed up by the ambiguity of his names. He is Gideon but he is also Jerub-baal, 'the Master Contends', which might imply serving Baal, or might imply defeating Baal, or might be a description of Yahweh as the Master. Is he really Gideon or Jerub-baal? Or which meaning of Jerub-baal is more significant? It's both a question about who he really was in himself and about what his long-term effect on Israel was.

You, Lord, are the one to rule over us, not some impressive human servant of yours.

7 The man who would be king
Judges 9

Jotham declaims his cheeky parable from the spot near Shechem where the clans stood declaring Yahweh's blessing when the Israelites first arrived in the country (see Joshua 8:33). But his words end up with a curse, not a blessing. Nobody who has a worthwhile job wants to be a leader, and anyone who wants to be a leader is a great danger to the people he (or she) leads. That is particularly so when the leader shows himself to be someone capable of acting with the ruthlessness Abimelek shows and when the people associate themselves with that ruthlessness. They can't call this acting in good faith in light of what Gideon did for them, can they? How can their action not backfire on both the leader and the people? Jotham prays that it may. The rest of the story shows how right he is and anticipates what often happens in Israel, in the church and in society.

It will not be at all surprising if an alliance rooted in ambition and violence falls apart. By a breaking of faith the violence done to Gideon's seventy sons 'came', as if it had been waiting and had eventually arrived to do its further work. In other words (it says), their blood was 'put on' Abimelek and the Shechemites. There is a sort of natural process whereby terrible wrongdoing brings about terrible consequences for the people who do it. So the Old Testament can describe things as involving the ordinary processes of cause and effect but also as something God is involved in.

While Abimelek is out of town, the Shechemite notables plan a coup d'état, but the mayor (presumably Abimelek's appointee) gets word to him. He returns with his private army and conducts a massacre in the city. He subsequently attacks a nearby city called Tebez (perhaps they took part in the rebellion), whose citizens take refuge in the tower that a city often had for precisely this purpose. This does not faze Abimelek; the Shechemites had done the same, and he had just set fire to their tower. But before he can do so, a woman drops a millstone onto his head and cracks his skull.

Yes, you, Lord, are the one to rule over us, not some man who aspires to be king.

8 The man whose promise makes the blood run cold

Judges 11

Jephthah is a complicated person with a complicated background. Everyone knows he is illegitimate, and when all his father's legitimate sons are grown up, they throw him out. Maybe exclusion drives him to achievement, and he becomes an outstanding warrior whom his clan therefore call back to lead them when the Ammonites are raiding Israelite territory east of the Jordan. In the negotiations that follow, he amusingly gives them a lesson in Israelite and Ammonite history, though his knowledge of Israel's story is chilling in light of his ignorance of Israel's principles in the story that follows.

God's spirit comes on him and he races through the region (presumably gathering forces) as he prepares to face the Ammonites. Then comes the fateful moment when he makes a promise. Is it a result of God's spirit coming on him? Who or what does he think will come out of the house to greet him? Does his promise work, causing God to give him victory? Why aren't we told his daughter's name? Isn't it monstrous that he blames her for what happens and sees her as bringing calamity on him? Why doesn't she resist implementing her father's promise? What is she weeping for when she weeps for her maidenhood? Why doesn't God intervene?

It's impossible to imagine that God intended Jephthah to sacrifice his daughter. That contravenes the Torah. And the Old Testament in general shows that promises to God tend to backfire. God doesn't intervene for the same reason as God doesn't usually intervene when (for instance) fathers abuse or kill their children; God leaves us as human beings to exercise our responsibility and doesn't go in much for intervening.

The story relates an aspect of the steady degeneration of Israel's life in Judges, a degeneration that especially affects the position of women. The story gives great prominence to the grieving that Jephthah's daughter does with her friends and the way they establish a practice of commemorating her. That offers scope to other young women to come together, stand together and reflect in a conscious way on their situation in a world where men can abuse women as Jephthah did, and on the way they handle the realities of their position in that world.

Lord, protect me from stupid promises, and protect other people from my stupid promises.

9 The insightful mother and the slow-witted father

Judges 13

Manoah's wife is another woman who has waited and waited and tried and tried, and each month has been disappointed, but now she is going to have a baby. She is going to make a marvellous mother, given her spiritual insight. Her husband needs to learn a thing or two, though. Yahweh's aide knows what he is doing in appearing to the wife rather than the husband.

Yet the story never names the wife, and she herself rather defers to her husband in the way she handles the aide's appearance to her. The story stands oddly in the tension between God's vision of husbands and wives having the same status in relation to God and society and one another, and the patriarchal reality whereby men count for more than women.

The word for someone 'dedicated' to God is *nazir*. Numbers 6 lays down some rules for people who want especially to dedicate themselves to God for a period of time as someone 'dedicated'; it doesn't say for what purpose they might want to do that. The story of Samson is distinctive because it implies his Nazirite vow will be lifelong. It involves abstaining from alcohol and letting your hair grow; the significance of the latter is not obvious, but we know in Western culture that letting your hair grow or shaving it can be a significant cultural statement. The vow also means being strict about taboos concerning what you eat, the taboos that people such as priests have to observe if their priestly ministry is not to be compromised.

'Train up a child in the way he should go: and when he is old, he will not depart from it' (Proverbs 22:6 KJV). Like other such promises, this one works much of the time but not all the time. You can be the best parents in the world, but that doesn't guarantee how your child will turn out. The story we shall read about Samson is a story that would have been painful to his parents. In the meantime, the present chapter comes to a beautiful close with its description of the boy growing up and God blessing him and God's spirit beginning to set him going on his vocation.

Lord, teach us what we are to do concerning our children.
(Judges 13:8)

10 Samson and a sequence of women
Judges 14 – 15

After the winsome story about his birth and the summary statements about his growing experience of God's blessing and the effect of God's spirit on him, it comes as a shock when the story fast-forwards to the time when Samson is thinking about marriage and relates how things then work out. The troubles of Samson and his bride needn't have been very serious, but Samson doesn't do things by halves, and he lacks the capacity to shrug his shoulders. Excess is his middle name.

The Israelites in Samson's area, on the opposite side of the country to Jephthah's, are in trouble. The Philistines are the problem, and Samson is the person God plans to use to deliver Israel from Philistine control. So Samson decides to marry a Philistine girl(!). In traditional societies, marriages are usually arranged, but this doesn't mean the parents arrange them without consulting the young people, and other Old Testament stories also indicate that the initiative may come from the couple. But marriage still isn't just a private arrangement between two people. So there's nothing odd in the young Samson fancying a girl and asking his parents to start setting up an arrangement. It's where he finds her that is troublesome. Other Philistines get honourable mention in the Old Testament story, but the presupposition then is that they have come to acknowledge Yahweh.

Yet, paradoxically, God is involved. Samson does what he wants to do; God is using that. God wants to end the domination of the Philistines over the Danites and intends to use Samson to that end. God doesn't insist on having honourable people as agents in bringing things about; if he did, it might mean waiting for ever. God uses people with all their human shortcomings. So when God's spirit comes on someone, its concern is with doing something powerful, not immediately with doing something moral. You could say Samson did wrong in striking down the Philistines in Ashkelon, but that could also contribute to the achieving of God's intention with regard to the Philistines.

Samson behaves in a fashion that denies his Nazirite vocation, but God just makes it all contribute to the fulfilling of his purpose. God will use Samson whether he does the right thing or the wrong thing.

Lord, do use us in our wilfulness, but do open our eyes to ourselves.

11 But blind Samson's hair begins to grow again
Judges 16

From a woman's perspective, the entire Samson story makes gloomy reading. First, there was the woman who bore him, who knew God's vision for him, made her commitment to God and to him, but then had to watch him make a mess of his entire life even while being unwittingly the means of God's will being put into effect. It must have been evident to her that he was never happy, and I imagine her grieving each day and each night about his fate.

Second, there was the wife. I have noted that there is no presumption that she became committed to Samson against her will, and he was evidently a hunk whom many a girl would regard as quite a prize. But she was everybody's victim, even God's victim as he looked for a way of causing trouble to the Philistines.

Third, there is the prostitute. What commonly drives women into the sex trade are some circumstances that mean the only way they can make a living is to sell themselves to satisfy the sexual desires of men, and it is reasonable to reckon that this is what makes this woman available to Samson.

Fourth, there is Delilah, who at least has a name. Samson falls in love with her. Does she love him? We are not told. Her perspective is again irrelevant. What matters is once more the role she is forced to play; she, too, becomes a victim of her fellow countrymen, and as a result Samson becomes her victim and theirs.

Samson becomes the fifth woman in the story, because he ends up grinding grain, conventionally women's work. But his hair begins to grow again. It could be a sign that his vow as a dedicated person is not done. And in Dagon's sanctuary, Samson is praying to Yahweh. You might think it's not much of a prayer; but then, God isn't always too concerned about how proper our prayers are.

Samson's story ends with him resting in peace. But he appears once more in the Scriptures, in the list of the heroes of faith in Hebrews 11. If there is room for Samson in the New Testament's list of the heroes of faith, there is surely room for any of us.

Lord, when necessary, remember us and strengthen us, just this once.
(Judges 16:28)

12 A Levite and his concubine
Judges 19

'There was no king in Israel.' Having some governmental authority will eventually lessen the prevalence of the social and moral chaos that this story describes. The kings will have responsibility for knowing the Torah and seeing that the people know it, and responsibility to see that the vulnerable are protected and the afflicted delivered. It's a magnificent vision of government's primary responsibilities of teaching and protecting.

In a social context like ancient Israel's, though, there's little scope for big government. Local communities have to be self-sufficient and responsible for themselves. The story holds up a mirror to cities and villages and challenges them to see their negative potential for the kind of abuse the story describes. It reminds individuals and families of the way communities can develop a demonic corporate personality.

The story describes the woman as the Levite's concubine, which means a wife of secondary status (it doesn't imply they are not properly married). Does he want her back because he has a 'first-class' wife who resents not having her household assistance? Anyway, like the Samson story, this one reminds men of their capacity to act in the barbarous way the story describes. After what happens, the Levite's father-in-law, the Levite's host and the Levite himself are in a position to say, 'If only I hadn't acted the way I did. If only I had seen this coming.'

The story also reminds women of the capacity of men to behave as these men did. The Old Testament provides women with role models of women who were not willing to work within the patriarchal assumptions of their society. It would add to this woman's suffering if we were to blame the victim for what happens to her, though it might take a tiny bit off the edge of it if she inspires other women to refuse to be pushed out of the door.

But further, this story is part of a wider story going back to Genesis and forward into Samuel and Kings, the story of God's involvement with the world and with Israel, an involvement that is committed to achieving God's purpose to bring into being a good world. This story is not the end of the human story or of Israel's story or of the story of women or of God's story.

Lord, have mercy. Lord, have mercy.

13 How Naomi's life falls apart
Ruth 1

Whereas Judges talks about things often going wrong because God makes them go wrong when Israel itself goes wrong, there's no suggestion here that the famine is an act of judgement. Anyway, Elimelek hears that things are better across the Jordan in Moab. Yet does he then die of a sense of failure or a sense of shame? Naomi in turn watches her sons get Moabite wives. Does that impose on her a sense of failure and shame? And what about when the young men then die? Is that God's judgement? Naomi's story parallels Job's. Blow after blow has devastated her life.

Then she hears that the famine is over. For the first time, the story mentions God. Mostly it proceeds in the way we experience our lives, recognising the importance of coincidences and of human initiatives, and believing that God is involved behind the scenes. At this point it affirms that God has got involved. The rains have come. The famine is over. Naomi can go home.

The two young women set off for Bethlehem with Naomi. Yet she points out they have alternatives not open to her. They have Moabite families they can go back to. 'Things are much harsher for me than for you,' she says, 'because Yahweh's hand has gone out against me.'

One can't blame Orpah for following Naomi's advice. But Ruth won't. She is committed to Naomi herself and to Naomi's people and to Naomi's God. It's impossible to guess why she should make this commitment. Naomi herself is pushing her away. Naomi's people is a people that looks down on Ruth's people. Naomi's God is the one Naomi has seen abandoning her and Ruth and Orpah. Yet this God is the one Ruth appeals to in her oath of allegiance to Naomi. In a film, Naomi might now burst into tears because she is overcome by Ruth's commitment. Not so much. She just gives in and stops trying to persuade Ruth. 'Whatever.'

Ruth does not appear in the list of the heroes of faith in Hebrews, like Rahab and Samson and Abraham, but she is a hero of faith like Abraham, and she does appear with Abraham and Rahab in the list of Jesus' ancestors in Matthew 1.

Lord, I thank you for the people who are unaccountably faithful in their commitment to me.

14 The Moabite
Ruth 2 – 4

Initially, the contrast between Naomi and Ruth that emerged when they were in Moab continues now they are in Bethlehem. Ruth is the person with the energy and initiative to take action to ensure they have something to eat. Naomi is too disheartened. But the new 'coincidence' when Ruth finds herself in Boaz's fields turns Naomi around and leads to her pressing an initiative on Ruth. Her plan and Ruth's execution of it seem risky. Ruth could look as if she is merely propositioning Boaz. But in effect she is proposing to him, when she points out that human life works on the basis of our finding protection under the skirts of another human being. That is what marriage involves. Yet there is a further nuance to her appeal to Boaz, given his position as a close kinsman.

In any decent romantic comedy, however, there have to be threats to whether the couple end up together. There is another kinsman with a prior moral and social obligation and right to take on Ruth, Naomi and the family land. While the gift of six measures of barley is another sign of Boaz's honour and generosity, it is more significant that at daybreak he goes off to the city to set going the process that will decide who gets Ruth.

For the anonymous kinsman, the trouble is that redeeming the land, taking on Ruth and fathering a child who will eventually inherit the land will involve him in significant expenditure and no long-term gain, and also in danger of imperilling the position of the family he already has. He faces a clash of responsibilities. He chooses to give priority to the responsibility he already has. We breathe a sigh of relief because we want the story to end the way we have projected.

As if there hasn't been enough excitement, the story of Ruth, Naomi and Boaz ends up as also a story about David. Until the closing paragraph, you could think you are simply reading about some ordinary people's ordinary lives and God's involvement in them. But God's involvement in their everyday lives relates to a much bigger purpose. It encourages them to raise their eyes to a bigger horizon, to God's concern with Israel and even his involvement with Moab.

Blessed be Yahweh, under whose wings we come for refuge!

15 Gaining a son and giving him up
1 Samuel 1 – 2

A need and desire for children will lie behind Elkanah's having two wives, as was the case with Abraham, Sarah and Hagar. Here, too, however, the apparent solution turns out also to be a problem. But every year Elkanah takes the family to Shiloh for a festival, and there Hannah prays. The trouble is, she looks as if she's been drinking too much festival wine. Fortunately, Eli gets his act together and then knows the right response to her prayer. 'Go in peace,' he says. And *shalom* means things going well in your life. They haven't been for Hannah, but they are destined to.

God has closed Hannah's womb (the Scriptures don't usually say that about a woman who can't get pregnant). But now God is mindful of her in the way she has asked, and he makes pregnancy possible. If you could look at her medical records, maybe you would find that her inability to conceive had some physiological or anatomical explanation and that her eventual conceiving was a surprise to the doctors. They would then say that sometimes 'miracles' (by which they would mean inexplicable events) happen. Unusually, the story attributes Hannah's infertility to God, and then attributes her pregnancy to God, though it specifically involves Elkanah, too.

Hannah's act of praise brings to its proper closure the interaction between her and God over her infertility. But her testimony is mostly addressed to other people, to encourage them to grow in their faith in God's being the kind of God of whom Hannah speaks, and to believe that what God has done for her might be an encouragement to them. But as is often the case in these stories, there's something bigger afoot. Hannah speaks as if she knows that her son's birth is of huge significance for Israel. It makes the sacrifice she makes at Shiloh more feasible: not only the slaughter of a bull but the giving up of her son. How could she do this? She knows that the meeting of her need relates not merely to her personally but to that much bigger purpose. So she can trust Samuel to Eli and the sanctuary – or rather, to God. His bowing down to God is a sign of his acceptance of his vocation.

There is no holy one like Yahweh, no one besides you!

16 A summons, not a call

1 Samuel 3

Samuel's summons is more or less the beginning of the story of the prophets in Israel. Before Samuel, 'Yahweh's word was rare; there was no vision spreading about.' The expressions are odd, but they make the point that prophecy was something occasional. You didn't regularly hear that someone had had a prophetic vision. This is about to change because of another imminent change: Israel is about to institute a central government. Prophecy will be needed in association with that.

Specifically, God has not yet spoken to Samuel, and thus Samuel doesn't recognise Yahweh. That is a chilling phrase, but Samuel has been growing up in God's presence, which implies growing up with a knowledge of God and in commitment to God. But God has not yet spoken to him in the audible way that now happens. An amusing scene thus unfolds. Perhaps Eli is no more to be faulted than Samuel for failing to realise what is happening, though the story may imply that the senior and experienced priest ought to have had more clue. Meanwhile, God waits patiently until the light goes on for Eli. When it does, Eli at least knows how a person needs to respond upon realising that God is summoning.

The idea of vocation can suggest finding fulfilment and the opportunity to exercise one's gifts, but this story emphasises divine sovereignty rather than human fulfilment. Being summoned by God provides the backing for being given an unpleasant task. Our instinct in reading about Samuel's call is to stop after 'Speak, because your servant is listening.' It's nice to identify with the process whereby God's call comes, but we'd rather not identify with its contents. Samuel is not stupid when he lies awake all night after God appears to him. Poor Eli has tried to get a grip of his sons, at least recently, but has evidently not tried hard enough or not taken firm enough action when they take no notice of him. It's too late now to change the waywardness that makes God's action necessary.

So God turns Samuel from a boy who does jobs in the sanctuary into someone through whom God speaks to Israel. There is nothing about Samuel that makes this happen. The Master just decides that this is the servant he intends to use.

Speak, Lord, your servant is listening.

17 You can't mess with the covenant chest
1 Samuel 4 – 6

The ironic aspect to the story of the Philistines and the Israelites lies in the theologies both sides work with. It's hard to decide whose theology is more mixed up. The Israelites are surely right that God wants them to be free of Philistine control and that God will likely expect them to fight for their independence. Yet they get defeated.

The Philistines' theology is more ironic. Like the Israelites, they think that bringing the covenant chest into the camp means bringing the deity into the camp. Yet their reaction is to determine to fight harder. And this works! Yahweh is quite prepared to risk seeming to be discredited. Actually, being prepared to let Israel be defeated avoids being 'credited' with being a different kind of deity from the kind Yahweh really is.

Back in Shiloh, Eli hears the people's cry when they realise what has happened, then the messenger reaches him and tells him about the defeat and about his sons' death and about the fate of the covenant chest. And this last piece of news makes him drop dead. The news jolts his daughter-in-law into labour and she dies in childbirth, while indicating that she, too, knows that the loss of the covenant chest suggests the departure of the covenant God. It's as if God has gone into exile.

The subsequent adventures of the covenant chest read like a cartoon – jokey, juvenile and scatological. But like one of Jesus' parables, the story then kicks the listeners in the butt, and they end up laughing on the other side of their faces. The Philistines find the chest a hot potato that they anxiously but futilely pass on from one city to another. The Israelites are no more reverent or wise in the way they treat it (and thus treat God) than the Philistines, and they pay a more serious penalty. Even the cows pulling the cart show more insight than them.

Do the people of Beth-shemesh think the people of Kiriath-jearim were a bit slow on the uptake in being willing to welcome this dangerous object into their midst? If so, the joke is on them. The people of that city know how to look after the chest with more reverence.

Grant, Lord, that the glory of God may abide with the people of God.

18 As far as this Yahweh has helped us
1 Samuel 7

It looks as if the defeat related in 1 Samuel 4 led to the Israelites' abandoning Yahweh to see if serving other gods would work out better, but it didn't. They are now 'mourning after Yahweh', which means (Samuel points out) that they must turn away from these alien gods. Samuel regularly shows himself capable of being a tough guy, and a mere show of weeping gets no one anywhere with him. Never mind the tears: what about your stance in relation to Yahweh and in relation to the Baals and the Ashtoreths, the Canaanite gods and goddesses?

The Philistines rightly perceive that the Israelites' gathering to pray portends trouble, and it makes them attack. The Israelites in turn panic, not believing Samuel's promise about God delivering them. Fortunately, this doesn't make God simply despair and go off, and fortunately they also again turn to Samuel. One implication and result is that the significance of Samuel grows by leaps and bounds. He started off as a sanctuary janitor. Then God turned him into a prophet. In this chapter he has become someone 'leading' Israel or exercising authority, the term that described the 'judges' and was also used of Eli. In addition, Samuel functions as a priest. He prays on the people's behalf, which he might do both as prophet and as priest.

God's answer to his prayer comes not in words but in action, in a thundering that reduces the Philistines to confusion, so that the Israelites do not have to fight them but just mop up. There could hardly be a sharper contrast with the earlier story. Yes, God 'helps' them, with the sort of help that means making something possible that would otherwise be impossible. When Samuel gives the name 'Help-stone' to the place where God delivers Israel from the Philistines, it's that kind of help that he is referring to. Actually, it was already called Help-stone. Now it has lived up to its name. God has helped (that is, delivered) them 'as far as this' in taking them toward their destiny as a people. They were not all the way there yet, but they were on the way, and experiencing God acting powerfully on such an occasion could embolden them about the certainty that God would take them there.

Lord, be our helper.

19 Appoint us a king!

1 Samuel 8

Samuel and his sons have been travelling around the country, maybe to teach, maybe to decide difficult cases in different cities. But Samuel is getting old, and his sons have given into the regular temptations of leadership, using their position to line their pockets. And the people give into the weird temptation that also characterises the modern world, the hope that a change of government will improve the situation. 'Appoint us a king, like everyone else has.'

In effect, Samuel points out that being governed by kings rather than by people without such a position will make no difference. For the most part, his realistic account of what it will be like to have a stable, fixed form of central government does not imply that this government will be characterised by gross abuse. But kings and presidents have to have a staff and the staff has to be paid for.

Before he comes to this point, Samuel is bidden to look at the situation theologically, not merely pragmatically. The people's request means they have rejected God as King, not just rejected Samuel. One might have expected God to tell Samuel, 'Don't yield to their request. Tell them I intend to reign over them.' Yet one of the terrible aspects of the way God runs the world is sometimes to give us what we ask for. So God says he will. Their request is not an aberration. It's in keeping with the way they have related to God since they came out of Egypt. So this is a moment at which God says, 'That's it. That's the last straw.'

In reaffirming their desire, they re-express it. They want a king to go out ahead of them and fight their battles. In one sense, this simply restates what it means to have a king. One theory about the very idea of central government is that its single indispensable job is to defend the nation's existence and freedom, its integrity and its borders, in relation to other nations that imperil these. The Israelites' experience of God's kingship in this connection has been mixed. Sometimes God has given them amazing victories. Sometimes God has let them experience notable losses. They want the freedom to safeguard their own destiny. OK, says God.

Lord, rule over us, and protect us from our other rulers and would-be rulers.

20 How Saul lost some donkeys and found more than he bargained for
1 Samuel 9 – 11

It is hard to piece together the story of how Saul became king. But first, the account of the donkeys and the anointing makes clear the interweaving of God's initiative, human actions and coincidence. It portrays Saul as having the physical characteristics appropriate to a king (like David) and the reticence appropriate when one is drafted by God (like Moses or Gideon), though as being a bit slow on the uptake, too. It also describes God's ability to turn him into a new person.

The gathering at Mizpah reaffirms that the idea of having a king is something God looks at with disfavour. This augurs ill for Saul's fulfilling the role. He will turn out to be a not-very-suitable candidate to do a job God doesn't really want done. Yet the story again emphasises God's involvement in the choice of Saul, indicated by the use of the lot. Although having a king is the people's idea, he is not democratically elected, because he is to be the means of God ruling, not the means of the people getting their will done. Samuel's laying down how the monarchy is to work goes along with that. On the other hand, Saul is democratically recognised. The story again notes how Saul has the reticence appropriate to someone God is going to use. God no more believes in people volunteering for service than in democratic elections.

If Saul has been designated king, what is he then doing ploughing? But the story about Jabesh-gilead provides another account of how he is shown to be the right person to be king. Once again God demonstrates a sovereign involvement in the process. Once again it involves God's spirit erupting on someone and making him act in a way that would not come naturally. God inspires a monumental anger in him; anger is here a fruit of the Spirit, an appropriate reaction to the enormity of the way the Ammonites propose to treat the men of Jabesh.

The magnanimous way Saul responds to people's desire to lynch the men who questioned his suitability to be king once again marks him as someone full of God's spirit.

Give us magnanimity and humility, Lord, especially when you achieve great things for us or with us.

21 The test

1 Samuel 13

We move almost straight from Saul's confirmation as king to his rejection as king, and there is more than one account of this rejection as there is more than one account of his becoming king. The way of telling the story of his reign compares with Luke's way of telling Jesus' story, when he puts the account of Jesus' rejection at Nazareth at the beginning of the story of Jesus' ministry, whereas the other Gospels put it much later. Luke recognises that it will help us read the story aright if he tells us at the beginning where it is headed.

You might be sympathetic with the position Saul is put in. Saul musters his army. The Israelites are then in a state of panic about the threat of a huge Philistine force and they start disappearing. Saul as the army commander-in-chief needs to take some action. Is he to wait for the Philistines to come down the mountains to attack, and to neglect to seek God's help? Is he to take the initiative and go into battle without seeking God's help? Is he to seek God's help as if he were a priest who could take the lead in offering sacrifice? Or is he to wait for Samuel to show up and risk his army dissipating until there is virtually nothing left and the force that is left gets slaughtered? Samuel sees his delay as a test of obedience. Perhaps it is also a test of trust.

So Saul's monarchy is rejected. God will appoint someone else in his place. Translations conventionally describe him as 'a man after God's own heart', which sounds as if it implies someone with the kind of character that pleases God, even someone whose own heart matches God's heart. Actually, it needs to mean only someone whom God's heart gets set on, someone God chooses. Indeed, Saul was such a person. But the man after God's own heart is David now, and he will be someone who will keep a steadfast commitment to Yahweh rather than to other gods, unlike many of his successors. But he will hardly be 'a man after God's own heart' in the sense of someone who in other respects lives the kind of life God looks for or has a heart like God's.

Lord, make me the man or woman whose heart does match your heart.

22 The fog of war
1 Samuel 14

Saul marches around in fog as he fights the Philistines. The story provides another perspective on why Saul's monarchy would inevitably fail. Ironically, it begins to show how Jonathan looks a much more promising candidate for leadership. Saul was capable of taking a spectacular brave initiative when God's spirit burst on him, but he was not this kind of person by nature. In contrast, it is in Jonathan's genes to behave thus.

While Jonathan doesn't wait for God's prompting before he takes some action, he knows there can be a difference between a merely harebrained idea and a stratagem that God will bless. Hence his 'perhaps'. You cannot take for granted that God will bless your schemes. Further, the fog of war means that on your own you may not be able to discern the difference between a great stratagem and a harebrained scheme. So Jonathan sets up the possibility of God's giving him a sign.

We know from the previous chapter that Saul and Jonathan have separate bases, and Saul is not to be faulted for being unaware of Jonathan's action. And at one level Saul knows as well as Jonathan does that you do not fight battles as if war is a purely secular enterprise. So Saul gets Ahitub to consult God. But before the consultation is over he concludes that he cannot afford to wait. He again needs to take decisive action. The chapter tells the same story as unfolded at Gilgal in chapter 13. The negative implication about Saul is clear. Yet his action does not stop God giving Israel victory. You can rarely second-guess God or know when mercy will triumph over what we deserve.

Unfortunately, Saul takes another false step that compromises the extent of the triumph. Saul's oath tempts his troops into gorging themselves when they at last have the chance to eat, after they have become famished. Then Jonathan unwittingly infringes Saul's promise in the way he finds some refreshment. Fortunately, even Saul's soldiers know that God is not a legalist and that it's possible to raise with God the question whether circumstances make it feasible to renegotiate a promise. So Jonathan's life is saved, but the victory fails to be the extensive one that it might have been.

Help me to keep my mouth shut rather than make rash promises, Lord.

23 Yahweh's good spirit and Yahweh's bad spirit

1 Samuel 16

Saul was good-looking, but his story implies that he had the outward qualifications to be king but not the inward ones. One might then think that God would ignore looks next time around, and the story at first gives the impression that this is what will happen. There are some other humorous notes in the story, such as God's willingness to collude with Samuel in being economical with the truth about the reason for his visit to Bethlehem, and the alarm of the city elders who know that the arrival of a prophet is usually bad news. And when Samuel is introduced to Jesse's eldest, he is told to take no account of his appearance or height, because God looks at the inner person. We then eventually meet Jesse's youngest, and we expect that he will be a little weed, but he too is tanned from spending his life out in the open, and good-looking. The story of his introduction to Saul adds to that account. He is strong and handsome, and a fighter, and also good with words and music.

We are told nothing about the inner person that God can see. David will manifest deep character flaws, but he has one great strength that will stand out. At least David will never look to other deities. There is something God can see about him. And God's spirit bursts on him.

David is the antithesis to poor Saul. The story juxtaposes God's spirit erupting on David with God's spirit leaving Saul, and (worse) a bad spirit from God attacking him. Translations talk about an evil spirit, but that's misleading. It's a bad spirit or a bad temper that afflicts him now. As a supplement to the music therapy David gives him, another therapist might be able to help him see how his bad spirit is a natural reaction to the way his life is unravelling, but Saul doesn't look to be the kind of person who would have the insight to face this.

Neither Saul nor David is the kind of person who grows in his human awareness as he gets older. Maybe the temptation of power is the reason. 'All power corrupts; absolute power corrupts absolutely.'

Lord, send upon us your good spirit, not your bad spirit.

24 How to recycle your killer instinct
1 Samuel 17

The Philistines have a sensible idea about how to wage war. The battle should be decided by one guy from each side fighting each other. Of course, they are convinced that they cannot lose, and it is not surprising that when their champion loses, they forget the sensible rule they proposed.

What bothers David is the reproach Goliath brings on Israel. But there is more to his concern than that. Goliath is bringing reproach and shame on the army of the living God. And David holds together his confidence in himself and his confidence in God. He is not a mere shepherd boy who has no experience of fighting. He has fought lions and bears and lived to tell the tale. Those battles will already have demonstrated to him that the outcome of a fight can be decided not by how big you are but by how clever and/or how brave you are. Yet David also knows that he might not have escaped from lion or bear unless God had also been with him. No courage and shrewdness: he dies. No involvement of God: he dies. He has needed both, and will need both again. In his argument with Saul, his experience of successful fighting has the first word, but his conviction that God will rescue him has the last word.

The basis for his conviction is that God is the Lord of Hosts, more literally 'Yahweh Armies'. David knows that God really does have all power in the heavens and on the earth, and that God is prepared to use it. God is not merely sovereign in people's religious and personal lives but in the world's political and military life. And God delights to turn odds upside down. David's story is good news for little people.

In a way, David's entire character comes out in this story. It shows how David could indeed be 'a man after God's heart'. David manifests a commitment to Yahweh and a trust in Yahweh the like of which we have hardly seen before in the Old Testament story. It is a shame that (as is the case with Saul) David's first moments are also his best moments.

Saul's problems as king and as father will now interweave.

We will go, Lord, in the name of the Lord of Hosts, the God who delivers.

25 How to be a dysfunctional family
1 Samuel 18 – 19

David and Jonathan are so like each other. It's hardly surprising that they became such friends. Saul's daughter Michal is smitten with David, too. In fact, everyone in Israel is. You would have to be a big man to cope with the situation, and Saul is not a big man. Now the bad spirit that comes on him threatens trouble for David.

You could say that God protected David, but the story just says that David evaded Saul. David knows how to watch his back. Human courage and sharpness and divine protection are both involved, otherwise things would hardly turn out the way they do.

When Saul hears that Michal has taken a shine to David, Saul sees he can use this as a means of getting David out of the way. The story incorporates a number of notes of humour, mostly at Saul's expense. The first is a note of coarse humour, of which the Bible is fond. Let David circumcise a few of the wild Philistines. Of course, he will have to kill them first. It's win–win for Saul: he hopes David fails, but if he wins, that will also be useful in its way. David of course succeeds, and doubles the number for good measure, and the story invites us to imagine David counting them out one by one. All to gain a wife. Who is this man? A man who wants to be king!

Saul can never see beyond the end of his nose. He can see that God is with David, and his appropriate reaction is to become more afraid of David. One might have thought that anyone with an ounce of good sense would see that there was no point fighting God, but it just makes Saul fight harder. Then he fails to see the further implications of the fact that Michal loves David. Once again, that word 'love' suggests commitment and loyalty as well as feelings. David is the one to whom Saul's daughter is committed.

Nor is Saul's son Jonathan any use to his father in connection with getting rid of David. But Saul has a bigger problem than his son and his daughter and his own stupidity being against him: God is against him.

Lord, give us courage and wisdom, and protect us yourself.

26 Friendship

1 Samuel 20 – 21

Both straight people and gay people have asked whether David and Jonathan had a physically homosexual relationship. Of course, the story never says, 'Oh, by the way, they weren't gay.' But its framework for describing the relationship between them is friendship and mutual commitment. This mutuality doesn't mean the relationship meant the same to both men. The relationship's energy comes from Jonathan. He 'loves' David, cares about him, is loyal to him rather than to his father, cares about him as much as he cares about himself. He has bound himself to David. It is his care and loyalty that lead to the making of a covenant between them.

In the West we may assume that a person's spouse is also his or her best friend. That puts extra pressure on a relationship that has all the other demands that apply to it. A relationship of friendship and mutual commitment with another person of the same sex avoids some of that complication.

The presuppositions of the story about Saul's dinner are that the beginning of the month is a special occasion celebrated before God, with a special dinner eaten in God's presence. But various things can make someone taboo and unable to come on such an occasion. Yet David's failure even to appear next day puts Saul on the track of the fact that something odd is going on.

Related considerations surface in the story of David's emergency visit to Ahimelech. As usual, it's worth asking why someone wrote this story. When David had become king, the story would function to assure its readers that the process whereby David came to the throne was entirely honourable.

The story also acknowledges expectations that would apply to David as king. He is to keep commitment to Jonathan not only during his lifetime but also after his death. For all David's popularity in his own circles, there will be many people still loyal to Saul who will assume that someone from Saul's family should succeed Saul. Such considerations mean that after a coup, a new ruler is tempted to make a point of eliminating potential rivals to the throne, which include Jonathan's sons. Actually, David will make a point of honouring his promises to Jonathan in this connection.

Lord, give us grace to keep our commitments to the people who become our friends.

27 The outlaw

1 Samuel 22 – 23

David hears that the pesky Philistines are raiding Keilah and plundering its harvest. But the one priest who escaped the massacre at Nob brought the ephod with him. So with its help, David can ask God whether to go and attack the Philistines, and God's answer is affirmative. It's a dangerous plan, and David consults God again, and God confirms that things will work out OK. They do.

Sometimes God does guide people about what to do, though not always, maybe not often. He often leaves us to make the decisions in our lives. How does God decide when to? How do you know when to ask God what you should do? The story suggests two insights. One is that there is something special about David. He is the man after God's heart – that is, the man God has chosen. He has a distinctive place in God's purpose as the person God intends to use as king. The encouragement in the story is that if ever God needs to guide you in order for you to fulfil your place in God's purpose, God will do so.

The other insight in the story is that even David doesn't ask God what to do every five minutes. Usually he makes his own decisions, takes responsibility for his own (and his men's) destiny. After escaping from Keilah, he runs for the hills, once again without showers or burgers or bars. God is protecting David, but there is no reference to supernatural guidance in this bit of the story. David just uses his human acumen. That can bring other problems, as the massacre at Nob shows. David knows the massacre issued from his action. We make decisions and we sometimes can't see their implications.

Two other things work in David's favour. One is a visit from Jonathan, who 'strengthens his hand by Yahweh', reaffirming that things are going to work out, that God will protect him, that he will end up as king. The other is that when Saul goes looking for him, 'God did not give David into his hands' – contrary to what Saul thought. 'Chance' events in which God is not directly involved work in David's favour, and one can imagine that God is glad.

Lord, guide us when we need guidance, and protect us when we have to make up our own minds.

28 Fool by name and fool by nature
1 Samuel 25

Nabal was a good catch in economic terms, but that was all. There are several Hebrew words that could lie behind his name. One is the word for a guitar. But another is a word meaning *fool*. I imagine it was not *nabal = fool* that his parents had in mind when they named him. But the name turned out to be curiously apposite. In some sense he must have been shrewd, otherwise he would not have done so well as a sheep farmer, unless perhaps he was unscrupulous.

Abigail has another sort of intelligence. She recognises that you don't mess with an outlaw like David. Further, she has the religious insight that her husband lacks. So David and Abigail make a marvellous if potentially fiery match, both of them good-looking, shrewd, insightful about what God is doing and capable of seizing the main chance. There is no suggestion of a love match; David is never said to love a woman, and the chapter closes by telling us about some of David's other marriages.

For David, there is no link between love and marriage, and neither is there any suggestion of such a link for Abigail. Whereas we have been told that Michal loved David (but then she lost him), we are not told that Abigail loved him any more than she loved Nabal. But she can see how events in Israel are developing, she can see that God is involved, and she does have her eye to the main chance. All through this story of human shrewdness, calculation and stupidity, God is again at work bringing about the fulfilment of an intention to keep David safe so that he can eventually be king.

The story declares that God strikes Nabal so that he dies. Yet it also implies that a post-mortem would reveal nothing odd about Nabal's death. He is a hard worker, a hard eater and a hard drinker (another word that his name could remind you of is the word for a skin of wine, which also features in the story). Then he has a major fright, and it's all too much for his heart. God uses that collocation of facts and events as God uses Abigail's shrewdness.

Lord, protect us from folly and give us wisdom.

29 The hunter and the hunted
1 Samuel 26

David here puts doing the right thing ahead of pursuing his personal interests, and he does it for the second time. He did it in chapter 24, an entertaining read. Engaged in trying to capture David, Saul goes into a cave to relieve himself, and it turns out to be where David and his men are hiding. They therefore have a chance to kill Saul, but David will only cut off the edge of Saul's coat while Saul is otherwise occupied.

David recognises that although God has abandoned Saul, Saul is still king, still the person God anointed, still marked out as God's servant. The point is underlined by David's critique of the way Saul's men fail to protect him, no matter that they are so deeply asleep that you could think they are in a coma that God has induced (it's the same word as is used when God puts Adam to sleep before borrowing one of his ribs).

The story neatly draws attention to the ambiguity attaching to our attitude to rulers who seem to have forfeited God's approval and our loyalty. In the Old Testament, there are times when God commissions a coup d'état. These two stories underline how horrifying such an event nevertheless is.

One can infer another reason why David would be glad to have similar stories told twice. It will not be in his interest to encourage the idea that people are free to assassinate the king when they become convinced that God has abandoned him. Saul's supporters will be able to accuse David of always having been disloyal to Saul and always plotting his way to the throne. David's declining more than one opportunity to kill Saul would be another basis upon which David and his supporters could confront the suggestion that he was somehow implicated in Saul's death.

It would be so simple for David to solve his problems and even keep his hands clean (because Abishai will do it). No, says David. Maybe God will strike him down, or he will die of natural causes, or he will get killed in battle (as actually happens). Let God's will be fulfilled in one of those ways. It's not David's job to fulfil it.

Lord, give me the trust and integrity to know when I must leave things to you.

30 What do you do when you are desperate?
1 Samuel 28

Most cultures have assumed that we can make contact with our dead family members, and that one reason this is worth doing is that they likely have access to information we do not. That assumption underlies this story. And in most cultures there have been people who were expert at making contact with spirits. No doubt some of them were charlatans, but the Bible doesn't say that making contact in this way is impossible; it simply says it's forbidden to Israel, because Israel has other ways of discovering God's will and God's plans. But the ordinary instincts of the people of God commonly triumph over what the Bible says.

It is now the eve of the last great confrontation between Saul and the Philistines. Saul needs God's guidance, but he cannot get it. So he is driven to seek guidance by that route which he has himself forbidden. When Samuel appears, something makes the medium realise who Saul actually is. After all, a prophet's most important job is to guide the king, so if Samuel is prepared to have his sleep interrupted, that suggests the visitor is someone important. Admittedly, Samuel doesn't like having his sleep interrupted. He is as brusque dead as he was alive, and also as tough with Saul.

Every time a prophet tells people that a terrible fate awaits them, the people have the opportunity to turn around, and when they do, God will relent, but most times they are too far gone and the prophetic word functions to announce what actually will happen. Saul has been too far gone for a long time. As we have read his story, we have kept wanting to shout out to him, 'Don't do it,' 'Turn around,' 'Let David have the stupid kingship.' But he can't hear. We can't reach him. Further, the Philistines are about to put him out of the way, and (ironically) about to open the way for another leader who will sort them out.

Saul collapses in terror. He has not eaten all day or all night. In a touching closing scene to the story, the woman and his servants persuade him to let her make him the final meal of his life, after which he returns to his troops to meet his fate.

Lord, give me grace to hear when you speak.

31 The fateful battle

1 Samuel 29 – 31; 1 Chronicles 10

Saul's suicide brings his tragic story to its close. There's a certain logic or inevitability about a tragedy. People bring about their own tragedy. But they can also be the victims of factors outside themselves. Tragedies are frightening stories that remind us how we can be our own worst enemies and how we may be responsible for our destinies, while also not being in control of them.

Saul is drafted to do a job that God doesn't really want done which he doesn't have the gifts for and doesn't really want, but he doesn't manage to evade it. God shows him he could be enabled to do it, but he doesn't give God the kind of obedience that God looks for. Saul cannot complain; his character flaws have been clear, and his tragedy issues from them.

When we come to the end of David's story, we will not exactly conclude, 'Oh how lucky David was to have lived the life he lived.' He too will end up in a mess. The more appropriate response on our part is gratitude for escaping being cast into important roles in God's big picture. We are likely to have our own tough experiences and we usually can't see what makes things happen in our lives, as we can with Saul's life. We can know that God can weave them into his bigger picture.

We like our Hollywood films to close with at least a tiny note of hope rather than unremitting bleakness, and Saul's story does, like Samson's. On the crest of the tell at Beth-shean, there used to be a gnarled old tree. I used to imagine it as the tree on which Saul's body might have been hanged. But the men of Jabesh-gilead will not let his body be consumed by the vultures there. The end of Saul's story reminds us of his finest hour, in the story told in chapter 11. In a strange sense, Saul and his sons are free to rest, under a tamarisk tree. Tamarisks are big shady trees with pretty blossoms.

Saul's death is also where Chronicles begins its alternative version of Israel's story, written for people in Judah when the exiles had returned and the nation had come back to life.

Lord, have mercy on us, and grant us rest at the end.

April

PROPHETS
AND KINGS

1 How the mighty have fallen
2 Samuel 1

The story of Saul's death at the end of 1 Samuel closes off the story of Saul's kingship. The story of Saul's death that begins 2 Samuel opens up the story of David's kingship. It does so in a way that continues to portray David as Mr Clean.

The narrative contains some ironies. The messenger who brings the news of Saul's death to David is an Amalekite. How did Saul come to have Amalekites in his army? The narrative does offer a piece of information that may partly answer such a question, because the Amalekite messenger explains to David that he is the son of a resident alien. Now he has already lied to David about killing Saul, in order to tell David a story he thinks David would like to hear, so who knows whether he is lying about his status? But the lie is nevertheless an interesting one. It presupposes that Israel has an open-door immigration policy. Anyone can join Israel, even an Amalekite. He just has to become a 'proper' Israelite in the sense of being committed to living by the Torah. Further (David assumes), he has to honour the king, and on his own false profession he has failed to do so.

His story records how David comes to possess Saul's crown and armband, which people sympathetic to Saul might find suspicious. But the integrity of David's relationship with Saul and Jonathan, the son whom Saul designated as his successor, finds further display in David's lament over them. The gazelle in its agility, speed and grace stands for Saul or Jonathan or both. The Hebrew word for gazelle is the same as a word for beauty or gracefulness or honour, so Israelites could understand the word either way, though they did like to use animal images for people – hence the poem's later references to the lion and the eagle. In the past Saul and Jonathan have been effective warriors but their demise is now summed up by the picture of Saul's shield stained in blood (his own), instead of cleaned up and ready for use next time. The elegy urges nature itself to mourn. David acknowledges that Jonathan's commitment to him was a matter of life and death.

Lord, how the mighty fall in war, how the handsome perish.

2 The struggle for power
2 Samuel 2 – 4

2 Samuel tells stories that are breathtakingly true to the way politics works. The Scriptures do not imply that God is involved in every assassination or act of deception. But was it God's will that David came to the throne? Yes. Did God devise a clean way for that to happen? No.

As is often the case, there are two sets of convictions here about how to approach a political question, and thus two sides involved in a political conflict. Both sides may believe they are right. Both sides may be concerned to pursue their own interests. Both sides are prepared to use violent means to bring about what they believe is right or to pursue their interests.

Individuals may pay with their lives for the violence in which they get involved. They may also suffer for it in other ways. Joab has had to watch Abner kill Joab's little brother. The women in the story suffer, too. Maybe Abner and Rizpah love each other, but more likely this is loveless sex imposed on a woman by someone with power. Abner is a guy who can be hardnosed about his own interests. In the ongoing conflict over who is going to be king of Israel as a whole, it is David's supporters who are winning. Abner knows which way the wind is blowing. So he changes sides. It looks a good idea, but he pays for it with his life.

Michal continues her life as a political football passed from one man to another. Like Abner, Ish-bosheth can see which way the wind is blowing, and he collaborates with David's demand for Michal. For Abner, being a political wheeler and dealer has its downside; Joab can plausibly claim that Abner cannot be trusted and can make that the basis for implementing his own desire to kill Abner in redress for Abner's killing his brother. Ish-bosheth will know that if his side loses, his own life will be in danger. His showing signs of willingness not to stand in David's way doesn't save him. But in all that happens, the stories can continue projecting David as Mr Clean. God makes things work out for David through the wrongdoing of the people around him.

Lord, be lord in the results of the wheeling and dealing that affects us.

3 King of all Israel

2 Samuel 5 – 6; 1 Chronicles 11 – 16

David got to the throne of Judah without trying. Now he is also anointed as king over the northern clans. The course of events points to the fragility of the unity between south and north and foreshadows the way they will fall back into being two peoples after Solomon. Establishing Jerusalem as capital of the united nation relates to that fragility. Jerusalem will later be described as the place God chose. Here it is simply the place David chooses, an obscure little Jebusite town in between north and south. But that means it is in neutral territory.

The Jebusites have to rely on a water supply some way down the hill on which they built their little town, and somehow the spring becomes the way David captures the town. So the Jebusite town becomes 'the city of David'. But David recognises that this all happens because Yahweh the God of Armies is with him. In tension with David's insight is the way he behaves in accumulating wives and children. These are the marks of a leader, so David behaves like a leader. The story makes no overt negative comment, but events will unfold in a way suggesting that David's attitude to women and children is his downfall.

In moving the covenant chest to Jerusalem, David is honouring Yahweh, but it is also another canny political move, a way of giving Jerusalem status. Poor Uzzah makes one understandable mistake, with the best will in the world, and loses his life. Israel will have assumed that Uzzah should have known better than to grab the chest, but maybe he just reacted instinctively, in a way that might have been designed to honour the chest rather than treat it irreverently.

At the end of the story there is Michal, who has been the political football between her father and two husbands and has now been taken away from the one who cared about her and given to the one who doesn't know what love means. She lets her feelings about him find expression and she gets as good as she gives. Then the storyteller tells us how she never has children. It doesn't connect the dots, but it suggests the grief that characterises her life as a whole.

I will dance before you, Lord, with all my might.

4 A house and a household
2 Samuel 7; 1 Chronicles 17

David has moved the covenant chest to his new capital, and next he wants to build a proper house for it. 'Of course,' says the prophet Nathan. For a prophet who is on the king's staff, it's easy to be the king's yes-man. But, deliciously, God taps Nathan on the shoulder that night. 'Err, excuse me, Nathan. You know this house. It's for me to live in, right? Do you think that perhaps I should be consulted about it? Actually, I don't care so much for houses. I like being on the move, you see.'

God's other problem is that David is getting too fond of taking initiatives for God. He is reversing the relationship between people and God. He wants to build God a house; God counters that declaration by announcing the intention of building David a house(hold). Later, when God has reestablished who has the sovereignty in this relationship by starting to build David a household, in the sense that his son has succeeded him as king, then this son can fulfil David's plan and build God the house that God doesn't really want.

Thus, when God agrees to the building of a temple, it has a similar significance to God's agreeing that Israel should have kings. God doesn't really want it, but God will let us have our way. Indeed, in both cases God goes much further than grudging agreement. The very commitment to the monarchy that God makes in this chapter shows how far God will go with us in connection with something that God doesn't really want.

'I myself will be a father to him and he will be a son to me.' The implication is that God can never cast him off. God envisages the possibility of chastising his son, and God will do a fair amount of chastising in relation to David and his successors over the next four hundred years, but when you adopt someone as your son, God presupposes, he becomes a real son, just as if he was born to you. You can never un-son him. After 587 BC no Davidic king ever sat on the throne of Jerusalem. But God's promise kept Israel hoping and kept Israel praying.

Who am I, Lord, and who is my household, that you have brought me as far as this?
(2 Samuel 7:18)

5 But the thing David did was displeasing in Yahweh's eyes
2 Samuel 11

David is at home when his army is out fighting. It would be OK if he were staying home to focus on exercising authority with justice in Jerusalem, the commitment he was fulfilling in 2 Samuel 8, the high point of his life. But he is doing no such thing now.

Yet you can't necessarily blame him for spotting Bathsheba bathing on the roof, nor Bathsheba for doing so. She is apparently undertaking the bath that the Torah requires at the end of her period, and the roof is where people go for privacy. While David is never said to love anyone, the number of children he procreates indicates that he has sex with various wives, yet (being a regular man) he's still capable of fancying another woman.

David and his agents are then the subject of a series of verbs that are chilling for Bathsheba – he saw, he sent, he inquired, he sent, they got, he slept with. She is then the subject of the verb that frightens her: she is pregnant. Even in traditional societies, there are ways of seeking to get an abortion, but the Old Testament's failure to mention abortion and the Torah's failure to prohibit it suggests it wasn't within the framework of thinking for Israelites. David's first thought is to try to get Uriah to sleep with Bathsheba so she can pass off the child as his, but Uriah won't cooperate.

It's horrible how one thing can lead to another. Finally, David has Uriah killed. After all, he's only a Hittite. Yet he is evidently a worshipper of Yahweh (his name means 'Yahweh is my light'). David turns the man himself into the messenger who carries the instructions for his own death. Joab knows that David won't mind the sacrifice of some warriors if Uriah is among them.

Problem solved. Bathsheba can fulfil the proper mourning for her husband, then David can send for her again. She is again the object of verbs; at no point is there any suggestion that she has any say in what happens. He is the king, after all. You don't say no to the king, whether it concerns a one-night stand or a marriage.

'But the thing David had done was displeasing in Yahweh's eyes.'

I have sinned against the Lord.
(2 Samuel 12:13)

6 The man who has learned how to be a prophet

2 Samuel 12

Initially, Nathan was David's yes-man. Here, he confronts David. Outside his parable, the punishment that God announces is not execution, as the Torah might seem to imply would follow, but a calamity arising within David's household. When you have let violence and sexual immorality loose, you may not be able to get them back into their cage.

Both David and God act and speak in jaw-droppingly mysterious ways. The first enigma is articulated in God's question to David. David has so much. Why on earth did he do what he did? The second question is raised by his reaction to Nathan: 'I have done wrong against Yahweh.' As Western readers with our stress on emotions, we think David should say how sorry he is, and we wonder if this acknowledgement is enough. Yet when public figures, caught guilty of some wrongdoing, go in for public hand-wringing, it makes us squirm. To an Israelite way of thinking, confession primarily means facing and acknowledging the facts. It is impossible to tell what is going on in David's mind, though the spare, bald acknowledgement contrasts with the impression of grief that will shortly be conveyed by his response to his son's illness.

It's also difficult to know what to make of God's response. God has 'removed' David's wrongdoing. Has God forgiven it? If so, in what sense? God doesn't cancel the sentence that Nathan has declared, and over the coming chapters what Nathan says will happen does happen. Perhaps that is not surprising. When a person guilty of a crime repents, we don't usually decide that therefore they needn't pay their penalty. Indeed, God imposes an extra punishment: Bathsheba's baby will die.

David has despised God's word. He has despised the kind of word that appears in the Ten Commandments, where God proscribes acts such as adultery and murder. Yet his story has made more reference to another kind of word, God's word of promise to him, which came in Nathan's previous message to him. One might think he has imperilled it, but God's removing David's wrongdoing means refusing to let it be an obstacle to the fulfilment of God's purpose with Israel through David. Maybe God's removing the wrongdoing isn't a response to David's confession at all.

Who knows? The Lord may be gracious to me.
(2 Samuel 12:22)

110

7 The price the family begins to pay
2 Samuel 13

The beginning of the price, then, is the horrific death of a baby. The sins of the father are visited on the child. Once again, events reflect the fact that the stakes are high when you are born into the family through which God's purpose is being put into effect. We may breathe another sigh of relief that we are just ordinary people and that God may not relate to us in the way God relates to David and to people close to him.

Tamar's story begins immediately to show that David has not sinned merely against God and Uriah and Bathsheba and the child who died and the Israelite troops at Rabbah and Israel as a whole. He has sinned against his daughter Tamar (and for that matter against his son Amnon), because the kind of person he is issues in the behaviour that appears in his family and because he brings down God's judgement on his own household as a judgement on himself.

It may be hard to imagine Tamar's hurt and shame. The best thing to do is go back more than once to read her story and keep listening to her words. In many cultures the mere fact of it becoming known that a young woman has had premarital sexual experience is inclined to bring great shame on her, whether or not she was a willing participant. She becomes used goods.

Her father is angry, but he does nothing about it. Once again the enigmatic mystery of David's character surfaces. Perhaps Amnon's being his eldest son is why David is so strangely inactive. Perhaps he sees himself in Amnon. Perhaps Amnon then lives for two years with the moral burden of his action and he is subconsciously willing to face his destiny. Yet over these matters the text is silent. It tells us little about people's feelings and motivation, but leaves us to reflect on them. It does the same in making no moral judgement on what goes on. It assumes we can work out that the events it relates are morally horrifying. In both connections (the psychological and the moral), leaving things unsaid draws us into making judgements and thus potentially involves us in reflection we might not undertake if it explicitly provided the answers.

Lord, protect girls and women from Amnons.

8 The coup
2 Samuel 14 – 15

It looks as if Absalom is right to think that his life is now in danger and that it would be a good idea to take refuge with his maternal grandfather. This time it is Joab who has to take the decisive action, though it contributes to Absalom being able to organise his subsequent coup, and to God's judgement being worked out in all these events. Once again David is the victim or the beneficiary of a parable.

The woman's story is fictional, like Nathan's parable, but once again it gets beneath David's skin. For the purposes of the story, David has just two sons, Amnon and Absalom; the others are ignored. One has killed the other and David's colluding with Absalom's self-banishment means Absalom is dead to David and to Israel. He agrees that if he would pardon the woman's non-existent murderer son, he should restore his own actual murderer son, though he does so in rather halfway fashion. This might seem reasonable, but it may be another aspect of the background to the further trouble that will follow.

With some irony, Absalom is now the clever political operator. He is made in the image of his father in being a hunk, and in the way he can get people to follow him. He is in Joab's debt for manipulating David into letting him come back from exile, but he makes clear that Joab cannot assume he is therefore Joab's underling. Joab had better take him seriously. Absalom's offer to people is an offer to do the thing David used to do, to see that decisions are taken in accordance with what is right. Absalom could hardly win support by making such an offer if David was still fulfilling that aspect of a king's responsibilities.

Absalom also wins over his father's adviser Ahithophel, whom the story describes as offering the kind of counsel that is as reliable as a message from a prophet. Absalom makes up a story to explain a need to visit Hebron, and with further audacity gets himself crowned in Hebron as David once did.

As David then flees, he demonstrates his trust in God. It is as if he can afford not to fight, because God is the basis of his position.

Lord, I trust you because of your promises, not on the basis of what I deserve.

9 Wise advice treated as folly
2 Samuel 16 – 19

While Absalom may be governed purely by self-interest and ambition, he has some excuses for his action, in David's dithering over Amnon and Tamar, and in David's (possible) neglect to see that authority was exercised in a fair way for people. Perhaps Ahithophel, too, can see no future for David the ditherer and feels some affront at David's failure to rule properly.

Anyway, Ahithophel's strategy was right; it is imperative to pursue and kill David now before he has chance to regroup and reprovision. Absalom's strategy is also right in seeking the advice of Hushai; the more advice you have, the more likely you are to make a good decision. Hushai's advice is plausible, too, plausible enough to mislead Absalom. Ahithophel's and Absalom's problem is that God is not on their side. God has made a commitment to David that God will not go back on, even though David is a ditherer and an incompetent father, even though David is a seducer and a murderer. Hushai's advice sounds good, but it is actually the opposite.

Why does Ahithophel commit suicide? Because of a sense of failure to bring about what needed to happen? Because he knows his number is up when David returns? Because he realises he has been opposing God?

The delay does give David chance to cross the Jordan, get supplies from allies there and organise his troops. He yields to pressure from his troops not to take part in the battle himself, but to stay safe in Mahanaim. As the troops leave for the battle, his last order is that they are to deal gently with his son. But in the battle, with some irony, Absalom's magnificent head of hair gets tangled in the branches of a tree he passes under. His donkey races on and Absalom takes refuge in the tree, but some of David's men see him and tell their commander, Joab. Notwithstanding David's orders, Joab and some of his men kill Absalom. That brings the battle to an end; Absalom's army flees. Joab sends runners to tell David the good news, and he is distraught. Once again his family relationships are a problem. Joab points out, 'It's as if you don't value your troops' bravery!'

Lord, give us the wisdom to be able to tell the difference between wise advice and foolish advice.

10 Last words
2 Samuel 23

We don't know in what sense these are David's last words (there is more of great importance in his story to follow). They do offer another look at his significance. There was a poem in chapter 22 that was like a psalm. This poem is more distinctively poetic.

Initially it is an objective, general statement about how leadership is supposed to work, with a ruler doing what is right and ruling in reverence for God. Once more there's some ambiguity or potential irony there. Following what is right along with mention of reverence for God could imply that doing what is right simply denotes the way David related to God. Yet the Old Testament's allusions to doing what is right commonly concern relationships with human beings as well as with God, and this concern lost priority in David's personal life and in his leadership as years went by.

Supposing a leader does fulfil God's vision by doing what is right and revering God. That's where the sun and rain image comes in. In nature, growth depends on both sun and rain. When you have both, then things flourish. In a parallel way (David knows), when you have leadership that makes a priority out of doing what is right and reverence for God, the society flourishes.

David continues to be ambiguous when he goes on to speak of his household's stability. Is he claiming that he and his household have been stable in relating to God? That's not the picture the story has been giving. Or does he mean that they are stable in the sense that God will keep them secure on the throne? Given that David and his household are not very stable in doing what is right and in revering God, it is just as well that they have God's covenant commitment to appeal to.

Ambiguity and irony continue into the last lines of the poem. Sun and rain make good things grow; they also make thistles grow. These are not only useless but harmful. Don't touch them, David notes. Just use something to gather them and burn them. That's what happens to people who manifest godless evil rather than doing what is right and revering God. You can't trust in God's graciousness in a way that suggests your response doesn't matter.

Lord, may my household be like that with God.
(2 Samuel 23:5)

11 I would rather fall into God's hands
2 Samuel 24; 1 Chronicles 21

God gets angry. Maybe he is angry for some reason we aren't told, or maybe this statement tells us where the story is going. The census is going to make him angry. In itself, there is nothing wrong with a census. But this is a census undertaken by the military, and the account of its results refers to the number of men drawing the sword. David is checking on the size of his army. The implication is that the size of the army is of key importance to the survival and flourishing of the nation. David has forgotten a consideration of key importance to a leader of the people of God. His story then keeps raising our eyebrows to the end, as his sinful act that issues in judgement leads into his building the altar around which Solomon will build the Temple itself.

With the typical boldness of his relationship with God, David challenges God about the epidemic God brings. Like us, David is offended at the way the people have to suffer for his wrongdoing. He too doesn't recognise how bad leadership can bring trouble to a people, as good leadership can bring them blessing.

Building an altar is something people can do when there is a crisis and they need to call on God. While it's possible simply to pray in those circumstances, building an altar and making offerings enhances the prayer. It indeed means that your worship costs something. It's not just words. Thus, burnt offerings and prayer often accompany one another.

Offerings always cost. That is especially clear with the burnt offerings that David offers, because they involve burning up a whole animal so that it goes up in smoke to God in its entirety. David also offers fellowship sacrifices, which God and offerors share – that is, some goes up in smoke, some the offerors eat in a fellowship meal with God. So even these offerings cost.

With God's responding to David's prayer and the cessation of the epidemic, 2 Samuel ends. It is not the end of a story. The last scenes in David's life appear at the beginning of 1 Kings. As usual, these narrative books stop rather than finish. We have to read on.

Lord, I will not make offerings to you that cost me nothing.

12 How to manipulate the old man to get things done
1 Kings 1

God's promise to David has established the principle of dynastic succession. God is committed to David's household. In the British monarchy the monarch's eldest offspring succeeds to the throne, and it looks as if Adonijah assumes this rule should apply. But God has not laid down that rule. David, too, has taken no action in connection with who should succeed him. It is an aspect of the way he has become irresponsible and feeble as years have gone by. The point is illustrated by the pathetic account of his dotage with which 1 Kings begins.

Adonijah could argue that someone needs to take decisive action rather than leave the nation with this apology for leadership, but he goes about it the same way as Absalom, by accumulating the outward trappings of kingship to add to his good looks. 2 Samuel has portrayed David failing his sons in not exercising any discipline in relation to them, and the point is here most explicit. David could confront his enemies but not his sons.

Israel's leadership is divided. Adonijah wins the support of some key figures. Solomon has the support of others. Maybe Nathan supports Solomon on the basis of the story of his birth. God struck down David's first son by Bathsheba; he then sent Nathan to tell David that Bathsheba's second son was someone God would love. So Nathan could connect some dots and conclude that God intends Solomon to be king.

This would link with the plan he presents to Bathsheba. It would be quite natural for her to hope her son would end up as king, and not simply for the usual motherly reasons. People who might look like rivals for the throne or might support such rivals are in a dangerous position. If Adonijah succeeds to the throne, both Solomon and Bathsheba may not live long. So Bathsheba might be quite willing to 'remind' the befuddled David of a promise that (as far as we know) he never made. And Adonijah will know that his number is up when David at last takes the decisive action that was needed long ago.

So God continues to work though people's manipulations, failures, fears and plotting. That doesn't necessarily mean they get away with them.

Lord, work through the manipulations and failures of our leaders.

13 Coping with the aftermath
1 Kings 2; 1 Chronicles 29

When you take sides, you take risks. Some of the violence here involves the continuing effects of events associated with David's own accession. Joab has a number of strikes against him from back then. Abiathar the priest just has the one strike, his support of Adonijah, but that is enough to take him into early retirement. The requirement that Solomon take action against Shimei looks a little mean. Adonijah's action in seeking to marry David's hot caregiver looks at best stupid. It is tantamount to an announcement that he still aspires to taking David's place.

So the way things work out issues from the stupidity of the people around Solomon, but it also issues from Solomon's own wisdom – at least David urges him to exercise his wisdom in the way he deals with the people David mentions. Solomon needs to be a person who reacts to people's action with insight and makes events work his way, who seizes opportunities, makes things happen, knows how to get things done. His doing so issues in the happy result that potential threats for his throne all disappear. Yes, Solomon's throne is securely established, and without Solomon's own hands getting stained with blood. Like David, he is Mr Clean.

How is God involved in all these events? The story's silence on this question is loud. That is all the more so when the storyteller reports many statements about God that other people make. The nearest the storyteller comes to associating God with what happens is to comment that Solomon's dismissal of Abiathar fulfils God's warning that Eli's descendants would lose their position as priests.

There is quite a contrast between the main body of this chapter and David's opening charge to Solomon, which recalls Moses' charge to Joshua. At this crucial moment of transition, the leader is given a commission to be strong and confident, an exhortation to stick by Moses' teaching and a promise that God will be faithful to him and that he will be successful.

There is another charge to which Solomon is heir: God's charge to David in 2 Samuel 7. It puts the emphasis more on God's promises, but David notes that the promise will depend on his successors 'walking before God in truth'.

We will keep your charge, Lord; will you establish your word?

14 Solomon dreams

1 Kings 3; 2 Chronicles 1

Solomon is asked, 'What would you like me to do for you?' and provides a model answer. Yet the account of God's appearing to Solomon and his making his request comes in a context that attaches some irony to it. The first thing we are told about Solomon, once he is secure on his throne, is that he has made a marriage alliance with Pharaoh king of Egypt. There are several reasons why this is a troublesome statement. In Western culture, we will be offended that marriage becomes subordinate to politics. Within the Old Testament, there would be more concern that Solomon is getting sucked into political alliances as a means of ensuring the nation's security and stability, rather than trusting in God. And there would be concern that bringing foreign wives to live in the city of David will mean making it possible for them to worship their gods there.

The subsequent verses indicate that there isn't an immediate problem, though they hint that there will be a problem in due course. Although David brought the covenant chest to Jerusalem and there is some kind of sanctuary there, apparently the sanctuary at Gibeon just up the road is more impressive and is thus chosen for this special occasion near the beginning of Solomon's reign.

Its significance leads to God appearing to Solomon with that testing question. The terms of Solomon's response are telling. He is concerned with the fact that his responsibility is to exercise authority over the people. It is the responsibility David accepted when he was at the peak of his achievement, before everything went south. In that connection Solomon knows he needs to be able to discern between good and bad.

Solomon's words thus clarify what he and God mean by wisdom. The key is a listening mind that submits one's thinking to God's way of thinking. The picture here sets before people (and especially before later kings) a vision of what a king is supposed to be.

So Solomon wakes up and realises it was a dream. In Western culture that would mean it was 'only a dream'. Here, to say it was a dream is to open up the possibility that it was a revelation from God.

Lord, give your servant an understanding mind, able to discern between good and bad.

15 Two mothers, one baby

1 Kings 3 – 4

As these women are prostitutes, were their pregnancies pure accident, or were they something they half-wanted? What were they planning to do when their babies were born? Would they help each other, taking turns to look after the babies in a house they shared and to ply their trade? In a Western context might they have had abortions? Might they have looked forward without enthusiasm or even with dread to the complications motherhood would bring? Did they then find their feelings changed when their babies were born?

How deep is the pain in the heart of the woman whose baby has died? How great is the fear of the woman who is in danger of losing her baby, or of watching him be slain? Yet her motherly instincts are her salvation and her baby's salvation. The Hebrew word for 'compassion' looks like the word for the womb. Compassion is the feeling a mother has for the child of her womb. The real mother's compassion saved her child.

Like many great insights, Solomon's solution to the problem is obvious as soon as he has enunciated it, yet it is a stroke of genius. It is an expression of wisdom because it is uttered in the course of his exercising authority for the community. The king's task is to see that decisions are taken in a proper way for people. His vocation does not focus on economics or international relations but on seeing that right gets done.

The ambiguity of Solomon's leadership appears further in the account of his necessarily complex administration. Solomon embodies Samuel's warnings about the cost of a monarchy. Adoniram's department of conscript labour is also worrying. We are a long way away from the Old Testament's vision for work.

The narrative does tell us that Judah and Israel are as numerous as the sand by the sea, eating and drinking and being happy. On the other hand, women are often driven into the sex trade by economic pressures, and these two are likely to be women who for some reason have no families and thus no livelihood. A troubling question the story thus raises concerns the way Israelite society has developed. The exercise of authority by David and Solomon has not produced a healthy society.

When the moment is especially crucial, give me wisdom, Lord.

16 The Temple

1 Kings 5 – 7; 2 Chronicles 2 – 5

Like the actual idea of having a temple, the plans for the Temple don't come from God. God again goes along with what seems natural to the people who want to relate to him. A temple needs to have an area where people can come into the Great King's presence. There needs to be a hall where the King meets with his staff. And the King needs to have his private quarters.

Outside the Temple are two pillars that symbolise what their names refer to, the fact that God establishes the world by his strength; it's therefore secure. If you thought your world looked insecure, looking at the Temple would remind you of an aspect of the good news concerning the God whose name dwelt there. If you turned around from looking at these pillars, you saw 'the Sea', a huge basin. Presumably it held water for the acts of cleansing required by the worship at the Temple. But the sea is an embodiment of threatening power that could overwhelm the land. This Sea constitutes another visual reminder that the world is established by God's strength.

The Sea stood in the courtyard, along with the main altar on which animals were burnt and offered to God, so the people could take part in making the offerings. Within the hall were the altar on which priests burned incense, the table on which was set the 'presence bread' that suggested the people's grain offerings and/or God's provision for the people, and ten lampstands. At the back of the hall was the inner room, the holiest place, where a priest went just once a year to purify it. There were two gold-plated figures, part animal and part bird, that symbolised the creatures that transported God's throne through the heavens and to the earth. They thus pointed to the presence of the invisible God, enthroned above them. In turn they stood over and protected the covenant chest. Its presence there underlined questions about the relationship between the covenant that went back to Sinai and about the way Israel had become a state like any other. Would the state be willing to shape its life by what was said on the two stone tablets (the Ten Commandments)? Answer: no, actually.

We will shape our lives by your expectations, Lord. Dwell among us.

17 Some things one can pray about

1 Kings 8; 2 Chronicles 6

Solomon's prayer at the Temple dedication deals with some of the mystery and the paradox involved in thinking about God's presence with us. I don't know how literally the story means us to take the picture of the cloud filling the Temple, but God certainly becomes present there. Solomon makes explicit his awareness that the idea of God's dwelling in a house on earth is silly. But his name will be there. They will proclaim it. When you say someone's name, it's as if it brings the person present.

Solomon's prayer is then a prayer about prayer. What can you pray about, and expect God to answer? You can pray for God to be involved in seeing that justice is done. You can pray about when things go wrong for the people of God. You can face your wrongdoing and talk to God about it and then plead with God for mercy. You can pray about what we might call natural disasters and such troubles affecting individuals. Solomon's prayer involves some bold requests, so the dramatic nature of his posture, lying flat on the ground, is appropriate.

It would be easy for the prayer to have no thought for anyone outside Israel. But Solomon's fourth request asks Yahweh to treat foreigners the same as Israelites, so that the world as a whole may come to revere Yahweh in the same way that Israel does. His closing blessing expresses the broader longing that all the nations may come to acknowledge Yahweh.

Then, before he finishes, Solomon starts talking about the possibility that the people may go so wrong in their relationship with God that God will get angry enough to let them be taken off into exile. Excuse me? But the people for whom this story in Kings is told are those who have gone through that experience and could be quite depressed about their situation. The story invites them to face some facts but also to hear some good news. They can turn around and ask for grace. Israel can appeal to God's own character, his power, his mercy and his consistency to his own purpose. Like Moses, Solomon argues that God can hardly give up on working with them now.

You have said you would dwell in thick darkness, Lord, but you also dwell among us!

121

18 The chance to be a servant leader
1 Kings 12; 2 Chronicles 10

The Scriptures usually talk more about leaders as servants of God than as servants of their people, and we haven't seen much indication that Saul, David or Solomon were concerned with serving people. The story of Rehoboam provides great talk of the idea of being a servant of the people, though it finally leads nowhere.

It's tempting for people in power to rely on power and to try to achieve things by force. Yet in Rehoboam's situation, presenting yourself as the people's servant would be a good idea. How can one explain Rehoboam's stupidity? I can see God behind it, says the narrator of the story. Rehoboam's foolishness will contribute to the fulfilling of God's plan. The situation parallels that in Egypt, when Pharaoh was stubborn, and he encouraged himself to be stubborn, and God encouraged him to be stubborn. You can look at what happens from different angles and see both the reality of human freedom and decision-making and the reality of divine sovereignty and the fulfilling of God's will.

You can also see God both operating in an interventionist way and making use of decisions people make for themselves. So when necessary, God sends a prophet to keep Rehoboam on the course God wants, if he shows an inclination to act contrary to the way God wants. Jeroboam's action reminds one of the exodus story, too. When the book of Exodus was written, and it came to the story of the gold calf that Aaron made, it seems to be nudging the reader to see the parallel with Jeroboam's action.

Jeroboam shares another problem with David and Solomon. For these kings, religion has become the servant of the state. There is a lot to be said for separation of Church and state, not to protect the state but to protect the Church. Jeroboam's building up Shechem makes sense; it is the obvious place for a capital city, at a crossroads between north and south, east and west. Nablus, the centre of the northern half of the West Bank today, is nearby. Penuel is east of the Jordan, so building up this city also makes sense, because it gives Jeroboam a major centre in that region.

If we are leaders, Lord, make us servant leaders.

19 Prophets, and when to ignore them
1 Kings 13; 2 Chronicles 10

Prophets are tiresome, and it is their destiny to be ignored. In Israel's history, they start coming into their own when there are kings. For Saul and David, they are ambiguous figures; they initiate the process whereby Saul and David become kings, and they confront them about the way they fulfil their role. They have the same function in relation to Jeroboam. It was a prophet who initiated the process whereby Jeroboam became king.

Sometimes God takes a person with no leadership ability and makes them a leader, as happened with Saul. Sometimes God picks out someone too young to have had a chance to show leadership ability and takes a chance on how things will turn out, as happened with David. Either way, the results are ambiguous. Sometimes God lets human wilfulness and plotting take their course, as happened with Solomon. The results are again ambiguous. Sometimes God harnesses human ability, as happens with Jeroboam. For there to be a king who is not David's descendant, there would need to be a prophetic word parallel to the ones that designated Saul and then David. Yet what happens in Ephraim is the fulfilment of God's word of judgement in light of Solomon's reign.

In terms of the reduction of oppression in Ephraim, Jeroboam's reign is an improvement on what Rehoboam planned, but in terms of relationship with God, it is hardly an improvement on Solomon's reign. Hence a man of God confronts Jeroboam with a prophecy, as prophecy initiated his reign.

The anonymous prophets later in the story are both ambiguous people, like those kings. One would guess that a northern, Bethel prophet would be a suspicious figure. Has he been supporting the regime? Is that why God sends a prophet from Judah? If so, he learns a thing or two through what happens. The Judahite prophet himself risks his life to confront Jeroboam, then loses his life because he relaxes and is insufficiently suspicious of another prophetic word. It would be inappropriate to infer that we should always trust what we think God has said to us, rather than what someone else says is a word from God. The opposite will often be the case. But gullibility doesn't pay, either.

Lord, grant us discernment over what claims to be a word from you.

20 The fate of a royal child and a royal father

1 Kings 14

When their child becomes ill, a king and queen may be no better off than ordinary people. They can only turn to God. So they turn to the prophet at Shiloh. The trouble is that they know from the Bethel prophet that they are in trouble with God. With some naiveté they try to circumvent this problem for their son's sake. They know that Ahijah may be able to tell them how they might avert any threat to their son's life. But they think that prophets may be able to look into the future but not be able to see the wrong things that are going on in the present. They are mistaken.

When bad things happen in people's lives, they are inclined to ask, 'Why has this happened to me?' and the Scriptures recognise that illness does sometimes result from wrongdoing (see 1 Corinthians 11:27–32), so it is a proper question. It's not explicit whether the king and queen ask the question, but Ahijah knows how profound, far-reaching and disastrous is the answer to the question they do ask. God's message to Jeroboam is now the same as the message to Solomon. His leadership is going to mean disaster for his people. The Old Testament is more hardheaded than Western thinking about how the destiny of children is tied up with that of their parents. If Jeroboam is to be punished for his action, the interweaving of the children's destiny with that of their parents means his children will suffer too. Once again, this principle is less threatening to ordinary people. A look at royal families in the modern world shows the price royal children may pay for their position.

The story does imply that the boy seems likely to die anyway. God does not need to intervene to make it happen. God needs only to decline to intervene to heal him. God's actual action is to give his death new meaning for his parents. But the story doesn't assume that the boy's death is inevitable. Once again, the prophecy has the capacity to make itself not come true. If someone repents in response to a prophet's word, the word need not come true.

But there is no talk of repentance here.

Lord, protect our children from paying a price for us being their parents.

21 The personal, the political and the religious
1 Kings 17

Ahab has encouraged political relationships with Tyre, the big power to the north, by marrying one of the king's daughters, Jezebel, which requires him to erect the necessities to facilitate the practice of her faith. Elijah then appears like a bolt out of the blue. He is almost like one of the divine aides who speak as if they are a kind of incarnation of God. In fact, at the close of the chapter the woman declares not that she now knows that Yahweh is God but that she now knows that Elijah is a man of God who truly speaks a reliable word from God. To recognise Elijah is to recognise Yahweh.

In light of Ahab's political and religious policies, Elijah declares that there is going to be a drought. And when there is no rain, nothing grows, and people have nothing to eat. During the drought, Yahweh takes Elijah himself to the far north into the very territory of Jezebel and her father and their gods. Elijah's being the means of Yahweh providing for a needy person there carries the conflict between Yahweh and Baal into enemy territory and demonstrates that Yahweh is truly God in Phoenicia as well as in Ephraim.

It's not quite clear whether the boy was then near death or had actually died. Either way, Canaanites and Israelites were inclined to assume that Baal was the lord of life and death, the god who decided whether children were born and whether people lived or died. There in Baal's territory Elijah demonstrates that it is Yahweh who has that power.

But the story focuses on the personal at least as much as the political or religious. Here is a woman who has committed herself to Yahweh's servant, letting this foreigner with his strange God use her spare room because he needs somewhere to live. She has pain in her heart and has the common human instinct to think that God is punishing her when things go wrong in her life. Will God really have her son die? God does not, which encourages Israelites to be open to the possibility that the God who definitely can do miracles of this kind might do one for them.

Lord, have mercy on your people for whom the flour jar and the oil jug threaten to run out.

22 Who is the real God?

1 Kings 18

Elijah and Obadiah exemplify two ways of rendering to Caesar what belongs to Caesar and to God what belongs to God. Elijah makes no compromises, gives in to no fears or pressures and takes no prisoners. Obadiah is also a loyal and committed servant of Yahweh, who seeks to work via the structures and the political realities. He is a kind of double agent. He is a member of Ahab's court and draws his pay from there. But he hides scores of prophets when Ahab wants to capture them. Subsequently, it is humorous for us but no joke for Obadiah that Elijah wants Obadiah to risk blowing his cover.

Elijah said there would be a drought because people had turned away from Yahweh. And there is a drought. But maybe it's a coincidence? Elijah requires the Ephraimites to make up their minds. It's a matter of guesswork why the contest takes place on Mount Carmel, the long mountain ridge that runs southeast to northwest from the heartland of Ephraim to the Mediterranean. Maybe the point is that this is border territory between Ephraim and Phoenicia, Jezebel's territory.

With scatological delight Elijah demonstrates that the Master's prophets cannot meet his challenge. In the summer Baal could seem to die; when the rains came in the autumn, it was a sign that he had come back to life. The prophets' gashing of themselves identifies with the dying Baal and seeks to bring him back to life.

I wish Elijah hadn't killed them all. Maybe God feels the same; the story doesn't say that God told him to, nor does it express an opinion on his doing so. But Elijah acts as a 'man of God', with scary power and authority. It wasn't usually what prophets or anyone else did, as it wasn't what God usually did. Like Jesus' warnings about hell, the story is meant to leave us horrified and to make us face the possible consequences of making the wrong choice about whether to follow the real God, who has made himself known to us.

The close of the story has Elijah continuing to manifest the supernatural power of a man of God. He knows rain is coming. He runs back to Jezreel quicker than Ahab can drive there.

Lord, let it be known that you are God.

23 God speaks in a gale and a whisper
1 Kings 19

Elijah comes to the conclusion that his work as a prophet is a total failure. He is inclined to see things as bleaker than they are. Does he know how to stand up to a man like Ahab but not a woman like Jezebel?

It would take some days to get to Beersheba, the effective southern boundary of Judah. Does he know where he is going? Is he just running like a maniac? After another day, for the first time he stops for breath, and for the first time talks to God. At some point he becomes set on travelling through the wilderness for another week or so to get to where God had long ago appeared to Moses.

The way God speaks to him there first involves wind, earthquake and fire, then a low murmuring sound. The King James Version has 'a still, small voice', but the expression is more elusive than that phrase implies. The story doesn't say that God is in the quiet sound though not in the earthquake, wind and fire, though one point the story makes is that you shouldn't just identify God with earthquake, wind and fire. But for Elijah, these reaffirm the power and might of his God, which he has been in danger of forgetting.

Having established that fact, God has a new, threefold commission for him. One aspect is that he is to anoint a new king of Ephraim in place of Ahab. This is not very surprising. Ahab has tested God's long-suffering to destruction. Either side of that anointing, however, are two more surprising anointings. First there is to be a new king in Syria. This act of Elijah signifies again that Yahweh is not merely a local god with power in Israel, but God on the international scale. And then, Elijah is to anoint Elisha as his successor. This is surprising, because anointing is a ceremony to set apart a priest or king and designate him as given authority by God. Perhaps God speaks metaphorically. At least, Elijah never actually anoints anyone. He does designate Elisha as his successor and thereby begins a chain of events whereby Hazael becomes king of Aram and Jehu becomes king of Ephraim.

Have mercy on me when I think I am the only one left.

24 Naboth and his vineyard
1 Kings 21

By Western standards, Israel has a revolutionary view about land. Land belongs to God. Human beings can't own land, can't buy it and can't sell it. But God is keen on people using it. In Israel, he had the nation allocate the land to the twelve clans by lot. It was then left to the individual clans to allocate the land to the groups and families within it. But once there is a central government and there are cities, things become more complicated. When the government needs land, it needs to be able to acquire some. Ahab makes that assumption. But Naboth is old school.

The rather childish way Ahab reacts to Naboth's refusal to sell his vineyard suggests he is a pathetic figure whose cluelessness contrasts with his wife's capacity to get things done. Further, as a Phoenician, Jezebel takes for granted some assumptions from her world. How can Ahab run an efficient administration if he can't make strategic decisions about the land that adjoins the palace? In insisting on holding on to his land when the king needs it, Naboth is resisting the religious and political basis on which a nation has to work. Jezebel just has to hire a couple of people to lie on her behalf. That shouldn't be too difficult.

But Ephraim is not an ordinary nation. It is part of Israel as the people of God. God does not send prophets to corruption capitals in Britain or the USA. They do not have a special place in God's purpose. God does send one to Ahab. There is then a kind of poetic justice about God's judgement. Ahab's blood will be shed where Naboth's blood was shed. There is also a consistency about God's judgement. That point is underscored by the wording that recurs from earlier declarations of judgement.

Jezebel is a woman who makes up her mind. She knows whom she serves. Ahab can be pushed this way and that, and Elijah pushes him. Elijah does not bid him to repent and he gives no hint that he has any way of escaping the judgement that Elijah declares to be imminent. But in some sense Elijah's words bring Ahab to his senses, which gives God the excuse to be merciful.

Give us wisdom, Lord, about when to be resolute and when to give in.

25 Who will entice Ahab?
1 Kings 22; 2 Chronicles 18

Elijah has momentarily disappeared, and even Ahab is unnamed at first in this story. But apparently he needs Judahite help if he is to realise his ambitions. While less important politically than Ahab, the Judahite Jehoshaphat is more aware of how to go about war. First, you ask God whether this war is one to undertake. So Ahab consults the prophets.

They behave like other prophets of whom we read in the Old Testament. 'Prophesying' implies something like speaking in tongues. And the sign that Zedekiah gives is the kind that Jeremiah or Ezekiel will give. His name indicates that he is a worshipper of Yahweh (the last syllable is a form of the name 'Yahweh'). Yet he shows how it is possible to think you are serving God and to manifest spiritual gifts but be deluded. Conversely, while a king like Ahab needs at least to go through the motions of consulting God, Jehoshaphat also wants to hear from the dissident voices.

In principle, Micaiah's picture of the decision-making process in heaven fits one that appears elsewhere in the Scriptures. God sits in the heavenly White House surrounded by the presidential cabinet and the various presidential aides, and together they decide on action to take on earth and on who is to take the action.

How dissident Micaiah's voice is! His understanding of God's way of working in the world may raise readers' eyebrows, though it again matches the way the Scriptures speak elsewhere. As God can bring judgement on people who have rejected the truth, by making it even more impossible for them to understand the truth (see Mark 4:12), so God can bring judgement by sending a message that isn't true. God uses people who are not really committed to bringing God's word as a means of bringing judgement on someone who doesn't really want to hear God's word.

Initially Micaiah behaves as if he belongs to the same company. He thus tests whether Ahab really wants to hear God's word. God continues to seek to get through to him by mercifully undermining the process of bringing judgement by explaining that dynamic to Ahab. He can choose how to react. Like Jeroboam, he thinks a disguise will work, but it doesn't.

Lord, protect us from lying spirits, and give us the insight to recognise them.

26 The cloak and the power of Elijah
2 Kings 2

Elisha is to be a prophet in the line of Elijah. Metaphorically speaking, Elijah anoints Elisha when he asks what Elisha wants him to do for him. The double share of someone's legacy is the share allocated to the firstborn son, in recognition of the fact that he has responsibility for the family's welfare and future, and for the fulfilling of its responsibility to vulnerable people outside it such as widows and orphans and immigrants. In effect, Elisha is asking to have the resources that will make it possible for him to be Elijah's successor. But Elijah knows he cannot decide that he will have them. It is God's business.

Elijah's parting of the waters shows him to be someone who stands in the line of Moses; Elisha's then being able to do the same shows that he comes next in this line. Elijah's disappearance also parallels that of Moses, though Moses did die. But it will be one reason why it is possible for him to appear with Moses to Jesus (see Mark 9).

In Hebrew the 'Dead Sea' is the 'Salt Sea', and the entire water supply in the Jericho area nearby could be affected by the mineral content of the water table, even though the Jericho area also boasts a pure fresh-water supply. Whether you have a good water supply is really a matter of life and death. As well as being a sign of God's caring for the everyday needs of his people, Elisha's purifying the water is another sign of his being a prophet in the line of Moses.

The story of the boys and the bears further underscores Elisha's importance as God's servant. The reference to his baldness suggests reference to a tonsure like that of a monk. While it implies a striking contrast to the assumption elsewhere that people who are devoted to God's service would grow their hair long, it fits the culturally widespread assumption that whether you wear your hair very long or very short, you may well be making a statement. So the boys are jeering at someone whom anyone could recognise as a servant of God, and in bidding him to 'go up' they are telling him to carry on past their city, to go away.

Lord, give us the anointing we need for serving you.

27 The ultimate sacrifice
2 Kings 3

Abraham's near-sacrifice of Isaac provided Wilfred Owen and Leonard Cohen with an image for their nations' strange willingness to sacrifice their children in war. It is both the most unintelligible and the most intelligible of acts. This Old Testament story also tells of someone making this sacrifice.

A great crisis has come to Moab. Moab has to pay taxes to Ephraim in return for the 'privilege' of living under its umbrella. Its king is a sheep breeder in the sense that he rules a country whose economy focuses on sheep. Maybe he pays his taxes in the form of wool. Or in the case of the lambs, maybe he pays it in the form of the animals themselves. It's not clear what Ephraim would do with all that wool, which would come to one or two animals' wool per person per year. Maybe Ephraim would use the wool in trading deals with other peoples.

A king's death and a new king's accession is a dangerous moment for a regime, and it is not surprising that Mesha takes this moment in Ephraim's history to declare independence from Ephraim. Equally, the new king of Ephraim knows he has to assert his authority in decisive fashion at this point, though Jehoram's attempt to do so comes unstuck. The combined forces of Ephraim and Judah join up with those of Edom, south of Moab and southeast of the Dead Sea; evidently Ephraim is also in a position to lean on Edom. They march down the west side of the Dead Sea and round the south end of it. For most of the way the country is extremely inhospitable, and it looks as if the kings have not thought through the logistics of their expedition.

Elisha is persuaded to seek a word from Yahweh. The word promises the water they need and promises a conclusive victory. Then Mesha offers his sacrifice. And it works. How so? What is this wrath that comes on Israel? It seems that the storytellers do not know and do not pretend to explain what they do not know. It is strangely encouraging that the Scriptures do not pretend to know everything; it is then easier to trust them when they think they do know things.

I will sacrifice only myself and only to you, Lord.

28 A tale of two women
2 Kings 4

You aren't necessarily protected from trouble by your husband's being a person truly devoted to God and involved in ministry, and there are no widow's benefits in Elisha's day. Evidently the woman (or her husband) took out a loan when they were in trouble in the hope that their situation would improve. It didn't. The collateral on the loan would be that the children's labour would pay back the loan. This didn't mean they would be slaves, but the arrangement wouldn't be much fun for mother or children. So what Elisha does for the woman is wonderful.

It looks as if the woman in Shunem has come to terms with not being able to have children and has directed her energy in other directions, like giving hospitality to a wandering prophet. It is another Old Testament story showing how women can be people of initiative and action – they are not confined to doing what their husbands say. Elisha's appreciation of the woman's care for him leads to his encouraging his servant to ask what he can do for her. She is reticent about saying, and it is Gehazi who points out that she has no son and that her husband is old. She will be left on her own sooner rather than later. Who will then look after her?

The miracle that follows is only half this story. Maybe it's sunstroke that overcomes the boy, out in the fields in the heat of harvest time. Again his mother is the one who exercises initiative, ignoring her husband's objections to her hastening to Elisha's base on Mount Carmel. He's there all right, but the man of God who did the miracle doesn't know what has now happened. The process whereby the boy is resuscitated again presupposes that Elisha's very person contains mysterious power. Life can flow from him to the boy.

It's tempting to wonder if these are 'just stories', and there is no way of establishing whether or not they are. Perhaps it makes little difference. If they relate things that happened, such things are unlikely to happen for us. One can't produce generalisations from them about the way healing works. They invite us to wonder at God's capacity to make extraordinary things happen.

Have mercy, Lord, on women who grieve over being childless or about their children's sickness.

29 The servant girl, the enemy general and the prophet

2 Kings 5

Translations traditionally refer to Naaman's problem as leprosy, but the word denotes a skin ailment, one that makes people wary of coming near you, maybe because you look like death. But there's a girl who's been captured in war who knows someone who can do something about it for Naaman. Ordinary people sometimes see things that leaders can't see.

It's also the ordinary guys who have the insight to see that Naaman has nothing to lose by following the prophet's instruction to go and bathe in a muddy river. And thus Naaman gets the cleansing. He gets it because God is demonstrating that there is a prophet in Israel – that God is speaking and acting there. The Jordan River is significant even though it is no more impressive than the rivers in Damascus. It is in the land where the God of Israel is especially at work.

So Naaman comes to recognise that there is no God in all the earth except in Israel. Yet he can hardly stay in Canaan as a resident alien, such as Ruth the Moabite or Uriah the Hittite. He has a job to go back to. He reminds us of the Middle Eastern sages who come to see Jesus and worship him, yet then have to go back to their homeland. How can Naaman possibly do that? He has been to the holy land, the land where Yahweh is especially active. So he takes back enough Israelite soil for him to be able to stand on it each day when he prays and offers sacrifice. It will be as if he is back in that holy land, and when he has to look as if he is worshipping the god of the Arameans, in his heart he will be worshipping Yahweh.

In Luke 4, Jesus hints at a different significance in Elisha's cleansing of Naaman with his disorder, rather than an Israelite: it is a kind of judgement on Israel itself. If this is one warning note in the story, another is the tailpiece about Gehazi. His action confuses the message that emerges from the action of the man of God and the action of the God who heals him, and he pays a terrible price.

I will no longer offer sacrifice to any God but Yahweh.

133

30 More chariots of fire
2 Kings 6

As a prophet, it seems that Elisha sometimes takes part in the meetings of Yahweh's heavenly cabinet, like Micaiah, and that is presumably how he knows about the Arameans' military plans which have been discussed there. This issues in the frustration of the Aramean king, to our amusement but not to his. He half-realises something of what is going on to frustrate his war plans, and he needs to do something about it. What chance does a prophet and his staff then have against the Aramean army? Answer: loads of chance when you realise the real dynamics of what happens on earth. There is a whole other realm of reality and activity that the assistant needs to take into account. What you see (with ordinary eyes) is not the only clue to what you get.

The dynamics enable Elisha to impose another frustrating experience on the Arameans in a way that is amusing for us but not for them. It's also a great example of how to be a peacemaker. Sometimes Elisha brings judgement down on people, though more often on Israel than on foreigners. In keeping with his mercy to the Aramean Naaman, he shows mercy to the Aramean army. But he gets God to demonstrate some power over them – not to 'blind' them (a word modern translations use) but to 'dazzle' them, just temporarily. Let's show them they have bitten off more than they can chew, then demonstrate magnanimity in victory and throw them a party, then send them home safe and sound. Imagine the story they will tell when they get home.

The model for how prayer works that emerges from a story like this and from the prophets' account of their experience is anthropomorphic. The same is true about their model for understanding the interrelationship of the activity of heavenly and of earthly forces. One might therefore seek to devise another model, but it needs to be one that accounts for the realities the story presupposes. What we see on earth is not all there is to reality, and prayer is not designed to change us but to change what happens. Until we have devised another model that represents those realities, we would be wise not to abandon Elisha's.

Lord, thank you that there are more with us than there are with them.

May

INTO EXILE
AND BACK

I Shoot the messenger

2 Kings 6 – 7

The account of the siege of Samaria makes clear that the effect of war back then was not so different from its effect in the twenty-first century.

The siege of a city was a central feature of warfare in the ancient world. You sat outside the city and cut off its supply lines, and eventually starvation made the city surrender or weakness made its people a pushover. In the meantime, people may experience moral breakdown. Babies are more vulnerable than adults and may die sooner than adults. But how desperate a situation is it when women can eat the bodies of their babies?

Indeed, it's worse here. The king is responsible to settle disputes among people in the community. Here, a woman is concerned with whether the king will fulfil his responsibility to decide a case of alleged deceit or fraud. She has lost any sense of the enormity of the women's action in eating their babies. In turn, her protest causes the king to reveal his own hidden sense of hopelessness and his resentment in relation to Elisha. Is he blaming Elisha as God's agent in bringing judgement on Ephraim? Is Elisha failing to use the power inherent in him as a man of God? Is lashing out at the prophet a way of lashing out at the God who is bringing terrible trouble on the city? Is it also thereby a refusal to take any responsibility, as if God's action has nothing to do with the way the king has been leading his people?

Whereas God previously closed the Arameans' eyes but opened the eyes of Elisha's attendant, now God opens the Arameans' eyes so that they see what the attendant eventually saw. Ironically, however, they assume that the chariots and horses belong to other earthly armies rather than to heavenly armies.

Unlike Naaman, some men with skin disorders are staying in isolation from their families. It's not quite clear why they are doing so; the First Testament hardly requires it. But it is then neat that the people in quarantine are the people who discover what God has done. Conversely, the man who can't believe that God is going to act on the city's behalf loses the chance to share in its results.

Even when things are desperate, we will continue to hope in you, Lord.

2 It was just a coincidence
2 Kings 8; 2 Chronicles 21 – 22

Coincidence has already played a part in the Shunammite woman's story. It was through coincidence that she knows Elisha, and as a result of the sequence of events that follows, she gets the heads-up to take refuge elsewhere during a famine. But she gets the heads-up because she is one of the few people who are responsive to Elisha.

It looks as if her husband is dead, and she is the effective head of the family, exercising responsibility for its destiny and its land as women often have to. This is background to a new coincidence. She and her family arrive back in the country, and she needs to appeal to the king for the restoration of their land, which has been taken over by someone else. She shows up to make her appeal at just the time Elisha's assistant is talking to the king about what Elisha did for her. So that encourages the king to do the right thing.

The background of the second story lies in God's instructing Elijah to anoint Hazael, which Elisha in effect does as Elijah's successor. It's not clear why Elisha is in Damascus, but his reputation has preceded him, and Ben-hadad sends Hazael to consult him. Like other international figures in the Old Testament story, such as his compatriot Naaman, he recognises that the power of Yahweh and the power and insight of Yahweh's prophet are not confined to Israel, whereas Israelite kings sometimes act as if the opposite is true – as if they don't really believe in Yahweh's power at all.

Does Elisha simply tell Hazael to lie to his master? The story in 1 Kings 22 has already illustrated God's willingness to send words of deceit to someone, as an act of judgement. But maybe Elisha's message contains a more subtle but chilling ambiguity and reflects the mysterious interplay between divine will and awareness on one hand, and human probabilities and initiatives and responsibilities on the other. It will also reflect the mysterious tension between God's willingness to chastise and God's grief in doing so. No, the king's illness is not fatal, so at one level the answer to his question is that he will recover. But no, he will not recover, because something else will intervene.

Lord, make coincidences work together for good for your people.

3 Jehu and Jezebel
2 Kings 9

God told Elijah to anoint Jehu, an army officer, and now Elijah's successor, Elisha, commissions the person who is actually to do it. The unnamed young prophet restates words of God from earlier. Jehu is to terminate the rule of the line of Ahab, the father of the current king, who was responsible for such degeneration in Ephraim. And he is to deal with Jezebel, now the queen mother, the widow of the previous king, who is often an important figure in the Middle East.

When the king asks Jehu whether things are well, more literally he asks, 'Is there peace?' He will be concerned with what is happening in Ramoth-gilead, where the army is engaged with the Aramaeans. He is hoping that it is in this connection that Jehu has raced to Jezreel. But there can be no more peace or well-being for Ahab's household.

Every trace of Jezebel is also to be eliminated, not explicitly because of the worship of false gods that Ahab encouraged as a result of her arrival, but because of the slaughter among the devotees of Yahweh that she herself encouraged. With poetic justice, her son's death comes about on the very plot of land that she enabled the king to acquire by engineering the death of its proper owner.

Like her son, Jezebel asks Jehu if things are well ('Is there peace?'), but she does so with more overt irony or calculation. She knows that the game is up and that Jehu's answer to Jehoram applies to her. She goes on to address Jehu as Zimri, which is actually the name of his predecessor and role model as an army officer who killed his king and assumed the throne. In effect, Jezebel is hinting that people who live by the sword die by the sword, though in Jehu's case she is wrong. Jehu's coup will result in the establishment of his own line in Ephraim.

Contrary to the impression given by the way Jezebel came to be turned into a sexual fantasy figure, the elderly queen mother is not hoping to seduce Jehu. She just wants to meet her death with the dignity appropriate to her position as 'the daughter of a king'. But she does not.

Lord, have mercy.

4 Two or three forceful women and two or three covenants

2 Kings 11; 2 Chronicles 22 – 23

Meanwhile in Judah, things are not much better. The king of Judah is Joram/Jehoram, and he married a woman from the Ephraimite royal family called Athaliah. Connecting some dots suggests she may be Ahab and Jezebel's daughter. She certainly shares Jezebel's religious commitments, her decisiveness and energy, her capacity to get her husband to do what she thinks is right, and her ruthlessness. While attitudes to Yahweh never get out of hand in Judah to the extent that they do in Ephraim, Athaliah takes them to a new low point.

Eventually a priest called Jehoiada makes a covenant with some army commanders and also sets up another covenant involving the people as a whole. Most covenants in the Bible involve God, and commonly God takes an initiative to establish them. In this story Jehoiada takes the initiative. But when you initiate a coup or a revolution, you put your life on the line. Jehoiada can count on some support, but the result is not guaranteed. The community is divided.

Jehoiada turns out to have calculated aright. He then needs to take the lead in connection with a third covenant, one that explicitly brings God in. The people have to make their commitment to God, in the hope that God may accept it despite the faithlessness that has characterised their recent history. So Jehoiada leads them in doing so, with some less obvious bravery – in fact, with two further forms of bravery. There is some risk involved in reaching out to God. And there is some bravery involved in encouraging Judah to make its covenantal commitment.

While Jehoiada would have no need to show his variegated bravery were it not for one woman, Athaliah, he would have had no opportunity to do so were it not for another woman. As well as being Jehoiada's wife, Jehoshabeath is the daughter of King Jehoram/Joram, apparently not by Athaliah but by one of his other wives. And she rescued her nephew from Athaliah's slaughter. She too would have put her life on the line in doing so. So would the nanny who looked after him. But it means he is alive to become king.

Thank you, Lord, for people who put their lives on the line for you. Protect them.

5 How to pray from inside a fish

2 Kings 14; Jonah 1 – 2

It is in 2 Kings 14 that Jonah appears in the story of Ephraim, as a prophet to whom Yahweh gives promises about Ephraim regaining territory it has lost. He is the first prophet to have a book named after him, but his book is not a collection of prophecies. It is a story. I assume it's 'just a story', but the reason isn't that it's impossible for someone to survive for three days inside a fish. 'Yahweh the God of the heavens, who made the sea and the dry land' (as Jonah magnificently calls him) could easily preserve someone inside a fish. The reason is rather the jokey nature of this story, which resembles many of Jesus' parables. The reason for attaching this story to Jonah is that a prophet who gives such a positive promise to Ephraim is the last kind of person to enthuse over Nineveh escaping God's judgement.

I like to picture God rolling his eyes when Jonah boards a ship going in the opposite direction from the one to which God pointed. Why does Jonah resist God's call? The second half of his story will explain. Preaching judgement to Nineveh, the capital of Assyria, may result in its repenting. Indeed, Jonah knows that the reason God has for sending him to preach judgement is a desire to find an excuse for cancelling the judgement. Jonah doesn't want judgement on the great Assyrian oppressor to be cancelled. In the story he continues to show his lack of insight into the truth about God. The pagan sailors understand more than he does, even if they too have some pretty primitive ideas.

Readers can be so preoccupied with the big fish that they miss the significance of the prayer Jonah prays when he's inside it. Inside the fish, one might have thought Jonah would be saying, 'Help, help, help,' and, 'Sorry, sorry, sorry.' He's actually saying, 'Thank you, thank you, thank you.' The fish is his means of salvation. When the sailors threw him into the deep, death seemed inevitable. But inside the fish he is safe.

Yet is there an irony in the prayer? Does his failure to say 'Sorry, sorry, sorry' suggest that he still has a lot to learn?

You brought up my life from the pit, Lord!

6 Mercy for the oppressor
2 Kings 14; Jonah 3 – 4

It boggles the mind to think of Jonah marching into Nineveh and achieving what he achieves. He has learned his lesson and realises it is wise to do as God says, but it will become clear that he has otherwise learned nothing. Yet any unwillingness he still feels makes no difference to his effectiveness. When you're God's mouthpiece, it may not matter what's in your heart.

Even the animals are involved in Nineveh's response to Jonah. They are part of the community. If the city is destroyed, they will pay the price, too. Jonah meets with a response that any prophet in Ephraim or Judah would give his eye teeth for, which is perhaps one of the points about the story ('Won't you Israelites learn from the Ninevites?').

What the Ninevites needed was to turn from their previous lifestyle. 'Turn' is a word commonly translated 'repent', and repentance also implies a change of attitude and a sense of sorrow. The Ninevites' outward observances show that they repent in this sense, too. They themselves entertain just a little hope that God himself may be prepared to 'turn' or repent and 'relent', to give up the idea of judgement and act in mercy.

Jonah knows that their tentative hopes are justified, and when God relents, he turns on God in a way that provokes a smile. 'I knew you'd do that. That's why I never wanted to come here.' He quotes back at God the words that God uttered at Sinai about being gracious, compassionate, long-tempered and vast in commitment (see Exodus 34). Apply them to the Assyrians? It's not that Jonah embodies a conviction that God is not open to being gracious to other nations, as if he has an exclusivist view of Yahweh. But Assyria, the oppressor?

Meanwhile, Yahweh provides some shade for Jonah, then adds insult to injury by letting the vine die as quickly as it grew. 'Excuse me?' says God. 'You feel sorry for the plant? What about the people in Nineveh? And for that matter, the animals there? Don't you think I care about animals?'

The book ends with that question. It doesn't tell us Jonah's answer, but leaves us as readers to answer the question.

Thank you, Lord, that you change your mind and relent over bringing judgement.

7 The end of Ephraim as a nation
2 Kings 17

We are on the way toward the end of the story of Judah and Ephraim with the fall of Jerusalem in 587 BC. These stories are not merely contemporary newspaper reports or journal entries. They are more like a memoir in which someone reflects with the benefit of some distancing on the significance of events. 1 and 2 Kings is Judah's later reflection on its own and its brother Ephraim's life, concerned not so much to understand Ephraim's story for its own sake as to discover what Judah needs to learn for its own life.

For the next century or so, Ephraim's story stands as a warning to Judah. It must learn from its brother's fate. It needs to read Ephraim's story in light of where it ended and of the religious and theological evaluation that this chapter offers. It doesn't do so: the next context for an edition of this memoir or a reading of it is the decades that follow Judah's consequent fall in 587 BC. A later one is the subsequent life of Judah, when it has to relate to the people living to its north later in that same century and following centuries.

At the hand of Assyria and Babylon, Ephraim and Judah go through analogous experiences. Assyria and then Babylon are the means of chastising the two nations, and one way they do so is by transporting part of their population. Thus the exiled Ephraimites become the 'ten lost tribes'. But the Assyrians also bring people from elsewhere to settle in their place. The population of Ephraim itself (which becomes Samaria) becomes mixed, combining adherence to Yahweh with adherence to the gods they bring with them from their homelands.

That mixing is then the background to relations between Judah and Samaria as described in Ezra and Nehemiah. This memoir provides Judah in their day with some rationale for their attitudes. In their relationships with Samaria, they need to remember the origins of the community there and the mixed nature of its religious commitment. And they still need to beware of becoming mixed up in that way. The Ephraimites didn't take anywhere near enough notice of the Torah or of the Prophets, this memoir says. Learn from their story.

Lord, give us grace to heed both the Torah and the Prophets.

8 The bird in a cage
2 Kings 18; 2 Chronicles 29 – 31

Hezekiah is more radical in his commitment to Yahweh than any other Judahite king so far, and he is initially successful in military and political affairs, but his rebellion against Assyria is a disaster. It provokes the Assyrian king into attacking Judah in 701 BC. King Sennacherib recorded his own account of the invasion in an inscription in his capital, Nineveh. He speaks of besieging and taking forty-six of Hezekiah's fortified cities, taking huge amounts of plunder and shutting up Hezekiah in Jerusalem 'like a caged bird'. The invasion brings to the surface the spiritual, religious and political issues Hezekiah has to face. 'It was on Yahweh the God of Israel that he relied.' The word 'rely' or 'trust' runs through this story.

Sennacherib is besieging Lachish, Judah's biggest city after Jerusalem. While doing so, he sends some lieutenants to give Hezekiah notice that the pincer is tightening. Jerusalem is the only remaining obstacle to the complete subjugation of Judah. It would be wise to surrender now. Sennacherib knows that Jerusalem will be his biggest challenge, located as it is in the mountains in a good defensive position. He will save himself trouble if he can get Hezekiah to surrender, and Hezekiah will get off more lightly than if he makes Sennacherib use up resources on a siege.

The question, 'What are you relying on?' is a telling one. Isaiah 30 – 31 makes clear that Judah is relying on Egypt as an ally when it rebels against Assyria. Isaiah points out theological considerations that make this a stupid policy; the Assyrians point to political considerations. The Judahites are behaving as if they think that the words of the Egyptians can be relied on and thus can be the key to military victory. It's not so. Without realising it, the Assyrians speak a prophetic word to the Judahites.

Some of the Assyrians' arguments are rather clever. But eventually they make a calamitous mistake. Even if Yahweh wants to rescue Judah from Sennacherib, would he be able to? The Judahite leaders return to their king in horror at Sennacherib's blasphemy, but in reality the blasphemy is good news. Surely Yahweh cannot resist the temptation to put Sennacherib in his place?

You, Lord, are the great God who can deliver your people out of the hand of people who attack them.

9 What to do with tricky mail
2 Kings 19; 2 Chronicles 32

The first time Assyrian forces made the trek up the mountains from Lachish, their leaders stood across from the walls of the city as they besieged it and declared how impossible it was that God should preserve Jerusalem. In one sense there is nothing new here to cause Hezekiah to tear his clothes and put on sackcloth. The city has been under siege for a while, though the determination expressed by the lieutenants threatens to push Hezekiah over the edge.

In addition to going into the Temple to stand before God, he sends his staff to discover Isaiah's reaction to the lieutenants' words. It's a nice touch that Isaiah refers to the Assyrian king's lieutenants as his 'boys'; it underlines their insignificance. God has nothing to fear of them, and therefore Judah has nothing to fear of them.

The point is implied in another way by Isaiah's introduction to his message: the phrase, 'Yahweh has said this' (in traditional translations, 'Thus says the Lord'). A story such as this one reflects the background of that phrase. When the Assyrian king's top lieutenant delivered his ultimatum to Hezekiah's aides, he introduced it by saying, 'The Great King, has said this...' Prophets who take up that form of expression are also relating messages that a king has formulated before they set off to deliver them; and this King is a much more impressive one than the self-styled 'Great King' of Assyria. God is in a position to get the so-called Great King simply to go home. He hears reports of trouble arriving from the south and then later returns home and gets assassinated.

Meanwhile, however, he sends Hezekiah a letter promising to be back, and Hezekiah takes the letter into the Temple so as to wave it before God and say, 'Have a look at this, then!' It is a great model for prayer. So is the way Hezekiah actually addresses God, reaffirming truths about Yahweh's being the Lord of the whole world (including the Assyrian empire), urging God to look and listen and deliver, leaving to God exactly what to do and closing with the reminder that delivering Judah from Assyria could contribute to the whole world's acknowledging Yahweh.

You, Lord, you are God, you alone, of all the kingdoms of the earth!

10 How to gain and lose God's sympathy
2 Kings 20; 2 Chronicles 29 – 32

Hezekiah here proves that prayer can change God. Isaiah tells Hezekiah what is going to happen as if it's fixed, but the way the story unfolds indicates that it's not fixed at all. When God wants to do something good for you but you don't respond with trust and commitment, that may change God's mind (it may not – in this respect, too, relationships with God, like other relationships, are not predictable). The good news is that when God tells you that things are going to turn out badly for you, your response may again change God's mind. Hezekiah has an illness that looks as if it will kill him, but actually it won't.

The story is also notable for the way Isaiah combines bringing a word from God with using traditional medicine. The 'treatment' in question would hardly be effective in countering a potentially fatal illness, but God seems to like using physical means in a sacramental way. The nature of the sign that Hezekiah gets is also unclear. There's no need to infer that God changed the movements of the planets, though of course God could do so. For the sign to work, some unusual changes in the process whereby the shadows of evening lengthened would be enough to provide Hezekiah with his sign.

Hezekiah is a more ambiguous person than is implied by some of the statements about him, as the last story about him shows. Babylon is going to take over from Assyria as the superpower, and the Babylonian embassy's arrival is likely related to Babylon's ambitions. Hezekiah's showing the embassy his resources is a sign that he is willing to be drawn into an alliance.

But Isaiah knows something Hezekiah does not know. Yes, Babylon is going to seize the reins of power in the Middle East. It might seem, then, that Hezekiah is backing the right horse in allying with Babylon. But Yahweh enables Isaiah to look beyond the rise of Babylon. Once it is the superpower, its relationship with Judah will be very different from the one it seeks now. It is Babylon that will terminate the life of Judah as a nation and take the Judahite leadership into exile. It's not clear how cynical Hezekiah's response is.

Lord, answer our prayers, even when we don't deserve it.

11 Last chance to take the Torah and the Prophets seriously

2 Kings 22 – 23; 2 Chronicles 34

Josiah's grandfather Manasseh was a kind of reformer, reasserting the traditional Canaanite-style religion of the land. Josiah undoes those reforms and engages in some positive innovations. They involve abolishing the 'high places', the shrines that were part of Israelite religion throughout its history. And they include a new style of Passover celebration, which could now more feasibly be held centrally as Judah is much smaller than it once was.

Maybe politics and faith come happily together for Josiah as they came unhappily together for Manasseh. Whereas it would have been hard for Manasseh to resist Assyrian pressure, and it was tempting for him to match his religious policy to the political pressures, Assyria is now in decline, and Josiah's actions could imply both doing the right thing by Yahweh and asserting Judah's independence.

But commissioning work on the Temple brings Josiah more than he bargains for – the discovery of a Torah scroll that both scares and inspires him. It seems to have been some form of Deuteronomy. Josiah's reformation seems to be the moment when Deuteronomy becomes a living force in Israel's life. As well as copious instructions about loyalty to Yahweh, Deuteronomy incorporates hair-raising warnings about what will happen to Israel as a consequence of the life Israel has been living.

Josiah sends to ask a prophet what action to take. The casual way the story refers to Huldah indicates that it takes for granted the activity of female as well as male prophets. Huldah has Temple connections, and if she is involved in ministry in the Temple, this would explain the fact that Hilkiah would go to her rather than someone better known to us, such as Jeremiah.

The combination of reading Deuteronomy and consulting Huldah stimulates the making of a covenant; Deuteronomy is the great covenant book within the Torah. A little like the unusual covenant in 2 Kings 11, this one involves God, king and people. Josiah knows he needs to make his commitment and that the people need to make theirs. His privilege and responsibility as a leader are to embody a proper response to God in his own life and then use his influence on the people so that they make theirs.

We will perform the words of the covenant, Lord.
(2 Kings 23:3)

12 The king who vacillates

Jeremiah 37 – 38

In due course, a sequence of kings fail to follow Josiah, the last being his son Zedekiah. It's twenty years later and Babylon is now the great power. Judah has rebelled against Babylon's authority and the Babylonian army has laid siege to Jerusalem.

This moment is one when the siege has been lifted, because the Egyptians are coming to take on the Babylonians and the Judahites see them as deliverers. Jeremiah knows the relief will be only temporary, but it gives him chance to pay a visit home to Anatoth. Unfortunately, a guard is suspicious about his motives in leaving the city, and Jeremiah ends up in detention.

Zedekiah believes in Yahweh, but he can't make up his mind whether to live as if he trusts in Yahweh. He's capable of treating Jeremiah as a true prophet, so he asks Jeremiah to pray for the people. He asks if there's a message from Yahweh, so he recognises the two sides to Jeremiah's significance as a prophet – a prophet represents the people to God, and represents God to the people. But Zedekiah doesn't want it to be generally known that he's consulting Jeremiah. Is it so he can decide not to follow Jeremiah if he doesn't like Yahweh's answer?

Anyway, he indeed doesn't take any notice of the message, and lets Jeremiah be put under house arrest. Then he lets him be put into a more unpleasant form of imprisonment, but subsequently releases him from there and provides him with basic rations for as long as food is available at all. Zedekiah's staff are prepared to be ruthless with Jeremiah and put him somewhere where he's bound to die. But he gets rescued by a foreigner, an African who works in the palace. The city gate is where a king would sit for judicial proceedings – citizens could come there to appeal to him.

What's the point of bringing Yahweh's message to a king who won't take any notice and will probably put you to death for your trouble? It will be the Babylonians who literally set fire to the city, but it will be Zedekiah who will have to carry responsibility for their doing so. In this sense, he'll set fire to the city.

Lord, protect your servants who are in danger because of the message they bring.

13 God is leaving
Ezekiel 8 – 11

While Jeremiah is a prophet in Jerusalem, Ezekiel is a prophet in Babylonia, in a little town where the Babylonians have already transported some people from Jerusalem – people like members of the administration and priests such as Ezekiel's father and thus Ezekiel himself. Yahweh then calls Ezekiel to be a prophet as well as a priest. And there Ezekiel's vocation is to enable his community to know what is happening in Jerusalem, so as to prepare them for what is going to happen to their home city.

In that connection, Yahweh transports Ezekiel in spirit to Jerusalem. In his vision he sees the polytheistic abominations in the Temple and he hears Yahweh commissioning some destroyers to cause devastation in the city, but also commissioning another aide to put a mark on 'the people who sigh and groan over the abominations' there.

Ezekiel's vision of the Temple building would remind his community of the awe-inspiring, transcendent aspect to God's presence there. In his vision, indeed, Ezekiel can see something of the glory or splendour of Yahweh on his throne, above the strange creatures that support it and transport it. The horror of the vision is that God's presence is pulling out of the Temple and the city. The appalling process begins when Yahweh's splendour, that glorious presence, moves to the Temple threshold. Then the creatures take off from the threshold and move to hover over the city, to the east, on the Mount of Olives. Yahweh hasn't totally left the Temple and city yet, but he is thinking about it, threatening it.

The departure of Yahweh's splendour is a horrifying event that hangs over Jerusalem, which (we know with hindsight) will become a reality shortly. The city will fall; the Temple will be destroyed. The encouragement to Judahites in Babylonia is that Yahweh isn't simply moving away from Jerusalem to reside somewhere inaccessible and unidentifiable in the wilderness. He has already become a small-scale sanctuary for these Judahites. He is present there among them, even though there's no building.

In Ezekiel's vision, Yahweh's splendour stops moving as it passes the Mount of Olives, east of Jerusalem. It's as if it's hesitating to leave. There's still the possibility of its not doing so, if the city turns back to Yahweh.

Lord, have mercy on us, and do not leave when we deserve that you should.

14 The end?

2 Kings 25; 2 Chronicles 36

It's obvious now that Judah's story had to end (for a while) with the fall of Jerusalem in 587 BC, but it wouldn't have been obvious in Josiah's day, or even in that of his sons Jehoahaz or Eliakim or Zedekiah, or of Eliakim's son Jehoiachin. At least, it would not have been obvious to these successive kings themselves. There is a sense in which it was self-evident to some of the prophets such as Jeremiah who were striving to give the story a different ending. Given the way the story has unfolded over the centuries, however, Judah's reaction to these prophets was all of a piece with its reaction to the prophets Yahweh had sent over the centuries.

Chronicles calls them God's aides. It's the only time it uses this word to describe prophets; the word more commonly denotes the aides of a human king or the supernatural aides of the heavenly King. It draws attention to the possibly frightening fact that prophets are more than messenger boys (and girls). They are people through whom God's decisions are put into effect. They can be means of blessing, but they are more often means of God's warnings being announced and (when they are not heeded) implemented.

By the end of the story, three of Judah's last four kings have been deposed by the Egyptians or the Babylonians as they vie for control of the area where Judah lives. Each of these kings earns the disapproval of these imperial powers or of God or of both. God keeps delaying the moment when the axe must fall, but eventually it has to do so. 2 Kings gives a ghastly account of the fate of Zedekiah and a grim account of what Nebuchadnezzar and his army do to Jerusalem.

Chronicles reports how the land lay desolate for seventy years – but at least not for ever. And Babylon duly falls to Cyrus the Persian in 539 BC. That is the means of God implementing a promise by Jeremiah that desolation would not last for ever. It is God who raises up Cyrus. Cyrus is doing what he wants to do and can do as the great leader he is, but all unknown, he is fulfilling God's purposes.

Lord, have mercy with your threats and implement your promises.

15 Lament for the fallen city
Lamentations 1

In the aftermath of Jerusalem's devastation, Lamentations begins with a bare exclamation, 'Oh!', a cry of pain. This word gives the book its title in Hebrew (the title 'Lamentations' comes from the old Greek translation). The cry of pain has twenty-two verses, each verse beginning with one letter in the Hebrew alphabet. The poem gives expression to grief and pain from A to Z.

The word *all* comes sixteen times. One should allow for hyperbole: the Old Testament makes clear that the Babylonians didn't actually transport the city's entire population (still less Judah as a whole), and many people who fled during the Babylonian invasion doubtless crept back when the Babylonian army was gone. Yet the contrast between past and present is horrifying. Jerusalem was not a great city like Ephesus, or Babylon. But with its Temple and its palaces, for its people it was a great city. And it was a great city because of the great God worshipped there.

The poem imagines the city as a person bewailing the loss of its people, as a mother bewailing the loss of her children. The roads to Jerusalem mourn because they're not full of pilgrims coming to its festivals. Instead, the sanctuary has been invaded by pagan feet (it would be no problem if these foreigners came to worship Yahweh, but they came to pillage).

Whereas the Psalms protest about invasions that Jerusalem did not deserve, Lamentations knows that this time the city cannot claim innocence. It's been characterised by rebellion. Its reference to friends and allies offers a further hint about the nature of its waywardness. Several prophets berate Judah for assuming that alliances with people such as Egypt are the proper safeguard for its destiny, that these people would support Judah in a crisis. The prophets' assessment has been vindicated.

The poem shows that knowing you got what you deserved doesn't mean you can't pray for mercy. It describes Zion as spreading out her hands in the posture of appeal. But she is finding no comforter. Is she spreading them toward Yahweh, or toward those other helpers in whom she has trusted? 'There's no comforter' is the truth about the situation. But things won't be that way for ever.

See, Lord, how distressed I am.

(Are there people for whom you might pray that way?)

16 On drawing the line
Daniel 1

Whereas Ezekiel is living in a small town some way from Babylon itself, Daniel and his friends get force-marched to the capital, and there they are going to have to work for Nebuchadnezzar. But they want to preserve their Judahite identity. They accept Babylonian names, even though the names make connections with Babylonian gods, as the four young men's original names make connections with the God of Israel. But as the names are reported, at least some of them make fun of the Babylonian gods.

The king's food isn't inherently defiling, but food links with identity, and they want to avoid eating it. Maybe what's important is that you draw the line somewhere. You have to avoid the defiling effect of a culture that worships different gods. The Babylonians 'determined' on names for the young men, but Daniel did some determining of his own in this connection.

It requires God's support if it is to work. And it gets that support. At the beginning of the story God 'gives' Jerusalem to Nebuchadnezzar, but later in the story God 'gives' Daniel favour and 'gives' all four men wisdom. They don't attempt to evade education in Babylonian learning, the learning that will fit them for jobs in the administration. The fruits of God's giving them superior insight will emerge in the stories that follow.

The opening and conclusion of this first story form a chronological bracket around the stories about Daniel. Near the beginning of Daniel's life, God does something strange in giving Jerusalem over to the Babylonian king. Among the horrifying consequences are not merely the transportation of some people, but the appropriation of some of the objects used in worship in the Temple. These things that were dedicated to Yahweh are deposited in a Babylonian god's temple. It looks as if the Babylonian god has defeated Yahweh, as the Babylonian king has defeated the king of Judah. But this first story closes with a note that refers to Daniel's old age – more than sixty years have gone by. Nebuchadnezzar has passed, and so have his four successors, and so has the Babylonian empire itself, taken over by Cyrus the Persian. Daniel is still there, having outlasted the Babylonian empire. Who would have thought it?

You, Lord, are the faithful God who honours the faithfulness of your servants.

17 After Nebuchadnezzar, what?
Daniel 2

Like any national leader, Nebuchadnezzar has hundreds of expert advisers. But can he trust them? He sets them a test. He's had a dream but he went back to sleep and has forgotten it. The advisers have dream books to help them see the significance of dreams, but they can't interpret a dream they don't know. Do they really have any superior knowledge?

They grant that the only thing they have is their dream books. They're experts, with technical resources, but they have no more supernatural insight than Nebuchadnezzar. Daniel knows a God who reaches down to our world, and he knows how to reach up to this God. He makes a risky commitment to find out about the dream from this God. He does, so he's able to tell Nebuchadnezzar what the dream was.

The phrase 'the end of the days', which in English can sound as if it denotes the end of history, isn't a technical term for the End. Nebuchadnezzar isn't asking that kind of question. He's asking what's going to happen after him. Given this basic clue to the dream's meaning, you don't need much insight to infer the significance of the metals in the statue.

Louis XV of France is credited with the phrase, 'Après moi, le déluge' – after me, the collapse of everything (the French Revolution came fifteen years after his death). Did he care very much? Nebuchadnezzar seems not to think that way. It's a shocking and troublesome revelation that a gradual decline will follow his reign, and eventually a collapse. But it's what happens to empires. Quite late on, it becomes apparent that they have feet of clay.

The vision doesn't say who or what is represented by the different metals. The second half of the book will refer to the Medo-Persian and Greek empires, but this understanding needn't apply here. The metals might stand for the kings who'll follow Nebuchadnezzar (none of them anywhere near as significant) before the empire falls to Cyrus. But the point doesn't lie in exactly who the metals stand for, but in the inexorable decline and collapse. When an empire's at the height of its power, it's hard to believe it could ever fall. The vision declares that it can and will. It will provide no legacy.

Blessed be your name, Lord, from age to age! Wisdom and power are yours!

18 But if our God does not rescue us

Daniel 3

There's no mention of Daniel in this story, perhaps because stories about Daniel and stories about the friends were told separately. This a story of a deadly serious recurring experience of Jewish people. But when you have to survive in a context where you're an unloved minority, it will help if you learn to laugh.

It's not clear what was the point about Nebuchadnezzar's statue, but anyway, the three men knew they couldn't bow down to it. Scorn for it is expressed in the very way the story is told. The repeated lists of officials and musical instruments make fun of the administration and of the important state occasion. The statue is a ridiculous size. The king's rage makes him an object of fun, as does the fate of the burly bouncers. The king ricochets from one stupidity to another in making it a capital offence to disdain Yahweh.

So the story is funny, but deadly serious. The idea of dying because you stand by the truth about God and about the state was not just a theoretical idea for Jews. The seriousness of the humorous story takes a new turn with the three youths' declaration about God. When they say, 'If he really exists,' they don't imply any doubt about the question; they speak that way because it's the question at issue between them and the king. They themselves know that this God could rescue them from the red-hot blazing furnace. Indeed, they're convinced that he's going to do so. But they're going to stay committed to this God whether or not he rescues them.

Did the story happen? I don't know. I'm inclined to assume that farces are more likely to be fictional than factual. I know that God can miraculously rescue people from their persecutors. God has many aides whom he can send to deliver people from red-hot furnaces of one kind and another. But I also know that he usually doesn't, and the story offers no promise that he'll do so for other people put in the position of these three youths. So it doesn't make a lot of difference whether it happened. Whether or not it happens to us, the story constitutes an encouragement to live by the principle the youths enunciate to Nebuchadnezzar.

We will not serve anyone else's gods, Lord, or the statues they set up.

19 The king who goes mad for a while
Daniel 4

Nebuchadnezzar is here giving his testimony. It relates to the way it's hard for someone in a position of power to hold on to integrity.

The king of Babylon really matters. The symbolism of the tree, which stands for Nebuchadnezzar, makes the point. A leader who gets to think of himself as important or fails to be faithful doesn't always pay the price, but it sometimes happens. Nebuchadnezzar's dream warns him about the possibility. So part of its point is to get him to change, so that the warning in the dream needn't come true.

Daniel acts like a prophet in confronting the king and exposing the problem in his attitude to his people, which goes together with a problem in his attitude to God. He doesn't tell Nebuchadnezzar that he needs to give up his pride. He tells him, 'Break with your offences by doing what is right, and your waywardness by grace to the weak.' In practice, leaders commonly look after themselves and other strong people. In effect, Daniel challenges Nebuchadnezzar to repent, though he doesn't use that word. Nebuchadnezzar needs to repent in the sense of changing the way he acts – specifically, how he exercises his leadership.

Otherwise, the consequences will be terrible and long-lasting, though not fatal or permanent. The deep roots of the tree will be left in the ground. The judgement will last 'seven periods' – how long that expression implies isn't clear, but the sevenfoldness means it's a 'perfect' time. It's a judgement not a discipline. It's designed to affirm publicly what's right and to condemn publicly what's wrong. In itself it's not a way of persuading Nebuchadnezzar to reform. It's designed to make clear that there's someone who rules the world, and it's not Nebuchadnezzar.

God doesn't seem to operate on the assumption that judgement changes people. Maybe it's unrealistic. The Bible assumes that, if anything, mercy and grace do a better job of changing people. But Nebuchadnezzar is restored because God decides that enough is enough. He's put under judgement until he learns to acknowledge Yahweh. But it's the fact that Yahweh brings the judgement to an end that leads to his making that acknowledgement. In his testimony he does so in rather splendid fashion.

Your kingdom, Lord, is an everlasting kingdom, your sovereignty from generation to generation!

20 The writing on the wall
Daniel 5

Belshazzar was the last ruler before the Medo-Persian empire took over the Babylonian empire. Technically, he wasn't king but a regent who ran affairs in Babylon when the last actual king, Nabonidus, had left the capital a decade earlier, for reasons that are unclear. Belshazzar was also not literally the son of Nebuchadnezzar, though as Nebuchadnezzar's effective successor he could be described thus. The queen who plays a key role in the story is the queen mother, maybe Nebuchadnezzar's widow, who'd be in a position to give the advice that this queen gives.

Belshazzar is evidently having a good time as 'king', along with his administration. A state banquet leads to a display that would seem quite reasonable to the Babylonians. A victorious army will show off its plunder on a state occasion. But these vessels are no ordinary plunder. They came from the Temple of the real God.

If the experts can't even read the writing on the wall (this story is where we get that saying from), the reason may be that that the alphabet in some Middle Eastern languages uses only consonants. If the words have no context or don't make a normal sentence, readers might make no sense of the letters in the message (if I write on a whiteboard 'th ct st n th mt', my students whose first language is English know it says 'the cat sat on the mat', but other students have a harder time reading it). Maybe they can tell that the words sound like a merchant's shout: 'Counted at a mina, a sheqel, and two halves' (mina and sheqel are weights). But so what? It's Daniel's supernatural insight that enables him to see another way of reading the words. They declare God's judgement on Belshazzar. Daniel again speaks like a prophet in confronting the king with God's perspective on his reign.

Once more, the point about God's warnings isn't merely to declare what's bound to happen. It's to challenge people to change so they escape God's judgement. Belshazzar doesn't respond that way. It's no coincidence that he loses his life that night. Is there internal intrigue as the Persians advance toward Babylon? The king pays the price for disdaining the true God and failing to respond to that God's warning.

You, Lord, the Most High God, have sovereignty over mortals.

21 The man who insists on praying
Daniel 6

As there's a link between the two stories about God issuing a warning to a Babylonian king (Daniel 4 and 5), so there's a link between the stories on either side about Judahites having to defy the king, the king sentencing them to execution and God miraculously rescuing them (Daniel 3 and 6). The lion pit story also resembles the furnace story in being funny, larger than life and designed to make fun of the Judahites' overlords.

The story is also another that's realistic about the nature of politics. There's jealousy among the politicians, and wheeling and dealing. Anyone who does well has to be wary of being stabbed in the back. A king, president or prime minister has to be wary of being manipulated by the people who are supposed to be his servants, but somehow the person who gets himself into that supreme position often isn't as bright as his subordinates, so he falls for manipulation.

The ministers' edict looks stupid, but it's the only way to catch Daniel out. The higher an ordinary person gets, the more careful they have to be to avoid giving hostages to fortune. If there's anything shady in their life, people will uncover it. It's quite a compliment to Daniel that they can't find anything, except that he thinks God is too important.

Daniel's action is the obverse of that of the three young men. The pressure there was to bow down to something other than God and thus do something that an Israelite couldn't do. The pressure here is not to bow down to the One to whom you must bow down and thus not do something that an Israelite must do. The Jerusalem Temple was the place where Yahweh had undertaken to live and be present to hear Israel's prayers. Solomon's prayer at the Temple dedication envisages Israelites being taken off into exile and praying toward the country and the Temple then, and he asks Yahweh to listen to such prayers. Daniel presupposes that Yahweh will do so.

Old Testament worship is designed to glorify God, and so it's offered in public. For Israelites in a foreign country, the temptation is to hide. Daniel doesn't fall for the temptation, and God honours his faithfulness.

You are the living God, enduring for ever. Your kingdom will never be destroyed.

22 The woman who won't play ball
Esther 1 – 2

In due course, Daniel finds himself in Susa, the capital city of the Persian empire, which is where we discover Esther a few decades later. King Ahasuerus, better known as Xerxes, gives a banquet, like Belshazzar. His banquet gets him into trouble in a different way from Belshazzar.

Queen Vashti has evidently had enough. Her husband has quite a harem, so we should not assume a loving exclusive personal relationship between the king and his queen. And perhaps it would seem quite natural for the king to parade one or two of his women in the way he does. Some further assumptions about marriage surface as the chapter unfolds. It's the job of the king's wife to obey her husband. The men in the Persian court assume it applies to all wives.

Confronted by sexism like that of Xerxes, a woman maybe has three possible reactions. She can simply accept it in the way Xerxes expects. She can simply say, 'No'; that is what Vashti does, doing what she has to do, willing to pay the price. Or she can accept it in an outward way but subvert it in more subtle ways; that is what Esther will eventually do.

Meanwhile, however, there is a beauty contest, no ordinary beauty contest, but one that leads to a place in a harem. Young girls are prepared there for a night of involuntary sex with the king, then they have the night of involuntary sex itself, then they transition to another harem. The two harems are naturally in the charge of eunuchs, which doesn't always mean men who have been castrated, but obviously does in this context, where they are men who have been rendered incapable of sexual activity. The entire Esther story is told in a way that entertains and amuses, but it is also a horror story.

It presupposes another complication. *Jewish* can be an ethnic term, a religious term or a bit of both. In Susa, being Jewish is the way you live as well as the ethnic group you belong to. That makes Jewish people vulnerable in Susa (as it regularly has elsewhere), which lies behind Mordecai's instruction to Esther to keep her Jewish identity secret.

Lord, have mercy on girls in situations like Esther's, and take action against their oppressors.

23 Faith and courage
Esther 3 – 5

Haman is scandalised not by Mordecai's belonging to a different ethnic group, but by his belonging to an ethnic group that keeps itself separate from other peoples and whose laws and conventions are different from those of other people. There is nothing in the Torah that would forbid Mordecai from bowing down to Haman, but perhaps the clue to his refusal lies in the pointed identification of Haman as an Agagite. Agag was an Amalekite, and the Amalekites were the epitome of a people irrationally and inhumanly hostile to Israel. You do not bow down to Amalekites.

But it will take a miracle to get Mordecai out of the fix he gets himself into. He gets a miracle, though nowhere does the Esther story actually mention miracles or God. It illustrates how God can be at work through human decision-making, human taking of responsibility and coincidences. Mordecai declares that relief and deliverance will arise for the Jews in Susa, but he doesn't say what will be its source.

Our characteristic human experience of God's extraordinary involvement in our lives is more that of the Esther story than that of the Exodus story, and that will also have been the case for Jews in Susa. People act in faith and with courage, as Esther commits herself to doing, and take the risk of doing so even though they know that the risk is genuine. Acceptance of responsibility doesn't guarantee that deliverance will come to us.

Esther with her hesitation manifests more realism about the situation than Mordecai does. But he points out that maybe the reason she finds herself in the position she has reached is that she has a role to play in ensuring that other people escape from the threat to their lives. Once again, there is no reference to God's having brought her to that position. This is presupposed but not stated, because it illustrates the way things often work out, without one being able to see the hand of God.

Esther's hesitation and fear make her faith and courage the more remarkable, illustrating the way courage and faith are not incompatible with fear and hesitation; they come into their own in the context of faith and hesitation.

Lord, make us people who act with faith and courage even when we see no prospect of a miracle.

24 The king's sleepless night
Esther 6 – 7

Xerxes thinks that reading from the royal archives may send him to sleep, and the result is that he is reminded of an earlier act of Mordecai's that ought to receive a reward. The king's sleeplessness thus becomes the crucial turning point in the story. In the destiny of the Jewish people in the context of the Persian empire, everything depends on this sleepless night.

People sometimes speak of God orchestrating events behind the scenes of our lives, but the image is a misleading one. An orchestrator decides what happens and gets the orchestra to play together in accordance with the score or the chart. The Bible can certainly portray God doing that. But sometimes God is doing something creative with actions and events after they happen, harnessing rather than orchestrating. Actually, the Esther story's omitting to mention God means one overstates even by talking in terms of harnessing. All you have is coincidence. We infer God's involvement in taking up the potential of Mordecai's doing the brave thing and Xerxes' sleeplessness, but the point the book overtly makes is that all we actually see is coincidences.

Haman gets caught by a further coincidence, this time laced with irony. His advisers then express an extraordinary insight about the danger of getting into conflict with Jews. They unwittingly agree with Mordecai's earlier declaration to Esther that deliverance will arise for the Jews from one place or another. It is because of God's commitment to them that an adversary like Haman is bound to fall before them. But once again, the narrative leaves that unstated.

The farcical element in the story is enhanced by the king's thinking that Haman is setting about raping the queen when Haman is actually trying to get her to take his side. Is one to feel sorry for Haman? The story surely does not imply so.

Is the execution of the would-be executioner right? The story doesn't quite ask that question. But maybe it assumes that people who wield the sword may die by the sword. Typically, the Old Testament looks at such events from the perspective of the victim. It frees its readers to be encouraged by the fact that justice is done to the Hamans of this world.

Lord, at least protect your people from the Hamans.

25 A celebration that will last
Esther 8 – 10

The poetic justice, the irony and the redress continue as Mordecai comes to be head of Haman's household in Haman's place, instead of Haman and his kind being able to appropriate the property of Mordecai and his compatriots after killing their households.

The new law doesn't give Jews the right to attack other ethnic groups. It does give them the right to self-defence. So other groups would be unwise to attack them, and many other peoples are so impressed at the way things have turned out for the Jews that they are clamouring to join them. On the other hand, there are some insane people who nevertheless do attack them, and find that Esther's people are quite adept at implementing the edict that permits them to defend themselves.

If the numbers of people who consequently get slaughtered seem high, that might suggest how many stupid Persians there were. But in Esther, as in Lamentations, we should allow for hyperbole. Another Jewish approach to Esther sees the slaughter in the story as its ultimate irony. It reminds Jewish readers (it might do the same for Christians) that they may be no more peace-loving and gentle than anyone else. Such an understanding fits the nature of the book as a whole, with its liking for humour and irony. Admittedly, the trouble with irony is that people often don't get it. Even if Jews do, antisemitic Gentiles might not.

Jewish people still repeat the celebration of this great deliverance each year, and read (not to say re-enact) the story. Jewish readers, again, may not assume that the story is fact rather than fiction. But one Jewish scholar who assumes it's fiction has commented that nevertheless, when he hears it read at Purim each year, he relives its truth and its actuality and knows that it is true.

Against the background of pogroms and Holocaust, the modern Jewish experience of Purim fulfils Mordecai and Esther's prescription for its observance. For Christians, the story fits the promise in Romans 9 – 11 that God will keep his commitment to the Jewish people, which is important for Christians (Paul implies) because if he doesn't keep his commitment to the Jewish people, maybe he won't keep his commitment to us?

Lord, you are the God who keeps his commitment to his people.

26 Exiles return
Ezra 1 – 2

Meanwhile, the Persian authorities are already allowing Judahites in their empire to return home – indeed, encouraging them to go – though it is a home that nearly all of them have never seen.

An agonising aspect of the fall of Jerusalem in 587 BC was the destruction of many of the precious and holy accoutrements of the Temple, and the Babylonian king's appropriation of what he did not destroy. Unintentionally, however, by putting these objects into his god's temple, Nebuchadnezzar made sure they would be kept safe and not end up on the Babylonian antiquities market and eventually in the British Museum.

Cyrus is therefore in a position to produce them and get the Temple treasurer to give them to the man who will lead the Judahites back to Jerusalem, so that they can again enter into Yahweh's service in the Temple. They will thus constitute one of the markers of the fact that the Second Temple will continue the worship of the First Temple. The people of God in Judah will continue the worship that their ancestors offered. Their story will be one with the story of Solomon, David and Moses.

As God aroused the spirit of Cyrus to issue his commission, so God arouses the spirit of some of the Judahites so that they want to make the journey to rebuild the Temple. It's not surprising that God needs to do some arousing. The Judahites in Babylon are not living in a refugee camp, itching to get back to the land where they were born. They have taken Jeremiah's encouragement to heart, built themselves houses and started families. It's not remarkable that many of them have no desire to leave Babylon, though they support people who do.

It is not just fellow Judahites who give this support, but the people's neighbours more generally. This motif recalls the exodus story. The move from Babylon to Judah is a repetition of the exodus, and when the Israelites left Egypt Yahweh made their neighbours favourably disposed toward them so that they gave them objects of silver and gold to take with them, which facilitated the making of the dwelling for God in the wilderness. The Judahites' Babylonian neighbours, like Cyrus himself, are likewise making a contribution to the worship of Yahweh.

You, Lord, are the God of heaven, and the God of Israel.

27 Shouts of joy and the sound of weeping

Ezra 3 – 6

The Judahites who make the move to Jerusalem from Babylon know that restoring the worship of the Temple is the first thing they have to do. Beginning the work of restoration, Jeshua and Zerubbabel embody the joint leadership of the Second Temple community. Zerubbabel is the grandson of King Jehoiachin, the king exiled to Babylon in 597 BC, and he is therefore a member of the line of David. Jeshua likewise belongs to the line of Aaron, so he can function as what would later be called the high priest.

The Babylonians set fire to the Temple in 587 BC but they had not demolished it. It would have been possible for some forms of worship to continue there during the exile – such as the grieving and the prayer for mercy expressed in Lamentations. While the Temple therefore needs substantial restoration, even now the community could build a new altar in it and thus make it possible to restore the regular routine of worship.

Beginning work on the Temple generates a mixed reaction of celebration and weeping in the community. The weepers are people who had seen the first Temple in its glory, which means they must be in their sixties or seventies. We are not told why they are weeping. Maybe some are depressed because they can't imagine that the Temple is going to be as glorious as it once was. Maybe some are appalled at the magnitude of the task they have set themselves. Maybe their tears are a paradoxical expression of happiness that the work has begun, a joyful disbelief that this moment has come. Both the shouts and the weeping thus have the same significance.

If they are appalled at the magnitude of the task that confronts them, they only know half of it, to judge from the chapters that follow. But eventually the work is finished, and they end up dumbfounded at the wonder of what God has made possible. There is the most stupendous celebration, which the story portrays as involving the whole of Israel – twelve goats sacrificed for twelve clans. Ezra 4 more realistically describes the people involved as 'Judah and Benjamin'. But this is a temple that needs to belong to the whole of Israel.

Lord, you are good, and your steadfast love endures for ever.

28 Ezra the priest, the theologian, the teacher

Ezra 7 – 10

It's now the reign of Artaxerxes, so it's at least half a century later. The story of the Temple rebuilding has emphasised the activity of priests in leading the Temple worship. But priests have a role in teaching the Torah, and Ezra is also a scholar or theologian, an expert in the Torah. When he comes to Jerusalem from Babylonia, he brings the Torah. It's a plausible idea that Ezra is associated with the process whereby the Torah in its final form came into existence and that his mission to Jerusalem is when this final version of the Torah comes to be implemented there.

One of the neatest compliments that could be paid him is that he has given himself to studying, observing and teaching the Torah. He isn't just a person who studies because he likes studying; his studying motivates him to teach. But neither is he someone who simply studies and teaches, but who could roll up his scroll at the end of the working day and forget about it. He is a person who lives by what he reads and teaches.

It turns out that he isn't the only one, to judge from some people's reaction when it emerges that Judahites have been intermarrying with people from other communities around. This isn't in itself against the Torah, and some upright people did it (Moses, for one). But it's a problem if these partners are not people who have come to commit themselves to Yahweh and to the Torah. These wives evidently haven't.

Ezra's first response is a public confession, in which he does not confess what *they* have done wrong, but what *we* have done wrong. His instinct is to associate himself with the offenders, not dissociate himself. And he knows that the action of some people brings defilement on the entire community. Following his confession, some of the offenders do come and acknowledge that they have broken faith with God. It seems that some then volunteer to give up these marriages, which others need to be leaned on to do.

It is tough action, but Ezra maybe realises that in the absence of such action, the community would soon assimilate out of existence.

Lord, give us grace to do the painful and costly thing when we must.

29 Nehemiah remembers

Nehemiah 1 – 2

Nehemiah apparently knows nothing about how things are back in Judah, but news arrives. While it's possible that Hanani is simply reporting that the city is still in the state it has been since its destruction by the Babylonians, the devastating effect of the news on Nehemiah suggests that some other disaster has happened more recently.

Nehemiah will turn out to be a practical, down-to-earth, bricks-and-mortar guy, but he is also a man who prays. He prays as someone who is himself committed to what he prays about, and he prays urgently to get God to take the action that only God can take; further, he recognises the failure of the people on whose behalf he prays.

His prayer actually begins with two forms of confession. First there is confession of who God is, the one who can be relied on to be faithful to his words and his undertakings. The sting in the tail that Nehemiah knows he needs to recognise is that you can only claim this if you are people who dedicate themselves to God and keep God's commands. It's a serious qualifier, because Nehemiah knows that his people have not been faithful to their side of the relationship. He knows he has to acknowledge the wayward history of Israel over the centuries. Yet he also knows that the same Torah that warned of the consequences of wilful failure also promised that chastisement need not be the end.

There is one further basis for his prayer, though it involves a paradox. Like Ezra, Nehemiah identifies with his people in their wrongdoing. Yet he also goes on to appeal to his being God's servant. Nehemiah wants God to put alongside the long-lasting failure of God's servants the commitment of servants like himself and Hanani, and even to take more account of the latter than the former.

He knows that the first practical thing he needs is for the king to feel some compassion for him. It's not a regular kingly virtue, though there is a possibility that his particular relationship with the king means Artaxerxes will care about something that Nehemiah cares about, when he might not care about the sorry state of an obscure city on the edge of his empire for its own sake.

Great and awe-inspiring God, keeping covenant and commitment! Do listen to your servant's plea!

30 Sword and trowel, confrontation and compassion

Nehemiah 3 – 5

We don't know enough of the extent and shape of Jerusalem nor of the location of its different gates to be sure of the route of Nehemiah's ride or of the course of the building works, though it is clear enough that the places are listed in anticlockwise order around the city. When the work starts, the priests naturally enough accept responsibility for the section near the Temple. The account of the work moves westward and then south, to the western gate where Nehemiah starts, and to the Rubbish Gate to the far south. It covers a broader area than Nehemiah surveyed, though the reference to abandoning part of the city suggests that Nehemiah's wall encloses a smaller area than Jerusalem covered before the exile.

Not for the last time, the story implies that Nehemiah is not put off by opposition any more than by the magnitude of the project. His opponents are right that his work threatens their interest in having control of Judah. In declaring that they will have no share or rights or honour in Jerusalem, he is affirming that they will be disappointed. The list of the people involved in rebuilding Jerusalem's wall would be significant for the readers of this story, reason for pride in what their parents or grandparents did.

In the order of the narrative, at least, the achievement of the building leads into the shame of the outcry by the ordinary people who are economically broken through taxation (by the government Nehemiah represents), famine and people with resources making a profit off people who are in trouble. One of the intriguing assumptions is the rule in the Torah that lending to people is not a way of making more money, as it is in in a Western economy, but a way of being compassionate to people who are in trouble. There are aspects of the story that are difficult to follow, but it looks as if Nehemiah himself is not guiltless. One has to recognise that he is caught by his position as the governor appointed by the empire that is partially responsible for the trouble that people are in. He has to do his best to square the circle of representing the empire and serving his people.

Listen to the prayer of people who are despised, Lord.
(Nehemiah 4:4)

31 Holy city
Nehemiah 11 – 13

Jerusalem is the holy city because the holy place, the Temple, is there. The city is identified with the holy God in a distinctive way. Its being the holy city then links with the awareness in Ezra and Nehemiah of a need to preserve the holiness of that which Yahweh has taken hold of. The need applies to the people, to the Temple and to the city.

But being the holy *city*, it needs a population. There will be the practical consideration that it will be vulnerable to attack by hostile neighbouring peoples. A population throbbing with life is as important as walls in this connection. Yet the deeper consideration is that it seems inappropriate for the holy city to be an impressively walled ghost town.

In the New Testament, it becomes even more the holy city, because Jesus died and rose from the dead in this city, and this city is the place from which the message about Jesus goes out to the world. Neither Rome nor Canterbury nor Geneva is the holy city. Jerusalem is.

From whichever direction you approach Jerusalem, you are sooner or later struck by the medieval walls of the 'Old City'. It's easy to imagine the rejoicing at the ceremony of the completion of the walls in Nehemiah's day, though it is surprising that they are also *dedicated*. It is usually an altar or a temple that is dedicated. And the Judahites are involved in thanksgiving, sacrifice and purification, as happens when a temple is brought into use.

It would be easy, and in a sense right, for the people to be congratulating themselves on their achievement. They bought into Nehemiah's vision. They have done the work. They have made the sacrifice involved in neglecting their regular work and imperilling their livelihood. They prepared themselves to fight against opponents if they needed to. Yet the dedication ceremony is one of thanksgiving, led by the Levites in their capacity as worship leaders, and involving marshalling Levites from a wide area in order to generate choirs big enough to match the importance of the occasion. There they offer sacrifices, evidently thanksgiving sacrifices of the kind that God and people share as they rejoice in what God has done, as well as in what they have done.

Give thanks to the Lord, whose faithfulness endures for ever!

June

WISDOM AND WORSHIP

I Job, the man ripe for a test
Job 1

Job's cup runs over. Moreover, he is a man of integrity, straight or upright, submissive to God, someone who turns away from evil, one who prays for his (grown-up) children.

But there in the heavenly cabinet someone raises the question, 'Why?' Most translations say this person is Satan, but *satan* is an ordinary Hebrew word for an adversary, and we shouldn't read the New Testament Satan into this figure. This is more someone who asks tough questions. Is Job committed to God only because of what he gets out of it? Can we test him to find out? So a series of disasters happen to Job's family and his wider household.

How does Job react? He doesn't pretend that nothing has happened. He falls prostrate before God. And he speaks. He was born naked and he will die naked, he acknowledges, speaking as if death means returning to one's mother's womb. Yahweh gave, Yahweh has taken.

Job's instinct in attributing the disasters to God contrasts with many people's instincts. We may like to let God off the hook of responsibility for what happens in the world by blaming human free will, though we may blame God for something when the problem does lie in human beings' use of their free will. Job has a rigorous doctrine of divine sovereignty and responsibility. There are points at which Job may see things too much in black and white (and the way he speaks about losing everything is a bit hard on Mrs Job), but the advantage of such a doctrine is that it can be the basis for prayer. If God is in charge, we can urge God to change things.

Job assumes that God is indeed the chair of the heavenly cabinet. God could take away all that he has, as well as give it. The statement could have been a protest, not an expression of submission. Yet the words that follow remove any ambiguity. Job praises Yahweh's name. Job's words to God suggest that the submission symbolised by his posture is the real thing. He really does bow down to God. He does not speak in a way that would constitute sinning against God by accusing God of acting improperly. Job recognises that God has the right to decide how to act.

You, Lord, give; you take away. Blessed be your name.

2 'Curse God and die'
Job 2

In another meeting of the heavenly cabinet, Yahweh again invites the adversary to report on what he has seen. Once again, one might have thought that God would know the answer to the questions about Job's integrity. Can't God work out everything without doing experiments? It's certainly true that God can look into people's hearts, but it seems that God doesn't always choose to.

Maybe God recognises that exercising a divine capacity to know everything that people are thinking before they say it would introduce a kind of unreality into God's relationship with people. Maybe God likes things to be established out there in public view. God doesn't just play games with people inside his head and he doesn't just imagine what they might do. God lets them be real and show themselves and show the world and show him.

On the other hand, I do assume that this is an imaginary story. That doesn't make it untrue. C. S. Lewis's fantasy stories about the lion, the witch and the wardrobe are not factual but they do embody truths about God and about God's relationship with us. Job is like that.

There is another question the story may raise. Does God relate to people like a cat playing with a mouse, or does he let the adversary play with them that way? Whether or not the story offers a literally factual account of a scene in heaven, does it offer a true account of God's relationship with people?

Now we will discover that part of the point of God's eventual appearing to Job is to say, 'Tough, deal with it.' But when we find the Scriptures saying something odd, it is at least worth asking whether this text is the only place where it says this particular thing, and whether then we are misinterpreting it. It would be unwise to base our understanding of God's way of working with us on the basis of one passage. And the dynamics of the Job story don't recur elsewhere. When Jesus tells parables, we don't base an understanding of their teaching on features that are present just to make the story work, and the opening of Job's story may be there just to make the story work.

Yes, Lord, we acknowledge that we can't complain if tough things as well as good things happen to us.

3 Job protests and argues
Job 3 – 27

Job's friends show up and sit silently with him for a week. It is the best thing they ever do. But then Job gives up being quiet. Maybe he has read the Psalms and he knows what you are supposed to do in a situation like his. What he does is to lament his life's beginning and long for its end. He calls down a whole sequence of futile curses on the day of his birth.

It's more realistic to long for death, and Job knows that the great thing about death is rest. Someone may be fighting an illness, but death means the person gives up striving and relaxes. A peace can come over the face when that moment arrives; the lines can disappear. A king may be carrying responsibility for a country or an empire, but death means he yields that responsibility. Workers may end each day in exhaustion and the next day have to drag themselves to work again, but for them, too, death means rest.

Toward the end of chapter 3, Job begins to speak overtly about himself instead of hiding behind the figures of 'small and great'. He is a man whose way is hidden: that is, he has no future, because God has hedged him in. He is stuck in this horrible present. The adversary commented on God's having hedged him around in a positive sense; Job identifies a new hedging. His closing description of himself as characterised by sighing, groaning, fear, dread and thunder (that is, the roaring trouble that assails him) rather than by peace, stillness or rest pungently expresses the nature of his experience as contrasting with everything he finds attractive about death.

While the content of his curse and protest are shocking, the chapter's greater shock lies in the suddenness of the transition from the opening of the story. Was more going on inside him than those earlier statements indicated? Has his friends' silence tipped him over the edge? Or are his lament and protest quite appropriate?

The bulk of the book that follows comprises a series of arguments between Job and his friends in which Job continues to protest and his friends keep urging him to admit that he deserves what has happened.

Where shall wisdom be found? Submitting to God, that's wisdom.
(Job 28:28)

4 God's answer (part one)
Job 38 – 39

Eventually God appears and responds to Job, but the content of God's response is nothing like what one might have expected. It points Job to the nature of creation and implies that we must accept our ignorance about many aspects of God's work in the world. In other contexts, confronted by the question why bad things happen to good people, an Israelite might have answered, 'I don't know, but what Yahweh did with Israel at the exodus helps me live with the question,' as a Christian might answer, 'I don't know, but what God did in Jesus helps me live with the question.' Here the implication is that looking at creation might have the same effect.

God points out, first, the obvious fact that Job was not present at creation, and notes the way God went about this building project. God made sure that this home had secure foundations. God notes how the very stars and the divine beings recognised the wonder of his creative work. The stars and heavenly beings were happy enough with the evidence that God could formulate a purpose and implement it in such a way as to give human life a secure foundation.

Second, the process of creation involved setting a limit to the power of dangerous and dynamic forces in creation. The sea is a common Old Testament symbol for such forces; its tumultuous power provides a vivid illustration and embodiment of them. While the sea's dynamic power gets out of hand from time to time, in principle God made sure it was under control.

Third, the process of creation involved establishing the rhythm of day and night. God's point is then that there is a relationship between the daily dawning of light in the world and the exposing of wrongdoers in the world. With the dawn, faithless people lose the 'light' they like (that is, what other people call darkness) and they can no longer exercise their violent power in order to do wrong.

God's account of creation recalls Genesis 1. But at each point, like a good preacher, God does not merely describe how something happened but draws out its implications for the audience – here an audience of one, plus people like us who listen in on the conversation.

Yes, Lord, you are the one who laid the foundations of the earth.

5 God's answer (part two)
Job 40 – 41

Job has found that the great but also solemn thing about confronting God is that God may respond, and may take as confrontational a stance as we do. So Job has given in. But then God starts again! I like to imagine Job thinking that his submission will bring to an end the confrontation that he no longer wishes for, now that God has put him in his place, and I imagine his heart sinking as he hears God start up again.

When Job spoke about asking for grace, in chapter 9, he described God as 'the one who makes decisions about me'. Here, God is not clear that Job's submission is more than a mere acknowledgement of God's superior firepower. God wants more. Job has questioned the way God exercises his authority in the world. It has looked as if Job thinks he could do better than God.

'Go on, then, Job,' in effect God says. The question is whether Job has an arm like God's to wield a weapon against the faithless, whether Job can roar like God as he charges into battle against the faithless. The people that need putting down are people in power, people in positions of eminence and majesty; does Job have the majesty to stand up to them? Does Job have the capacity for well-directed anger that God has?

Pointing Job to Behemoth, the Monster, puts flesh on the point. Job cannot hope to tame or control such a creature, but it is one of the creatures God made, as he made Job. Then there is Leviathan. Strange creatures, especially strange sea creatures, have long been symbols of frightening and threatening power, and in the Middle Eastern world, Leviathan is one of them. Such figures symbolise extraordinary and frightening negative power. Scholars in the Middle East in ancient times thought of the most powerful, frightening, uncontrollable creatures they could, and invited people to picture the power that encouraged disorder and turmoil in the world as an enhanced version of such creatures. OK, says God, think of Leviathan as the embodiment of turmoil and disorder in the world. Then look at the world. I tell you, I have it under control. And ask yourself if you could do better.

Lord, do please keep the forces of chaos in the world under control.

6 So they all lived happily ever after
Job 42

Evidently Job's second concession speech satisfies Yahweh in a way that the first did not. Job has acknowledged not only that God is bigger than he is but also that God is right. The truth is as God has said. God can do what he wishes to do and God can implement plans that he makes in a way that Job can't.

Job has surely passed his test. Furthermore, compared with his three friends, he is a man of understanding. God compliments him on that, and urges a further reversing of positions between Job and his friends. The restoration of the relationship between God and them requires a move on their part as well as a move on God's part. Simply forgiving them won't achieve that restoration. If they ask Job to make an offering and pray on their behalf, then the relationship can be healed.

The nature and the magnitude of Job's subsequent restoration raises an eyebrow or two, and one wonders what Mrs Job thought about bearing another ten children (unless there was more than one Mrs Job). Maybe we should allow for Middle Eastern hyperbole and assume we don't have to take the details of the story too literally. On the other hand, the countercultural note about Job giving property to his daughters means the book almost ends with a final testimony to what an extraordinary man Job was, capable of sitting loose to social norms and filled with love and commitment for the daughters of his restored life.

With a final irony in this book full of irony, the story's last scene asserts that the traditional teaching affirmed by the friends and by Job (and subsequently by Jesus) is right. Those who honour God, God honours. Submission to the Lord is insight, turning from evil is understanding. Not that the book's ending disposes of the questions that it has raised. It has considered various ways of looking at suffering, none of which applies in every case, but all of which may sometimes apply, and all of which are worth thinking about before disaster hits us. That's a better use for the book than encouraging someone who is suffering to read it. It's a bit late then.

I know that you can do all things, and that no purpose of yours can be thwarted.

7 You have a choice
Psalm 1

The book of Psalms begins in an unexpected fashion, not really with a psalm, a song of praise or a prayer, but with a challenge and a promise to have in the back of your mind through the book of Psalms.

Psalm 1 believes in the importance of choice, believes that the key choice we have to make is enormously important, but also believes that it is straightforward. There are two ways that open up before us as individuals; Jesus takes up the idea in Matthew 7 when he speaks of the broad and narrow way. We are like people on a journey who face a split in the path and have to decide which way to take. One of these ways involves 'walking by' Yahweh's Torah. The image suggests a way to walk that is well signposted. It's a bit like having GPS or a satnav.

Walking this way is both easy and difficult. The kinds of things the Torah says are, 'Bow down only to Yahweh, don't make any images, keep the Sabbath, don't commit adultery, tell the truth in court, don't fancy other people's belongings.' It's not very complicated. Yet the Torah's expectations also constitute a narrow way; they go against human instincts.

If you want to follow the Torah and stick with the company of the faithful, you need to watch who you walk with, where you stand around and who your friends are. And you need positively to make Yahweh's teaching what you delight in and talk about. The Hebrew word for 'talk about' suggests meditation, but a meditation that does not happen simply inside our heads. God's teaching is on our lips.

If you need encouragement to delight in Yahweh's teaching, then one encouragement is the promise that the route with those signposts that could seem so limiting (don't you ever get annoyed when GPS or a satnav keeps telling you what to do?) is the route that leads to blessing. Jesus again takes up the psalm's perspective when he comments on the blessing that comes to people who hear God's word and keep it (Luke 11:28). In contrast, the route that looks like the open road with lots of freedom and good company is actually a route that leads nowhere that you would really want to go.

Lord, watch over my way as I seek to walk your way.

8 Thus far and no further
Psalm 8

When the Old Testament talks about babies and sucklings, they are usually victims of oppression, war and death. Might the abuse of children become all-pervasive in the world? Could some Herod do for the world what the historical Herod did for Bethlehem?

The psalm proclaims that God has set limits to humanity's capacity in that connection. In effect, God has said, 'Thus far and no further.' God has established a barricade to restrain people and forces that oppose God's purpose in the world, like the barricade shepherds would build to protect their sheep from wolves. Thank God, then, that God has set a limit to our capacity to wreak our own justice.

The psalm thus constitutes a sigh of relief that God's name is mighty in all the earth – that is, that God himself is mighty. It is a sigh of relief that God has established his majesty in the heavens, indeed above the heavens. The Scriptures recognise how rebellion against God and resistance to God's ways is not merely an earthly phenomenon. It has a supernatural aspect. But neither earthly wilfulness nor heavenly wilfulness can get totally out of hand. It is as if before the very creation God anticipated the cry of babies and sucklings, the most wretched victims of that wilfulness, and heeded that cry by declaring, 'Thus far and no further.'

The cry of babies and sucklings might make it seem the more extraordinary that God paid attention to humanity and gave us a power in the world that is almost Godlike. God might even seem to have been rather irresponsible in giving humanity a role to play in the created world. Yet it is a consistent pattern of God's work in the world that God takes risks in delegating responsibility and power to people who are then supposed to work as his agents, though they are inclined to abuse their power. Certainly a result of God's giving humanity authority in relation to the animal world has led to our abusing it in a way that is now more far-reaching than it has ever been before. Yet the psalm implies that God's majesty and might will finally have their way. God takes risks, but God is committed to taking creation to its destiny.

Lord, how majestic is your name in all the earth!

9 The wretched of the earth
Psalm 10

The 'why' that opens this psalm isn't the 'why' we ask concerning why people suffer. It's a 'why' that challenges God to action. Human beings should not be allowed to do what they like in the world. The Hebrew word for 'human being' in this psalm denotes humans in their relative feebleness and insignificance. The psalm says to God, how can such creatures be allowed to behave in the way they do? The word for humanity in its insignificance contrasts with the talk of 'eminence' and 'exaltedness'. The psalm is talking about people in positions of importance, and when you are important, it is easy to forget that you are a mere limited human being.

But God has the capacity to take action when such people misuse their position. God ought to be taking some decisions about these people, the psalm says. Instead, God is letting events take their course. God has the power to intervene in the world, but he doesn't intervene very often. He's like a father, and fathers don't interfere every time their children have an argument. They know that children need to learn to sort things out for themselves. But sometimes a situation reaches a point when parents have to intervene. Similarly, it would compromise God's purpose in making the world if God intervened in every conflict, but the psalm implies that it is quite proper for us to say to God, 'Can't you see this is one that requires your intervention?' The 'why' of the Psalms is not a request for information but a challenge to action.

The psalm shows that it is fine to challenge God to take action to punish people for their wrongdoing, as the New Testament also assumes (see God's reaction to the plea of the martyrs in Revelation 6:9–11). It assumes that taking redress is God's business, not ours, but that we are free to urge God to act. Turning the other cheek does not mean passivity in relation to God. Confronted by the wickedness of human oppressors and their unwillingness to acknowledge God as God and to acknowledge fellow human beings as fellow human beings, it is weird if we don't press God to put evil down.

Lord, will you listen to the longing of the meek, do justice for the orphan and the oppressed?

10 In the dark of the canyon
Psalm 23

I used to live in the foothills of some mountains with deep canyons that often had streams running through them. They were thus densely wooded. They had the water supply lacking in the countryside outside the canyons. But they were thus dark and a bit sinister, and their deep darkness contrasted sharply with the bright sunshine above them.

Maybe their swiftly running water would be a bit scary for sheep, but the shepherd would know where the water becomes quieter pools. He would know where the presence of moisture makes some grass grow and where the presence of shade stops it withering in the blistering heat. He would know where there are some wild olive trees or other bushes whose fruit he can knock down with his cane. So the flock is secure and provided for. The shepherd is faithful in his care for the flock.

So it is for a human being who has Yahweh as shepherd. Yahweh is the God who is faithful, active in seeing that his people are provided for and protected. He acts in this way 'for the sake of his name', in order to be the person his name proclaims him to be.

In the second half of this psalm, literal reality pokes through. The psalm is encouraging us to declare our trust that we can face being threatened by the human equivalent of bears, rattlesnakes and cougars because God protects us with his club like a shepherd protecting his sheep. Like a shepherd providing his sheep with pasture, Yahweh provides us with what we need – indeed, provides for us abundantly. The psalm imagines the enemies outside our camp able to see us within it, clean-shaven and smart and enjoying our meal, and unable to get access to us, like animals on the edge of a clearing unable to get to the sheepfold. Whereas sheep can be chased by wild animals and human beings can be chased by their enemies, on the battlefield we are chased only by two of God's agents, goodness and commitment. On the battlefield we are cut off from the place of worship where we meet with God and from the place of fellowship where we meet with God's people, but we know this will not be the end of the story.

You, Lord, are my shepherd. I will not lack.

11 How to give your testimony
Psalm 30

This psalm tells a story in three parts about how things went wrong, how I prayed and how God answered. It also illustrates another feature that recurs in some psalms: it says what it needs to say, then says it once more. It could have stopped after verse 5 and we wouldn't have thought that it was truncated, but then it starts again. Maybe the psalmist felt that verses 1–5 just didn't say enough to do justice to what God had done.

When the second half of the psalm tells the story again, it goes behind the first account by recalling how fine things were before trouble struck. Maybe the words imply that the psalmist was over-confident then. At least the opening line in version two of the testimony raises a question we should think about. Version two also gives us more information on the way the psalmist prayed.

The psalm illustrates three other interrelated aspects to giving one's testimony. First, it assumes that an experience of God's deliverance is not a mere one-off, odd event. It constitutes a concrete illustration of who God really is. God is one who puts down, but his anger lasts only a moment, and loving acceptance of his people is more characteristic of him. Second, experiencing God's deliverance isn't something that just affects you at the time. It changes you, and changes the way you pray, for ever. Third, you are not the only person it affects. A thanksgiving psalm is also a testimony psalm because it is designed for other people to hear and for them to join in, because the facts about God that it illustrates are relevant to the rest of the congregation as well as to the person who is healed.

What about the psalm's introduction? The house is presumably the house of God. So maybe the psalm was used at the dedication of the Temple after the exile, or at its rededication after its desecration by Antiochus Epiphanes in 167 BC. The Hebrew word for dedication is *hanukkah*, and that is the name of the Jewish festival celebrating that deliverance from Antiochus. Either way, a psalm devised as an individual's testimony became a means of giving the congregation's testimony, which illustrates the flexible way the psalms could be used.

Lord, I will give you thanks for ever!

12 The lowly will inherit the land
Psalm 37

Don't get worked up about people who are doing well when you or other people you know are doing badly, Psalm 37 says. They won't be doing well for ever. We may find this exhortation and promise annoying or encouraging. Anyway, the psalm says, instead of getting worked up, trust in God on the basis of what you know about him. There's a calm about trust.

Psalm 37 is one for people who feel powerless and helpless. It is designed to help them see that being powerless and helpless doesn't mean being hopeless. The lowly will inherit the country, it says, and Jesus puts that into the Sermon on the Mount. It's a psalm for people in government and business leaders to read, so as to overhear what God says to powerless people and work out what they therefore need to do. It's also a vision or a prophecy. Jewish use of the psalm in thanksgiving prayers after a meal suggests it gives us means of expressing our gratitude for our own actual experience of being provided for.

Its perspective is one Job's friends have, and it is thus the kind of statement that the book of Job questions. Indeed, one doesn't have to go as far as the book of Job to look for statements that conflict with it. The Psalter is full of them. All Psalm 37 does is affirm particularly concretely the promises in Psalm 1, which also recur throughout the Scriptures. The statement in this psalm is no more untrue than Jesus' promise that people who seek God's reign will have food, drink and clothing; Jesus says he agrees with Psalm 37.

We can be unimaginative in the way we read the Scriptures. If we read the Psalms' statements about suffering in a literalistic way, it will give us an unreal impression of people's experience and assumptions. The Scriptures love hyperbole, as appears from the accounts of slaughter in Joshua or the size of armies in Chronicles. 'Everything is possible for the person who believes' (Mark 9:23)? Really? If our objections to Psalm 37's unrealism had been made to the psalmist, he or she might just have looked blank.

Lord, be with the people who find it hard to believe that this psalm is true.

13 Praise, thanksgiving and prayer
Psalm 40

Prayer issues from thanksgiving. The awareness that God has previously answered your prayer encourages you to believe that you can come to God again with your plea for help, and it gives you a basis for leaning on God like a child or a grandchild ('You did it before; you could do it again').

So this prayer psalm spends more than half its time recalling something God did in the past, and one could easily think it is simply a thanksgiving psalm, though maybe its covert agenda as an introduction to a prayer pokes through the first part. There is less detail on the nature of the answer to prayer than appears in some thanksgiving psalms, though it presupposes that death was threatening the person. It stresses how the prayer reached out to Yahweh rather than to other people who had themselves turned away from Yahweh and who looked to other, false gods. It stresses how the person praying had then given testimony to what the one true God did.

'Sacrifice and offering you didn't want' in the sense that these were not all that Yahweh wanted. As words need offerings, offerings need words that (in this case) give account to other people of the way God has answered prayer. Thus the psalmist can say, I was not just thankful inside; I was thankful outside. I wasn't shy. I didn't make my sacrifice at a moment when no one else would be there. I gave my testimony to what God had done for me. ('Digging ears' may refer to God making the holes in our head where our ears go.)

It's on that basis that the psalmist can ask God to show compassion and commitment once more. The declarations in the first part of the psalm needn't imply a claim that the trouble that has come to the psalmist was undeserved, but neither does it presuppose that guilt means we can't plead with God to rescue us. Maybe the implicit irony is that the psalmist had not maintained trust in Yahweh and that the waywardness of which the psalm speaks consists in a turning to other gods; if so, the psalmist has now come back and rejoined the circle of people who seek help from Yahweh rather than from anywhere else.

You are my help and my deliverer: do not delay, Lord!

14 Against you alone have I sinned
Psalm 51

The introduction to this psalm encourages readers to set the psalm and David's story in 2 Samuel 11 alongside each other. It is then illuminating in the questions it raises. If David prayed in this fashion after the Bathsheba and Uriah affair, then there are ways in which it illustrates how he needed to pray, but, 'Against you only have I sinned'? Like other psalms, it drives us to examine ourselves and not simply assume that our discernment about ourselves is genuine discernment.

Starting from the other end of the psalm offers some complementary insights. The plea to God to build up Jerusalem's walls doesn't fit with David's day, either. The walls were intact then. The end of the psalm suggests some later time when Israel's praying 'against you alone have I sinned' makes sense. The 'I' of the psalm might then be the ordinary Israelite or an Israelite leader, acknowledging that they have turned to other gods or other allies.

In that situation, offering sacrifices doesn't get you anywhere. Sacrifices can deal with problems of uncleanness, but not serious sin; and sacrifices expressing praise and commitment are nonsense when your relationship with God has broken down. When your wife has caught you out for being unfaithful, a gift of flowers or even a new car is not going to get you anywhere. When you have committed serious sin, you can only cast yourself on God's grace, as someone crushed and broken by the price you have paid for your wrongdoing, as Jerusalem needed to do. Then, if God forgives you and answers the prayers in the psalm and sees to the city's rebuilding, you can recommence your regular life of worship, in which sacrifice has its proper place as an expression of praise and commitment.

In Psalm 51, then, the people of God casts itself on God's mercy and compassion. And God seems to have answered the psalm's prayer as prayed by Judah. The Temple and the walls got rebuilt, the community over the succeeding centuries showed more signs of being indwelt by God's spirit, and it was in a position to share what it knew about God in surrounding countries, so that there were Jewish congregations attracting Gentile believers widely spread by Roman times.

Have mercy on us as your people, Lord, in accordance with your steadfast love!

15 How to pray for the government
Psalm 72

There is a phrase associated with Bill Clinton as US president, that 'it's the economy, stupid', and Psalm 72 agrees, though on a less cynical basis than might be implied by that phrase. It recognises that the economy is indeed the responsibility of governments.

But its vision is, first, that government involves the exercise of authority or the taking of decisions with faithfulness in relation to God and to the people. Governance is concerned for the good of the people as a whole. If it has a concern for particular groups, it is not for the people who are wealthy and powerful, who include the members of the government themselves (and who can look after themselves), but for the lowly, the needy and the poor, and for their protection from the vicious, the violent and the extortioner. In practice, it is often the people with power who can be the extortioners, so there is a further bite to the psalm's words about what people in power are supposed to do.

Sandwiched in the midst of this emphasis is the reference to the land producing well-being, as an expression of God's faithfulness, with the implication that the government's giving priority to faithfulness and a concern for the lowly will issue in God's ensuring that prosperity follows for the country as a whole. The faithful will flourish. Both in his governing with faithfulness and in his opening up the possibility of this prosperity, the king will be like rain on the land.

Also alongside this emphasis is the note about people revering God through the ages. The exercise of authority in faithfulness will be an expression of obedience to God. Foreign policy, the vision implies, will then look after itself in the same way as the flourishing of the crops. The promise to Abraham will be fulfilled; foreign peoples will see the way God blesses, and they will pray for similar blessings.

Indirectly, then, the psalm lays before the government God's vision for how it should work, and makes promises about where implementing the right priorities will lead. But directly the psalm is a prayer, and it appears in a book of prayers and praises. What it directly does is set agenda for our praying for the government.

May the government make decisions for the people with faithfulness, Lord!

16 Talking to yourself about worship
Psalm 103

Whereas worship may sometimes come naturally, Psalm 103 implies that we may need to stir ourselves up to worship, to argue with ourselves. So 'I' tell 'my soul', my inner being, that it must worship God.

So what do you say to your heart or self? It's not that you tell yourself to feel things you don't feel or to sing loudly when it doesn't seem natural. It's rather that you remind yourself of the reasons for worship. You remind yourself of the way God acts toward us. In making the point more specific, the psalm points to two actions, pardon and healing, on which much of the following lines give more detail.

God, you remind yourself, isn't the kind of person who holds on to things, as if he is waiting for the strategic moment to come down on you like a ton of bricks. Rather, he dismisses our rebellions so that they go into exile as far as east is from west. Whether or not the psalmist knew it, that distance is infinity.

'Heals all your sicknesses' might seem an exaggeration. But at least God *can* heal all sicknesses, and he is the origin of any healing that does come – no one else can heal. And the kind of healing the psalm has in mind involves rescuing people when they were bound for the grave pit, and it involves putting a celebratory garland around their neck because there is something spectacular to rejoice in. It's as if they are twenty years younger.

Talk of pardon and healing could make it sound as if God is interested only in people's individual personal needs. Actually, God is also one who acts on behalf of the oppressed, as Israel's experience under Moses illustrates. How could a psalm of praise omit that fact? These and all God's actions are expressions of magnificent commitment and compassion, of grace and long-temperedness. The psalm is picking up God's own self-description in Exodus 34:6 and saying to God, 'Yes, you are what you said you are.' Given that 'compassion' is the term for a woman's womb and that it suggests a woman's feelings for her children, it's noteworthy that the psalm assumes that compassion can also be a fatherly characteristic.

We bless you, Lord; everything within us blesses your holy name!

17 God of light and God of darkness
Psalm 104

Psalm 104 paints a big picture of God's relationship with our ordinary world, and draws us into worship for that relationship.

It starts with a vivid, poetic portrayal of how God went about creation at the beginning. But then it goes on to talk about God's activity in the world now. God makes the springs come out of the earth. God sits in the heavens with his watering can, watering the slopes where trees and crops grow. Plants, trees, animals and human beings are all part of one whole, of which God takes ongoing care. The provision of bread, wine and male make-up is part of this care. The movements of sun and moon form an aspect of this ecology, signalling to the creatures of the night when to go about their work, and signalling to human beings as creatures of the day when to go about theirs.

The richness of God's creative work is not confined to the plants and animals that lie close at hand for humanity. There is the sea with its ships and its exotic plenty, including (the psalm notes with a smile) a creature like Leviathan, elsewhere a figure for immense power asserted against God, but here a joke figure, like the Loch Ness Monster. The sea creatures, like the land creatures, look to God for their food. Even if they don't literally do so, they are actually dependent on God every day. When God provides, they live on; when God withholds, they die. God is Lord equally of life and death. Only God has life in himself to give. If God gives living breath, creatures live; if God withholds it, they die.

The psalm thus recognises the dark side to creation – darkness as well as light, hunger as well as sufficiency, death as well as life, earth's quaking as well as earth's stability. Maybe there is a link between that resolute double recognition and the surprising note with which the psalm almost ends, a plea for sinners and faithless to disappear from the earth. Human rebellion and waywardness spoil the world that God created and keeps in being. The prayer also means that the people singing this psalm cannot take the risk of being faithless and sinners themselves.

Lord my God, you are very great!

187

18 God knows
Psalm 139

God can find out anything about us and can do anything with us that he wants to. It can be encouraging to know that we can never get beyond the realm of God's care for us. Yet Amos 9 uses the same imagery as the psalm to remind Israel that it can't escape God's judgement. Every breath you take, every step you take, God will be watching you. It's almost as if the psalm is daring us to decide whether it's good news or bad news.

It goes on to wonder at the process whereby we come into existence. Israelites knew that conception and birth is a natural process, yet they also knew that it is God who works through the natural process. And the psalm knows that there is a sense in which everything we will be and do is shaped before we are born – what kind of person we will be, with our strengths and weaknesses. It's not that everything is predetermined, but the possibilities and constraints are already set. And God knows them.

It's tempting to focus on the psalm's first three sections, and to find the last part embarrassing. How could such a spiritually sensitive person as this psalmist segue into the harshness of the last part? Very easily and naturally, is the answer, once we see the ominous side to God's having the kind of access to us that the psalm describes.

The last part of the psalm implies that it is an expression of commitment to Yahweh's ways. The psalmist knows about faithless people who live murderous lives, people who take the name of Yahweh on their lips in their oaths and in their testimony in court but do so in connection with lies. The psalmist's closing invitation to God to examine him or her is then an opening of the self to God's checking whether this commitment is real. The earlier sections of the psalm add bite to this self-opening. There is no fooling God about the nature of our commitment to God's ways. There is no escaping God if we pretend to be something other than we are.

Augustine commented that we are called to love our enemies but not to love God's enemies.

Lord, you have searched me out and known me. Do search me and know my heart.

19 Praise him, shining stars
Psalms 148 – 149

We may think of worship as something that essentially involves minds and hearts. Psalm 148 thinks of worship being offered by sun and moon, sea monsters, fruit trees and cattle. Apparently, words are less essential to praise than we may assume, and the involvement of the body is more important than we may assume, so that it is not odd to think of trees as worshipping when their branches sway and of animals worshipping as they roar or low or shriek.

The psalm expands our horizon in a different way by reminding us that the community summoned to praise includes all God's aides and armies. There are entities in the heavens and on the earth that are more interested in resisting God than in praising him. The psalm has a vision of them all being drawn into praise. Then the psalm closes with a complementary reason for Israel's own praise. How extraordinary that the God of such majesty should have elevated little Israel.

Psalm 149 widens our perspective further. It assumes that dancing is a natural part of worship, as is the use of instruments such as the tambourine and the guitar. Worship indeed involves the whole person; how could you express enthusiasm for your Maker and King if you stood still? The smooth transition from dancing to wielding the sword also makes us feel uncomfortable. While the New Testament makes no reference to dancing in worship, or to the use of musical instruments in worship, it does refer to the use of the sword in God's service (e.g., Romans 13).

The psalm's freedom about worship is thus refreshing, as is its commitment to seeing that wrongdoing is put down. It does not expect the people of God to sit by when wrong is done. When Israel itself is under attack, the Psalms assume its job is to trust God and not seek to defend itself. But it is a different matter when there is wrongdoing to be opposed and defenceless people to be rescued. The assumption that a little people like Israel can put down kings and empires is crazy, though not if you believe in God and know there is a decision God has made that needs to be implemented.

Lord, we will join sun and moon, mountains and hills, fruit trees and cedars, and praise you!

20 The praise of God, the Eternal Creator, is finished and completed
Psalm 150

The heading above for this final psalm is the rabbis' footnote to the Hebrew text of the Psalms. We have come a long way from Psalm 1, with its exhortation to pay heed to Yahweh's teaching, and Psalm 2, with its promise to the king. One could say that the second psalm from the end (Psalm 149) corresponds to the second psalm from the beginning, in its assertions about nations being rebuked and kings being put down, while the very last psalm then contrasts with the very first psalm.

It also contrasts with the development of the book of Psalms after that opening, because the first half of the book is dominated by prayer and protest, but praise is more prominent in the second half, and its ending in Psalms 146 – 150 simply comprises praise. The Hebrew title of the book of Psalms, 'Praises', is not very apposite to the book as a whole, but it corresponds to where the book ends, where pain and abandonment and disappointment have been forgotten. There are people who need to be reminded that the Scriptures are interested in our showing compassion to the needy and not just offering enthusiastic worship. There are other people who need to be reminded that the Scriptures are interested in our offering enthusiastic worship and not just showing compassion to the needy.

The praise of the Psalms commonly involves two features – an exhortation or self-commitment to praise, and the reasons for or content of this praise. Psalm 150 alone comprises only the first feature, the feature that elsewhere comprises something more like an introduction. Psalm 150 is not an introduction to anything; it is more like a conclusion. In effect, it says, 'We have said a lot about God in all these psalms; in light of all that we have said, you know all the reasons to praise God. Just do it.'

The actual expression 'Praise the Lord' comes at either end of each psalm from 146 to 150; these are the words commonly transliterated as 'Hallelujah'. This Hebrew word for praise, *halal*, suggests in particular ululating, going lalalala. If words are less essential to praise than we think, then just make a noise!

We praise you, Lord, for your mighty deeds, in accordance with your surpassing greatness!

21 Proverbs' dictionary

Proverbs 1

The opening paragraph of Proverbs comes to a climax by declaring that the first principle of knowledge is awe for Yahweh, whereas stupid people despise wisdom and discipline (1:7). Now, Proverbs' opening chapter refers to knowledge six times, but the knowing it's interested in isn't expressed merely in achieving a high IQ score. Proverbs assumes a connection between what goes on in the head and what goes on in the life.

Its dictionary is selectively expressed in its opening verses, and it includes a number of words that make one think. 'Shrewdness', for instance, is the capacity attributed to the snake in Genesis 2. It suggests being able to get people to do what you want them to do. It can have a bad or a good connotation. 'Discretion' suggests skill in thinking things through and formulating plans, which in other contexts can be evil plans. But alongside the references to wisdom and knowledge come references to doing the right thing or faithfulness, to the exercise of authority and to uprightness. Knowledge, shrewdness and discretion need to be in the service of these moral qualities.

In the modern world, questions about economics, business, education, counselling or foreign policy can be treated as issues in their own right that should not be mixed up with questions about religion or ethics. Proverbs would think it unnatural to consider policy questions, ethics and God as separate spheres. It begins by urging its readers to let them interweave. Christians and Jews cannot adopt from the world theories or practices of business or counselling or education without setting them in the context of what we know about ethics and about God. Proverbs models how to go about learning from the secular world: we are open to such learning, but we set the secular world's theories and findings into a framework that includes God and ethics.

Maybe that fact links with the further promise that Proverbs' teaching is designed to help people understand parables and puzzles. Parables are straightforward-sounding stories whose real meaning is rather enigmatic; puzzles are the mysterious topics that the wise seek to understand, such as the nature of creation and the problem of evil. We'll never understand everything about such topics, but we'll gain more understanding if we take ethics and God into account.

We commit ourselves to live in awe of you, Lord, so we may be wise.

22 Ms Wisdom
Proverbs 8

'Leaders rely on wisdom – shouldn't you?' wisdom asks. Proverbs personifies wisdom as a woman asking the question. 'As God's wisdom, I was involved in the world's creation – shouldn't you rely on me too?' It's as if God had given birth to his wisdom at the beginning of everything. God thus 'acquired' his wisdom back then (Proverbs uses the verb that Eve used of her 'acquiring' Cain as her son in Genesis 4). Wisdom is the design principle that made and makes things work in the world; Ms Wisdom is a member of the divine cabinet that God consults, which takes part in decision-making about the world and keeps watch over the world.

There is a further aspect to her claim and testimony. Wisdom sounds like something serious, but it turns out to be something playful. It's not certain whether Ms Wisdom describes herself as a 'child' – different translations have 'confidant' or 'craftworker'. But it's clear from the lines that follow that she was having a playful, enthusiastic, animated, childlike time when God was creating the world. You could infer that creation was itself an outworking of joy; that joy created the world. Ms Wisdom was excited in the creation that God was bringing into being, and excited not least with humanity itself. Genesis 1 describes each element of creation as good, but does so rather solemnly. Ms Wisdom claps her hands and dances. This chapter is playful, though serious, as the last paragraph shows when it returns to solemnity and sobriety.

When early Christians needed to speak about Jesus as existing before he became a human being and as divine yet distinguishable from the Father, they picked up the idea of God's Wisdom, which a passage such as Proverbs 8 describes as divine yet pictures as distinguishable from God (of course, in the context of Proverbs this picture is more metaphorical than it is when we speak of Jesus as the embodiment of God's Wisdom). The description of Jesus as God's Word in John 1 picks up the terms that describe God's Wisdom in Proverbs 8. The implication isn't so much that we should read Jesus into Proverbs but that we understand Jesus in light of Proverbs. Jesus' teaching is an expression of the wisdom written into creation.

Lord, give us the gift of wisdom by which you yourself worked in creation and work still.

23 Even in laughter a heart may grieve
Proverbs 14

It's unwise to assume that the emotions people show are the ones they feel. People can be good actors. Even if you do know the true nature of someone's feelings of sadness or joy, don't think you actually share them, says Proverbs. There's perhaps a sense in which each of us is alone with our inner experiences; there are limits to empathy.

'A healthy heart is life for the flesh, but passion is rot for the bones' (14:30). It's another saying that sounds as if it's declaring an unvarying truth when it's a generalisation that works by and large but not invariably. Sometimes passions such as jealousy and anger are correct reactions to situations and make people take action that needs taking. But bottling up such strong feelings rather than owning them may indeed be hurtful to the whole person, body as well as spirit.

Biblical usage matches English usage in referring to the heart in various connections. But whereas we often refer to the heart in speaking of the emotions, the Bible more often refers to the heart in speaking of the mind or the will. Both usages see the heart as the centre of a person's inner being, the well-spring of who a person is. Wisdom's residing in the heart implies it resides in the mind, but also that it permeates the inner being more broadly. It affects the emotions and the will. And there's an inner wisdom that can somehow know what is wise independently of thinking things through intellectually.

To describe the mocker as seeking wisdom (14:6) is paradoxical; perhaps the idea is that mockers may know they need to make sensible decisions, but their arrogance prevents their acquiring the wisdom to do so. Their insight concerning the action that they should take turns out to be deception (14:8). They are hot-headed and confident where trepidation would be wiser (14:16, 29). Their shortness of temper can get them into trouble, though their considered deceptiveness can have worse consequences (14:17). Making themselves unpopular may then be an irreversible development; there's no way their attempts to make up for their stupidity can succeed and generate the friendly relationships that happen between the upright (14:9).

Lord, give me a heart of discernment and a mind of insight.

24 Faithful are the wounds of a friend
Proverbs 27

Who knows whether I shall be able to fulfil the schedule required by my agreeing to take on this *Daily Bible Meditations for Everyone* project? I could get too confident. Who will tell me that I take myself too seriously or get angry too often or get consumed by envy? It will be my friends' job (27:5–6). You can assume that you should trust a friend's hurtful statements as well meant and likely reliable.

Conversely, the principle of wariness about effusive displays of purported support provides one context in which to apply the saying about honey (27:7). In turn, maybe the saying about leaving home (27:8) complements the one about friends. Proverbs would then compare with two attitudes that surface in Western culture. We have some sympathy with the Greek and Roman view that a man's friends are likely to be men and that a woman's friends are likely to be women.

Yet we may assume that our spouse should be our best friend and may yearn for it to be so, and I can be sure that my wife will not let me down when I need a friendly, straight rebuke. Perhaps the saying about the contentious wife (27:15) reminds a man of the danger of receiving loving rebuke as contentiousness, or of ignoring such rebukes and having them turn into contentiousness.

The companion saying (27:16) may also be double-edged. A wife might take it as a compliment that trying to control your wife is like trying to control the wind. The inadvisability of leaving home may also underlie the double saying about abandoning your friend or your father's friend (27:10), if the idea is that a friend near home is a wiser resource in a crisis than a brother far away.

Our friends' rebuke and counsel are important safeguards against trusting our own instincts (27:9); they are even sweeter than expensive luxuries. It might not be surprising if some Israelites found incense got into their eyes and up their noses and thus didn't find it sweet, and a friend's counsel may not seem sweet. But if the only counsel you get is sweet, do you have any real friends? Or are you just choosing to hang out with flatterers or people whose nice words counteract your poor image of yourself?

Lord, give me faithful, straight-talking friends.

25 The strong woman
Proverbs 31

Proverbs presupposes a family living in a small town, or a village that might comprise a couple of hundred people belonging to three extended families that each comprise a number of households. In any one household or extended family, the senior woman is a vital figure. When you're looking for a wife, then, Proverbs advises a young man, don't just focus on her looks. Ask how smart she is. Look at the size of her muscles and at her capacity to burn the midnight oil.

If the man and the woman are lucky, there are other, more romantic aspects to their relationship than the ones this poem highlights (the kind that feature in the Song of Songs), but the focus here lies on practical considerations. The woman operates from the home base in managing the family's affairs, but she is like a warrior going out to battle and coming home with the spoils for the family's benefit. The poem appeals to the imagination, but this implies that readers should not be too literalistic about the picture it paints. While a woman could be encouraged by the range of responsibility expected by it, she could also be daunted. Remember, it's a poem.

There's nothing lazy about this woman, unlike some of the men we meet in Proverbs. It means she doesn't have to worry about her own appearance or about the family's provision for next year. In a village or town, the acquisition of fabric and foodstuffs, and their manufacture, will involve bartering (money hasn't been invented). A family will not necessarily be self-sufficient but will use its surplus to obtain things it needs but doesn't produce. The woman is in charge of this process and of the process whereby the family spots a way of extending its land and planting an extra vineyard.

She sees that the family doesn't just care for itself. She makes sure it looks after other people in the village. Nor does her provision limit itself to material needs. If we were in any doubt about the question whether mothers share in the teaching of their family, this poem removes such doubt. It's related to the fact that she isn't merely a hard worker and a dedicated teacher but also someone in awe of Yahweh.

Lord, grant us to find expression for our gifts as men and as women.

26 Empty, empty
Ecclesiastes 1

'Vanity of vanities,' says the usual translation of the opening words of Ecclesiastes (KJV). Everything is totally empty. Ecclesiastes keeps saying things that you wouldn't have thought a teacher or preacher would say. It keeps raising questions, not the questions of an atheist or an agnostic, but the questions of a believer who wants to keep faith honest.

The word for vanity or emptiness literally means a breath. It declares that things are evanescent; they have no substance. In Ecclesiastes it describes pleasure, achievement, work, wealth and politics. The evanescence of everything suggests the uselessness of all the effort that people put into their lives. The important thing is not to think that those things can give life ultimate meaning. Enjoy them, and they can be worthwhile, but don't make that mistake.

There's no point putting effort into trying to achieve things, because you can never know whether you achieve anything in the long run. It's chance that determines things. You can only see how things are 'under the sun'. Ecclesiastes looks at life resolutely from the perspective of what you can see. It doesn't mean leaving out God or leaving out right and wrong. It does mean focusing on what we can experience as human beings in the now, on the earthly plane. It doesn't talk about the exodus or the covenant, about heaven or hell, or about a coming messiah. It asks, 'What can you learn by focusing on what you can see now?' Here, randomness often rules. That fact is one aspect of how things are 'under the sun'.

Another feature of life 'under the sun' is that there's nothing new there, Ecclesiastes says. Things just go around and around. The nature of its observations introduces another feature of the book. You could think that its comment that nothing new ever happens is bad news or good news. In Western culture we are inclined to put a positive estimate on new things. Advertisers seek to get us to buy things because they are new. But the reliable cycle of sun and moon and the unchanging circulation of water (evaporation, rain, rivers, sea) provides important undergirding for human life. There being nothing new there is good news. Everything depends on how you look at the phenomena.

Face the facts, people!

But you, Lord, are the single non-evanescent one!

27 For everything there is a season
Ecclesiastes 3

There is a time or a moment for all the activities that the poem in Ecclesiastes 3 describes. Ecclesiastes follows up the poem with a long reflection on how God has made everything fitting in its time. Birth and death, weeping and laughter, silence and speaking, peace and war – they are all part of human life as God created it, part of human life 'under the sun'. The poem is not a series of exhortations but of descriptions. In most cases, perhaps in all, one of the pair of verbs denotes an activity that is preferable to the other, and one effect of the poem is to rub people's noses into the reality of human life. Death is as integral to it as life, slaying as healing, hating as loving. The equal status of positive and negative is further suggested by the random order in which they appear – sometimes the positive comes first, sometimes the negative. In other words, Ecclesiastes itself isn't evaluating them as positive and negative. They are just realities.

The evaluation comes in the prose reflection that follows. The sovereign God's lordship lies behind all these activities, but he hasn't made it possible for humanity to make sense of them as aspects of some whole. Enigmatically, Ecclesiastes declares that God has put 'eternity' or 'permanence' or 'a sense of past and future' into our minds. God has created us with a yearning to understand the big picture about human life and about God's activity in the world, and Ecclesiastes implies that there is such a big picture. But from our position within the context of earthly life 'under the sun', we can't perceive what it is. All we can see is the apparently random collocation of the contrasting activities that the poem describes. Fortunately, we know that God knows what the big picture is and that we can trust him for it.

Its realisations don't make the author of Ecclesiastes inclined to despair and suicide. It generates an exhortation to people to settle for what we can have and do – enjoy our life, do what is good, eat and drink, enjoy the fruit of our labour and accept the gifts God has given us, but also the limitations God has placed upon us.

Thank you, Lord, that you do know the big picture – in fact, you paint it.

28 Face the fact that you are going to die
Ecclesiastes 11

Ecclesiastes issues this exhortation not in order to inhibit people from enjoying life but to encourage them to enjoy it in a way that doesn't ignore the fact that they are going to die. Remember that 'God will bring you to judgement'. Death itself is a kind of judgement, the implementing of God's decision to terminate a life, which eventually comes to everyone.

The context also hints that God's judgement is his evaluating whether we've made the most of enjoying our lives. The inevitability of death isn't to make young people fail to enjoy the youth they are given. Yet neither should they fail to keep their creator in mind during their youth, because he's eventually going to undertake that evaluation and bring about that judgement.

Ecclesiastes gives a vivid poetic description of old age. It's when you stop enjoying life because your physical frailty makes it impossible to do so. It's when gloom falls upon your life. It's when your arms fail, your legs grow weak, your teeth fall out, your eyes grow dim. It's when your ears become deaf and your voice becomes faint. It's when you wake up with the birds because you can't sleep but you can't properly hear girls singing. It's when you're afraid of heights and of the danger of going out. It's when your hair grows white like almond blossom and you shuffle along like a grasshopper and your desires fail. All these experiences indicate that you're on your way to your eternal home in the grave, in Sheol; indeed, the mourners are already gathering like rival undertakers looking for business. It's the moment when the thread of life snaps. It's when dirt and spirit return whence they came.

People need to be mindful of how life will end before they get old. It's almost as if Ecclesiastes is warning against the idea of deathbed repentance, or deathbed regrets and resentments, but the dynamics of his concern are different. He isn't saying that deathbed repentance is impossible or that death may take you before you get around to repenting, but that he wants people to live authentic human lives, and it's such lives that need to be characterised by enjoyment of what God gives, but truthfulness in respect of where our lives will lead.

Thank you, Lord, for our life.

29 You are beautiful, my love
Song of Songs 1

The Song of Songs is a set of dialogues between a man and a woman (not necessarily the same couple all the way through). The couple who speak in this first poem want to get away. How can they be together for some time during the day? In the poet's imagination, they are both shepherds. The woman wants to know where she'll be able to find her man, particularly when he has his break for lunch and his siesta. Maybe her brothers' anger results from her desire to spend time with this young man. Further, she doesn't want the embarrassment of having to negotiate her way through other groups of shepherds, veiled in order not to be caught out. So he tells her which track he intends to follow as he finds pasture for his sheep, so she can follow with her goats.

Each tells the other how lovely the other is. The woman herself doesn't think she's lovely, but the poem recognises how someone who loves sees the beloved differently from other people. To the woman, in a culture that values a fair skin, she's unattractive because her skin has been darkened by the sun. But in the Song, a vineyard can be an image for a woman's personal self, especially her sexual self, and the ensuing comment implies that having to look after the literal vineyard has meant she hasn't been able to look after her physical self.

The poem also pictures the couple as a king and a princess. They are sitting outside in the shadow of the trees, but it's as if they are reclining in royal apartments. Little girls have often thought of their weddings as coronations or royal-like ceremonies, as the time when they get to be 'queen for a day'. The appearance of this new image reminds us to be wary of taking even the first image too literally. The poems are poetry.

One implication of the presence of the Song in Scripture is a recognition that natural human love is God's gift, including the love of ordinary people like a shepherd girl and a shepherd boy. Our instinct to love, our sexuality and our sexual enthusiasm are part of the way God created us, and something God rejoices in.

Thank you, Lord, for the gift of love and relationships.

30 Love as fierce as death
Song of Songs 8

Love is as fierce as death; passion is as tough as Sheol. It's quite a comparison. When death gets hold of you, it doesn't let go. Love has the same power. It's like an archer who shoots burning arrows at you, arrows that burn so ferociously that you couldn't find enough water to put them out. It's as if they shoot a supernatural flame. Literally, they are 'a flame of Yahweh'. It's the only time God is named in the Song of Songs. Love is stronger than any other earthly force. When love comes along, you're done for.

You don't mind, the Song implies. At least you may not mind the fact that you are overwhelmed. You just want this other person to be clearly marked as yours, soul and body: the seal goes on the heart and on the arm. The image of a seal that is outward as well as inward suggests a reference to marriage, a public, outward relationship as well as an inward one. The Song excludes the idea that marriage means the man owns the woman, except as one side of an arrangement whereby the woman also owns the man. Her seal of ownership is on his inner being and on his body for all to see.

Yet a couple who want to make their mutual commitment may well not be able to marry straightaway, and waiting is agonising. If her man were her brother, she could express her affection for him by kissing him and embracing him, but such a display would be unacceptable in her culture except between members of the same family. How long might they have to wait until the families have completed their negotiations and the arrangements for the celebration have been completed?

The woman repeats several times an exhortation not to arouse love until it wishes. A couple must not get too overwhelmed by love when they are not yet in a position to act on their feelings and spend their lives together. Yet the fierceness of the flame makes such a declaration useless.

The Song ends the way it has been all the way through, with longing, not fulfilment. He is still far away from her, and she can't wait for them to be together.

Give us grace to wait when we have to wait, Lord.

July

PROPHECIES
AND VISIONS

I How to frighten people into repentance

Isaiah 6

Isaiah's account of his vision tells how he came to be declaiming the message that Isaiah 1 – 5 have already reported. His vision came in the year that King Uzziah died. His not naming the new king puts this king in his place and draws attention to Isaiah's focus on another King. In his vision of Yahweh's palace in the heavens, the seraphs are attendants, creatures that combine some animal-like, some bird-like and some human-like features. Their declaration of Yahweh's holiness links with the distinctive importance of this theme in Isaiah. Yahweh is supremely holy.

Isaiah's problem, however, is that he is an impure human being living among an impure people. His associating himself with his people's defilement implies a recognition that as individuals we are all inevitably implicated in the wrong done by the group we belong to (family, church, city, nation). But God cleanses Isaiah's lips by a sacramental action that will enable these lips to become a means of serving Yahweh. Whereas Yahweh drafted Moses and will draft Jeremiah, Isaiah is the prophet who responds to a request for volunteers.

But Yahweh is looking for someone to declare judgement on this polluted people. The judgement will take the form of telling them they're never going to understand what God is saying to them and doing with them. Not surprisingly, Isaiah is appalled. He is perhaps regretting the way he volunteered without knowing what the commission would be. His question, 'For how long?' is the question that recurs in the Psalms when someone protests about how long God intends to let some calamity continue. The answer makes things even worse, until we reach the last phrase, about the holy seed. It promises that the end will not be the end. A holy seed will survive.

On the surface this story implies that judgement is inevitable. But Yahweh's aim in telling people what he intends to do is to provoke a response. The aim of a message of judgement is consistently that it should make it possible for God not to implement it, though that aim may fail and then the judgement will indeed happen. When Jesus quotes this passage in Mark 4 to provide the rationale for his speaking in parables, the same framework applies.

Holy, holy, holy, Lord of Armies: The whole earth is full of your glory!

2 Light dawns
Isaiah 9

When Judah has experienced darkness, defeat and oppression, the birth of a son in the royal household is a sign of hope. After the promise with which Isaiah 9 begins, the chapter speaks of Yahweh's act of restoration as if it's already happened, but it hasn't yet. Isaiah speaks by faith concerning what he knows God is going to do. He can speak as if the events have happened because they have begun; it's a common feature of the way the Scriptures work. The event that has happened is the birth of this son to the king, perhaps the birth of Hezekiah to Ahaz. People would indeed look back to his birth as a significant moment, given his greatness as a reformer and as one who saw Yahweh marvellously preserve Jerusalem from falling to Assyria.

Whoever he is, this child has a complicated name, a string of expressions that make best sense taken as a pair of sentences: 'A wonderful counsellor is the mighty God. The everlasting Father is the prince of peace.' It's not the kind of name that is someone's everyday name. When the New Testament says that Jesus will be called Immanuel, 'God with us', it doesn't mean this expression is Jesus' everyday name. Rather, in some way the person who has the name stands for whatever the name says. God gives him as a sign of the truth of the expression attached to him. Here, the name doesn't mean that the child who has been born *is* the mighty God or the everlasting Father. Rather, he is a sign and guarantee of this truth about God. It's as if he goes around bearing a billboard with that message and with the reminder that God commissioned the billboard.

So the name makes some declarations about who God is, as one who makes plans and fulfils them; who acts with power as a warrior; who is an everlasting father; who is going to bring *shalom*, peace, well-being, for his people. This prospect is what the child's name promises Judah. The child's birth is a sign that God will restore his people. In his mind's eye Isaiah can see light dawning over the whole land, light that contrasts with the darkness presupposed by the opening of the chapter.

Yes, Lord, you are 'Wonderful counsellor, mighty God, everlasting Father, prince of peace'.

3 New growth from a stump
Isaiah 11 – 12

In a vision, Isaiah has seen the felling of Jesse's tree. Jesse was David's father; the vision presupposes the fall of David's dynasty. But Isaiah has also seen beyond that catastrophe, seen a new shoot growing from the felled tree. The new shoot will lack the weaknesses that the Davidic kings have usually shown; he will realise the Davidic ideal in demonstrating both compassion for the weak and toughness toward the oppressor. The context suggests that the picture of killers in the animal world being turned into pets is another image for the same deliverance.

There's more that Yahweh intends to achieve through this new shoot. His significance will extend beyond Israel to the entire world. The sequence here implies the idea going back to God's promise to Abraham, that what God does in Israel will be so impressive that the world will flock to Jerusalem to seek blessing and guidance from Yahweh. Here the draw is the achievement of the Davidic shoot in bringing about a transformation of Judahite society.

Isaiah also talks in terms of a signal summoning the nations, but he does so in connection with another aspect of Israel's own need. There's need for social renewal, and also need to bring back to the country Ephraimites and Judahites who have been or will have been transported all over the known world. The vision even goes beyond the return of people to the land. It envisages a healing of the longstanding tension within Israel between Ephraim and Judah, a tension going back to the split within the nation more than a century before Isaiah's day.

The final paragraph gives Judah a song to sing 'on that day', a song rather like the thanksgivings or testimonies that appear in the Psalms, for singing when God has done something amazing for people. This 'psalm' also assumes that God's acts for his people are not significant just for them. Their praise deserves to be heard among other nations, so that they're drawn to acknowledge Yahweh.

It's disheartening that after 2,700 years, Isaiah's vision has been fulfilled only in little ways. But Jesus' coming did constitute God's 'Yes' to his promises. It thus makes it the more possible to keep believing in them and to keep singing the song in anticipation.

We will give thanks to you, Lord. You, Lord, are our salvation.

4 The downfall of the pretender
Isaiah 14

The Gospels describe Satan entering Judas and Jesus addressing Peter as Satan (Luke 22:3; Matthew 16:23). How did Satan become able and inclined to act the way he did? John Milton's poem *Paradise Lost* took Isaiah 14 to provide the answer. Satan's pride had got him thrown out of heaven for pretending that he was God's equal.

Isaiah is indeed talking about someone trying to usurp God's position of authority, but he isn't describing a supernatural being. He is talking about the Babylonian king as the head of the superpower. Our word 'superpower' gives the game away. The claim to be a superpower is a claim to have usurped God's authority. Isaiah sees the desire to control the entire world as a desire to have a godlike position over it.

Isaiah makes the point by taking up a theme people would have known. Each morning Venus gets very bright just before dawn, so that it can be called the son of dawn, the morning star. The New Testament applies that term to Jesus (Revelation 22:16). But the actual planet Venus is eclipsed by the sun's own brightness. Now Middle Eastern religions saw the planets and stars as representing the gods and representing things going on between the gods, and a Canaanite story saw these events in the sky as reflecting Venus's failed attempt to become top god, to become president of the assembly of the gods. The Latin equivalent of 'morning star' is Lucifer, so 'Lucifer' became a name with negative connotations.

Isaiah is using that story to describe the king of Babylon attempting to achieve a godlike position over the world, trying to become top dog or top god. The irony in Milton's use of the story is that he reverts to its significance in Canaanite myth.

In Isaiah's vision, the king of the superpower has been cast down from the godlike position over the world that he sought. He has gone from the height of heaven to the depth of Sheol. He doesn't get the splendid burial that other kings get. His corpse is lying on the battlefield in a heap of corpses. Isaiah has seen the superpower's downfall, and his people are invited to live in the certainty that rest will come. And the superpower did fall.

Lord, you are the great God who puts down people who pretend to be superpowers.

5 Comfort my people
Isaiah 40

Jerusalem's fall to the Babylonians happened some time before God put out this message. The book of Lamentations keeps grieving that the city 'has none to comfort her'. God now responds with the commission to 'comfort, comfort my people'. The message doesn't say who the comforters are. The point is that some comforting is commissioned.

The first element in the comfort lies in the words that follow: 'my people' and 'your God'. Another bit of background to the prophecy is the way Hosea long ago reported God's words to Israel: 'You are no longer my people and I am no longer your God' (Hosea 1:9). That declaration was a death knell. But God also promised through Hosea that the moment would come when God would again say, 'my people' and 'your God' (see Hosea 2:23). The moment has now arrived.

The reason is that God knows when enough is enough. The people resemble an army unit who have been on a demanding tour of duty; the tour is over. They needed to pay for their waywardness, and 'double for all your offences' underlines the adequacy of the payment. Yahweh abandoned Jerusalem. Now he intends to return, and another voice commissions freeway contractors to carve out a highway to take him back.

Then someone is commissioned to preach. But the potential preacher can't imagine preaching. How can someone preach to people who are like plants withered by the hot desert wind? But when God speaks, things happen. God said way back that he would not simply abandon Israel as 'not-my-people'.

Another commissioning voice restates the commission to preach. It's as if the preacher is to soar to the top of a mountain higher than Zion itself, higher than the Judahite mountains. From that perspective the preacher could see God coming along that highway. And God isn't on his own. He has a flock of sheep, the flock of Israel, for whom he is caring with power and compassion as he brings them with him. The prophecy turns out to have in its mind not only Jerusalem and Judah and the people living there, praying those desperate prayers in Lamentations. It has in mind the people who were taken off to Babylon decades ago. They're coming back with God.

You are the Lord God who comes with might, feeding his flock like a shepherd.

6 Have you not known?
Isaiah 40

'My way is hidden from the Lord,' the Judahites are lamenting. It might seem that one could hardly blame them. God abandoned them, let the Babylonians take many into exile, and had then let the people mark time in Judah or in Babylon for half a century. Yet the prophecy does rebuke them for lamenting – or at least it wants them to see that the moment has arrived to stop.

It begins by bringing out into the open four other realities they are tempted to trust in or be overwhelmed by. The first is the empire itself, 'the nations', which had defeated them, destroyed their capital and exiled many of them. So the prophet begins with an outrageous assertion of how unimpressive the empire is. Suppose you compare it with God, the God whose power is expressed in the world that he created and whose history he controls? They aren't a threat to him.

What about the images of gods that the Babylonians had? Excuse me, says the prophet, have you thought about how images are made? They're made by human craftworkers, made of wood and then overlaid and provided with chains so no one can steal them. It's embarrassing if someone steals your god or it falls over.

What about the empire's kings? These sovereigns are no more impressive than the rest of the grasshopper-like creatures that God looks down on from the heavens. God can put them down in a moment if he chooses.

What about the planets and stars that the Babylonians see as ruling what happens on earth? But who is in charge of them, the prophet asks. The planets and stars are the army of which Yahweh is the commander-in-chief.

In light of all those considerations, it's foolish to entertain the idea that Judah's destiny could have escaped God's purview. Yahweh is about to act to put down the empire, restore Jerusalem and bring the exiles home. Events you could watch unfolding on the television news were the ones in which Yahweh was involved in order to fulfil these intentions. If you know who God is and what God is going to do, you can look to those events that are coming, and then it energises you in the present.

You, Lord, are the everlasting God, the creator of the ends of the earth.

7 The man who kept his mouth shut
Isaiah 52 – 53

This vision portrays a servant of God who has gone through extreme suffering at the hands of other people. He declines to be a victim and instead turns his experience into a kind of offering to God.

Specifically, he turns it into a reparation offering. This kind of sacrifice was one you made when you needed to make amends for something you'd done. The servant himself has no need to make amends for anything. But he lives among a people who indeed need to make amends to God. They were taken into exile because of the way they turned to other gods, trusted in politics rather than God and let people with power and resources take advantage of people without power and resources. Much of the generation that lives in exile has continued the same pattern. They have a desperate need to make amends to God, though as far as we can tell they don't yet see that point.

So someone who doesn't have that need offers his obedient life to God on their behalf, to see whether God would accept his offering of his life as a compensation for their lives that lack such commitment. Maybe it could work, and be the means whereby the servant could bring Israel back to God.

It's Israel that is the 'we' who speak in the main part of the vision. They took the servant's being ignored and despised as a sign of his being punished by God. They have now realised they had the picture upside down. It was because of *their* wrongdoing that he was suffering, not his own. What enabled them to come to see the picture right was the way he coped with their treatment of him. He simply accepted it and didn't complain. That's not what people usually do. It's not even what the Psalms expect you to do. It raised the question, 'Who is this man?' and eventually they saw the answer (in the vision, that is; in the real world there's no such movement yet).

This vision of what God might achieve through his servant helped the New Testament to understand what Jesus was about and to understand the Church's vocation. It has helped the Jewish people to understand their own suffering.

Lord, you revealed your own arm in your servant's accepting affliction.

8 High and holy
Isaiah 57

God is high and lofty, and holy. But that statement's importance lies also in what it goes on to, that the one who dwells on high and holy also dwells with the crushed and low in spirit, bringing life to the spirit of the people who are low, to the heart of the crushed. Either part of the statement on its own is disastrously misleading.

People who have returned to Jerusalem or never left Judah found life tougher than they hoped. It was as if they were continuing to be objects of the divine wrath that destroyed the city and deported many of its people. Yahweh speaks in a way designed to make clear that this is not so. He is commissioning aides to clear the obstacles that separate the people from their destiny, and assuring them that anger belongs to the past, not the present. His lips are going to speak of well-being for this mourning people, the community here in Jerusalem and the community who are still far away in Babylon.

They do need to be people who turn to Yahweh, otherwise there will be no well-being for them. That applies to their leaders, which the end of the previous chapter described as lookouts or shepherds who are more like dogs than shepherds – sleeping dogs, too busy indulging themselves to keep an eye open on their people's behalf. The result is that their people who are faithful can lose their lives to ruthless people who deprive them of their land and livelihood, without anyone noticing or caring. Ironically, the prophecy adds, losing one's life, being gathered to one's ancestors, might be a kind of deliverance from the events one would otherwise see and experience when judgement comes.

But there's not much faithfulness among the people in general, either. They think they can combine commitment to Yahweh with adherence to the traditional religious practices of the country. They have to make a choice. The entities they're turning to cannot save them. They must turn to Yahweh to the exclusion of these practices. It would be tempting to doubt whether they can ever be in secure possession of the land again, and thus truly be a people. The promise declares that it is possible.

You are indeed the high and lofty one, who also dwells with the crushed and low in spirit.

9 Blown over and anointed

Isaiah 61

When Yahweh's breath blows you over, it leaves you without options. The talk of also being anointed makes one think of the prophet as like a priest or king – anointing isn't usually linked with being a prophet. But it is a sign of being commissioned and given authority.

Both those claims, to have been bowled over by Yahweh's wind and to have been anointed, buttress the message that follows. We are again reminded that the people to whom the prophet ministers are lowly and broken in their inner being. They're like people in prison. It's as if they're still in exile. They're mourning Zion, mourning its broken state. Their city lies in ruins, as it has done for years. Their spirit is flickering. They live with shame at the way their devastated state reflects their downfall to Babylon and their abandonment by God that lay behind their disgrace.

The commission doesn't mean the prophet has to do anything. Characteristically, all a prophet does is preach. This prophet's task is to bring news, to declare that the people's release is imminent, that God's year of favour and his day of redress is here. These are two sides of a coin. God's action will mean that redress against Israel is replaced by favour and that God's using the superpower's instinct for destruction is replaced by bringing judgement on its destructiveness.

It's by bringing this message that the prophet will bind up the people, bring them comfort, make it possible for them to give up the clothes of mourning and put on celebration garments. God's purpose for them will be fulfilled. Instead of being humiliated they will be able to take on their proper role as priests looking after the worship of Yahweh. Other peoples will support their work by looking after the shepherding and farming and otherwise providing for them, as within Israel the clan of Levi looks after the worship and the other clans support its work. The other peoples will come to be astonished at God's blessing of Israel instead of being astonished at their shame.

Jesus takes up the opening lines of the prophet's testimony to describe his ministry as he comes to bring good news to the lowly Jewish community of his day, living as they were under Roman overlordship (Luke 4:18–19).

You are the Lord of the everlasting covenant.
(Isaiah 61:8)

10 Straight talking meets straight talking
Isaiah 65

Person-to-person communication is often fraught, and that can be true about person-to-person communication between people and God. In Isaiah 64, Israel has complained at Yahweh's inaction and hiddenness. 'You've got a nerve,' Yahweh retorts. 'You're the ones who've been hiding.' Their self-portrait in that previous chapter was disingenuous. Maybe they see themselves as worshippers of Yahweh. They certainly see themselves as deeply committed to their faith (hence the line about warning people to be wary of coming too near to them because of their consecrated state). But their expression of their faith is totally unacceptable to Yahweh.

They will pay for it. But Yahweh allows here more explicitly than usual for the possibility of distinguishing between the faithful and the faithless in the community. The faithless have surrendered any right to be designated 'my servants'. That expression applies only to people who dissociate themselves from the faithless. The prophecy's aim is thus to encourage the faithful and also to push the faithless to changing their ways, so that the coming judgement doesn't fall on them.

But yes, Yahweh is to intervene positively in Jerusalem's life in the way that their prayer urged. And the fruit of that intervention will be 'a new heavens and new earth'. That doesn't denote a new cosmos. There's nothing wrong with the cosmos. The later lines in the prophecy make clear that creating a new heavens and new earth is an image for creating a new Jerusalem, where the problems about human life in the present Jerusalem are put right. At the moment, babies die in infancy and people who survive to grow to adulthood die by middle age. Then, the person who might have died as a youth will live to a hundred, while the sinner who lives to a hundred instead of dying young as he should will still die and be humiliated. People will build houses and live in them and plant vineyards and live in them, instead of leaving the houses and the vineyards to the next generation. Flocks will be safe from wild animals and people will be safe from attackers. Life will be more the way God intended from the beginning. And communication with God will be real instead of being short-circuited.

Thank you, Lord, that you are ready to be sought out by us, ready to be found by us.

11 The prophet who is told not to pray

Jeremiah 7

Jeremiah delivers his message in the Temple concourse in Jerusalem. It wasn't as large as the enclosure around the Dome of the Rock today, but it was similar in function in that its courtyards provided a natural meeting space. As is the case in the context of Jesus' ministry, it was a natural location for a preacher who wanted to be heard.

People think that the presence of Yahweh's Temple, the King's palace, in Jerusalem guarantees the city's security. What king is going to let his palace be destroyed, let alone is going to take an initiative to destroy it? The King of Israel is the answer. He's done it before. The sanctuary at Shiloh, north of Jerusalem, was once an important one. It was where Hannah prayed for a son and where Samuel was then based. But in Jeremiah's day it is evidently a ruin. And Jerusalem could go the same way if its people continue to live the way they are.

Even more shocking is the King's instruction to Jeremiah not to ask him to hold back from this action. A prophet mediates between King and people. He brings the King's words to the people, and he brings the people's words to the King. But Jeremiah is told not to speak to him. The King has heard enough about the life of the people Jeremiah represents. There's no basis for any more talk about giving them more time.

This doesn't mean Jeremiah has to agree and shut up. Maybe he will still insist on representing his people. We don't know. Bringing the people this frightening news that Yahweh has told him not to pray for them any more constitutes another attempt to get through their thick skulls. 'Can't you see: your attitude is so horrifying, I can't even pray for you any more? *Now* will you turn back to Yahweh?'

Jeremiah speaks more specifically about the way they are turning away. We know from archaeological discoveries that as well as making images of Yahweh, many people in Israel assumed that Yahweh had a consort, as the Canaanites would assume a god would have, and they prayed to her, too. They're offending Yahweh, of course. They're also hurting themselves.

We will obey your voice; we will be your people: be our God!
(Jeremiah 7:23)

213

12 The potter and the clay

Jeremiah 18

One might have thought that clay was simply malleable raw material that a potter can shape at will. Yet, like wood or stone that a sculptor works, it can seem to have a mind of its own, so it's the potter who may find himself having to be flexible as he does his work. He doesn't throw the resistant clay away, but he does roll it up and start again. The insight that comes to Jeremiah in the potter's workshop isn't that Israel *must* be clay in the potter's hand. It's that Israel *is* clay in the potter's hand, so it had better get used to the idea.

It might seem that sovereignty would imply inflexibility, and politics speaks as if changing your mind is a weakness. It suggests you didn't foresee the factors you should have taken into account in making your decision. The Bible sees it a different way. It's happy with the idea that there's an interaction between divine sovereignty and human reaction. It implies that when someone (like God) is confident about his ultimate sovereignty, he can afford to be flexible and to take the long view. That assumption makes sense of Israel's history and of the Church's history, which don't look as if they're simply the outworking of an ideal divine plan.

Translations sometimes speak of God 'repenting', which would be odd, as it would seem to imply that God had done something wrong, but 'relenting' or 'having a change of mind' better conveys the force of the Hebrew verb. Sometimes it can mean 'regretting', more in the sense of being sorry that one had to do something than in the sense of wishing one hadn't done it.

The 'response' of the clay, then, can lead to the potter relenting or having a change of mind about how to shape the clay, which is good news. All Judah has to do is turn back and God will change his mind about the threat of judgement. Even when Jeremiah reports the Judahites as saying that the situation is hopeless and that there's no way they're going to turn back to Yahweh, Jeremiah is seeking to break through to get them to change their mind.

You are the potter: as the clay, we submit ourselves to you to make something out of us.

13 The prophet's lament
Jeremiah 20

The division between chapters 19 and 20 looks odd, but it's illuminating. Jeremiah is capable of being confident and straight with a priest or a prophet who opposes his message, but it doesn't stop him being distraught about the ministry he has to fulfil. Yahweh drafted him against his will to preach a message about violence and destruction coming from Yahweh's hand. It put Jeremiah in a dangerous position in relation to people who didn't like his negativity. It also made him look stupid because his message failed to come true.

In bringing your experiences before God, however, you can find your understanding reframed. Although prayer is designed to change God, not you, it can also change you. The point is not that letting it all hang out makes you feel better. It's that bringing your experience before God can enable you to get a fresh angle on it, or to regain the angle you had before your troubles knocked you off balance. God enables you to see things a different way. You see the implications of God being part of the picture.

Here, Jeremiah realises afresh what God had told him, that God is with him even when it doesn't look like it, and that God will protect him. Jeremiah can therefore make the transition to praise that also appears at the end of psalms, on which he models his prayers. Sometimes psalms make that statement by faith, knowing God will make it true. Maybe Jeremiah also recognises that it has in fact been true. He's still alive and praying, after all.

Whichever way he means it, however, the next paragraph places him back where he was, or rather places him in an even worse position. Through these chapters that incorporate his prayers, his anguish gets deeper and deeper. It here reaches its lowest point. The chapter closes with no word from Yahweh and no statement of hope or faith. It thus follows the model of other psalms that make no transition to hope or praise.

One can hardly fault Jeremiah. The experiences that he describes persist throughout his ministry, until the moment forty years after his original commission when some of his compatriots take him to Egypt by force, never to be heard of again.

Lord, be with your servants who are pressurised and attacked and tempted to give up.

14 The new covenant
Jeremiah 31

Rachel's tomb is not far from Jerusalem. Jeremiah pictures her having wept there as she watched her Ephraimite 'children' trudge off into exile (Matthew 2:18 will picture her weeping again). But Yahweh hasn't forgotten them, and he responds to Rachel's weeping. They're not gone for ever. Motherhood may cost a mother her life – it did Rachel. But her hard work won't be fruitless.

This chapter makes creative use of a verb that can mean turn, turn away, turn back and bring back. People turned away from Yahweh in order to turn to other deities or other political resources. Therefore Yahweh let them go. 'See how that works out for you, then.' But himself having the instincts of a Rachel, Yahweh can't finally let them go. He will bring them back to their own country.

There's no doubt that parents eat sour grapes and their children's teeth get set on edge, with that weird feeling around your gums when you eat something tart. The sins of parents get visited on the children all right. It's therefore strange that Jeremiah should say it won't happen any more. Maybe it's partly because he has to grant that people in his day are particularly paying a price for their parents' faithlessness. Jeremiah's promise is then that Jerusalem's fall in 587 BC doesn't set a pattern. Maybe it's partly because these children mustn't and won't make their parents' waywardness an excuse for what they themselves are. Every generation stands before God responsible for its destiny. If it turns back to God, God responds. No, God doesn't punish the children for their parents' sins irrespective of their own response to God.

Alongside that promise and related to it is the promise of the new covenant. How will God achieve the inner change he wants to see? Maybe the answer lies in the closing line of the promise, in the statement about God pardoning their wrongdoing. Being forgiven by someone is a powerful thing. God intends to pardon the people's waywardness and restore them to their country. Maybe that has the power to change them? To some extent things did work out that way when God restored them and brought people back from exile and they were more faithful than they had been before.

Thank you, Lord, that your people are as secure as the sun by day and the moon by night.
(Jeremiah 31:35)

15 Yahweh's shadow side and his dominant side

Lamentations 3

We looked at Lamentations after reading the story of the fall of Jerusalem. Now we will look at another chapter at another appropriate point, following Jeremiah. He didn't compose Lamentations, as far as we know, but it would fit him.

Here, someone who can speak on behalf of the people of Jerusalem declares that he has seen affliction, seen the terrible trouble that has come on the city. And line after line of the poem has Yahweh as the subject of punitive action – he drove, he broke, he walled in, he shut out, he mangled.

Yet the speaker knows that Yahweh's afflicting is only half the story. When we go through tough experiences, the challenge is to own two sets of facts: the facts about the hard things that have happened and the facts about God's love and compassion that are still facts. It's easier to deny one set of facts: either to avoid facing the tough realities or to abandon the truths about God.

Lamentations insists on being real about both sets. It goes on from the facts about God's afflicting to the facts about God's commitment, compassion and steadfastness, which are 'new every morning'. The verses have inspired several hymns and songs, but people who sing these may not realise the dynamic of the words' setting, as affirmations made in the context of the experience of affliction.

Both evil things and good things (that is, blessing and trouble) can come from the one God. Yet whereas people sometimes picture God as equally balanced between love and justice, Lamentations declares that God isn't balanced in that sense. God's heart, God's dominant or major side, is commitment, compassion and steadfastness. At the very centre of the poem, which is itself the central of the five poems that make up Lamentations, it declares that God 'does not afflict from his heart' (verse 33). He has a shadow or minor side, a capacity to make himself act in judgement, and that does just as truly come from God. But it's from somewhere nearer the edge of God's character. His dominant side is love and compassion and commitment.

The poem in effect invites Judahites not to be so overwhelmed by God's recent abandonment that they forget the central nature of Yahweh.

Your steadfast love never ceases. Your compassion never comes to an end.

16 God shows up where you don't expect
Ezekiel 1

Meanwhile, in Babylonia... Ezekiel's community are people who had been transported there in 597 BC, and five years have now passed. Their feelings might parallel those expressed in Lamentations after the later fall of Jerusalem in 587 BC. But they have forfeited any right to expect anything from God.

Out of the blue, in a literal sense, Yahweh appears. Maybe Ezekiel sees a literal storm approaching, with wind, cloud and lightning. If so, Yahweh turns the literal storm into an appearance of his own cloud carriage. Yahweh is coming to his people in Babylonia, of all places.

There are limits to what God dares let Ezekiel see. Too direct an appearance of God would blind a mere human being. Mostly what God lets Ezekiel see is his carriage pulled by four creatures – not mere horses but combinations of human being, animal and bird (so they can fly and transport God through the heavens). Their combined features give them great manoeuvrability, as do the crisscross wheels on the carriages that can turn this way or that way. But they're driven by one will.

The creatures support a platform on which there stands a throne; on the throne is a human-like figure. Ezekiel is looking from below, so he sees little of the figure. His experience parallels that of Isaiah, who saw only the hem of God's robe (Isaiah 6:1). While God can be pictured as lion-like or rock-like, more often he is described as human-like. It links with the fact that human beings are made in God's image, to represent God in the world. Ezekiel's account further safeguards God's transcendence (it won't let people think of God in too human terms) by using the name Shadday, of which the traditional translation is 'Almighty' (though admittedly that is a guess). But the Hebrew word links with a verb meaning destroy, so Shadday might suggest destroyer.

It's also a solemn fact that the storm comes from the north. That's the direction in which people often locate God's abode. But it is also the direction from which invaders come. God's appearing to Ezekiel is both good news and solemn news. For Ezekiel's audience and for people reading his messages in written form, it also indicates that we'd better take his words seriously.

You are the Lord, the Almighty, potentially the destroyer.

17 Yahweh prepares to leave Jerusalem
Ezekiel 10 – 11

Ezekiel has another vision of God in his glory, now in the Temple in Jerusalem. The horror of this vision when he relates it is that God's presence is pulling out from the Temple and the city. This glorious presence has already moved to the Temple threshold. Now the creatures take off from the threshold and hover over the city, to the east, over the Mount of Olives. Ezekiel notes now that the 'creatures' in that earlier vision can be identified as 'cherub[s]', but biblical cherubs are not 'cherubic'.

The link with the vision that led into his commission as prophet suggests that there might be some good news as well as some bad news. The appalling prospect is that Yahweh is abandoning the Temple in Jerusalem, but he isn't simply going off no one knows where. Indeed, at the moment he is lingering just across from the city. There's still a possibility that he might stay.

But the departure of Yahweh's splendour is a horrifying event that hangs over Jerusalem, which (we know with hindsight) will become a reality in four or five years' time. The city will fall; the Temple will be destroyed. If the community does not turn back to Yahweh, people in Jerusalem and people already in Babylonia need to prepare for it in their thinking. An encouragement to Judahites in Babylonia is the fact that Yahweh isn't merely moving away from Jerusalem to reside somewhere inaccessible and unidentifiable in the wilderness. He has already become a small-scale sanctuary for them.

These exiles may have thought about building a sanctuary in Babylon, and may have done so, but Yahweh speaks not of dwelling in a sanctuary there but of *being* a sanctuary there. He is present there, even though there's no building. In a sense there's nothing new here. Israelites never assumed that Yahweh was only present in the Temple (which would mean most of them could hardly ever be in his presence). There was a special guarantee of his presence there, but he was present throughout the country, and also present in Babylonia. Being in Jerusalem doesn't guarantee that people are in Yahweh's presence, and being in Babylonia doesn't rule out being in Yahweh's presence.

We thank you, Lord, that if the usual signs of your presence disappear, it doesn't mean you are not there.

18 Dem bones, dem bones, dem dry bones
Ezekiel 37

The city has now fallen and the Temple has been destroyed, and it's hard for Judahites in Jerusalem or in Babylonia to imagine that they have any future. When Israelites roll away the stone from the family tomb because someone in the family has died, they can see how all that remains of people who died earlier is their dry bones. That fact provides a metaphor for the community's understanding of itself. Its hope is perished. While Ezekiel may include an allusion to their subjective hope (the hope they feel), he's at least as concerned about their objective hope. They're finished as a people. They have no future.

It's regularly a prophet's job to disturb the comfortable and comfort the disturbed. Prophets exist to disagree with their people. When his people thought they had a future, Ezekiel's job was to tell them they had none. Now they think they have no future, his job is to tell them that they have one. They feel like a people who are dead and buried. OK, says God, I shall open your graves and bring you back to life. Ezekiel is not talking about the resurrection of individuals but the resurrection of the nation. When the people of God seems to be finished, it's not finished.

The Hebrew word *ruah* means wind, breath and spirit. By 'spirit', it denotes the dynamic life power inherent in a person, which finds expression in dynamic action. It suggests extraordinary, forceful liveliness. So the same word can mean wind, a mysterious embodiment of extraordinary, forceful power; it's invisible, yet it can fell a tree. And because spirit suggests dynamic life power, the same word means breath, the mysterious movement of air that's much less dramatic yet also vital and life-giving; if there's no breath, there's no life.

In this vision, Ezekiel sees the remains of a defeated army scattered over a plain, their bones glistening white in the sun. There's no prospect of this army ever fighting again. But he's told to preach to the bones, which is silly. He's to tell them that Yahweh is going to reconstitute them as bodies and then put *ruah* into them so that they're living bodies, He prophesies and it happens. They stand up, an army ready to fight again.

Lord, you know. And you have dynamic life-giving power.

19 The big mouth is silenced
Daniel 7

Daniel was in Babylonia, like Ezekiel, but this vision covers the sequence of empires that unfold over four succeeding centuries, beginning with Babylon and ending with Greece. The original Greek 'animal' was Alexander the Great. He died in 323 BC when he was still only thirty-two, and his empire broke up and came under the rule of his generals.

In the 160s BC, Judah was under the control of one of these domains, based in Syria. The king was now Antiochus IV, who called himself Epiphanes; the title suggested he was a manifestation of God. Truly he spoke things against the God who is actually the One on High. The Judahites didn't endear themselves to him by wheeling and dealing about who was to be high priest, while also playing the Syrians to the north against the Egyptians to the south. The Judahites' seditiousness eventually led Antiochus to impose direct rule. He 'made war on the holy ones and overcame them' and banned worship in accordance with the Torah.

This vision promises one of those moments when God intervenes. Its climax describes a scene in God's heavenly court. God is pictured as an august senior figure. Another human figure is presented to him and is given supreme authority in the place of the four empires. The Aramaic expression for 'one like a human being' is literally 'one like a son of man', which is a poetic way of saying 'human being'. Later Jewish thinking pictured this 'human being' or 'son of man' as an actual individual, which is part of the background to the use of the expression 'Son of Man' in the Gospels. But here the person like a human being stands for 'the people of the holy ones on high'. God has decided for this people and not for Antiochus's empire, symbolised by the small horn.

Antiochus stayed in control of Jerusalem for a little over three years, from 167 to 164 BC, but then the Judahites rebelled. You wouldn't have bet on the Judahites, but they won. Antiochus's forces fled. For the first time for centuries, Judah was free. It didn't get everything that the vision pictured, but it did get something spectacular, a first instalment of a final fulfilment that will come one day.

You are the Most High, the one who has lived from eternity and will fulfil his purpose.

20 A time of anguish and a time of deliverance

Daniel 11 – 12

In the context of that same crisis, there were people who stayed faithful to God and to the Torah, and people who didn't. You had to decide which side you were on. In the last part of this last vision in Daniel, the description of the way the crisis will reach a climax takes up imagery from passages in the Prophets and the Psalms. It's not a literal prediction of what will happen. It compares with the book of Revelation, which doesn't paint a literal description of things but takes up Old Testament imagery – including Daniel's! – in order to describe them.

This is the only passage in the Old Testament promising that many people who have died will come back to life. Like the New Testament's promises, it involves a bringing back to life that will mean new life for some but a second death for others. The background is a sense that God can hardly leave unresolved a situation in which faithful people have been martyred and faithless people have got away with their unfaithfulness. The vision promises that things won't stay like that. The faithful will be vindicated and honoured, the faithless exposed.

The timing envisaged by the revelation corresponds to that envisaged earlier – a time, two times and half a time. You wouldn't be compelled to take this formula to denote three and a half years, but when the crisis did last that kind of time, you could hardly resist the temptation to see a link. The subsequent references to 1,290 days and 1,335 days fit that inference, but we don't know what exactly these figures refer to. Perhaps they correspond to stages in the unfolding and resolution of the crisis.

As far as we know, people didn't actually come back from the dead after the city's deliverance from Antiochus. Yet evidently Judahites were impressed enough by the correspondence in principle between the promise of deliverance and the event of deliverance that they recognised this vision as a divine revelation. Once again, God's great act of deliverance doesn't bring the actual end of everything, but it does bring an instalment of the end, and a confirmation that God's ultimate purpose will find fulfilment.

Yes, Lord, you are the one who keeps your promises and will bring about the fulfilment of your purpose.

21 The persisting nature of a mother's love
Hosea 11

Whereas Yahweh speaks elsewhere as a betrayed husband, here he speaks as a betrayed mother. Perhaps Hosea learned from his wife Gomer how a mother feels about her son. Whereas a husband can divorce his wife, it's harder for a mother to divorce her children. Whatever they do, they remain her children. So Yahweh is torn between refusing to have anything else to do with his children and yielding to the instinct to comfort them, like a mother.

Perhaps the comfort will need to be the kind that a mother gives after severely chastising her children. We don't know much about Admah or Zeboim except that they were near Sodom and Gomorrah and were devastated, like those cities (see Deuteronomy 29:22). How could Yahweh treat Ephraim as if it were an obscure place like those?

God cannot do it because he is the Holy One, not a human being. Our human instinct is to act in wrath when we have been deceived, let down and betrayed. And people often make God in their image and assume that God is the same. Does being the Holy One mean God is austere and tough and certain to act in wrath? This belief isn't exactly wrong, but Hosea turns such logic on its head. The holiness of Yahweh lies in his refraining from acting in wrath because of our faithlessness.

But he may not refrain for ever. Maybe we have to see God as combining a mother's finding that it is impossible to divorce her children and a father's capacity to discern when throwing them out becomes necessary (of course, those are gender stereotypes and they may work the other way around).

The last lines of the chapter would fit with that, because they presuppose that actually God will throw Ephraim out, but also that this will not be the end of the story. They promise another expression of Yahweh's comfort. Exile will come, but people will at last follow Yahweh, and Yahweh will bring them back to their country. Yahweh's roaring like a lion will make them tremble and thus submit to him, but the lion will be mainly concerned to roar against the overlords in the countries from which he's bringing them home.

You loved us, you summoned us, you taught us to walk, you healed us, you led us.

22 The years the locust has eaten

Joel 2

Judah's crops have been devastated by a locust epidemic. It's as if Judah has been subject to invasion by imperial powers, to its people's slaughter and to its communities' destruction and displacement. Of course, it has been, in the past. And the trauma of the locust invasion brings back to life the trauma of invasion. Prophets were accustomed to describing that kind of event as the arrival of the day of the Lord.

Here, Joel superimposes the description of an invading army on the description of invading locusts. An insect epidemic might seem trivial compared with an enemy invasion, but the implications of a locust invasion are in their own way as devastating as the implications of a military invasion. But when people re-experience trauma, even a trivial experience can trigger a reaction like the one caused by the original experience.

By portraying the locust invasion in this way, Joel heightens the impact of his message, and heightens the impact of his exhortation concerning the appropriate reaction. The reaction needs to be more than a formal gesture such as ripping one's clothes. It needs to involve fasting, weeping and lamenting, and also the turning of the inward person. It needs to involve the whole person, inward and outward.

Joel heightens the power of his appeal by pointing out some key aspects of who Yahweh is. Turning to him can be done in hope because Yahweh is 'gracious and compassionate, long-tempered and vast in commitment'. Joel picks up Yahweh's own self-description in Exodus 34:6, and thus reminds Judah about some basics of its knowledge of God. While Joel has assumed that Yahweh was in control of the locusts, he hasn't emphasised that fact – it's the horror of their action that he has stressed. So he hasn't talked about the disaster as an act of judgement. But whatever its cause, Yahweh's revelation of himself means they can turn to him, and they need to.

Yahweh goes on to promise more than Joel explicitly bids people ask. Yahweh will repay them for the years the locust has eaten. Joel can pass on to the people the good news that Yahweh has heard their prayer and said 'Yes' to it. And he will pour out his spirit over them.

Lord, you are indeed gracious and merciful, slow to anger and abounding in steadfast love.

23 When the exercise of authority becomes poisonous

Amos 5

The exercise of authority is designed to protect community and individual by providing a way of resolving conflicts. The elders gather at the city gate, and when there's a dispute, they listen to the case and resolve it. It's a great theory that looks as if it might have advantages over the Western system, but it's just as amenable to being perverted by human selfishness. The exercise of authority can turn to poison.

At the beginning of this chapter, Amos tries a rhetorical manoeuvre, taking the form of a mourning song over someone who's died. The audience wonders who's died, and realises the answer is that they have. Amos is mourning the death of the community, which he wants them to see is inevitable unless they change.

Then he speaks like a priest inviting people to come to Yahweh to seek what they need. But merely going to a worship service doesn't count. Seeking Yahweh has to be expressed in seeking good. The words good and evil are nicely ambiguous. If the community seeks what's morally good, it will experience good in the form of blessing. If it seeks what's morally evil, it will experience evil in the form of trouble.

Amos's reference to the day of the Lord is the first one in the Scriptures, but the idea is evidently familiar to people. That day will be when Yahweh's purpose is fulfilled and people experience the fullness of his blessing. That experience would naturally include the crushing of their oppressors. On Yahweh's day the superpower will get put down.

Amos turns such ideas on their head. The nature of Ephraim's life means that the day when Yahweh's purpose is fulfilled and evil is put down will be when Ephraim itself is crushed, not when it's blessed. They think worship is so important, but Amos reminds them that at the beginning of their story as Yahweh's people, when they were still on their way to settled life, they had no permanent sanctuary where they could sing praise to Yahweh morning and evening. The relationship between Yahweh and the people can survive the absence of singing and offerings. It can't survive the absence of the faithful exercise of authority, which needs to 'roll'.

Give us grace to seek you and to seek good, Lord.

24 'Who could bring me down to earth?'
Obadiah

The time is long after Amos, and the exile of Judah has happened. But Obadiah links with the ending of Amos, where Amos refers to Edom, Israel's neighbour to the southeast. Israel was aware of a family link with Edom. Israel traced its ancestry back to Jacob and traced Edom's ancestry back to Jacob's big brother Esau – hence Obadiah's references to Esau.

The prophets refer a number of times to Edom's wrongful treatment of Judah. We don't have Edom's version of events, but it's plausible to think of the Babylonians engaging Edomite support in their attack on Jerusalem and to imagine Edom having an eye to the main chance for itself. More certainly, the exile and succeeding decades saw gradual Edomite occupation of Judah's southern territory.

Yahweh's promise through Obadiah is that Edom's takeover of Judahite land won't continue for ever. As Mary puts it (Luke 1), lifting up the people who have been down has as the other side of the coin putting down the people in power. Obadiah draws attention to two of Edom's assets that it won't be able to rely on. One is its mountainous position. The other is its learning, for which it has a reputation that in theory finds expression in practical expertise.

Edom's being a thorn in Judah's side might be enough to explain Obadiah's focus on Edom. But later, Edom becomes a cipher for a nation that opposes Yahweh's purpose and Yahweh's people, such as Rome (like Babylon in the New Testament). The transition to talk about 'the nations' toward the end of the prophecy hints at a similar understanding (the drink to which Obadiah refers is a cup of poison).

Similarly, Obadiah generalises the promises concerning Judah. Judah is a sad little people, under pressure from all sides. It could seem to have no future. Yahweh promises it has one. It will regain its land on all sides. In this period, Ephraim or Samaria is a grey area – the people there might claim to be worshippers of Yahweh, but the Judahites aren't sure they could be trusted religiously or politically. The renewed Israel will embrace them, too.

But the last word concerns Yahweh's reigning in the world. Not Edom, not Judah, not Israel, not a Davidic king, but Yahweh.

Yes, Lord, the kingdom, the kingship, the rule is going to be yours.

25 Let's go up to Yahweh's mountain!
Micah 4

The prophets think more in terms of people being attracted to Israel, being drawn to recognise that the true God is active there, than in terms of Israel going out to convince people that they should recognise this God. This way of thinking is expressed in Micah's vision of nations flocking to Jerusalem. The prophecy also appears in Isaiah 2; maybe it's original there, or maybe here, or maybe it wasn't associated with a specific prophet and it found its way into the collections of both prophets. Evidently God was happy with that development because it's so important.

Its opening phrase is commonly translated 'at the end of the days', which can give the impression that it explicitly refers to a time way after Micah's day. Actually, it's not looking that far forward. The preceding chapters have been depressing and have ended with Zion as a ploughed field. But, like the opening chapters of Isaiah, the book of Micah alternates warnings with promises. Perhaps there's an element of stick and carrot about the arrangement – people's response decides which type of future they experience. But most readers of the book of Micah will live after the disaster that fulfilled his earlier warnings, and the promise will encourage them with the assurance that God is still to achieve what the vision portrays.

Israel usually lived in the shadow of the world of nations that surrounded it, a divided, threatening and depressing world. It was in no position to make a difference in that world. The prophecy makes astonishing promises to it. God will be the one who makes a difference. God will do so by drawing the world to Jerusalem. Insofar as Israel had to do anything, it was simply to walk in the name of its God. Of course, there's an irony here, because that obligation was one that Israel found hard to fulfil.

Three 'now' prophecies that follow put us back in the middle of the pressures upon the city. Even in the midst of a life-threatening crisis, Judah is challenged not to be hopeless. If the nations think they'll have their way with Jerusalem, they'll find they have to rethink things. And Ms Zion is now to turn itself into an army that can stand firm.

We will walk in your name, Lord our God, for ever and ever.

26 The fall of the bloody city
Nahum

The time is a little after Micah's day and Judah is an underling of Assyria, which controls its relations with other peoples and extracts taxes for the privilege of being part of the Assyrian empire. Nahum declares that Assyria will fall. He was proved right, which will be one reason why his prophecies were included in the Scriptures.

Prophets such as Nahum give no encouragement to Judah to attempt violent resistance to Assyria. It's not because they think violence is wrong but because the task of the people of God is to trust in God and let him sort out its future. But they want to discourage their people from accepting their fate as inevitable. They want to encourage their people to live in hope. That is Nahum's aim.

The prophets can see a power such as Assyria as both God's agent and God's enemy. It's God's agent because it's God's means of chastising Israel for rebelling against God. But Assyria acts in this way not because it wants to serve God but because it wants to extend its power and wealth. Nahum declares that God's not one who simply sits on the side when an empire oppresses other peoples, even if it assures itself that it's also bringing benefits to the people it conquers.

Nahum takes up the style and some of the words from God's self-revelation in Exodus 34, where God declares himself to be gracious and forgiving, and points out that this revelation doesn't mean Yahweh is indifferent when nations behave in a way that demands redress. Yahweh has passion to arouse in those circumstances. How stupid to make plans against Yahweh! He also has an army to muster. Nahum may be referring to the army of another nation that Yahweh will marshal (in which case, the literal referent will be Babylon, which will in due course take on Assyria). But maybe more likely he's referring to Yahweh's heavenly forces.

Nahum actually names Assyria only once in his messages, and names Nineveh only twice. His prophecy thus lies open to being applied to other cities as well as Nineveh. If Jerusalem is also a bloody city, as the prophets say it is, the prophecy could apply to it...

Lord, we acknowledge that you are the passionate God who is slow to anger but doesn't acquit the guilty.

27 'You can't do that!'
Habakkuk 1

The time is similar to that presupposed by Nahum, when Assyria exercises oppressive rule over Judah. But Habakkuk's talk about violence and oppression suggests that his concern relates to Judah's own internal life.

A distinctive feature of Habakkuk is that it takes the form of a dialogue between the prophet and God. Habakkuk's opening protest parallels protests in the Psalms. Habakkuk protests not for himself but for people he sees being wronged, in a situation where he's in no position to do anything about it. Being a prophet doesn't give him power to take any action. Again, the protests in a psalm may presuppose that a prophet who hears the protester speaking in the Temple has the vocation of bringing a response from God. Here in Habakkuk it's explicit that God responds. Habakkuk is both the person who prays and the person who reports God's answer.

The response is that God intends to take action against the wrongdoing in the city. That's where the Chaldeans, the Babylonians, come in. They will invade Judah, besiege Jerusalem and eventually destroy the city. That might seem just as bad news for the victims of wrongdoing as for the wrongdoers themselves. But when it happened, at least it meant that the people in power were taken off into exile while the ordinary people were able to reclaim the land that the powerful people had swindled them out of.

Habakkuk has a different worry. His rejoinder to God's response first affirms some truths about God and acknowledges the good news in God's acting by means of Babylon, but he then points out that this action raises a further question. God's own words have pointed to the ruthless nature of the Babylonian military machine. Babylon in its military might is its own god. Can God simply use it as he says? Do two wrongs (the wrongdoing of the people in power in Jerusalem and the wrongdoing of the Babylonians) make a right? The Babylonians, too, are the faithless devouring the faithful. They're like people involved in fishing, who are amassing 'victims' in their dragnet.

Habakkuk declares his intention to wait to see how God will reply. God takes the point. He will deal with the Babylonians, too, in due course.

Lord, how long will we cry for help for the oppressed, and you do nothing?

28 In the midst
Zephaniah 3

Like Habakkuk, and again in about the same period, Zephaniah focuses on the community in Jerusalem. He begins once more from the degenerate aspects of the city's life. Here, a key motif is the expression 'in the midst' or 'from the midst', which comes more times in this chapter than in any other chapter in the Old Testament. Initially, it's another way of expressing Zephaniah's prophetic critique: the city's officials 'in its midst' are roaring lions. They're supposed to serve their people, but they consume them. They don't gnaw until morning: they eat up everything overnight.

In contrast, Yahweh 'in its midst' does the right thing in relation to people. He operates each day like a faithful leader, not a faithless one. It's both good news and bad news. If you want to see the implications, Yahweh says, think again about what I'm doing to those other nations. I thought you'd be sensible enough to learn the lesson and thereby avoid that fate, but you declined.

Zephaniah goes on to extend the parallel between what Yahweh will do to the nations and for Judah. It begins with what looks like the nations' total destruction, but then segues into talk of their speech being purified so that they call on Yahweh's name. Likewise, the devastating judgement on Judah will turn out not to be the end, because Yahweh will bring back survivors of his scattered people so that they too can bring their offerings to Yahweh. The judgement will turn out to be a cleansing that removes the powerful who are faithless and arrogant 'from your midst'. It will leave 'in your midst' a lowly and poor people who will live honourably in their relationships with one another.

So Yahweh, Israel's King, is 'in your midst', and you need no more be afraid of imperial powers such as Assyria. Yahweh your God being 'in your midst' is a basis for hope. Only here does the Old Testament apply the nouns 'rejoicing' and 'resounding' to Yahweh himself. He is celebrating with the uninhibited enthusiasm that Jerusalem shows at a festival. Yahweh being able also to hold his peace perhaps reflects the fact he no longer needs to rage at his people. If Yahweh will so rejoice over the city, it can surely rejoice itself.

Lord, you are in our midst!

29 A new splendour
Haggai 2

We've jumped a century forward. Jerusalem has fallen, then Babylon has fallen, and the people who were taken into exile there have been able to go back with a commission to rebuild the Temple, under the leadership of a prince from David's line and a high priest from Aaron's line. But it was hard for people to imagine the Temple's former glory returning. The answer to the question, 'How many of you saw that glory?' would be, 'Only a handful.' But everybody's parents had told them how glorious it was.

They have to remember a few things. There's the fact that the Lord of Hosts is with them. He's going to act. To put it another way, God's spirit is with them, as was the case at the exodus. That presence, too, meant not merely a feeling but a dynamic reality. The covenant that God sealed with them back then still holds. So they can have confidence that the work they put into rebuilding the Temple will be fruitful. The people need rebuilding, too, and Haggai goes on to that. The congregation can bring pure offerings into the Temple, but if they themselves aren't pure or the Temple building isn't pure, the impurity will spread to the offerings.

They already have evidence of Yahweh's fulfilling his promise of blessing. The tide has already turned. Haggai's final prophecy declares that this development is just a harbinger of blessing to come. Like David, Zerubbabel is Yahweh's chosen and Yahweh's servant, and Yahweh is going to treat him like the signet ring with which a king seals things.

Yahweh didn't make Persia fall in the lifetime of Haggai or Zerubbabel, nor did he make the second Temple more glorious than the first. Apparently, these facts didn't trouble the Judahites, who held on to Haggai's prophecies. They knew that prophets' messages were sometimes larger than life, for ill and for good. They did see the Temple rebuilt and reconsecrated, and they knew that Haggai's ministry had been decisively important in making it happen. There was thus no doubt that Yahweh called Haggai and worked through him. When Persia fell two centuries later, perhaps they said to one another, 'You see, Haggai was right that it would come, the same as he was right about the other things.'

You are the Lord of Hosts, and you are with us.

30 Plenty of guilt to go around
Zechariah 2 – 3

In the vision that comes to Zechariah, Haggai's contemporary, the young man is like a city employee who has to plan the rebuilding of the city's walls. Walls? What use are they, when the city will be growing so fast they can never keep up? And why do you need walls when you have God's protection and God's fire within?

There's a link between this promise of exponential growth and the words that follow. While some Judahites have returned to Jerusalem, others have stayed in Babylon, which might seem more attractive than returning to Jerusalem. Zechariah declares that it's not as safe as it might seem. Yahweh has not finished with Babylon. Judahites will find themselves scattering from there. They'd be wise to leave while they have the chance. Jerusalem, after all, is the city Yahweh chose. Babylon may have looked like the centre of the world. Actually, Jerusalem is.

In the second vision, Joshua is on trial. It's another prophecy in which Yahweh is meeting with his staff. Like the king in many traditional societies, he also functions as supreme court. Joshua is accused of being unclean. Perhaps Joshua stands for the priesthood; there are certainly priests who have been unfaithful to Yahweh. The question is, what's the court to do about this uncleanness?

Like a president, the King has the right to issue pardon, but some people think the King should take a tough line. There in the meeting is the official prosecutor who features in Job, whose task is to press charges, but maybe gets too enthusiastic about his responsibility. Yahweh has decided that this is one of those occasions when he must risk making an exception. Joshua is to be restored in his position as senior priest.

The accuser is right that the King has to be careful about issuing a royal pardon. But Joshua's pardon is a sign that the whole community can be pardoned. Yes, the re-establishment of the priesthood as a whole is a sign of God's grace and God's commitment. At the moment David's 'tree' is cut down, but Yahweh is going to make it produce a new Branch, and bring the new age when people will relax under their vine and fig tree.

Lord, we acknowledge you as the one who has the power to pardon, and uses it.

31 A full and frank exchange of views
Malachi 3 – 4

God and Israel could be pretty straight with each other. Mutual confrontation and questioning characterises Malachi. Here, the people have just now raised a familiar question: why doesn't God intervene, if he is supposed to be sovereign in the world?

'OK,' says God, 'I'll intervene, but you may not like it.'

Malachi warns Judah that God's acting to implement his righteous purpose in the world will be an uncomfortable experience for God's people, like smelting, even if this work will finally be positive.

There's a link with Yahweh's subsequent comment, 'I haven't changed,' and, 'You haven't come to an end.' Throughout Israel's story, Israel has been inclined to weary Yahweh by the way it has conducted its life. It's amazing that it continues in existence, but it does so, notwithstanding the chastisements and the cutting down to size. In other words, Judah hasn't changed, either. The Hebrew word for 'cheat' is similar to the name Jacob, who cheated Esau out of his birthright as firstborn.

Here's another complaint about God. Serving God doesn't get you anywhere. This time it leads into a description of an appropriate response when God doesn't act in the way we need. It's that people talk to one another. This is a different kind of talking from the complaining. It's talk by people who continue to be in awe of Yahweh. They don't hide from the reality of their hardship, but neither are they in danger of giving up on Yahweh. Yahweh can take a different stance toward them from the one he takes toward the people who have surrendered to cynicism. He takes steps to make sure they're not forgotten. Meanwhile, the first important thing to be mindful of is Moses' teaching (the Torah).

Solemnly, the last word in the Old Testament is *annihilation*. It's the word that most often refers to God's command to the Israelites regarding the annihilation of the Canaanites. But the Hebrew Bible tells people to repeat the verse about God sending Elijah, after this worrisome ending, so that the book ends on a note that affirms God's involvement with us. Yet people who are sure that they belong to God need the reminder that God's judgement starts with God's household (1 Peter 4).

Thank you that you are the God of justice and that you do not change.

Part 2

THE NEW TESTAMENT
FOR EVERYONE

TOM WRIGHT

August

SCENES FROM THE
LIFE OF JESUS

I The Word made flesh
John 1:1–18

Approaching John's Gospel is a bit like arriving at a grand, imposing house. Like many a grand house, the book has a driveway, bringing you off the main road, telling you something about the place you're getting to. The gateway to the drive is formed by the unforgettable opening words, 'In the beginning was the Word…' At once we know that we are entering a place that is both familiar and strange. 'In the beginning' – no Bible reader could see that phrase and not think of the opening words of the Old Testament. John wants us to see that this is about the creator God acting in a new way within his much-loved creation. It is about the way in which the long story that began in Genesis reached the climax the creator had always intended. And it will do this through 'the Word'. In Genesis 1, the climax is the creation of humans, made in God's image. In John 1, the climax is the arrival of a human being, the Word become 'flesh'.

When I speak a word, it is, in a sense, part of me. It's a breath that comes from inside me. And yet our words have a life that seems independent of us. When people hear them, words can change the way they think and live. Think of, 'I love you,' or, 'It's time to go,' or, 'You're fired.' These words create new situations. Similarly, in the Old Testament, God regularly acts by means of his 'word', and that's part of what lies behind John's choice of 'Word' here, as a way of telling us who Jesus really is.

But perhaps the most exciting thing about this opening passage is that we're in it too: 'To anyone who did accept him' (verse 12) – that means anyone at all, then and now. God wants people from everywhere to be born in a new way, born into the family he began through Jesus and which has since spread through the world.

Anyone can become a 'child of God' in this sense. Something can happen to people in this life that causes them to become new people, people who (as verse 12 says) have 'believed in his name'. Somehow the great drama of God and the world, of Jesus and Israel, of the Word who reveals the glory of the unseen God – this great drama is a play in search of actors, and there are parts for everyone, you and me included.

Lord, we thank you for coming to dwell with us in Jesus and inviting us to play our part as your adopted children.

2 The birth of Jesus
Luke 2:1–20

If you try to point out something to a dog, the dog will often look at your finger instead of at the object you're trying to point to. This is frustrating, but it illustrates a natural mistake we all make. It's the mistake many people make when reading the Christmas story in Luke's Gospel. What do people know about Jesus' birth? The manger – the Christmas crib. The most famous animal feeding-trough in all history. But to concentrate on the manger and to forget why it is mentioned is like the dog looking at the finger rather than the object. Why has Luke mentioned it three times in this story? The answer is: because the feeding-trough was the sign to the shepherds. It told them which baby they were looking for.

Why is that significant? Because it is the shepherds who are told *who this child is*. This child is the Saviour, the Messiah, the Lord. The manger isn't important in itself. It's a signpost, a pointing finger, to the identity of the baby boy who's lying in it.

We have to assume that the shepherds, like other Palestinian Jews at the time, would have known what a saviour, a messiah, a lord was to do. Luke has introduced the story by telling us about Augustus Caesar, way off in Rome, at the height of his power. Augustus was the adopted son of Julius Caesar and he turned the great Roman republic into an empire, with himself at the head. He proclaimed that he had brought justice and peace to the whole world; and, declaring his dead adoptive father to be divine, styled himself as 'son of god'. Augustus, people said, was the 'saviour' of the world. He was its king, its 'lord'. Increasingly, people worshipped him, too, as a god.

Meanwhile, far away, on that same eastern frontier, a boy was born who would within a generation be hailed as 'Son of God'; whose followers would speak of him as 'Saviour' and 'Lord'; whose arrival, they thought, had brought true justice and peace to the world. The point Luke is making is clear. The birth of this little boy is the beginning of a confrontation between the kingdom of God – in all its apparent weakness, insignificance and vulnerability – and the kingdoms of the world. So when you see the manger on a card, or in church, don't stop at the crib. See what it's pointing to: the baby lying there is already being spoken of as the true King of the world.

Jesus, Son of God, we worship and adore you as the true King of our world.

3 The boy Jesus
Luke 2:41–52

Perhaps the first remarkable thing about this story is that Mary and Joseph were happy to set off with their large group from Galilee without checking that Jesus was with them. That tells us a lot about the kind of world they lived in, where extended families of kinsfolk and friends lived together in close-knit mutual trust. But by the same token, once they had left Jerusalem, and when they returned to it without the rest of the party, the city was a large and potentially dangerous place, full of dark alleys and strange people, not a place where one would be happy to leave one's son for a few days.

The agony of Mary and Joseph, searching for three days, contrasts sharply with the calm response of Jesus when they found him. Mary blurted out an accusation, perhaps tinged with that mixture of guilt and relief that most parents will recognise. Instead of saying, as she might have, 'How could *I* have done this to *you*, leaving you behind like that?', she said, 'How could *you* do this to *us*?' Jesus accepted no blame, and indeed issued a gentle rebuke that speaks volumes, in Luke's portrait, for his own developing self-awareness.

'Your father and I,' said Mary, 'have been looking for you.'

Jesus replied, 'I have been busying myself in my Father's work.'

Some families today keep notebooks of the striking things their children come out with. Mary kept her notebook in her heart, and this remark in particular will have gone straight there with a stab.

As we read this story prayerfully, then, we can probably identify quite easily with Mary and Joseph – and perhaps with Jesus, too, quietly asserting an independence of mind and vocation, while still returning home and living in obedience. We may want to remember times when we thought we'd lost someone or something very precious. We may want to reflect on whether we have taken Jesus himself for granted; if Mary and Joseph could do it, there is every reason to suppose that we can too. We mustn't assume he is accompanying us. But if and when we sense the lack of his presence, we must be prepared to hunt for him, to search for him in prayer, in the Scriptures, in the sacraments, and not to give up until we find him again.

We must expect, too, that when we do meet him again, he will not say or do what we expect. He must be busy with his Father's work. So must we.

Lord, may we be devoted to you and to your work at all times.

4 Jesus' baptism and genealogy
Luke 3:21–38

The New Testament, surprisingly, presents us with not one but two quite different family trees for Jesus. Matthew begins his book with a list of names from Abraham to Jesus; Luke now includes a list of names working back from Jesus, through Abraham, to Adam and thence to God himself. And the odd thing is that the lists don't match. Even the name of Joseph's father is different. In any case, what is the point of a genealogy of *Joseph*, when both Luke and Matthew insist that he was not in fact Jesus' physical father?

Obviously, in a small and close-knit community, there is every probability that someone could trace their descent from the same source by two or more different routes. This is so even in modern Western society. After my own parents married, they discovered that they were distant cousins with one remove of generation. Think of the little country of Israel in the period between David and Jesus; similar things could easily have happened. Many could have traced their descent to the same ancestors by at least two routes.

For Luke, the link between the family tree and what goes before and comes after is the final phrase: Jesus is the Son of God. Perhaps it is best to see the family tree, stretching back to the creation of the world, as a way of saying that, though Jesus is indeed the Messiah of Israel, he is so precisely for the whole world.

This global scope to God's purposes is in the background as Jesus comes to the Jordan to be baptised by John. It's often suggested that the baptism was the moment when Jesus received his first inkling of a messianic calling, but this can hardly be correct; the voice from heaven comes to confirm and give direction to something that has been true all along. The Spirit and the word together give Jesus the encouragement and strength he needs to begin his short public career. They also give an indication of where that career will take him. The heavenly voice echoes words of Isaiah the prophet (42:1), commissioning the Messiah as the Servant, the one who will suffer and die for the people and the world. The voice is at the same time a wonderful affirmation of Jesus' vocation and a clear reminder of where it is to lead.

Father, send us your Spirit and bless us with the affirming love you bestowed on your beloved Son.

5 Temptation in the wilderness
Luke 4:1–13

Luke has just reminded us of Jesus' membership in the family of Adam. If there had been any doubt about his being really human, Luke underlines his sharing of our flesh and blood in this vivid scene of temptation. If Jesus is the descendant of Adam, he must now face not only what Adam faced but also the powers that had been unleashed through human rebellion and sin.

In particular, after his baptism, Jesus faced the double question: what did it mean to be God's Son? And what sort of messiahship was he to pursue? The three temptations can be read as possible answers to this question. The story does not envisage Jesus engaged in conversation with a visible figure; the devil's voice appears as a string of natural ideas in his own head. They are plausible, attractive and make, as we would say, a lot of sense. God can't want his beloved son to be famished with hunger, can he? If God wants Jesus to become sovereign over the world, then why not go for it in one easy stride? If Jesus is Israel's Messiah, why not prove it by spectacular displays of power?

Jesus responds to the devil by quoting Scripture. The passages he draws on come from the story of Israel in the wilderness: he is going to succeed where Israel failed. Physical needs and wants are important, but loyalty to God is more important still. Jesus is indeed to become the world's true Lord, but the path to that status, and the mode of it when it arrives, is humble service, not a devilish seeking after status and power. Trust in God doesn't mean acting stupidly to force God into performing a spectacular rescue. Jesus' status as God's Son commits him to the strange path of humility, service and finally death. The enemy will return to test this resolve again. For the moment, an initial victory is won, and Jesus can begin his public career knowing that, though struggles lie ahead, the foe has been beaten on the first field that really matters.

We are unlikely to be tempted in exactly the same way as Jesus was, but every Christian will be tested at the points that matter most. It is a central part of Christian vocation to learn to recognise the voices that whisper attractive lies, to distinguish them from the voice of God, and to use the weapons provided in Scripture to rebut the lies with truth.

Lord, help me to see through the lies and corruption that temptation offers, and to stay focused on your truth.

6 The healing of a paralysed man
Luke 5:17–26

This is the first time Luke has introduced us to the Pharisees, and here they are in force, from all over the small country. This may seem a bit excessive; why should they gather like this to check out a young prophet who is doing and saying strange things? The answer is that their particular cause was the coming kingdom of God; and if someone else appeared on the scene who seemed to be talking about the same thing *but was getting it all wrong*, they wanted to know about it.

The Pharisees' kingdom-plan was to intensify observance of the Jewish law, the Torah. That, they believed, would create the conditions for God to act: to judge the pagans who were oppressing Israel and to liberate his people. In addition, some of the more militant believed that it was their duty to use violence to kick-start the process of revolution. Jesus' kingdom-vision was very different.

Luke emphasises that Jesus was powerful, and that it was God's power at work in him. This, of course, was why people came in such numbers, and when the unwieldy little procession of people arrived at the door, carrying a paralysed friend on a makeshift stretcher or mattress, they couldn't get in. Jesus saw their resourcefulness in opening up the roof-tiles and letting him down as a sign that they really believed God was at work. Again and again, Jesus made a connection between faith and the power of God.

In fact, when people don't believe, they can look even at the evidence of their senses, as the Pharisees did that day, and still grumble. 'Your sins are forgiven': that did it. Only God can forgive sins, and the normal way he did it, within their system, was through the Temple and all that went on there – the sacrificial system, the rituals of cleansing. If anyone could speak for God, declaring to the people that God had forgiven their sins, it would be the Temple priests.

Jesus was slicing through all of that and declaring that this particular man was now right with God. It isn't so much that Jesus was 'claiming to be God'; he was claiming to *speak for* God, in a way that undercut the normal channels of authority. No wonder the crowds were amazed. The combination of healing, authority-claims and the sharp dispute with the Pharisees was beyond anything they'd known before.

When people come to Jesus today with even a grain of faith, the unexpected still can and does occur.

We thank you, Lord, that if we turn to you in faith, you will always hear us.

7 Water into wine

John 2:1–12

This is one of only two occasions when we meet Jesus' mother in this Gospel, the other being at the foot of the cross (chapter 19). This is important, because Jesus' strange remark in verse 4, 'My time hasn't come yet,' looks on, through many other references to his 'time', until at last the time does come and the glory is revealed fully as he dies on the cross. That event, for John, is the ultimate moment when heaven and earth meet. That is when it takes all the faith in the world to see the glory hidden in the shame: the creative Word present as a weak, dying human being.

But events like this one point on to that moment. The wedding is a foretaste of the great heavenly feast in store for God's people (see Revelation 21:2). The water-jars, used for Jewish purification rites, are a sign that God is doing a new thing from within the old Jewish system, bringing purification to Israel and the world in a whole new way.

The wedding itself, in the town where Nathanael comes from, would probably involve almost the whole village, and several people from neighbouring ones too; which is why Mary, her son and his friends have been invited. Running out of wine is not just inconvenient, but it is also a social disaster and disgrace. The family would have to live with the shame of it for a long time to come; bride and groom might regard it as bringing bad luck on their married life. Though Jesus hereafter addresses himself to other kinds of problems, we are already witnessing the strange compassion that comes when people are in need and he deals with that need in unexpected ways.

The transformation from water to wine is, of course, meant by John to signify the effect that Jesus can have, and can still have today, on people's lives. He came, as he says later, that we might have life in all its fullness (John 10:10).

You might want to pray through this story with your own failures and disappointments in mind – remembering that transformation only came when someone took Mary's words seriously: 'Do whatever he tells you.'

One final point. What do you think John is hinting at when he says that all this took place 'on the third day'?

Lord Jesus, we thank you for your life-transforming love.

8 Jesus and Nicodemus
John 3:1–13

Some people experience their entry into Christian faith as a huge, tumultuous event, with a dramatic build-up, a painful moment of decision and then tidal waves of relief, joy, exhilaration, forgiveness and love. They are then easily tempted to think that this moment itself is the centre of what it means to be a Christian, as though what God wants is simply to give people a single wonderful spiritual experience to be remembered ever afterwards with a warm glow.

But that's a bit like someone framing their birth certificate, hanging it on the wall and insisting on showing it to everyone who comes into the house. What matters for most purposes is not that once upon a time you were born, but that you are alive *now*, and that your present life, day by day and moment by moment, is showing evidence of health and strength and purpose.

So when Jesus talks to Nicodemus about new birth, we shouldn't suppose this means that we should spend all our time thinking about the moment of our own spiritual birth. It matters that it happened, of course. But where there are signs of life, it's more important to feed and nurture it than to spend much time going over and over what happened at the moment of birth.

In fact, what Jesus says here to Nicodemus is more sharply focused than we sometimes imagine. The Judaism that Nicodemus and Jesus both know has a good deal to do with *being born into the right family*. What matters is being a child of Abraham. Of course, other things matter too, but this is basic. Now Jesus is saying that God is starting a new family in which this ordinary birth isn't enough. You need to be born all over again, born 'from above'.

The new birth Jesus is talking about is the same thing that has been spoken of in John 1:33. 'Water and spirit' here must mean the double baptism: baptism in water, which brings people into the kingdom-movement begun by John the Baptist and continued by Jesus' disciples (John 3:22; 4:1–2), and baptism in the Spirit, the new life, bubbling up from within, that Jesus offers. As with John 1:12–13, the point is that God's kingdom is now thrown open to anyone and everyone. The Spirit is on the move, like a fresh spring breeze, and no human family, tribe, organisation or system can keep up with it.

Lord, let us move with your Spirit, and so help us grow stronger each day in your love and grace.

9 The woman of Samaria
John 4:1–15

Samaria is the name given to the land in between Galilee to the north and Judaea to the south. Jesus and his followers are travelling through Samaria, and there, in the heat of the day, Jesus finds himself alone by Jacob's well, when along comes a woman.

Now, in that culture, many devout Jewish men would not have allowed themselves to be alone with a woman. If it was unavoidable, they would certainly not have entered into conversation. The risks, they would have thought, were too high – risk of impurity, risk of gossip, risk ultimately of being drawn into immorality. And yet Jesus talks to this woman.

The woman is, of course, a Samaritan. Ever since some of the Jewish exiles had come back from Babylon to find that the central section of their ancient territory was occupied by a group who claimed to be the true descendants of Abraham, and who opposed their return, there had been constant trouble. Sometimes it had broken out into actual skirmishes. But mostly it was simply a matter of not mixing. The Jews wouldn't have anything to do with the Samaritans. They would, especially, not share eating and drinking vessels with them. And yet Jesus asks this woman for a drink.

In doing so, Jesus tells the woman that *she* should have asked *him* for one. She is, of course, bound to think he means it in the ordinary sense. The clue that he doesn't is found in the phrase '*living* water'. What Jesus says about this water makes it clear that he's talking about something quite different, something for which all the water on earth is just a signpost. Not only will the water he's offering quench your thirst so that you'll never be thirsty again, but it will also become a spring bubbling up inside you, refreshing you with the life of the whole new world God is making. Later, Jesus will say something like this again, and John will explain that he's referring to the Spirit (John 7:37–9). Here the promise remains teasing, cryptic and puzzling.

But it's enough for the woman. She doesn't know exactly what he's talking about, but she wants to know more. What other meanings she might be thinking of, we cannot now fathom. But she's in for a shock – as is everyone who starts to take Jesus seriously. He has living water to offer all right, but when you start to drink it, it will change every area of your life.

Lord, may we drink deeply from the well of your Spirit and be refreshed on our journey.

10 Opposition to Jesus in Nazareth
Luke 4:14–30

'Inspiration': we use the word loosely. We imply that 'it just came over them', that they suddenly became someone different. Of course, we know that it doesn't happen like that. The brilliant athlete has been training and practising, week after week. The musician has been playing exercises, perfecting technique for long hours. Then, when the moment comes, a surge of adrenalin produces a performance we call 'inspired' – but is actually the fruit of long, patient, hard work.

When Jesus says, 'The spirit of the Lord is upon me,' Luke has already let us into the secret. His years of silent preparation. His life of prayer leading up to his baptism. The confirmation of his vocation – and then its testing in the wilderness. Now, with years of prayer, thought and the study of Scripture behind him, he stands before his own town. He knows everybody there and they know him. He preaches like a man inspired; indeed, in his sermon that's what he claims. But what he says is the opposite of what they were expecting. If this is inspiration, they don't want it.

What is so wrong with what he says? What makes them kick him out of the synagogue, hustle him out of the town and take him off to the cliff edge to throw him over? The crucial part comes in Jesus' comments to his hearers. He senses that they aren't following him; they are ready to taunt him with proverbs, to challenge him to do some mighty deeds for the sake of show. By way of defence and explanation, Jesus points out what happened in the days of the great prophets Elijah and Elisha, and in doing so identifies himself with the prophets. Elijah was sent to help a widow – but not a Jewish one. Elisha healed one solitary leper – and the leper was the commander of the enemy army. That's what does it. That's what drives them to fury. Israel's God was rescuing the wrong people.

The earlier part of Jesus' address must have been hammering home the same point. This message was, and remains, shocking. Jesus' claim to be reaching out with healing to all people, though itself a vital Jewish idea, is not what most first-century Jews want or expect. Here, as at the climax of the Gospel story, Jesus' challenge and warning brings about a violent reaction. The gospel still does this today, when it challenges all interests and agendas with the news of God's surprising grace.

Lord, may we always remember that your saving grace extends to all people, including to those we may disdain or even count as enemies.

11 Jesus' authoritative healings
Luke 4:31–44

The little town of Capernaum, a fishing village on the north shore of the sea of Galilee, had never seen anything like it. Jesus had evidently decided to make it his base of operations after he'd left Nazareth. It was where the two pairs of brothers, Peter and Andrew, and James and John, had their homes and their small fishing businesses.

You can still walk into the ruined synagogue there, where some of Jesus' first remarkable healings took place. The buildings you can see date from some while after Jesus' time, but it's the correct site and you can get a sense of it all: a small town, gathering in its main public meeting-place. That's where we find Jesus' first encounter with a shrieking, yelling, demon-possessed man.

Many people in the modern world don't believe in demons. They are inclined to say that this sort of thing was simply a medical condition that people hadn't diagnosed in Jesus' day. Many others, however, in several parts of today's world, know only too well that strange forces seem able to invade a personality so that the person talks with a strange voice and has a peculiar, one might say haunted, look in the eye. It's more than just an illness of the mind, though some of the signs are similar. And sometimes people in that condition seem to know things that nobody else does.

Whatever we say about such a condition, there is no historical doubt that Jesus dramatically healed a good many people who were regarded as 'possessed'. Such cures were not unusual. Elsewhere in the Gospels, and in Acts, we find mention of exorcists working from within Judaism. But the strange thing about Jesus, here and elsewhere, is that he did what he did by simple commands. He just told the spirits to go, and they went. That was what astonished people. He didn't have to summon up stronger powers than his own; he just used the authority he already possessed in himself.

Once again, Luke wants us to recognise what all this is saying about Jesus. Those with special insight can see behind his work and teaching, where he appeared to most people as a prophet. He was 'the Son of God', here in the sense of 'the Messiah'. He was God's anointed. The Lord's Spirit was indeed resting on him, as he said at Nazareth, to release the oppressed, to give sight to the blind, to loosen the chains of the prisoners.

Lord, we thank you for the saving power of your Spirit – then and now!

12 Jesus calls the disciples
Matthew 4:18–25

If you go to Galilee today, you could well be shown a boat that might have belonged to Andrew and Peter, or perhaps the Zebedee family. The boat is a vivid reminder of the day-to-day existence of Jesus' followers – and of what it cost them to give it all up and follow Jesus. They were, in today's language, small businessmen, working as families not for huge profits but to make enough to live on and have a little left over. Fish were plentiful and there were good markets. In a cosmopolitan area, with soldiers, wayfarers, pilgrims and pedlars coming and going, as well as the local population, people would always want what they were selling. But it was hard work, and sometimes dangerous. Their lives were modestly secure, but hardly luxurious.

So why did they give it all up to follow a wandering preacher?

The same question faces people today. Why did this person give up a promising legal career to become a preacher, throwing away a lifetime of high earnings for the insecurity and relative poverty of pastoring and teaching a church? Why did that person abandon her remarkable gift as a singer in order to study theology and be ordained? Why did this person become a teacher, that one a prison governor, this one a monk, that one a missionary? And – since these more obvious callings are only the tip of the iceberg of Christian vocation – why do Christians in millions of other walks of life regularly give up lifestyles and practices that look attractive and lucrative in order to maintain honesty, integrity, faith, hope and love?

The answer can only be in Jesus himself, and in the astonishing magnetism of his presence and personality. This can be known and felt today, as we meditate on the stories about him and pray to know him better, just as the first disciples knew and felt his presence two thousand years ago. Sometimes his call comes slowly, starting like a faint murmur and growing until we can no longer ignore it. Sometimes he calls people as suddenly and dramatically as he called Peter and Andrew, James and John. When that happens to you, by whatever means and at whatever pace, you will know. Jesus has a way of getting through, and whatever we are engaged with – whatever nets we are mending or fish we are catching – somehow we will be sufficiently aware of his presence and call to know what it is we're being asked to do.

Be with us, Lord, and show us the path you are calling us to follow.

13 Sheep among wolves
Matthew 10:16–23

Jesus knew that he was running into opposition. It hadn't come as a surprise. He knew that the agendas his contemporaries were following, particularly those who were eager for violent revolution against Rome, were diametrically opposite to the message he was advocating. Now he has the difficult task of warning the disciples that it's going to happen to them, too.

Those of us who live in the Western world have become used to living in a tolerant society. We don't expect people to haul us off into court for what we believe. We don't expect to be beaten up because we speak about Jesus. But Jesus' message was truly revolutionary, and like all true revolutionaries he and his followers were regarded as very dangerous.

The story of the early church bears out Jesus' solemn warnings. The disciples were indeed persecuted, beaten, imprisoned and killed. The message of Jesus did indeed divide one family from another, and even split up parents from their children, brothers from brothers and sisters from sisters. But Jesus doesn't think it will take very long for all this to happen. Though he's sending them out urgently now, the strange event which he refers to as the coming of the Son of Man will happen all too soon.

What exactly Jesus meant by this has been much discussed and puzzled over. Some have thought that it refers to Jesus' second coming, but this is unlikely. The phrase echoes Daniel 7:13, where the coming of the Son of Man is not his coming from heaven to earth, but his coming from earth to heaven: exalted, after suffering, to be the judge and ruler of the world. What seems to be meant here is that the disciples will face harsh persecution, but eventually God's judgement will fall on those who oppose them. In particular, it will fall on Jerusalem, which will reject Jesus and his gospel. When that happens, they will be 'rescued' or 'delivered', because this means that 'the Son of Man' has been vindicated, has 'come' to his father (see Matthew 16:27).

Faced with this awesome challenge, Jesus' sharp advice to his followers was to be shrewd like snakes, but innocent like doves. Christians often find it easy to be one or the other, but seldom both. Without innocence, shrewdness becomes manipulative; without shrewdness, innocence becomes naivety. Though we face different crises and different problems from those of the first disciples, we still need that finely balanced character, reflecting so remarkably that of Jesus himself.

Lord, help us to hold a balance between shrewdness and innocence in our lives, just as Jesus did.

14 Jesus calms the storm
Mark 4:35–41

Behind stories like this, Mark's readers would probably have heard older echoes. Think, for example, of the Psalms that speak of the creator God who rules the sea, telling its rough and threatening waves to quieten down (e.g. Psalm 65:7; 89:9; 93:3–4; 107:23–30).

Apart from fishermen, the Jews were not a seafaring people; they left that to their Phoenician neighbours to the north. The sea came to symbolise, for them, the dark power of evil, threatening to destroy God's good creation. In books like Daniel, the sea is where the monsters come from.

So when Jesus rescues the disciples from a storm, we are witnessing something that says, in concrete terms, that God's sovereign power is being unleashed; that is, God's kingdom is at hand. It isn't like people thought it would be, but this is the real thing. It's the same power that made the world. And this power is now living in Jesus and acting through him. Just as in Daniel 7 the monsters who have come up from the sea are finally put to flight by 'one like a son of man' (Daniel 7:13), so here Jesus assumes the role of God's agent in defeating the forces of chaos.

The forces of evil are roused, but Jesus is so confident of God's presence and power that he can fall asleep. The disciples are cross: doesn't he care that the boat is about to go to the bottom and take them with it? Jesus quizzically reverses the question, putting them on the spot: don't you yet have faith?

Imagine this as a blockbuster film – it would need a big screen to do it justice – and you are auditioning for a part. Make it *your* story. Actually, if you sign on with Jesus for the kingdom of God, it will become your story whether you realise it or not. Wind and storms will come your way. The power of evil was broken on the cross and in the empty tomb, but, like people who have lost their cause and are now angry, that power still has a shrill malevolence about it.

Mark's first readers probably knew that better than most of us. They would have identified easily with the frightened men in the boat. That's Mark's invitation to all of us: OK, go on, wake Jesus up, pray to him in your fear and anger. And don't be surprised when he turns to you, as the storm subsides, and asks when you're going to get some real faith.

Lord, give us faith to trust in your salvation whenever the sky is dark and the storms gather.

15 The healing of the demoniac
Mark 5:1–20

The politics of Jesus' day were every bit as complicated as those of our own. After the death of Herod the Great in 4 BC, when the country was divided up between his sons, Philip got the bit to the northeast of the Sea of Galilee. But the bit to the southeast, where this story takes place, had never really been Jewish territory. The point for our purposes is clear: it wasn't Jewish land, and the people weren't Jews. Why, if they had been, would they have been keeping pigs? Everyone knew the Jews regarded them as unclean.

While we're on about uncleanness, graveyards were also considered places of contamination. For Jews, contact with the dead, or with graves, made them unclean. The man who rushes out to meet Jesus is about as unclean as you could get.

For the century or so before Jesus' time, the whole area had been overrun by the Romans. The legions had marched in and taken over, as they did everywhere from Britain to Egypt. Whoever got in their way was crushed. A few people – local politicians, tax-collectors, call girls – did all right out of the Romans. Most people saw them as The Enemy. As satan incarnate.

And some people found that they were gripped by that evil force internally as well as externally. It seems as though this poor fellow had become, from one point of view, totally obsessed by the powers that had taken over his country; from another point of view, totally possessed by the troop of phantom invaders that had taken over his humanity.

So what was going to happen when the man who was announcing God's kingdom, God's sovereign rule over all human rule, came face to face with someone obsessed and 'possessed' by Rome and her unclean legions? God's kingdom is to bring healing, restoring justice to Israel and the world. If unclean beings are fouling up human lives, the answer is plain: into the sea with them.

This story shows that underneath the pain and injustice of political enslavement there is a spiritual battle. Leave that out and you simply go round the endless cycle of violence and counter-violence. Mark sees Jesus' kingdom-movement, which reached its climax in his death, as the means by which all earthly powers are brought to heel, even though the messengers of the kingdom may suffer in the process. Those who follow Jesus are now to put into practice the victory he achieved.

Lord, help us to bring your healing peace to people possessed by mental and physical pain today.

16 The woman with chronic bleeding
Mark 5:25–34

Jesus is on his way to a house where, as we already suspect, he will find a corpse. Thoughts of sorrow would mingle with the threat of impurity, since contact with a dead body is one of the chief sources of impurity in Jewish law. Here, on the other hand, is a woman who has chronic internal bleeding; one of the other main causes of impurity was bodily discharges and those who had them (especially women).

The woman's perpetual uncleanness (with all its consequences in her family and social life) explains her fear both of openly requesting help and then of being discovered after she's received it. But one of the most remarkable things about the story is the way in which Jesus knows at once that power has gone out of him.

Healing by touch, not least when the healer isn't expecting it, is such a strange phenomenon that we probably can't probe much further about how such things work. But they highlight for us the intimate nature of the contact between the individual and Jesus that Mark expects and hopes his readers to develop for themselves. When life crowds in with all its pressures, there is still room for us to creep up behind Jesus – if that's all we feel we can do – and reach out to touch him, in that odd mixture of fear and faith that characterises so much Christian discipleship.

Then the other odd thing: was it Jesus' power that rescued the woman, or her own faith? Clearly it was Jesus' power; but he says, 'Your faith has rescued you.' The answer must be that faith, though itself powerless, is the channel through which Jesus' power can work (compare Mark 6:5–6). He is not a magician, doing conjuring tricks by some secret power for an amazed but uninvolved audience. He is (though the onlookers don't yet realise this) God's Son, the one through whom the living God is remaking Israel, humans, the world. And faith, however much fear and trembling may accompany it, is the first sign of that remaking, that renewal, that new life.

Where are you in this story?

Lord, we thank you that despite our spiritual uncleanness you are there, ready to heal and save us.

17 The Syrophoenician woman
Mark 7:24–30

This very odd story has all the trappings of a dangerous event for Jesus, and Mark helps us to understand it by the way he's linked it to what Jesus has just been saying in this chapter. Jesus has presented a fresh view of cleanness and uncleanness; now here is a girl with an unclean spirit. We've just heard Jesus say something which, when decoded, undermines the protective fence that first-century Jews maintained around their own identity; now here he is, in a decidedly Gentile town, trying to lie low for a while and then doing, with a healing miracle, what he's just done with his cryptic sayings.

This explains the very odd exchange between Jesus and the woman. The tone of voice throughout, though urgent and (on the woman's part) desperate, is nevertheless that of teasing banter. Some have tried to make out that the woman put Jesus straight, correcting and indeed rebuking his restricted viewpoint, but this is hardly what Mark intends. She accepts, after all, the apparent insult and turns it to her own advantage.

The point at issue is rather that Jesus is conscious during his ministry that his personal vocation is not to spread the gospel to the Gentile world, but to tell the Jewish people themselves that their long-awaited deliverance is at hand, and indeed to bring it about by completing his vocation in Jerusalem. He is careful not to be drawn away to an extension of his work into other areas, which would divert him from the difficult and dangerous tasks to which he has been called.

Nevertheless, what Jesus does here is seen by the disciples, and written up by Mark, as a sign that he means what he has said about cleanness and uncleanness. The old barriers, the old taboos, are being swept away. The dogs under the table are already sharing the children's bread; pretty soon they will cease to be dogs and will become children alongside the others.

Mark, we may be sure, has one eye at least on his own community, in which Gentiles have come to share in the kingdom-blessings promised to Israel. Precisely because we must understand Jesus' words as referring to a temporary, short-term urgency in which Israel needs to hear the gospel before it is too late, we must also see that this short-term situation comes to an end with the crucifixion, never to return. From that moment on, what is anticipated in the Syrophoenician woman becomes universally true. The King of the Jews becomes the Saviour of the world.

Lord, we give thanks for the offer of salvation that Jesus has made possible for all.

18 God's Son breaks the Sabbath!
John 5:9–18

It is as though Jesus and his Judaean opponents are working in two different time zones. Not geographical time zones, of course, but what we might call different *theological* time zones. Basically, the Judaeans think it's still time for rest, but Jesus is wide awake and has already started the business of the day. The issue concerns the Sabbath. As we discover in the Old Testament, the Sabbath was originally intended to highlight the seventh day as the time when the creator God rested from his work in making the world. Week by week, the law-observant Jews kept a strict day without work – defining quite carefully what 'work' might include so there would be no doubt.

Jesus, however, seems to have continued doing things on the Sabbath that could be understood as deliberate 'work'. After all, in the present case he didn't have to heal the man that day. The man had waited nearly forty years to be healed; another day wouldn't have hurt him. But Jesus seems deliberately to have chosen to do it that day. And though what Jesus himself has done was hardly 'work' – all he did was to issue a command – what he told the man to do, to carry his mattress, certainly is.

At the heart of this story is Jesus' belief that Israel's God was then and there in the process of launching the *new creation*. And somehow this new creation was superseding the old one. Its timescale was taking precedence. God was healing the sorry, sick old world, and though there might come a time for rest, at the moment it was time for the work of new creation to go forward.

But if Jesus' work of healing and new creation was going forward, what was holding it up? The answer lies in the short, sad statement in the Gospel Prologue (John 1:10–11): 'He came to what was his own, and his own people did not accept him.' They were not ready for new creation, for the living Word of God to come to them with new things to say. They were living in the old time zone, and were angry with Jesus for, as it were, waking them up too soon.

This battle still continues today, though in another form. With Jesus' resurrection, God's new creation project is launched upon the whole world. People still react angrily to it. Where are the followers of Jesus today who are prepared to say, 'Jesus is at work, and so am I'?

Lord Jesus, help us to keep awake and work for the new creation that you launched and which is still moving forward.

19 True greatness
Mark 9:30–7

I don't know whether Mark wants us to feel sorry for the disciples at this point, but quite frankly, I do. Earlier in the Gospel Jesus said things to them in code, and they didn't understand them. They struggle to get their minds round the fact that he often says things that have a clear meaning at the surface level, but what he wants is for them to find a hidden meaning somewhere else.

At this stage we can not only sympathise with the disciples, but we must also ask ourselves whether we do the same thing. When God is trying to say something to us, how good are we at listening? Is there something in Scripture, or something we've heard in church, or something going on around us through which God is speaking to us – and if so, are we open to it? Are we prepared to have our earlier ways of understanding taken apart so that a new way of understanding can open up instead?

A sign that the answer may still be 'no' is if, like the disciples, we are still concerned about what's in it for us. If we are thinking that by following Jesus we will enhance our own prestige, our sense of self-worth, then we're very unlikely to be able to hear what God is actually saying. Certainly, Jesus must be frustrated and disappointed that the disciples could only worry about their own relative status. That's the trouble with understanding half the message – the half they want to understand: if Jesus is Messiah, then we are royal courtiers-in-waiting!

To try to jolt them out of their upside-down thinking, Jesus, not for the last time, uses a child as a teaching aid. Aside from normal family affection, children were not rated highly in the ancient world. The point Jesus is making here is that the disciples won't gain particular favour or social standing because they are his followers; anyone who receives even a child in Jesus' name will receive Jesus himself, and thereby will receive also 'the one who sent me'. In other words, anyone at all associated with Jesus can become the means of access to royalty, and even to divinity; the disciples aren't special in that sense at all.

This lesson resonates out into the present. Jesus is also turning upside down the way people, including Christians, still think. If we feel sorry for the disciples in their confusion, we should ask ourselves just how confused we ourselves still are.

Lord, help us to clear our minds of all thoughts of self-importance so that we may hear your voice clearly.

20 Feeding the five thousand
John 6:1–15

The whole of the sixth chapter of John's Gospel is dominated by the theme of Passover, or rather by one aspect of it: the fact that God fed the children of Israel, during their wilderness wanderings, with 'bread from heaven'. The story is told in Exodus 16, where the manna is provided by God because the people are grumbling and complaining. Both sides of this story provide part of the important background for John 6.

The chapter opens with this story, which is told in all four Gospels, of Jesus' own provision of food for a large crowd out in the wilderness area, across the sea of Galilee and away from towns where food might be found. As well as providing the starting point for the long discussion of 'the bread from heaven', this passage is full of deft little touches that invite us to enter into the scene imaginatively and, perhaps, identify with one or other of the characters.

The exchange between Jesus, Philip and Andrew – and the unnamed boy with the bread and fish – is told far more intimately than in the other Gospels. Indeed, Philip and Andrew are not given speaking parts at all in the other Gospels; John has retained a sense of their different personalities and roles, as he has with some of the others. Here it's Andrew who has got to know the boy with the food and introduces him to Jesus.

Philip doesn't know what to do. Andrew doesn't either, but he brings the boy and his bread and fish to Jesus' attention. The point is obvious, but we perhaps need to be reminded of it: so often we ourselves have no idea what to do, but the starting point is always to bring what is there to the attention of Jesus. You can never tell what he's going to do with it – though part of Christian faith is the expectation that he will do something we hadn't thought of, something new and creative.

Lord, whenever we feel lost and uncertain about what to do, help us to remember we can turn to you for guidance.

21 Jesus walking on the water
John 6:16–25

The account of Jesus walking on the water is recorded by Matthew and Mark (Matthew 14:22–33; Mark 6:45–52) as well as by John – with all three of them locating it immediately after the feeding of the multitude. There is no way of rationalising it (although people used to suggest that maybe Jesus was standing on a sandbank near the shore, or something equally banal). You either come to the text with a view of what is and isn't possible in the world – which is not, perhaps, the best way of approaching a book like John's Gospel, which is all about the challenge to existing world views – or you come with at least an open mind to possibilities hitherto unimagined.

This isn't the same as being gullible. Nor are the extraordinary stories in the Gospels designed, as some seem to have imagined, to portray Jesus as being able to do anything at all, simply for the sake of making a supernatural display. They are there, rather, as moments in the text when the strange glory of the Word-made-flesh shines through, because this particular thing is so closely associated with what Israel's God does at a key moment in Israel's history.

The reaction of the crowd is explained in detail by John. He wants to rub our noses in the fact not only that the disciples saw what had happened but also that the crowds are puzzled. They know Jesus didn't set off on the boat, and yet, when they manage to get to the other side of the lake, they find he's already arrived in Capernaum. It would have been difficult to make the journey by land in that time, round the northeast side of the lake. As so often, John leaves us with their puzzled question, to which Jesus will now give what seems an even more puzzling answer.

The story of Jesus walking on the water can easily be used as a theme for meditation. There are many times in our lives when, metaphorically speaking, suddenly the wind gets up and the sea becomes rough. As we struggle to make our way through, sometimes we are aware of a presence with us, which may initially be more disturbing than comforting. But if we listen, through the roar of the waves and the wind, we may hear the voice that says, 'It's me! Don't be afraid!' And if we are ready then to take Jesus on board, we may find ourselves , sooner than we expected, at the harbour where we will be calm and secure once more.

Lord, we will never be afraid, knowing you are with us.

22 Bread from heaven
John 6:26–35

At first sight, Jesus' warning seems almost churlish. He has done something remarkable, they are excited and come to him wanting more, and he all but rebukes them for having the wrong motivation. What else could you expect from them? But underneath the warning of verses 26 and 27 is his recognition that after the feeding in the wilderness they were only a moment away from making him king (verse 15). And they would have meant him to be a king like other kings, a strong, this-worldly figure. Jesus is indeed a king, but the type and manner of his kingship will be very different from what the crowds expect or want.

Here, his charge against the crowds is that the 'sign' of the feeding is meant to lead them to the true food: the food that *is* Jesus himself. What matters is not just what Jesus can do for you; what matters is who Jesus *is*. Only if you're prepared to be confronted by that can you begin to understand what he really wants to do for you.

The question of who Jesus really is now comes to the fore. First, he is the one upon whom the Father has set his seal: God has stamped this person with the mark that declares not only where he comes from but also that he carries God's authority. What Jesus is doing, in other words, bears the marks that say: this is the kind of thing that, in Israel's Scriptures, God himself does. The wilderness feeding and the walking on water speak of this in ways that are both related to the Exodus story.

Second, the crowd realise that Jesus is pointing out that they can't just expect bread on demand, that if this really is a heaven-sent renewal movement there will be a new standard to which they must sign up. God is making this demand on them: that they believe in Jesus. No new exposition of the commandments of the law; rather, a command which, if it is to be obeyed, will require a change of heart.

The passage ends, climactically, with the first of the famous 'I am' sayings in John's Gospel. In this case the particular emphasis is on nourishment. Until they recognise who Jesus really is, they may be fed with bread and fish, but there is a deep hunger inside them that will never be satisfied. Verse 34 can be used as the prayer that we all need to pray if our deepest needs are to be met.

Lord, feed us with the bread of life, this day and every day, and we will be satisfied.

23 Division among Jesus' followers
John 6:60–71

I once went to a lecture that was supposed to be an introduction to philosophy. It quickly appeared that the great philosopher wasn't interested in introducing the subject, but rather in talking about it at a high level to the small group of eager postgraduates who already knew the basics and wanted to go further. I didn't go back.

That is not, I think, the problem in verse 60. It isn't that Jesus is talking at too abstract a level – though no doubt there are some who find their heads spinning after the long discussion in the Capernaum synagogue. It is more that what he said has made a huge hole in their world view, and when that happens some people prefer not to think about it any more.

This new teaching is 'difficult' in the sense that it is demanding not just to get their minds round it but also to get their hearts and souls into it. For anyone brought up in one of the varieties of first-century Judaism, all that Jesus has said is demanding in every sense, but most particularly in that, whereas they might be prepared to follow a prophet like Moses or a would-be Messiah as long as such figures keep within the bounds of the agendas and aspirations they have in mind, the thought of someone who would speak as Jesus has spoken is too much.

There is therefore a division among his followers. It looks as though the majority refuse to go with him any longer. The Twelve, however, remain. They are prepared to say out loud that Jesus is God's holy one, his Messiah. He is the one who is not only speaking *about* God's new age, the age to come, but is, by his words, already bringing it into existence: 'You're the one who's got the life-giving words of the age to come!' Jesus knows that one of them will turn traitor, and, worse than traitor, become an 'accuser' (the word can mean 'devil', but here and elsewhere John seems to refer to what Judas is actually going to do in handing Jesus over to the courts). But for the moment the Twelve stand as representatives of the faith, the belief, that Jesus has been looking for: the recognition that in him, his words and his deeds, Israel's God is at last bringing into being the new exodus, the great movement that would set the whole world free from sin and death.

Lord, we thank you for the words of eternal life that you speak into our hearts.

24 Adultery and hypocrisy
John 8:1–11

This chapter begins with people wanting to stone a woman to death; it ends with them wanting to stone Jesus.

The story turns on the trap that the scribes and Pharisees have set for Jesus. They suspect that he will want to tell the woman that her sins have been forgiven; but that would mean he would be teaching people to ignore something in the law of Moses.

Already we can sense the temperature of the situation rising, and with it Jesus' anger. They are using the woman, however guilty she might be of serious sin, simply as a tool in their attack on him. And in so doing, they are enjoying their sense of moral superiority over her, as well as their sense of having put Jesus in a corner he can't easily escape from.

Nobody knows, of course, what Jesus writes on the ground. But his answer when it comes, though apparently risky (supposing one of them had the arrogance to go ahead?), is devastating. When you point the finger at someone else, there are three fingers pointing back at you. He hasn't said the law of Moses is wrong; only that, if we're going to get serious about it, we should all find ourselves guilty. And one by one they get the point and go away.

The story certainly doesn't mean – as some people have tried to make it mean – that adultery doesn't matter. That's not the point at all. Jesus' last words to the woman are extremely important. If she has been forgiven – if she's been rescued from imminent death – she must live by that forgiveness. *Forgiveness is not the same thing as 'tolerance'.* Being forgiven doesn't mean that sin doesn't matter. On the contrary: 'forgiveness' means that sin *does* matter – but that God is choosing to set it aside.

And the sin that matters even more is the deep-rooted sin that uses the God-given law as a means of making oneself out to be righteous, when in fact it is meant to shine the light of God's judgement into the dark places of the heart.

Lord, save us from the self-righteous sin of hypocrisy.

25 The healing of the centurion's servant
Luke 7:1–10

The heart of this story is the centurion's faith. Here he is, a middle-ranking military officer, stationed in Capernaum. He would be receiving regular orders from a commander, probably in Caesarea, about fifty miles away. And he would have soldiers responsible to him for performing tasks locally, perhaps including peacekeeping. Often soldiers in that position would despise the local people as an inferior race, but this man doesn't. He has come to love and respect the Jewish people, and has even paid for the building of the local synagogue. Luke presents him to us as a humble Gentile, looking in at Israel and Israel's God from the outside, opening himself to learning new truth from this strange, ancient way of life.

Jesus is astonished at the centurion's message; and we are astonished at his astonishment! Normally in the Gospels Jesus does and says things that surprise people; this is one of the few places where Jesus himself is surprised. And the reason is the sheer quality of the man's faith. This faith isn't an abstract belief about God. It is the simple, clear belief that when Jesus commands that something be done, it will be done. The centurion recognises that there is a power at work in Jesus that can carry all before it.

For all his lack of appropriate religious background, the centurion has grasped the very centre of the Jewish faith: that the one true God, the God of Israel, is the sovereign one, the Lord of heaven and earth. And he has grasped it in its shocking new form: *this one true God is personally present and active in Jesus of Nazareth.* Luke presents this Gentile as a model for all those who will come in by faith from outside God's ancient people to share the blessings of healing and salvation.

Contrast the prayer of this centurion with the prayers we all too often pray ourselves. 'Lord,' we say (not out loud, of course, but this is what we often think), 'I might perhaps like you to do this...but I know you may not want to, or it might be too difficult, or perhaps impossible...' and we go on our way puzzled, not sure whether we've really asked for something or not. Of course, sometimes we ask for something and the answer is No. God reserves the right to give that answer. But this story shows that we should have no hesitation in asking. Is Jesus the Lord of the world, or isn't he?

Lord, we thank you for the privilege of prayer, and that you hear us when we ask in faith.

26 Peter's declaration of Jesus' messiahship
Luke 9:18–27

Jesus was known as a prophet, and when people asked what he was up to they found themselves remembering the stories of prophets old and new, from Elijah to John the Baptist. Some may have been trying to identify Jesus with the Elijah who, according to Malachi 4:5, would return to herald 'the great and terrible day of the Lord'. Certainly they believed that Jesus was behaving like someone through whom some great act of God was about to take place.

But Jesus was more than that. Prophet he certainly was, but he was not simply pointing to God's kingdom in the future. He was causing it to appear before people's eyes, and was setting in motion the events through which it would become established. And sooner or later he had to put the question to the disciples. They marked themselves out from the crowd by piercing the disguise; even though Jesus wasn't doing everything they had expected the Messiah to do, the combination of authority, power, insight and fulfilment of the Scriptures was too potent to mean anything else. To have called them, as the deeply symbolic Twelve, was important, too; but anyone could have done that, and been mistaken. To have equipped them to go out and do what he was doing was something else again. Their own identity had come to depend on his, and there was only one answer they could give: You're the Messiah, God's anointed King.

Jesus at once told not just the Twelve but anyone who would want to follow him that there was a dark and dangerous time ahead. The world would be turned upside down, and anyone who wanted to come through would have to be prepared to be turned upside down and inside out with it. Despite what many well-meaning evangelists and preachers have said, Jesus didn't come with the message that if we follow him we would have an easy life. Just the reverse. To save your life, you have to lose it. To avoid having the Son of Man be ashamed of you, you have to acknowledge him. In other words, when the Messiah is installed as judge of God's world, then only those who have been prepared to follow him when it was dangerous and shameful to do so will be acknowledged by him in return.

Jesus' swift movement, from asking who they think he is to summoning them to follow him even to the death, shows clearly enough that we cannot separate thinking from action in the Christian faith.

Lord, may my faith be strong and true, showing itself in actions as well as words.

27 The Transfiguration
Luke 9:28–45

All the Gospel writers follow the story of the Transfiguration with the story of a boy who is desperately ill, so sick that the disciples haven't been able to cure him. They seem to be telling us that the two go together: the mountaintop experience and the shrieking, stubborn demon. Many people prefer to live their lives without either, to be people of the plateau, undramatic and unexciting. God seems to call some to that kind of life. But for many, dramatic visions and spiritual experiences are balanced by huge demands. The more open we are to God, the more we seem to be open to the pain of the world.

Luke has highlighted throughout this passage the way in which the Transfiguration is preparing Jesus himself not just for one human tragedy but for the greatest threat of all. Moses and Elijah, says Luke, are speaking with Jesus about 'his departure, which he was going to fulfil in Jerusalem'. The word for 'departure' is *exodus*, and Luke means us to understand that in his death Jesus will enact an event just like the great exodus from Egypt, only more so. In the first exodus, Moses led the Israelites out of slavery in Egypt and home to the promised land. In the new exodus, Jesus will lead all God's people out of the slavery of sin and death, and home to their promised inheritance – the new creation in which the whole world will be redeemed.

Jesus himself, then, goes through the mountaintop experience, knowing that it is preparing him to follow where the Law and the Prophets (here represented by Moses and Elijah) pointed: down into the valley, to the place of despair and death, the place where the Son of Man will be handed over to sinners.

The disciples are overwhelmed by the Transfiguration, and they are unable to understand how it is that the glory they have glimpsed on the mountain, the glory of God's chosen Son, will finally be unveiled on a very different hill, an ugly little hill outside Jerusalem.

We, too, often find it completely bewildering to know how to understand all that God is doing and saying, in both our times of great joy and our times of great sadness. But the word that comes to us, leading us on to follow Jesus even when we haven't a clue what's going on, is the word that came from the cloud on that strange day in Galilee: 'This is my son, my chosen one: listen to him.'

Lord, we thank you for being with us through the light and shade of our existence.

28 The nature of discipleship
Luke 9:46–62

Jews in Galilee regularly made one journey: the pilgrimage to Jerusalem (about three or four days' walk). And all Jews, wherever they were, would tell the story of the great journey of the exodus, when their ancestors travelled from Egypt to the promised land. Luke has all this in mind as he tells us about Jesus' plans to go to Jerusalem, where he is to 'fulfil' his 'exodus'. But before they even set off, the disciples are having a private row about which of them is the greatest. Whenever any project is launched, people discover that their own ambitions get mixed up with it.

All James and John can think of is that they are now in the same position as Elijah in the Old Testament. If they meet opposition, they want to call down fire from heaven (2 Kings 1:10–12). But that's not what Jesus' journey is like. It's not a triumphant march. It is the progress of the gospel of the kingdom and, as we know from Luke 4, that means the message of love – of a grace so strong and surprising that many will find it shocking.

Including, it seems, many who see Jesus and think it would be a fine thing to follow him. The people who speak to Jesus on the road want to follow, but they attach conditions. Are they ready to come right away? The obligation to bury one's father was regarded by many Jews of the time as the most holy and binding duty of a son, but Jesus says that that, too, is secondary to the call to announce God's kingdom.

The challenge to journey on with Jesus comes over loud and clear in the last line. Many today don't work the land, and perhaps don't appreciate what happens if you're trying to plough a straight furrow and then look back to see how you're doing. Even if what you see is a straight line, the act of looking back will mean that the next bit will become crooked. Think of other pictures. If you're singing a song, it's no good wondering whether you sang the previous line all right. You've got to concentrate on the next line. If you're on a journey, the map you need is the one that tells you where to go next, not the one for the road you've just travelled.

The question comes home to us. Where is Jesus asking us to travel, not yesterday but tomorrow? Are we ready to follow him wherever he goes?

Lead us, Lord Jesus, and help us to keep our eyes firmly focused on the road ahead.

29 Ten lepers healed
Luke 17:11–19

In this story Luke focuses on Jesus' attitude to the outsider. This time it is a Samaritan who puts to shame the Jews who have been healed but who don't say 'thank you'. Perhaps, once they've seen the priest, they are afraid to go back and identify themselves with Jesus, who by now is a marked man. Perhaps, having realised they have been healed, they are so eager to get back to their families that they simply don't think to look for Jesus. Luke doesn't say that they are any less cured, but he does imply that they are less grateful. After the lesson in humility comes the lesson in gratitude. Humility, of course, is still built in: only the foreigner gives God the glory.

It is not only the nine ex-lepers who are shown up. It is all of us who fail to thank God 'always [and] for everything', as Paul puts it (Ephesians 5:20). We know with our heads, if we have any Christian faith at all, that our God is the giver of all things. Every mouthful of food we take, every breath of air we inhale, every note of music we hear, every smile on the face of a friend, a child, a spouse: all that, and a million things more, are good gifts from his generosity. There is an old spiritual discipline of listing one's blessings, naming them before God and giving thanks. It's a healthy thing to do, especially in a world where we too often assume we have an absolute right to health, happiness and every possible creature comfort.

Jesus' closing words to the Samaritan invite a closer look. The word for 'get up' is a word early Christians would have recognised as having to do with 'resurrection'. New life, the life Israel was longing for as part of the age to come, arrived in his village that day, and it called out of him a faith he didn't know he had. Once again (compare 5:20; 8:48, 50), faith and healing go hand in hand. Once again, 'faith' here means not just any old belief, any generally religious attitude to life, but the belief that the God of life and death is at work in and through Jesus, and the trust that this is not just a vague general truth but that it will hold good in *this* case, here and now. This rhythm of faith and gratitude is simply what being a Christian, in the first or the twenty-first century, is all about.

We give you thanks, O Lord, for the blessings you shower on us each day of our lives.

30 The rich young ruler
Mark 10:17–31

If you'd asked any Pharisee, or any member of one of the other sects of the time (such as the Essenes), what you should do to inherit the age to come, they would almost certainly have given two sorts of reply. First, they would have given you their own interpretation of the Jewish law. The law itself defined Israel as God's people; but granted that Israel as a whole was (as the prophets had said) full of sinners, it was necessary to follow a more precise understanding of the commandments. Rabbinic law and the Dead Sea Scrolls have plenty of material like that.

Second, they would probably have urged you to join their own group: to become a Pharisee, an Essene, or whatever. Then you would be able to enjoy the security of knowing that you would inherit the age to come.

The question is, then: what is Jesus' attitude to the basic Jewish law? And what sort of a movement might he be leading? Jesus' reply must puzzle the young man greatly. Jesus' basic demand is not for some extra observance, some tightening of definition here, some sharpening of exact meaning there. It is for idols and covetousness to be thrown to the winds: sell up and give to the poor! And it is for a radical rethink on what putting God first might mean: Why do you call me good? No one is good but God; come and follow me.

Jesus' new movement is indeed a radical revision of what it means to be God's people. Because he, Jesus, is here, a whole new world opens up: the age to come is not now simply in the future (though it is that, too); it is bursting through into the present.

The discussion that follows the rich man's sad departure reflects the disciples' shock at being told that wealth won't buy you a place in the age to come. Their surprise only makes sense if we assume that they regard wealth as a sign of God's pleasure – a common view in both Judaism and paganism, though there is already much in the Old Testament to challenge that attitude.

Jesus slices through their amazement. Riches can no more go into the age to come than a camel can go through a needle – a typical and deliberate overstatement, like saying, 'You'll get your riches into God's kingdom when you can put the entire ocean into a bottle.'

Lord, let us not put our trust in money or what it can buy, but may we instead set our hearts on the riches of your love and the promises of the age to come.

31 Humility and danger
Matthew 18:1–7

In this passage, Jesus is concerned not just with helping his followers to learn a lesson about humility and the dangers of pride and arrogance. He doesn't just want them to see that becoming like children is central to their growing in grace and wisdom, in kingdom-greatness. He is, of course, also concerned for children themselves. He doesn't have a romantic, cosy vision in which children can just play happily. Precisely because they are so trusting, so eager, they are of all people the most at risk. This remains as true today as ever it was.

So Jesus issues a stark warning, with typical exaggeration. There must be easier ways of drowning someone than making them carry an enormous millstone around their neck and taking them in a boat far out to sea so that they can sink into the deepest part; but that's what his picture suggests, like a vivid and overdramatised cartoon. Large circular stones, with a central hole for the mechanism, were used to grind corn; the biggest were so large it took a donkey to work them. That's the type Jesus is talking about, the type he says you should imagine having round your neck as a collar. And he doesn't just talk of people being thrown into the sea; he is talking of the deep sea, far out, away from the shore.

If this seems violent or extreme, perhaps it's because we, too, have undervalued the 'little ones' Jesus is talking about – children in particular, of course, but also all those who are powerless, vulnerable, at risk in our world. Exploitation of such people is inevitable, granted the way the world now is. But those who indulge in it are given this warning, far sterner than anything Jesus ever says about what we think of as the 'big' sins such as murder, adultery and theft. They matter, but causing one of the little ones to 'stumble' or 'trip up' matters even more. Harsh words to address a harsh reality. Learning about God's kingdom means facing the real evils of the world and realising that God hates them far more than we do.

Lord, let us not turn a blind eye to the abuse of children, but show us what we can do to help them.

September

STORIES AND
TEACHINGS
OF JESUS

1 The Beatitudes
Matthew 5:1–12

This passage is the beginning of the famous 'Sermon on the Mount', which runs through chapters 5, 6 and 7 of Matthew's Gospel and sets out the main themes of Jesus' proclamation. People often say what wonderful teaching the Sermon on the Mount is, and that if only people would obey it the world would be a better place. But if we think of Jesus simply sitting there telling people how to behave properly, we will miss what was really going on. These 'blessings', the 'wonderful news' that he's announcing, are not saying, 'Try hard to live like this.' They are saying that people who already *are* like that are in good shape. They should be happy and celebrate.

Jesus is not suggesting that these are simply timeless truths about the way the world is, about human behaviour. If he is saying that, he is wrong. Mourners often go uncomforted, the meek don't inherit the earth, those who long for justice frequently take that longing to the grave. This is an upside-down world, or perhaps a right-way-up world; *and Jesus is saying that with his work it's starting to come true.* This is an announcement, not a philosophical analysis. It's about something that's starting to happen. It is *gospel*: good news.

'Follow me,' Jesus says to the first disciples; because in him the living God is doing a new thing, and this list of 'wonderful news' is part of his way of saying that God is at work in a fresh way. Jesus is beginning a new era for God's people. In our world, still, most people think that wonderful news consists of success, wealth, long life, victory in battle. Jesus is offering wonderful news for the humble, the poor, the mourners, the peacemakers.

The word for 'wonderful news' is often translated 'blessed', and part of the point is that this is *God's* wonderful news. God is acting in and through Jesus to turn the world upside down, to pour out lavish 'blessings' on all who now turn to him and accept the new thing that he is doing.

That's the point of the Sermon on the Mount, and of these 'beatitudes' in particular. They are a summons to live in the present in the way that will make sense in God's promised future, because that future has arrived in the present in Jesus of Nazareth. It may seem upside down, but we are called to believe, with great daring, that it is in fact the right way up. Try it and see.

Lord, help us to live and act now in ways that reflect the values of your coming kingdom.

2 The Lord's Prayer
Matthew 6:7–15

What does the Lord's Prayer tell us about our regular approach to God? First, and so obvious that we might miss it, the prayer is deeply *meaningful*. It isn't a magic formula. It is something we can mean with our minds as well as say with our lips. It implies strongly that we humans can and should use our ordinary language in talking to the creator of the universe.

Second, everything is set within our calling God 'Father'. For Jews in Jesus' day, this title for God went back to God's action in the exodus, rescuing Israel from Egypt and so demonstrating that 'Israel is my son, my firstborn' (Exodus 4:22).

Third, this God is not a man-made idol. He is the living God who dwells in 'heaven' and longs to see his sovereign rule come to birth on 'earth'. This is, in fact, a prayer for the kingdom of God to become fully present – for the glory of heaven to be turned into earthly reality as well. When that is done, God's name will be held in honour everywhere.

Fourth, because this God is the creator, who loves his world and his human creatures, we can ask him for everything we need in the safe knowledge that he is far more concerned about it all even than we are ourselves.

Fifth, we pray for forgiveness. Jesus assumes that we need to ask for forgiveness not on one or two rare occasions but regularly. This is a sobering thought, but it is matched by the comforting news that forgiveness is freely available as often as we need it. There is, however, a condition: we ourselves must be forgiving people. The heart that will not open to forgive others will remain closed when God's forgiveness is offered.

The prayer ends with a sombre note. Jesus believed that the great time of testing was coming upon the world, and that he would have to walk alone into its darkness. His followers should pray to be spared it. Even now, in the light of Easter and with the guidance and power of the Holy Spirit, we still need to pray in this way. There will come yet more times of crisis, times when all seems dark. If we follow a crucified Messiah, we shouldn't expect to be spared the darkness ourselves. But we may, and must, pray to be kept from its worst ravages, and to be delivered from evil, both in the abstract and in its personified form, 'the evil one'.

Father, help us to make the prayer that Jesus gave us our own, and to live it as well as say it.

3 Jesus' invitation
Matthew 11:25–30

There is a deep mystery here that takes us right to the heart of what it meant to be Jesus. As he announced God's kingdom and put God's powerful love to work in healing, forgiving and bringing new life, he obviously realised that the people he met, including the religious leaders, his own followers and the ordinary people, didn't have the same awareness of his Father that he did.

Imagine a gifted musician walking around among people who can only just manage to sing in tune. That must have been what it was like for Jesus. He must have known from early on that there was something different about him, that he seemed to have an inside track on knowing who Israel's God truly was and what he was wanting for his people.

This must have made it all the more galling when he discovered that most of his contemporaries didn't want to hear what he was telling them. Most of them, alarmed at the direct challenge he presented, were either resisting him outright or making excuses for not believing him or following him. Opposition was mounting. And, strangely, this gave Jesus a fresh, further insight into the way his Father was operating. This, in turn, resulted in a burst of praise as he glimpsed the strange, unexpected way God was working.

Jesus had come to know his Father the way a son does: not by studying books about him, but by living in his presence, listening for his voice and learning from him as an apprentice does from a master, by watching and imitating. And he was now discovering that the wise and learned were getting nowhere, and that the 'little people' – the poor, the sinners, the tax-collectors, ordinary folk – were discovering more of God simply by following him.

When Jesus declares here, in the old King James translation, that he is 'meek and lowly of heart', he isn't boasting that he's attained some special level of spiritual achievement. He is encouraging us to believe that he isn't going to stand over us like a policeman, isn't going to be cross with us like an angry schoolteacher. And the welcome he offers, for all who abandon themselves to his mercy, is the welcome God offers through him. This is the invitation that pulls back the curtain and lets us see who 'the Father' really is – and encourages us to come into his loving, welcoming presence.

Thank you, Lord, for welcoming us as your children, and for showing us who you really are.

4 The Servant

Matthew 12:15–21

Here we see Jesus surrounded by pressures on all sides. His own followers don't yet really understand what he's doing. People are badgering him from every direction to heal them, to cast out evil spirits, to be there for them in their every need. At the same time, opposition is growing. Herod is not far away. Religious pressure groups are stirring up trouble. Some are even saying he's in league with the devil. He knows where it's all leading. And still he goes on.

And he goes on because he has a story in mind. The story of the Servant: Isaiah's story, the most famous story of the most famous prophet. The story of the Servant begins in the passage Matthew quotes here: Isaiah 42. The 'Servant of Yahweh' is a strange figure in Isaiah: one who will bring Yahweh's blessing and justice to the world – the task which, earlier in Isaiah, was assigned to the Messiah, the coming King. But how is the Servant to accomplish his task? Not, it seems, by bullying Israel and the nations. Rather, with a gentle work of healing, bearing the love and grace of God to the dark parts of the world.

Matthew looks back over the ministry of Jesus, knowing where it would lead. He sees Jesus as the Servant, not only when he dies a cruel death, wounded for our transgressions and bruised for our iniquities, but also in the *style* of what he was already doing in Galilee. He was going about bringing God's restoration wherever it was needed, by gently leading people into God's healing love.

This is the story of one in whose name the nations will hope. Well, they would, wouldn't they? The nations – and, alas, Israel as well – are bent on violence and arrogance. Those who want peace and who work for it are always, in the end, shouted down by those who want more money, more land, more security, more status, and are prepared to fight to get it. Those who are great and mighty in this world's terms make sure their voices are heard. Those who shout loudest get obeyed the soonest. But that's not the Servant's way.

So, too, those who want to get ahead in this world tend to push others out of the way. If they see a weak link they will trample on it without a thought. That's not the Servant's way. The nations are used to arrogance. Here is a Servant who is the very opposite. He is the one shining light, the one hopeful sign.

Lord, we thank you for showing us that your power lies in humility and peaceful service.

5 Judging others and true obedience
Luke 6:39–49

One picture is worth a thousand words. Here, in quick succession, are five of Jesus' most vivid word-sketches. Each is a warning about rival teachings, rival visions of the kingdom, about 'solutions' that leave the depths of the problem untouched. They applied to rival teachings in Jesus' day, but they apply just as well to some of today's theories about what human life should be like.

The riddle about the speck of dust in the other person's eye and the plank in one's own (it is meant to sound ridiculous; Jesus was deliberately sketching a verbal cartoon, a caricature) is asking the question: can you see clearly enough to criticise, let alone lead, someone else? What people criticise in others is frequently, though not always, what they are subconsciously aware of (or afraid of) in themselves. The speck and the plank are a classic case of what psychologists call 'projection'. The person knows there's something seriously wrong with his or her own eye, so tries to avoid the problem by telling someone else there's a tiny problem with theirs.

But, of course, Jesus' picture continues to be relevant to new situations long after his own day. There must be many churches where a huge fuss is made about small details, while the main point of the gospel and of radical Christian witness in the world is missed altogether. It has been claimed that the leaders of the Russian Orthodox Church in 1917 were having a long debate about vestments at the very moment when the Bolsheviks were launching their revolution. Whether that is true or not, the very thought of it serves as a dire warning to other churches at other times. There's nothing wrong with getting the details in place; the story ends with removing the speck, after all; but first you've got to deal with the plank.

Lord, help me guard against the hypocrisy of pointing the finger at the trivial faults of others while ignoring my own larger faults.

6 The good Samaritan
Luke 10:25–37

The best-known stories are sometimes the hardest to understand. Often this parable is simply taken in a general moral sense: if you see someone in the ditch, go and help them. Sometimes, when people remember that in Jesus' day the Samaritans and the Jews hated each other like poison, this is expanded into a further moral lesson about the wickedness of racial and religious prejudice. But if we are to have any chance of understanding what Jesus himself means – and what is at stake in the wider conversation with the lawyer – we need to go deeper.

What lies at the heart of the confrontation with the lawyer is a clash between two quite different visions of what it means to be Israel, God's people. The lawyer's question about the key requirements for entering the age to come is a standard rabbinic question, to which there are standard answers. His own summary is exactly the same as that which Jesus himself gives in Mark 12:29–31 and Matthew 22:37–40. But what the lawyer has in mind is the way in which the law provides a definition of Israel. He wants to put Jesus on the spot, and force him into saying something that might appear heretical.

When Jesus makes him reveal his own summary and then simply agrees with it, the lawyer now aims 'to win the point', to justify himself. The question he asks about the neighbour is designed to smoke out Jesus' supposedly heretical views on God's wider plans, and so to show that the lawyer is right to challenge him. It does indeed produce from Jesus an answer about the wide-reaching grace of God, but the story Jesus tells makes it clear that these views are not heretical, but rather the true fulfilment of the commandment the lawyer claims to regard as vital.

What is at stake, then and now, is the question of whether we will use the God-given revelation of love and grace as a way of boosting our own sense of isolated security and purity, or whether we will see it as a call to extend that love and grace to the whole world. No church, no Christian, can remain content with easy definitions that allow us to watch most of the world lying half-dead in the road. Today's defenders of the gospel must find fresh ways of telling the story of God's love which will do for our day what this brilliant parable did for Jesus' first hearers.

Lord, help me to live and act in ways that reflect your love for all humanity, especially those who suffer at the hands of others.

7 The rich fool
Luke 12:13–34

The modern Western world is built on anxiety. It thrives on people setting higher and higher goals for themselves and for each other so that they can worry all day and all year about whether they will reach them. If they do, they will set new ones. If they don't, they will feel they've failed. Is this really how we are supposed to live?

We now know that anxiety itself can be a killer. Stress and worry can cause disease, or contribute to it, producing the enchanting prospect of people worrying about worrying, a downward spiral that perhaps only a good sense of humour can break. As with so much of his teaching, what Jesus says here goes to the heart of the way we are. To inhale a bracing lungful of his good sense is health-giving at every level. But his warnings and commands go deeper as well, down to the roots of the problem he faces in confronting his contemporaries with the message of God's kingdom. This isn't just good advice on how to live a happy, carefree life. This is a challenge to the very centre of his world.

The man who wants Jesus to arbitrate in a property dispute with his brother is typical in his attitude, the attitude that many of Jesus' fellow Jews take toward the Holy Land itself. The land isn't just where they happen to live; in the first century, as in the early twenty-first, possession of the land is a vital Jewish symbol. Families cling to their inheritance for religious reasons as well as economic ones.

Jesus comes with the message that God is changing all that. He isn't tightening up Israel's defence of the land; he is longing to shower grace and new life on people of every race and place. Israel, as far as he can see, is in danger of becoming like the man in the story who wants the security of enough possessions to last him a long time. Societies and individuals alike can think themselves into this false position, to which the short answer is God's: 'You fool!' Life isn't like that. The kingdom of God isn't like that.

Lord, help us to see that our real and lasting security is found by trusting you and what matters to you.

8 The great banquet
Luke 14:12–24

The first level of meaning of this parable should be clear. Jesus has been going around Galilee summoning people to God's great supper. This is the moment Israel has been waiting for! At last, the time has arrived; those who were invited long ago must hurry up now and come! But most of them have refused, giving all kinds of reasons. But some people have been delighted to be included: the poor, the disadvantaged, the disabled. They have come in and celebrated with Jesus.

The second level is what this might mean for Luke in particular. Once again, the expected guests are the Jews, waiting and waiting for the kingdom, only to find, when it arrives, that they have more pressing things to occupy them. Of course, in Luke's day many Jews became Christians. The detail of the parable can't be forced at this point: it isn't true, at this level, that 'none of those people who were invited will get to taste my dinner', since clearly many Jews were part of Jesus' kingdom-movement from the beginning. But the majority of the nation, both in Palestine and in the scattered Jewish communities in the rest of the world, were not. Instead, as it must have seemed to those first Jewish Christians, God's messengers had gone out into the roads and hedgerows of the world, getting all kinds of unexpected people to join in the party – not just Gentiles, but people with every kind of moral and immoral background, people quite different from them culturally, socially, ethnically and ethically.

But there is a third twist to this parable, in which it bends back, as it were, on itself, returning to the challenge Jesus gave in verses 12–14. The party to which the original guests were invited was Jesus' kingdom-movement, his remarkable welcome to all and sundry. If people wanted to be included in Jesus' movement, this is the sort of thing they were joining.

Once again, therefore, the challenge comes to us today. Christians, reading this anywhere in the world, must work out in their own churches and families what it would mean to celebrate God's kingdom so that the people at the bottom of the pile, at the end of the line, would find it to be good news. It isn't enough to say that we ourselves are the people dragged in from the country lanes, to our surprise, to enjoy God's party. That may be true, but party guests are then expected to become party hosts in their turn.

Lord, help us to find fresh and appealing ways of inviting people of all backgrounds to join your kingdom-movement.

9 The lost sheep and the lost coin
Luke 15:1–10

The parables in Luke 15 are told because Jesus was making a habit of having celebration parties with all the 'wrong' people, and some others thought it was a nightmare. At the heart of the trouble were the characters of the people Jesus was eating with on a regular basis.

In the stories of the sheep and the coin, the punchline in each case depends on the Jewish belief that the two halves of God's creation, heaven and earth, were meant to fit together and be in harmony with each other. If you discover what's going on in heaven, you'll discover how things are meant to be on earth. That, after all, is the point of praying that God's kingdom will come 'as in heaven, so on earth' (Matthew 6:10).

As far as the legal experts and Pharisees were concerned, the closest you could get to heaven was in the Temple. The Temple required strict purity from the priests, and the closest that non-priests could get to copying heaven was to maintain a similarly strict purity in every aspect of life. But now Jesus was declaring that heaven was having a great, noisy party every time a single sinner saw the light and began to follow God's way. If earth-dwellers wanted to copy the life of heaven, they'd have a party, too. That's what Jesus was doing.

The particular sheep and the particular coin weren't themselves special. In one of the late, corrupt versions of Jesus' teaching circulated in subsequent centuries, Jesus is made to say to the lost sheep, 'I love you more than the others.' But the whole point of the parable is that the *only* thing different about this sheep is that it was lost. Imagine the impact of this on the repentant sinners who heard the stories. They didn't have to earn God's love or Jesus' respect. He loved coming to look for them, and celebrated finding them.

The real challenge of these parables for today's Church is: what would we have to do, in the visible, public world, if we were to make people ask the questions to which stories like these are the answer? What might today's Christians do that would make people ask, 'Why are you doing something like that?', and give us the chance to tell stories about finding something that was lost?

Lord, we thank you that you search for us when we're lost, and that you celebrate us when you find us!

10 The prodigal
Luke 15:11–24

The parable of the prodigal son, as it's usually known, hardly needs an introduction. When the father divides the property between the two sons and the younger son turns his share into cash, this must mean that the land the father owns is split into two, with the younger boy selling off his share to someone else. The shame that this would bring on the family would be added to the shame the son has already brought on the father by asking for his share before the father's death; it is the equivalent of saying, 'I wish you were dead.' The father bears these two blows without recrimination.

In modern Western culture, children routinely leave homes in the country to pursue their future and their fortune in big cities, or even abroad; but in Jesus' culture this would likewise be seen as shameful, with the younger son abandoning his obligation to care for his father in his old age. When the son reaches the foreign country, runs through the money and finds himself in trouble, his degradation reaches a further low point. For a Jew to have anything to do with pigs is bad enough; for him to be feeding them, and hungry enough to share their food, is worse.

But, of course, the most remarkable character in the story is the father himself. One might even call this 'the parable of the running father': in a culture where senior figures are far too dignified to run anywhere, this man sets off at a run as soon as he sees his young son dragging himself home. His lavish welcome is of course the point of the story: Jesus is explaining why there is a party, why it's something to celebrate when people turn from going their own way and begin to go God's way. Because the young man's degradation is more or less complete, there can be no question of anything in him commending him to his father, but the father's closing line says it all: 'This son of mine was dead, and is alive again! He was lost, and now he's found!' How could this not be a cause of celebration?

From the moment he generously gives the younger son what he wants, through to the wonderful homecoming welcome, we have as vivid a picture as anywhere in Jesus' teaching of what God's love is like, and of what Jesus himself took as the model for his own ministry of welcome to the outcast and the sinner.

Lord, we thank you for being a Father who longs to forgive and welcome us home.

11 The rich man and Lazarus
Luke 16:19–31

We all know Lazarus. He is our neighbour. Some of us may be rich, well dressed and well fed, and we walk past him without even noticing; others of us may not be so rich or so finely clothed and fed, but compared with Lazarus we're well off. He would be glad to change places with us, and we would be horrified to share his life, even for a day.

Jesus' story about Lazarus and the unnamed rich man works at several levels. It is very like a well-known folk tale in the ancient world; Jesus was by no means the first to tell of how wealth and poverty might be reversed in the future life. But in the usual story, when someone asks permission to send a message back to the people who are still alive on earth, the permission is granted. Here, it isn't, and the sharp ending of the story points beyond itself to all sorts of questions.

The parable is not primarily a moral tale about riches and poverty – though it should be heard in that way as well. If that's all it is, some might say that it is better to let the poor stay poor, since they will have a good time in the future life. That sort of argument has been used too often by the careless rich for us to want anything to do with it. No; there is something more going on here. The story, after all, doesn't add anything new to the general folk belief about fortunes being reversed in a future life. If it's a *parable*, that means once again that we should take it as picture-language about something going on in Jesus' own work.

The ending gives us a clue, picking up where, a chapter earlier, the story of the father and his two sons ended. 'Neither would they be convinced, even if someone rose from the dead'; 'This brother of yours was dead and is alive again!' The older brother in the earlier story is very like the rich man in this: both want to keep the poor, ragged brother or neighbour out of sight and out of mind. Jesus, we recall, has been criticised for welcoming outcasts and sinners; now it appears that what he's doing is putting into practice *in the present world* what, it was widely believed, would happen in the future one. 'As in heaven, so on earth' remains his watchword. The age to come must be anticipated in the present.

Lord, help us to see what your welcoming of the poor and outcast means, and how we can follow your example.

12 The persistent widow and the tax-collector
Luke 18:1–14

In the ancient Jewish lawcourt, if someone had stolen from you, you had to bring a charge against them; you couldn't get the police to do it for you. If someone had murdered a relative of yours, the same would be true. So every legal case in Jesus' day was a matter of a judge deciding to vindicate one party or the other: 'vindication' or 'justification' here means deciding in their favour.

These two parables, very different though they are in some ways, are both about vindication. The first is more obviously so, since it is actually set in a lawcourt; but here we are puzzled at first glance, since, though Jesus clearly intends the judge to stand for God, this judge is about as unlike God as possible. He has no respect for God, and he doesn't care whether he does the right thing for people or not. The point of the parable is then to say: if even a rotten judge like that can be persuaded to do the right thing by someone who pesters him, then of course God, who is Justice in person, will see that justice is done.

The second parable looks at first as though it is describing a religious occasion, but it, too, turns out to be another lawsuit. Or perhaps we should say that the Pharisee in the Temple has already turned it into a legal contest: his 'prayer', which consists of telling God all about his own good points, ends up exalting himself by the simple expedient of denouncing the tax-collector. The tax-collector, however, is the one whose small faith sees through to the great heart of God, and he casts himself on the divine mercy. Jesus reveals what the divine judge would say about this: the tax-collector returns home vindicated.

These two parables together make a powerful statement about what, in Paul's language, is called justification by faith (see Romans 3:21 – 4:25). The wider context is the final lawcourt, in which God's chosen people will be vindicated. But this doesn't mean that one can tell in the present who God's elect are simply by badges of virtue, and in particular the observance of the Jewish law. If you want to see where this vindication is anticipated in the present, look for where there is genuine penitence. 'He was the one who went back to his house in the right before God'; those are among the most comforting words in the whole Gospel.

Lord, help us to remember that only by confessing our sins and throwing ourselves on your mercy can we hope to be justified in your eyes.

13 The king, the servants and the money
Luke 19:11–27

For most of Church history, this parable has been taken as a picture of the last judgement, the time when, at the end of history, Jesus returns as King to reward his followers and punish the disloyal. But we can be sure that Luke doesn't think of it like that. Luke believes, of course, in Jesus' second coming (see Acts 1:11), but he does not intend us to read this story as a reference to it. The parable is about something happening much closer to Jesus' own day.

Jesus is telling a story about the king who comes back to see what his servants have been doing, and he tells it for the same reason as he tells almost all his parables: to explain what he himself is doing, and what it means. He is going to Jerusalem. And he is challenging his hearers to see and understand this event as the long-awaited return of Israel's God, the rightful King.

The darkest strand in the story concerns the citizens who don't want this man to be their king. This almost certainly echoes the story of Archelaus, the older brother of Herod Antipas. After the death of their father, Herod the Great, in 4 BC, Archelaus went to Rome to be confirmed as king, followed by a delegation of Judaeans who didn't want him. Now, Jesus is implying, the unwanted king is coming back in power: not another wicked Herod, but the true King, the King who comes with a message of grace and peace, the King who was rejected because his people wanted to keep the kingdom for themselves.

The story therefore says three things to Jesus' hearers. First, to the people who suppose God's kingdom is coming immediately, it declares that it is indeed coming, but with judgement as well as with mercy. Second, it indicates that as Jesus arrives in Jerusalem, the city that is already rejecting his message, God's judgement is being prepared. Third, it brings together dramatically Jesus' own journey and the return of God himself, and thus unveils the secret inside so much of the gospel story. Jesus is not just speaking about God, God's kingdom, God's return to Zion. *Jesus is embodying it.* Concealed within his own messianic, royal mission is the ultimate, and more fateful, mission: Israel's God himself, in human form, is returning at last to the city and the Temple dedicated to his honour, to put to rights, at every level, that which has gone wrong.

Lord, as we await the final day of your judgement, help us prepare to welcome Jesus as our one and only rightful King.

14 The light of the world

John 8:12–20

The idea of God calling someone to be the means of bringing light to the world is rooted in ancient Judaism. There, in the prophet Isaiah in particular, it is Israel who will be the world's true light. But, ultimately, it is the Lord's Servant who is anointed to bring God's truth and justice to the world, and who at the climax of the book dies a cruel death to achieve the goal (Isaiah 42:6; 49:6; 53; 60:1, 3). The claim to be the world's true light, like so much that Jesus says in this Gospel, is not in itself a claim to be divine (though John believes that, and wants us to believe it too); it is a claim to be Israel's Messiah. It is, in principle, a claim that we can imagine other would-be messiahs of the period making. After all, the last great would-be messiah in this period was Simeon ben-Kosiba, who led a revolution in AD 132–5 and who became known as bar-Kochba, 'son of the star'.

But the light that God intends to bring illumination to the whole world is the same light that shines relentlessly into the world's dark corners. And when it does so, it brings judgement. Throughout the Gospel it's clear that Jesus has not come to judge the world, or Israel, or individuals; but it's also clear that the fact of his coming to bring rescue, salvation, life and hope would inevitably have the effect of condemning those who don't want those things.

As Jesus has come to realise, at the heart of the Israel of his day there is a single great problem: they have forgotten who their God really is. Their behaviour, their attitudes and their ambitions indicate that they don't know the one Jesus called 'Father'; and that is why they can't recognise him as having come from this one true God.

This highlights the problem that runs through the whole chapter. Israel is supposed to be the light of the world; but Israel is providing only darkness. If Jesus is now shining the true light into that darkness, there could only be one result: a head-on clash. That is what we find.

As you read John 8, do you ever find yourself siding with the Pharisees? Have we all, perhaps, allowed ourselves to forget just how deep the darkness goes within each of us, not least when we are called to be God's people for the world but decide to turn this calling into a privilege for ourselves?

Lighten our darkness, O Lord, and let us reflect your light into the world.

15 The truth will make you free

John 8:30–6

This saying of Jesus rings like a great bell through so much Christian language: free from sin, free from slavery, free from the law, free from death, free from injustice, free from debt, free from tyranny… It's needed today as much as ever, in all of these senses and more. The way to freedom is through the truth, and what matters therefore is to know the truth. Tyranny and slavery of every sort thrive on lies, half-truths, evasions and cover-ups. Freedom and truth go hand in hand.

So Jesus is offering – we might have thought – what everybody in Israel is longing for! Freedom at last! And at an even deeper level than they have imagined. Surely this will catch people's attention. Surprisingly, no. They hear straight away that he is offering a freedom that goes far beyond the national hope of freedom from Rome, and they react against the idea. 'How can you say such a thing? We are Abraham's children, and we've always been free!'

Jesus doesn't point out, as he might, that the foundation of their national life and faith is not just Abraham, but the exodus that took place after their slavery in Egypt. He goes straight to the heart of what he means. There is a worse slavery than that which they suffered in Egypt, or the semi-slavery they are suffering under the rule of Rome. It is the slavery that grips not only individuals but also groups, nations and families of nations. It is the slavery we know as 'sin'.

The charge Jesus is putting to his contemporaries is that they are confusing two sorts of family membership: being children of Abraham and being children of God. They have been assuming that being children of Abraham means automatically being children of God, but Jesus insists that this isn't so. In fact, the children of Abraham have been deeply and seriously infected by the disease of sin. But there is still a chance. If only they would hear and receive Jesus' words, they could themselves be set free from the slavery they don't even know they are in.

Save me, Lord, from the complacent assumption that sin has no hold on me because I'm a Christian and go to church.

16 Before Abraham, 'I Am'

John 8:48–59

The point Jesus has been making throughout the chapter is that the Father, Israel's God, the one whom the Judaeans claim to worship, is operating in and through him in a decisive and unique way to summon Israel back to a genuine knowledge and allegiance to himself. The Father is the one who alone gives life; he has given his words to Jesus; so if someone keeps Jesus' words, death will go by them without making any difference.

In making claims like this, Jesus is talking about 'the father who sent me' (John 8:18). This, however, is so striking that his hearers convince themselves that it constitutes evidence of demon possession. All four Gospels tell us that Jesus' hearers accuse him of being either possessed by or in league with the devil (see Matthew 12:24; Mark 3:22; Luke 11:15). Clearly, this isn't something the early church would make up; equally clearly, then, Jesus must have been saying and doing things that were disturbing enough to make people throw such an accusation at him.

Jesus could answer the question of verse 53 by simply saying that God gives life to the faithful departed – a life with him in the present and a newly embodied life in the resurrection to come (see John 5:25–9). But he doesn't. He goes further, claiming that the one true God is at work in and through him, and that Abraham himself, in trusting in this one God and his promises for the future, celebrated the fact that he would see the day of Jesus. This seems to mean that Abraham, in trusting God's promises that through his family all the peoples of the earth would be blessed, was actually looking ahead to the day when Jesus would bring that promise into reality. He is claiming, in other words, that he, Jesus, is at last embodying what the one living God, Abraham's God, envisaged and promised.

What, then, does he mean in the crucial verse 58? He is identifying himself so closely with the one true and living God that he can speak of himself as being there 'before Abraham existed'. In other words, Jesus is so conscious of the Father with him that he can speak, in a kind of ecstasy of union, in the name of the Father. 'I Am': one of the central meanings of Yahweh, the secret and holy name of God. Jesus has seen himself so identified with the Father that he can use the name as a way of referring to himself and his mission. 'Before Abraham existed, I Am.'

Lord, thank you for perfectly revealing who you are through Jesus.

17 The good shepherd
John 10:1–10

To this day, in the Middle East, a shepherd will go into a crowded sheepfold and call out his own sheep one by one, by name. They will recognise his voice and come to him. The shepherd, after all, spends most days in their company. He knows their individual characters and markings. What's more, they know his voice. Someone else can come to the sheepfold and they won't go near him, even if he calls the right names. They are listening for the one voice that matters. When they hear it, he won't need a sheepdog to keep them in order. He won't walk behind them, driving them on. He will walk ahead, calling them, and they will follow him. I've seen it done.

The first paragraph of this section (verses 1–5) is a parable, as John tells us in verse 6. In the Bible, the picture of the shepherd with his sheep is frequently used to refer to the king and his people. The ideal king is pictured as a shepherd (Ezekiel 34), perhaps modelled on the shepherd boy David, who became the king after God's own heart (see 1 Samuel 13:14). In a world where they knew about the intimate contact between shepherd and sheep, this was their preferred way of talking about kingship.

This is the image that Jesus chooses to explain his own claim to be the true King of Israel. But, faced with blank stares, Jesus continues with further explanations. The first, in verses 7–10, highlights another part of the shepherd's role. He is the gate, or door. In many Eastern sheepfolds, the shepherd lies down at night in the gateway, to stop the sheep getting out and to stop predators getting in. Here Jesus seems to indicate the way in which the shepherd keeps the sheep safe and, like God himself in Psalm 121:8, watches over their going out and their coming in. The emphasis is on the safety of the sheep. The shepherd's priority is those sheep. Find a king like that, and you've found the Lord's anointed.

The promise of full life, 'full to overflowing', is as relevant for us today as it was then. The modern Western world has discovered how unsatisfying materialism really is, and is looking for something more. Many thieves have told lies, stolen the sheep and left them for dead. The call today to Jesus' true sheep is to listen for his voice, and to find in him and him alone the life that is overflowing indeed.

Let me hear your voice loud and clear, O Lord, and I will put all my trust in you.

18 The sower
Matthew 13:1–9, 18–23

Many of Jesus' parables are like mazes, designed to challenge his listeners to work out for themselves how to get to the heart of things. But sometimes the hearers simply get lost, and Jesus then provides a map. The point of the map is, first, to help people see where they are, and then to help them see how to get where they ought to be. As with most mazes, there are several ways of going wrong, but only one way of going right. Jesus has already seen, in the responses of many people to his announcement of God's kingdom, that there are certain common reactions that all lead to dead ends.

It's important to notice how surprising and puzzling this parable is to the disciples. They have expected, like many Jews of the time, that when God finally acted to bring the kingdom to birth, this would happen in a movement that would sweep through Israel, bringing freedom, justice and peace wherever it went. The suggestion that instead it might come, as it were, by stealth, not only through the puzzling words of a riddling preacher but also through the mixed response of his hearers – this must seem very strange. But this is, and remains, God's way of working. And that's why the *word* is so important as a theme in Jesus' ministry. Jesus speaks God's word, the word that announces the kingdom. As Isaiah saw, the word goes out and does its own work in people's hearts and lives (see Isaiah 55:10–11). That's what some kinds of words do: they change the way people are, giving them an internal map.

But, back then, not everyone who heard Jesus' words used them like this. Still, today, not everyone who hears them has the right reaction. The interpretation of the parable is, therefore, both very specific to Jesus' own context and very relevant to our own day. Some allow the evil one to snatch the words away at once. Most of us have experienced cynical and sneering reactions. Some seem to be enthusiastic, but when the gospel starts to make demands they quickly show that the word never really became rooted in their hearts. Some really do have a deep-rooted hearing of the word, but then allow other things to take root as well; like thorns, the other things choke the delicate plant of the word. As we read the parable today, we should ask ourselves: are we, too, stuck somewhere? Are we in danger of any of these reactions?

Lord, may your word take root deep inside me so that I bear good fruit for you and your kingdom.

19 The weeds
Matthew 13:24–33

'Why doesn't God *do* something?'

These parables are all about waiting, and waiting is what we all find difficult. The farmer waits for the harvest time, watching in frustration as the weeds grow alongside the wheat. Not only the farmer, but also the birds wait for the tiny mustard seed to grow into a large shrub. The woman baking bread must wait for the leaven to spread its way through the dough until the whole loaf is mysteriously leavened. And that's what God's kingdom is like.

Jesus' followers, of course, don't want to wait. If the kingdom is really present where Jesus is, coming to birth in what he is doing, then they want the whole thing at once. They aren't interested in God's timetable. They have one of their own, and expect God to conform to it.

At the heart of the parable of the weeds and the wheat is the note of patience – not just the patience of the servants who have to wait and watch, but also the patience of God himself. God didn't and doesn't enjoy the sight of a cornfield with weeds all over the place. But nor does he relish the thought of declaring harvest time too soon, and destroying wheat along with weeds.

Many Jews of Jesus' time recognised this, and spoke of God's compassion and the delaying of his judgement so that more people could be saved at the end. Jesus, followed by Paul and other early Christian writers, took the same view. Somehow Jesus wanted his followers to live with the tension of believing that the kingdom was indeed arriving in and through his own work, and that this kingdom would come, would fully arrive, not all in a bang but through a process like the slow growth of a plant or the steady leavening of a loaf.

When today we long for God to act, to put the world to rights, we must remind ourselves that he has already done so, and that what we are now awaiting is the full outworking of those events.

Lord, help us to understand the need to wait in patience for your purpose to unfold.

20 Reconciliation and prayer
in the community
Matthew 18:15–20

Reconciliation is a huge issue today. We see clearly the results of *not* doing it: suicide bombs, campaigns of terror, heavy-handed repression by occupying forces. That's on the large scale. On the smaller scale, we see broken marriages, shattered families, feuds between neighbours, divided churches. Many of us prefer to pretend there isn't a problem. We can refuse to face the facts, swallow our anger or resentment, paper over the cracks and carry on as if everything is normal while seething with rage inside. Many Christians have taken the paper-over-the-cracks option, believing that this is what 'forgiveness' means – pretending that everything is all right, that the other person hasn't really done anything wrong. That simply won't do. If someone else – another Christian in particular! – has been offensive, aggressive, bullying, dishonest or immoral, nothing whatever is gained by trying to create 'reconciliation' without confronting the real evil that's been done.

Forgiveness doesn't mean saying 'it didn't really happen' or 'it didn't really matter'. In either of those cases, you don't need forgiveness, you just need to clear up a misunderstanding. Forgiveness is when it *did* happen and it *did* matter, and you're going to deal with it and end up loving and accepting one another again anyway. That's why the sequence recommended by Jesus here is vital.

Together with this hard and high challenge there go dramatic promises. We aren't left on our own as we struggle to become the sorts of communities, families and churches that Jesus is describing. God's presence is with us; our actions on earth have an extra, hidden dimension: the heavenly counterpart of what we do here. And, when we pray together in Christian fellowship, we are therefore assured of being heard and answered. Because, in a promise that remains central to everything that Christians ever do together, 'Where two or three' (or two hundred or three hundred, for that matter, but it's often the small groups that need this encouragement most) 'come together in my name,' says Jesus, 'I'll be there amongst them.'

That's not just a promise that we will sense his presence. It's a promise – and a warning! – that he will see and know the innermost truth of everyone's heart. If we take that seriously, engaging in reconciliation will still be costly. But it will always be done in real hope, with joy waiting round the corner for those who persevere.

Lord, give me the wisdom and courage never to back away from seeking or fa-cilitating reconciliation when the challenge presents itself.

21 The challenge of forgiveness
Matthew 18:21–35

Why does Jesus solemnly say, in the last verse, that those who refuse to forgive will themselves be refused forgiveness? Isn't that, to put it bluntly, so harsh as to be out of keeping with the rest of the gospel? Can't God override our failings at exactly that point?

Apparently not. At least, I don't know about 'can't', but it seems that he won't. The New Testament speaks with one voice on this subject. Forgiveness isn't like a Christmas present that a kindly grandfather will go ahead and give to a sulky grandchild even if the grandchild hasn't bought a single gift for anyone else. It isn't like the meal that will be waiting for you back home even if you failed to buy a cheese sandwich and a cup of tea for a tramp on the street. It's a different sort of thing altogether.

Forgiveness is more like the air in your lungs. There's only room for you to inhale the next lungful when you've breathed out the previous one. If you insist on withholding it, refusing to give someone else the kiss of life they may desperately need, you won't be able to take any more in yourself, and you will suffocate very quickly. Whatever the spiritual, moral and emotional equivalent of the lungs may be, it's either open or closed. If it's open, able and willing to forgive others, it will also be open to receive God's love and forgiveness. But if it's locked up to the one, it will be locked up to the other.

This is a hard lesson to learn, in our thinking and also in our acting. It goes back, like everything else in Matthew 18, to the picture of the child. What is it that stops us saying either 'sorry' or 'I forgive you'? Isn't it just that unchildishness, that I'm-too-important-to-do-that-ness, which shows that we have forgotten, or never perhaps learned, that the greatest in the kingdom of heaven is the one who has been turned inside out and has become like a little child?

Peter's question and Jesus' answer say it all. If you're still counting how many times you've forgiven someone, you're not really forgiving them at all, but simply postponing revenge. 'Seventy times seven' is a typical bit of Jesus' teasing. What he means, of course, is, 'Don't even think about counting; just do it.'

Lord, save me from the sin of feeling too important to forgive, and open my heart that I may always be ready to forgive when the right moment arrives.

22 The workers in the vineyard
Matthew 20:1–16

It's important to realise that Jesus doesn't intend this story to serve as a comment on the social justice of his day. How likely such an incident is to have happened we can only guess, but most people who have studied that world think it is very *un*likely. Jesus is accepting, for the purpose of the story, the social and economic power of the landowner in order to say something about God.

But what is he saying about God, and why is he saying it here? To answer this we need to look a bit more closely at the last group of workers, the ones who were hired when only one hour of the day was left. It is curious, we may suppose, that they hadn't been spotted before. Had they not been in the marketplace earlier? The vineyard-owner questions them: why haven't you been working? Their answer is revealing: nobody has given us a job. Nobody, in other words, wanted them. They were, perhaps, the sort of people everybody tried not to hire.

But the landowner hired them, and he paid them the same as the people who had been slaving away all day in the heat of the sun. As in so many of Jesus' stories, the landowner is obviously standing for God, and the workers for Israel, and Jesus is saying that God's grace isn't the sort of thing that one person can have a lot of and someone else only a little.

The point of the story is that what people get from having served God is not actually a 'wage' at all. It's not, strictly, a reward for work done. God doesn't make contracts with us, as if we could bargain or negotiate for a better deal. He makes covenants, in which he promises us everything and asks of us everything in return. When he keeps his promises, he is not rewarding us for effort, but doing what comes naturally to his overflowingly generous nature.

There is always a danger that we get cross with God over this. People who work in church circles can easily assume that they are the special ones, God's inner circle. In reality, God is out in the marketplace, looking for the people everybody else is trying to ignore, welcoming them on the same terms, surprising them (and everybody else) with his generous grace. The earliest church clearly needed to learn that lesson. Is there anywhere in today's Church that doesn't need to be reminded of it as well?

Lord, help us to see and accept that your grace is for everyone, regardless of effort or merit.

23 The tenants
Matthew 21:33–46

Once upon a time there was an ancient king who had a strange dream about a huge statue. (The story is told in Daniel 2.) The statue's head was made of gold, its chest and arms of silver, its middle and thighs of bronze, its legs of iron, and its feet of a mixture of iron and clay. Then there came a stone that struck the statue on its feet of iron and clay and smashed them into pieces. But the stone itself became a great mountain and filled the whole earth.

Daniel's interpretation of the king's dream lived on in the memory of the Jews from that day to the time of Jesus and beyond. It was all about the kingdoms of the world and the kingdom of God. The kingdoms of the world were the successive kingdoms of gold, silver, bronze and iron. Each would be less glorious than the one before. Finally, there would be a brittle kingdom, like iron mixed with clay. Then there would come something different altogether. A Stone would smash the feet and the whole tottering structure of the empires of the world would come down with a crash. The Stone itself would grow to become a mountain: a new sort of kingdom.

No Jew of Jesus' day would have any difficulty figuring out what it all meant. The kingdoms of the world, starting with Babylon and Persia, had gone on until at last it was Rome's turn. And now, surely, was the moment for the Stone to appear! The Stone, they thought, meant God's Messiah, who would set up the kingdom of God by destroying the world's kingdoms and starting something new.

What has all this to do with the parable of the wicked farmers killing the owner's son? Just this: Jesus, interpreting his own story, quotes from two biblical passages, Psalm 118 and Daniel 2. The stone the builders rejected has become the top cornerstone. And the stone will crush anything that collides with it. He is the Stone, the Messiah.

And why is that an interpretation of the parable? Because the Stone and the Son are the same. The Son the farmers rejected is vindicated when the owner comes and destroys them and gives the vineyard to someone else. The Stone the builders rejected is vindicated when it goes in place at the top of the corner. The whole story is therefore Jesus' perspective on the very events he is involved in – rejected by those he has come to, but destined to be vindicated by God.

Lord, we thank you for sending Jesus to explain and fulfil the prophecies of old.

24 The wedding feast
Matthew 22:1–14

This parable often bothers people because it doesn't say what we want it to. We want to hear a nice story about God throwing the party open to everyone. We want to be 'inclusive', to let everyone in. We don't want to know about judgement or about demanding standards of holiness. We want to hear that God loves us just as we are.

People often say this when they want to justify particular types of behaviour, but the argument doesn't work. When the blind and lame came to Jesus, he didn't say, 'You're all right as you are.' He healed them. They wouldn't have been satisfied with anything less. When the prostitutes and extortioners came to Jesus, he didn't say, 'You're all right as you are.' His love reached them *where* they were, but his love refused to let them stay *as* they were. Love wants the best for the beloved. Their lives were transformed.

Actually, nobody really believes that God wants *everyone* to stay exactly as they are. God loves serial killers and child molesters; God loves ruthless and arrogant businessmen; God loves manipulative mothers who damage their children's emotions. But the point of God's love is that he wants them to change. He hates what they're doing and the effect it has on everyone else – and on themselves, too. Ultimately, if he's a good God, he cannot allow that sort of behaviour, if they don't change, to remain for ever in the party he's throwing for his Son.

That is the point of the end of the story, which is otherwise very puzzling. Of course, within the story itself it sounds quite arbitrary. Where did all the other guests get their wedding costumes from? If the servants just herded them in, how did they have time to change their clothes? Why should this one man be thrown out because he didn't have the right thing to wear? Isn't that just the sort of social exclusion that the gospel rejects?

Well, yes, of course, at that level. But that's not how parables work. The point of the story is that Jesus is telling the truth that political and religious leaders often like to hide – that God's kingdom is a kingdom in which love and justice and holiness reign unhindered. They are the clothes we need to wear for the wedding. And if we refuse to put them on, we are saying we don't want to stay at the party. That is the reality. If we don't have the courage to say so, we are deceiving ourselves.

Clothe us, O Lord, with the garments of salvation and with the robe of righteousness.

25 The wise and foolish girls
Matthew 25:1–13

This story is rooted in the Jewish tradition of contrasting wisdom and folly – being sensible or being silly. The writer of Proverbs treats Wisdom and Folly as two women, and describes them calling out to men going by, and offering them their respective lifestyles (see Proverbs 8 – 9). Now, in this story, Lady Wisdom and Mistress Folly have each become five young girls, and the story invites its hearers to decide which they'd rather be. Obviously, wisdom in this case means being ready with the oil for the lamp, and folly means not thinking about it until it's too late.

There is one other aspect to this particular story that has roots deep in the Jewish context and has given rise to a tradition of hymn-writing about the coming of the bridegroom. Already in Matthew's Gospel Jesus has referred to himself as the bridegroom (Matthew 9:15). In a previous parable Jesus spoke of the kingdom as being like a king making a marriage feast for his son (Matthew 22:2). Mention of a bridegroom hints again at Jesus' messiahship, which has of course been a central issue in the previous chapters.

This highlights the fact that the parable isn't just about the very end of time, the great and terrible day for which the world and the Church still wait. Throughout his ministry, Jesus is coming as Messiah to his people, Israel. They are the ones invited to the wedding feast. They, in this story, are divided between the wise, who know Jesus and make sure they keep alert for his coming, and the foolish, to whom at the end Jesus will say, 'I don't know you' (echoing Matthew 7:23).

It is tempting to move away from this conclusion, because saying that parts of Jesus' teaching relate particularly to a unique situation in his own time might make it look as though they are irrelevant for every other time. But that's not so. It is because what Jesus did was unique and decisive, changing for ever the way the world is and how God relates to it, that we have entered a new era in which his sovereign rule is to be brought to bear on the world. And in this new era, no less than in the unique time of Jesus and his first followers, we need as much as ever the warning that it's easy to go slack on the job, to stop paying attention to God's work and its demands, to be unprepared when the moment suddenly arrives.

Lord, may we keep the lamps of our hearts and minds trimmed and constantly prepared for your service.

26 Clean and unclean
Mark 7:14–23

Popular religion and philosophy, from at least the time of Plato, have often suggested that the physical world is bad and the spiritual world is good. So when Jesus says that food doesn't matter and the heart does, what some people hear is that 'externals – physical things – don't matter; what matter are the internal, spiritual things'. And so, since what Jesus says looks like that at first glance, we assume he's said what we expected him to say. And since we can fit that view into several other things many people today believe, the passage doesn't disturb us.

But we would be wrong. The passage should disturb us. Jesus is precisely *not* saying that external and physical things are irrelevant or bad and that internal or spiritual things are good. He is not saying that if we get in touch with our deepest feelings or learn to listen to what our heart is truly telling us, we will find our real identity and thereby discover happiness, fulfilment or whatever. He is insisting that good and bad external and physical actions come from internal and spiritual sources, and that therefore the poisoned wells of human motivation are the real problem to which the purity laws are pointing.

Is Jesus therefore setting aside Scripture, which is where the laws about clean and unclean food come from? Yes and no. Yes: the Bible says don't eat pork (and lots of other things), and Mark at least thinks Jesus is saying this doesn't apply any more. No: Jesus' basic point is that purity laws, including food laws, don't actually touch the real human problem, and that is what the kingdom of God addresses. The Scriptures spoke of purity and set up codes as signposts to it; Jesus is offering the reality. When you arrive at the destination you don't need the signposts any more, not because they were worthless but precisely because they were correct.

Learning to read the Old Testament this way wasn't easy in the early church, and it isn't easy today. The starting point is to realise that the Jewish Scriptures aren't to be seen as a timeless code of behaviour, but as the story that leads to Jesus. This doesn't mean we can casually set aside bits we don't like or understand. When things are set aside, as the purity laws are here, it's not because they're irrelevant but because the deeper truth to which they pointed has now arrived.

Create in me a clean heart, O Lord, and renew your Spirit within me.

27 Warnings about sin
Mark 9:38–50

John's attitude in this passage is a symptom of a disease that afflicts the Church to this day. How easy it is for any of us, especially professional clergy and theologians, to assume that the Church belongs to us. How easy, too, for people who have always worshipped and prayed within one particular tradition or style to feel that this is the 'proper' way. That isn't to say, of course, that some styles may not be richer or more satisfying than others. But out there in the world, beyond even rudimentary theological education and training, there are millions of Christians whom Jesus may be referring to as 'little ones who believe'. If those who have training and education do anything that excludes such people, they are in deep trouble.

This probably gives us the right focus for the sayings about cutting off hands and feet and plucking out eyes. Virtually all readers agree that these commands are not to be taken literally. They refer to precious parts of one's personality – to aspects of one's full humanness – which may from time to time cause one to stumble, which may, that is, bring about one's ruin as a follower of Jesus. Anything that gets in the way must go.

Such sayings, though, demand that we apply them in various ways to wider issues. The first thing to note is that discipleship is difficult, and demands sacrifices. Many today write and speak as if the only purpose in following Jesus were to find complete personal fulfilment and satisfaction, to follow a way or path of personal spirituality that will meet our felt needs. That is hardly the point. There's a war on. God is at work in our world; so are the forces of evil; and there really is no time or space for self-indulgent spiritualities that shirk the slightest personal cost, or even resist it on the grounds that all the desires and hopes one finds within one's heart must be God-given and so must be realised.

The second thing, within that, is that what we are asked to give up is not always something that is sinful in and of itself. Of course we should reject sin; there's nothing special in that (difficult though it may be), but that's just the beginning. We should also be prepared to reject something that is good and God-given – as hands, feet and eyes are! – but which, at the moment at least, is leading us down the wrong path.

Lord, give me the wisdom to know when I need to give up something, even something good, in order to follow you more faithfully.

28 On paying taxes to Caesar
Mark 12:13–17

Here, the Pharisees and Herodians are acting together. Their trap is clear. They are trying to force Jesus either to support the paying of taxes to Rome, thus alienating the crowds, or to denounce the tax, in which case they could tell the governor, Pontius Pilate, that Jesus is guilty of a straightforward capital charge, namely inciting revolt. But they reckoned without Jesus' brilliant response.

'Give Caesar back what belongs to Caesar,' can be taken, of course, as a way of saying, 'Yes, pay the tax,' but without the sting of, 'Yes, submit to the Romans as your masters.' The fact that Jesus has drawn attention to the blasphemous image and writing on the coin gives his command the flavour of, 'Send this filthy stuff back where it came from!' It is contemptuous, without opening Jesus to the charge of sedition.

At the same time, the command to give God what belongs to God opens all kinds of questions. Does he mean, because humans bear God's image, that all humans owe themselves, their very lives, to God and should give those lives back, as one might give a coin back to Caesar? Does he mean, standing there in the Temple courtyards, that the sacrificial system, which is supposed to be the way of giving God his due, needs to be superseded by a more complete worship? Does he mean – against the normal revolutionaries – that if you really give your whole self to God you will discover that using violence to fight violence, using evil to fight evil, simply won't do? I think he probably means to hint at all of that, and perhaps even more.

What he doesn't mean – despite many attempts to squash his words into this shape – is that you can divide human life, and the world, into two segments (the 'religious' part and the 'political' or 'social' part). That's a much later idea, which is increasingly being seen today as at best inadequate and at worst dangerous. It would prevent, for instance, any Christian critique of public policy, including economic policy, which is sometimes sorely needed in our world. Jewish thought, and Christian thought as it emerged within Judaism, have always seen the entire world and everything in it as created by the one God. All aspects of it fall under his sovereign and saving rule.

Lord, grant us wisdom to see to the heart of things, and to give ourselves wholly to our true God and King.

29 The most important commandments
Mark 12:28–34

The Jewish law begins with worship, with the love of God, because if it's true that we're made in God's image we will find our fullest meaning, our true selves, the more we learn to love and worship the one we are designed to reflect. No half measures: heart, soul, mind and strength – that is, every aspect of human life – is to be poured out gladly in worship of the one true God. Whatever we do, we are to do for him. If we were to truly live like that for a single day, God's kingdom would have come on earth as it is in heaven. And – this is the point – Jesus seems to think that through his kingdom-work this commandment is now within our reach.

Nor does Jesus stop there. He adds, 'Love your neighbour as yourself.' This doesn't mean loving others *instead of* ourselves, but showing to all people the same respect and care that we show to ourselves. Elsewhere in the Gospel stories (such as in Luke 10), this is developed and applied in more detail. Again, if people were to live by this rule, most of the world's greatest problems would be solved overnight.

The lawyer draws out a meaning that Jesus hasn't said out loud but which is certainly there. If these commandments are the primary ones, if this is what worshipping, loving and serving God is all about, then all that the Temple stands for, the daily, weekly and annual round of sacrifices and offerings, is virtually unnecessary. When a crisis comes, loving God and one's neighbour still matter; sacrifices don't.

At one level, then, this passage enables us to understand more fully what Jesus thinks his work is all about, and how his overall mission is bound to challenge the centrality of the Temple – a highly controversial, not to say dangerous, thing to suggest. Jesus really does believe that through his kingdom-mission Israel's God will enable people to worship and love him, and to love one another, in a new way, the way promised in the Prophets, the way that stems from renewed hearts and lives.

At another level, this comes as a challenge to all contemporary Christians. Would anyone looking at us – our churches, our lives, the societies that claim in some sense to be 'Christian' – ever have guessed that the man we claim to follow sees his followers as being people like this? Or to put it another way: when the crisis comes, what remains solid in your life and the life of your community?

Lord, help us to show our wholehearted love for you through the love we show to others.

30 Watching for the Son of Man
Mark 13:28–37

Jesus' main concern in this passage is to warn his followers of the signs that will immediately herald the end of the Temple, which happened when Roman armies laid siege to Jerusalem in AD 70. He uses the image of a fig tree in leaf, signalling that summer is almost here, as an illustration of how his hearers are to react. They need to watch for the crucial events, especially the arrival of pagans taking over the holy city and the Temple itself. That will be the sign that the end is not far away.

And Jesus is quite clear that this will take place within a generation. Jesus, however, does not know the precise day or hour. He, the Son, does not know it, because only the Father does. Like a good deal of Jewish thought on God's control of history, this implies that God has planned the right time. But unlike a good deal of 'apocalyptic' writing, ancient and modern, which tried then and tries now to figure out precise timings for events, this passage insists on leaving the issue to God.

The resulting command, then, is not, 'Sit down and work out a prophetic timetable' – always a more exciting thing to do – but 'Keep watch, stay awake.' The little church in the first generation cannot afford to settle down and assimilate itself to either the Jewish or the pagan world. It must constantly remind itself that terrifying times are just ahead.

But what does this mean for us, who look back on the events of AD 70 as a distant tragedy? Partly, it is important for us simply to absorb the once-for-all significance of that moment in history. Christians increasingly need to realise that unless we understand the first century, we will not understand our own times, or what sort of people we ourselves are called to be.

But it is also important for us to remind ourselves of our own call to watch. The judgement that fell on the Temple is a foretaste, according to other passages in the New Testament (for example, Hebrews 12:25–9; 2 Peter 3:7–10), of the judgement that will fall on the whole world. This time there are to be no advance warnings. Just the ongoing command to be faithful to Christ, not to compromise with the standards of the present age, but to watch for the day to dawn, in whose light the dim flickering candles of the present age will be needed no more.

Help us to keep awake, O Lord, especially when it seems as though the dark forces of this world are closing in.

October

THE WAY TO
THE CROSS

I The cup he had to drink
Matthew 20:17–28

At the heart of the story is the head-on clash between what Jesus is trying to explain to the disciples and what they assume their journey to Jerusalem is all about.

James and John come with their mother to Jesus. She's had a bright idea (or perhaps it was theirs all along): when Jesus sits on his throne, as they all know he's going to do, why not have her two sons on either side of him?

This request opens a window for us on the whole sordid business of power. Young politicians try to guess who's going to be powerful. They attach themselves to him or her, so that if they've guessed right they will be rewarded handsomely for their early allegiance. People play such games all the time. They produce cheap 'loyalty' that's not worth a thing, hollow 'friendships' that don't go deeper than the outward smile, and easy betrayals when things go wrong. That's the level the two brothers are working at. When the other disciples are cross with them, it's probably not because they are all too pure-minded to have similar thoughts, but simply because James and John got in first.

Jesus' curious answer to them opens a very different window: on the biblical roots of the calling he is following. The Old Testament prophets speak darkly about the 'cup of Yahweh's wrath' (Isaiah 51:17, 22; Jeremiah 25:15–29 and several other passages). These passages talk of what happens when the one God, grieving over the awful wickedness of the world, steps in at last to give the violent and bloodthirsty, the arrogant and oppressors, the reward for their ways and deeds. It's as though God's holy anger against such people is turned into wine: dark, sour wine which will make them drunk and helpless. They will be forced to 'drink the cup', to drain to the dregs the wrath of the God who loves and vindicates the weak and helpless.

The shock of this passage – and it becomes more shocking as we go forward from here – is that Jesus speaks of drinking this cup himself. No wonder the disciples can't grasp the idea! They are eager to become rich and famous themselves. They are bent on power, position and prestige. They are becoming... yes, just a little bit like the arrogant, the rulers of the world, the people the gospel is meant to overthrow. Have they, so soon, forgotten the Sermon on the Mount?

Lord, help us to remember that the only power worth having is the power to serve you and your kingdom.

2 Martha and Mary
Luke 10:38–42

In describing Jesus' journey to Jerusalem, Luke has chosen this incident as part of his introduction.

The real problem between Martha and Mary isn't the workload that Martha has in the kitchen. That isn't the main thing that is upsetting Martha. Nor is it (as some have suggested) that both the sisters are romantically attracted to Jesus and Martha is jealous of Mary's adoring posture, sitting at Jesus' feet. If there is any such feeling, Luke neither says nor hints at anything about it. No: the real problem is that *Mary is behaving as if she were a man*. In that culture, houses were divided into male 'space' and female 'space', and male and female roles were strictly demarcated. Mary has crossed an invisible but very important boundary within the house and within the social world.

The public room was where the men would meet. The kitchen, and other quarters unseen by outsiders, belonged to the women. For a woman to settle down comfortably among the men was bordering on the scandalous. Who does she think she is? Only a shameless woman would behave in such a way.

In the same way, to sit at the feet of a teacher was a decidedly male role. 'Sitting at someone's feet' doesn't mean a devoted, dog-like posture. When Saul of Tarsus sat and 'studied at the feet of Gamaliel' (Acts 22:3), he wasn't gazing up adoringly; he was listening and learning. To sit at someone's feet meant, quite simply, to be their student. And to sit at the feet of a rabbi was what you did *if you wanted to be a rabbi yourself*. There is no thought here of learning for learning's sake. Mary has quietly taken her place as a would-be teacher and preacher of the kingdom of God.

Jesus affirms her right to do so. This has little to do with the women's movements in the modern West. They do have some parallels with Jesus' agenda, and the two can make common cause on several issues; but they should not be confused. Jesus' valuation of each human being is based not on abstract egalitarian ideals, but on the overflowing love of God, which, like a great river breaking its banks into a parched countryside, irrigates those parts of human society which until now have remained barren and unfruitful. Mary stands for all those women who, when they hear Jesus speaking about the kingdom, know that God is calling them to listen carefully so that they can speak of it too.

Lord, grant us the will to hear and respond in faith to the boundary-breaking call of Jesus.

3 The calling of Zacchaeus
Luke 19:1–10

Nobody in Jericho likes Zacchaeus. He is exactly the kind of man every-body despises. Not only a tax-collector but a chief tax-collector; that is, not only does he make money on the side, in addition to his legitimate collections, but he almost certainly makes more money from the tax-collectors working under him. Wherever money changes hands, whether across a grubby table in a tin shack in a dusty small town or across a sparkling computer screen in a shiny office on the ninety-ninth floor of a Wall Street skyscraper, the hands all too easily get dirty. Whenever money starts to talk, it shouts louder than the claims of honesty, respect and human dignity. One can only imagine the reaction of neighbours, and even of friends and relatives, as Zacchaeus's house becomes more lavishly decorated, as more slaves run about at his bidding, as his clothes become finer and his food richer. Everyone knows that this is their money and that he has no right to it; everyone knows that there is nothing they can do about it.

Until Jesus comes through the town. Inquisitiveness gets the better of the little rich man, an unspoken question emerging from behind his hard, crafty look. Jesus sees straight through the layers of graft and greed, of callous contempt for his fellow citizens. He has met enough tax-collectors already to know exactly what life is like for them, and how, even though they can't resist the chance to make more for themselves than they should, there is a sickness at the heart for which he has the remedy.

So once again Jesus finds himself relaxing in the company of the wrong sort of people. And once again the crowd outside grumble. But this time, instead of Jesus telling a parable, the tax-collector himself speaks to Jesus in public, and gives evidence of his extravagant repentance. Repentance here isn't just a change of heart; as in Judaism in general, repentance involves restoration, making amends. Zacchaeus is determined to do so lavishly. He doesn't offer to sell all his property, nor does Jesus demand it. But by the time he gives half of it away and makes fourfold restitution where necessary, we can imagine that he will find himself in seriously reduced circumstances.

But he doesn't care. He has found something more valuable.

Lord, if we have cheated or taken advantage of others for our own gain, show us how we can truly repent and make amends.

4 The man born blind

John 9:1–11

If something in the world seems 'unfair', but if you believe in a God who is all powerful, all loving and all fair, one way of getting round the problem is to say that it only *seems* 'unfair', but actually isn't. There is, after all, some secret sin being punished.

Jesus firmly resists any such analysis of how the world is ordered. The world is stranger than that, and darker than that, and the light of God's powerful, loving justice shines more brightly than that. But to understand it all, we have to be prepared to dismantle some of our cherished assumptions and to let God remake them in a different way.

We have to stop thinking of the world as a kind of moral slot machine, where people put in a coin (a good act, say, or an evil one) and get out a particular result (a reward or a punishment). Of course, actions always have consequences. Good things often happen as a result of good actions (kindness produces gratitude), and bad things often happen through bad actions (drunkenness causes car accidents). But this isn't inevitable. Kindness is sometimes scorned. Some drunkards always get away with it.

In particular, you can't stretch the point back to a previous 'life' or to someone else's sins. Being born blind doesn't mean you must have sinned, says Jesus. Nor does it mean that your parents must have sinned. No: something much stranger, at once more mysterious and more hopeful, is going on. The chaos and misery of this present world is, it seems, the raw material out of which the loving, wise and just God is making his new creation.

New creation always seems puzzling. Nobody in the story can quite figure out whether it is the same man or not. Sometimes when people receive the good news of Jesus it so transforms their lives that people ask the same question: is this really the same person? Can someone who used to lie and steal, to cheat and swear, have become a truthful, wholesome, wise human being? The answer is yes. New creation does happen. Healing does happen. Lives can be transformed. And the question then is the one they asked the man: how did it happen? How *does* it happen?

The answer given throughout the Gospel is, of course, 'through Jesus'.

Lord, we thank you for the creative, healing, life-transforming grace you offer us through Jesus.

5 The resurrection and the life
John 11:17–27

When did you last say, 'If only…'?

With those two words we express a kind of nostalgia, not for the past as it was, but for the present that could have been, *if only* the past had just been a little bit different. Like all nostalgia, it's a bittersweet feeling, caressing the moment that might have been, while knowing it's all fantasy. All of that and more is here in Martha's 'if only' to Jesus. She knows that if Jesus had been there he would have cured Lazarus.

Instead of looking at the past and dreaming about what might have been (but now can't be), Jesus invites her to look to the future. Then, having looked to the future, he asks her to imagine that the future is suddenly brought forward into the present. This, in fact, is central to all early Christian beliefs about Jesus, and the present passage makes the point as clearly and vividly as anywhere in the whole New Testament.

First, he points her to the future: 'Your brother will rise again.' She knows, as well as Jesus does, that this is standard Jewish teaching. They share the vision of Isaiah 65 and 66: a vision of new heavens and new earth, God's whole new world, a world like ours only with its beauty and power enhanced and its pain, ugliness and grief abolished. Within that new world, they believe, all God's people from ancient times to the present will be given new bodies, to share and relish the life of the new creation.

Martha believes this, but her rather flat response shows that it isn't at the moment very comforting. But she isn't prepared for Jesus' response. The future has burst into the present. The new creation, and with it the resurrection, has come forward from the end of time into the middle of time. Jesus has not just come, as we sometimes say, 'from heaven to earth'; it is equally true to say that he has come from God's future into the present, into the mess and muddle of the world we know. 'I am the resurrection and the life,' he says. 'Resurrection' isn't just a doctrine. It isn't just a future fact. It's a *person*, and here he is standing in front of Martha, teasing her to make the huge jump of trust and hope.

Lord, we thank you for coming into our world, into our pain and sorrow and death, and for bringing with you the world-transforming hope of life in your new creation.

6 The triumphal entry
Mark 11:1–11

Imagine the sense of excitement, the feeling that Jewish pilgrims coming south from Galilee would have every time they go up to Jerusalem for a festival. They are coming to the place where the living God has chosen to place his name and his presence. They are coming to celebrate the great Jewish stories of the past, which are mostly stories of freedom and hope. They will meet with relatives and old friends. There will be singing, prayer, dancing, feasting.

Now add to that anticipation and gladness the mood of Jesus' followers as they come up the hill. It's Passover time – freedom time! But it's also, as far as they are concerned, kingdom time. The long climb up through the Judaean wilderness is the climb to the kingdom. Everything Mark tells us in this account of how they arrive at Jerusalem is designed to emphasise this.

Then comes the climax. You don't spread cloaks on the road – especially in the dusty, stony Middle East! – for a friend, or even for a respected senior member of your family. You do it for royalty. And you don't cut branches off trees or foliage from the fields to wave in the streets just because you feel elated; you do it because you are welcoming a king. The disciples believe that Jesus is the true and rightful King of the Jews, on his way to the capital city to be hailed as such. This is the moment for his royal reception.

The shout of the crowd brings this out exactly. 'Hosanna' is a Hebrew word which mixes praise to God with the prayer that God will save his people, and will do so right away. The beginning and end of their cheerful chant is taken from Psalm 118:25–6, which is itself all about going up to Jerusalem and the Temple.

This passage raises questions for us in our own following of Jesus and loyalty to him. Are we ready to put our property at his disposal, to obey his orders even when they puzzle us? Are we ready to go out of our way to honour him, to find in our own lives the equivalents of cloaks to spread on the road before him, and branches to wave to make his coming into a real festival? Or have we so domesticated and trivialised our Christian commitment, our devotion to Jesus himself, that we look on him simply as someone to help us through the various things we want to do anyway?

Lord, we welcome and celebrate you as our one true King, and rejoice in being your loyal subjects!

7 Jesus cleanses the Temple
Mark 11:12–25

Many people have read this passage and concluded that Jesus was simply protesting against commercialisation. On this view, he only intended to clean up the Temple – to stop all this non-religious activity and leave it as a place for pure prayer and worship. But Mark makes it clear that he sees Jesus' actions as a dramatic acted parable of judgement.

The key comes in the biblical quotations that sum up Jesus' charge against the Temple. Harking back to the old prophetic books of Isaiah and Jeremiah, Jesus is reminding his hearers that the Temple has always been ambiguous. Right from the time it was built and dedicated by Solomon, it was clear that it could never in fact be the full and final dwelling-place of the true God (1 Kings 8:27). Although God promised to bless Israel through the Temple, if Israel began to take it for granted, to use the Temple as an excuse for immoral behaviour, then the Temple itself could be judged. That's what the early chapters of Jeremiah are all about, including the quotation that comes here: God's house has become 'a brigands' den'.

In what sense was it a brigands' den? Not in the sense that people were using it to make money on the side. The word 'brigand' in Jesus' day wasn't a word for 'thief' or 'robber' in the ordinary sense, but for the revolutionaries, those we today would call the ultra-orthodox, ready to use violence to bring about their nationalist dreams.

Part of Jesus' charge against his fellow Jews is that Israel has used its vocation to be the light of the world as an excuse for a narrow, nationalist piety and politics in which the rest of the world is to be condemned. The Temple was intended to symbolise God's dwelling with Israel for the sake of the world; yet the way Jesus' contemporaries have organised things, it has come to symbolise not God's welcome to the nations but God's exclusion of them. The holy brigands who are bent on violent rebellion against Rome – which in Jesus' view is exactly the wrong way to bring about the kingdom of God – look to the Temple as the central focus of their ideology. And the guardians of the Temple itself are notorious for their oppressive lifestyle. Violence toward outsiders; injustice toward Israel itself: that is what the Temple has come to mean. As a result, Jesus' only word for the place is one of judgement.

Lord, deliver us from the temptation to use our religion in the service of a narrow nationalism that seeks to exclude and condemn people of other nations.

8 Jesus is anointed at Bethany
Mark 14:1–11

It always happens, when people decide to worship Jesus without inhibition – to pour out their valuables, their stories, their dancing, their music, before him just the way they feel like doing – that others looking on find the spectacle embarrassing and distasteful. Not everyone is called to pour out expensive ointment over Jesus' head; but if someone is, the rest should respect it.

The grumbles of the bystanders call forth from Jesus a quite astonishing double comment. To their suggestion that the ointment might have been sold for a huge sum and the proceeds given to the poor, Jesus, in spite of all his other teaching about the poor, makes his own imminent death the prime consideration. He is trying to tell them something, though they still aren't listening.

The second half of Jesus' comment places a startling interpretation on the woman's action. She has, he says, anointed his body for burial. She has done it ahead of time, presumably because, as Jesus knows, he will be killed in such a way that there may not be a chance for a proper anointing at the time. He is not implying that the woman has any actual knowledge of his coming fate. She has simply acted spontaneously, out of the fullness of her heart. She has, in fact, gone intuitively right to the heart of things, cutting through the male objections on the one hand and contrasting with the male plots on the other. Not for nothing is this story sometimes held up as an example of a woman getting it right while all around her men are getting it wrong.

In particular, the contrast of reactions as Jesus goes to the cross invites Mark's readers to ponder their own position, feelings and attitudes. 'Were you there,' asks the old song, 'when they crucified my Lord?' Yes, but the more important question is: what was going on inside you? Were you one of those who wanted to look the other way because some people were so exuberant in their devotion? Were you, like Judas, hoping that, if Jesus was determined to die anyway, you at least might make something out of it? Were you glad to be rid of such a troublemaker? Or were you ready to give everything you had to honour this strange man, this unexpected Messiah, this paradoxical Passover-maker?

Lord, may my devotion to you be without embarrassment or inhibitions!

9 Passover and betrayal
Matthew 26:14–25

The figure of Judas is one of the darkest, not only in the Gospels but in all literature. People have written whole books trying to get to the bottom of what precisely he did and why. I suspect that even if we were to transport all we now know of psychology back to the first century and gain an interview with Judas on the day of the Last Supper, and even if he were to answer all our questions, we still wouldn't get to a single identifiable motive that would make us say, 'Of course! That's why he did it.' Evil isn't like that. It's ultimately absurd. That's part of its danger.

It wasn't just the money, though that may have helped. If he was going to break ranks with the others, he would need something to help him get started on a different life. But the decision to hand Jesus over probably came first. It may have been partly an angry disappointment at the fact that Jesus, having caused such a stir in Jerusalem, was now talking again about going to his death, instead of planning the great moment when he would become king. Maybe Judas had hoped, as James and John had hoped, that he would be Jesus' right-hand man in the new regime.

In the middle of the picture once more, almost serene though deeply sad, is Jesus himself, arranging a secret Passover celebration with an unnamed supporter, then sitting with the Twelve and telling them what was about to happen. The sorrow of his approaching ordeal was overlaid with the sorrow of betrayal. And in that moment we glimpse one element of the meaning of the cross.

Jesus was going to his death, wounded by the wounds common to humanity. Greed, lust, ambition: all kinds of natural drives and desires turned in on themselves rather than doing the outward-looking work the creator intended them to. When we say that Jesus died 'because of our sins', we don't just mean in some abstract sense. We mean that what put him on the cross was precisely the sins that we all not only commit but also wallow in.

'It isn't me, is it, Teacher?' Only when you've said that, knowing that it might well be you, can you begin to appreciate what it meant for Jesus to sit at that table and share that Passover meal with them, with Judas too. Or what it means that Jesus has promised to share his feast with us as well.

Help me, O Lord, to examine my motives for everything I do, even when I'm sure that what I'm doing is right.

10 The Last Supper
Matthew 26:26–35

As far as the disciples were concerned, it was a Passover meal. That's what they had prepared. To this day, when Jewish families all over the world celebrate Passover, there is special food and drink, prescribed by custom going back thousands of years. And there are particular words to say. The words tell the story of how God's people, Israel, came out of Egypt through the Red Sea, leaving behind their slavery and going on to freedom in their promised land. The food and drink are carefully chosen to symbolise and express aspects of that great event, the exodus.

All this would have been second nature to the disciples. They would, of course, have been expecting Jesus to take the part of the leader in this regular, annual celebration of God's promised freedom. And so he did. But in doing so, he drew the meaning of the whole meal on to himself. He offered a new direction of thought which, for those who followed him and came to believe in him, took Passover in quite a new direction, which has likewise continued to this day. We can perhaps imagine the shock of the disciples as they realised he was departing from the normal script and talking about... *himself.*

'My body, my very self... here it is!'

'My blood, my life, my death, all for you, all so that sins can be forgiven... here it is!'

Somehow, identifying the bread with his body (about to be broken in death) and the wine with his blood (about to be spilt on the cross), and inviting his followers to share it and find in it the gift of forgiveness of sins – somehow this action had then, and still has today, a power beyond words. A power to touch and heal parts of our broken and messy lives.

But, perhaps because that power always remains mysterious and never in our own control, many people found then and find still that it's all too much. The disciples, instead of being heartened and encouraged, were all about to be scattered, as Jesus went alone to face the darkest night of the world. Peter – big, strong, blustering Peter – was about to be reduced to a spluttering, lying, weeping fool. Perhaps that tells us something, too, about the power of Jesus' action. Perhaps when it starts to have its effect, the first sign is that we learn just how weak we are, and how much we need God's redeeming love.

Lord, we thank you for the bread and wine that speak to us so powerfully of your sacrificial love.

11 The way, the truth, the life
John 14:1–11

Within the Western world of the last two centuries or so, this saying of Jesus has become one of the most controversial. 'I am the way and the truth and the life!' How dare he, people have asked. How dare John, or the Church, or anyone else, put such words into anyone's mouth? Isn't this the height of arrogance, to imagine that Jesus or anyone else is the *only* way? Don't we now know that this attitude has done untold damage, as Jesus' followers have insisted that everyone else should give up their own ways of life and follow his instead?

The trouble with this is that it doesn't work. If you dethrone Jesus, you enthrone something or someone else instead. The belief that 'all religions are really the same' sounds nice and democratic – though the study of religions quickly shows that it isn't true. What you are really saying if you claim that they're all the same is that none of them is more than a distant echo of reality. You're saying that 'reality', God, 'the divine', is remote and unknowable, and that neither Jesus nor Buddha nor Moses nor Krishna gives us direct access to it. They all provide *a* way toward the foothills of the mountain, not *the* way to the summit.

It isn't just John's Gospel that you lose if you embrace this idea. The whole New Testament – the whole of early Christianity – insists that the one true and living God, the creator, is the God of Israel; and the God of Israel has acted decisively within history to bring Israel's story to its proper goal, and through that to rescue the world. The idea of a vague general truth to which all 'religions' bear some kind of oblique witness is foreign to Christianity.

The real answer is that, though of course it's true that many Christians and churches have been arrogant in the way they have presented the gospel, the whole setting of this passage shows that such arrogance is a denial of the very truth it's claiming to present. The truth, the life, is Jesus himself: the Jesus who washed the disciples' feet and told them to copy his example, the Jesus who was on his way to give his life as the shepherd for the sheep. Was that arrogant? Was that self-serving? Only when his followers are themselves continuing to do what Jesus did may they be believed when they speak the earth-shattering truth.

Lord, be with us as we follow your way, as we rejoice in your truth and as we hope in the eternal life you have promised us.

12 Another helper

John 14:12–21

Jesus has promised to send us his own Spirit, his own breath, his own inner life. Here he uses a special word to describe the Spirit. He says that the Father will give us 'another helper'. This 'helper' is the Spirit.

The word I've translated 'helper' is rich and many-sided. It doesn't simply mean someone who comes to lend assistance. It certainly does mean that as well: the Spirit comes to give God's people the strength and energy to do what they have to do, to live for God. But it means two other things as well.

One word sometimes used is 'comforter'. Comfort is a strange and wonderful thing. Have you noticed how, when someone is deeply distressed, the fact of having other people with them, hugging them and being alongside them, gives them strength for the next moment, then the one after that, then the one after that? Outwardly nothing has changed. The tragedy is still a tragedy. The dead person won't be coming back. But human support changes our ability to cope. It gives us strength. When the Spirit is spoken of as the 'comforter', this kind of extra strength to meet special need is in mind.

But there is something quite different as well. An equally good translation for the word is 'advocate'. An advocate stands up in a court of law and explains to the judge or jury how things are from his or her client's point of view. The advocate pleads the case. Jesus assumed that his followers would often find themselves, as he found himself, on the wrong side of official persecution. He saw the situation, as centuries of Jewish tradition had before him, in terms of the heavenly lawcourt with God as the judge. In that court, his people can rest assured that their case will be heard, that God will constantly be reminded of their plight, because the Spirit will plead on their behalf. (Paul says much the same in Romans 8:26–7.)

The last three verses of this section present a wonderful circle of promises that are ours because Jesus is with us by the Spirit. We will 'see' him, plain to the eye of faith. We will live with his new life. We will know the deepest theological knowledge of all: that he and the Father are 'in' each other, and that we are 'in' him and he 'in' us. And we will be joined to Jesus and the Father by an unbreakable bond of love.

Lord, we are so grateful that Jesus is with us now through your Spirit, joining us to your holy circle of love.

13 My peace I leave with you
John 14:22–31

When Jesus in John's Gospel speaks of 'the world', he is speaking of the whole created order; but he is also speaking about the people who inhabit it and who have rebelled against their creator. Jesus has, however, come 'into the world' (John 1:9), because 'God loved the world' so much (John 3:16) that he sent his son to rescue the world. Confused? You might well be. But the confusion isn't John's fault. It comes from the way human wickedness has distorted everything. God's proper answer to this is *both* that he rejects wickedness and remains totally opposed to it *and* that he loves the world and the people that he made. Jesus' coming into the world brings both of these divine answers onto the stage of human history. He comes as the light of the world; yet many prefer the darkness.

There is, then, a sharp distinction between the followers of Jesus and 'the world'. Only when that is recognised can the next word be heard. Those who hold fast to Jesus will find that his peace comes to them as a gift, a peace of a kind that 'the world' can never give. This peace will assure them of his presence and support, gladdening them with the knowledge that the Jesus they love is indeed one with the Father.

The way to this peace, however, is through the sharp conflict that is about to come. 'The ruler of the world' is on his way, even now, coming to arrest Jesus. Who is this 'ruler'? At one level it is Caesar, whose soldiers will take Jesus to his death. At another level it is the dark power that stands behind even Caesar, the spiritual force of wickedness now using Judas as a poor accomplice. The phrase 'the world' gets its negative force in John's Gospel from the fact that the present world, though loved and claimed by the Father, remains under the rule of this dark lord. Jesus' approaching death and resurrection will inflict a huge wound on this rule, from which it will never recover; but the disciples are to be sent out into the world where opposition is still powerful and deadly.

Their courage is to be sustained by remembering what Jesus has done. He did what he did so that 'the world' might know that he loves the Father. Called to follow him, we too are to act in such a way that 'the world' will know that we love him.

Lord, we thank you for giving us your peace, the peace that gives us the courage to overcome the darkness of this world.

14 The true vine
John 15:1–8

Within Jewish tradition, the vine was a picture of Israel. God brought a vine out of Egypt and planted it in the promised land (Psalm 80:8–18). It had been ravaged by wild animals and needed protecting and re-establishing. The vineyard of Israel, said Isaiah in chapter 5, has borne wild grapes instead of proper ones. Other prophets used the same picture.

Now Jesus is saying that *he* is the 'true vine'. This can only mean that he is, in himself, the true Israel. He is the one on whom God's purposes are now resting. And his followers are members of God's true people – if they belong to him and remain 'in' him. The picture of the vine isn't just a clever illustration from gardening; it is about who Jesus and his people really are, and what is now going to happen to them as a result.

Within the farewell discourse as a whole, this section opens up a new dimension of what Jesus wants to say as he takes his leave of his closest associates. He has already spoken of them being 'in' him, as he is 'in' the Father (14:20). Now we see more of what this means. On the one hand, it is a way of speaking of himself as Israel-in-person and of his followers as members of God's true people because they belong to him. On the other hand, it is a way of speaking of the intimate relationship with him that they are to enjoy and (so to speak) to cultivate.

Branches that decide to 'go it alone', to try living without the life of the vine, soon discover their mistake. They wither and die and are good for nothing but the fire. But branches that remain in the vine, and submit to the pruner's knife when necessary, live and bear fruit. That is the prospect that Jesus holds out to his followers, to all of us.

The urgent question, then, is this: how do we 'remain' in him? What does it look like in practice? Both of the meanings above come into play. We must remain in the community that knows and loves him and celebrates him as its Lord. There is no such thing as a solitary Christian. We can't 'go it alone'. But we must also remain as people of prayer and worship in our own intimate, private lives. We must make sure to be in touch with Jesus, knowing him and being known by him.

Lord, help us to be fruitful as well as faithful followers of Jesus.

15 Obeying and loving
John 15:9–17

We can't legislate for love; but God, through Jesus, can command us to love. Discovering the difference between what law cannot achieve and what God can and does achieve is one of the great arts of being human, and of being Christian. In the present passage we are brought in on the secret of it all.

The 'command' to love is given by one who has himself done everything that love can do. When a mother loves a child, she creates the context in which the child is free to love her in return. When rulers really do love their subjects, and when this becomes clear by generous and warm-hearted actions, they create a context in which the subjects can and will love them in return. The parody of this, seen with awesome clarity in George Orwell's book *1984*, is when the totalitarian ruler ('Big Brother'), who has done nothing but oppress and terrify his subjects, nevertheless orders them to love him. And the devastating climax, after the initially resisting subjects have been brainwashed, is that it works. At the end of the book, the hero is, in a sense, happy. 'He loved Big Brother.' And the reader knows that at this moment the hero has ceased to be truly human.

Jesus, though, issues the command that we are to love one another, and so to remain in his love, because he has acted out, and will act out, the greatest thing that love can do. He has come to make us more human, not less. He has come to give us freedom and joy, not slavery and a semi-human stupor. Love makes both the lover and the beloved more truly human.

At the heart of it all is the humility that comes from knowing who's in charge. 'You didn't choose me. I chose you.' I was once asked, on the radio, which religion I would choose if I could. I pointed out that the idea of 'choosing your religion' was a mistake in the first place. Religions are not items on the supermarket shelf that we can pick and choose – though many today try to run their lives that way. Or, if they are, you'd have to say that following Jesus wasn't a 'religion'. It is a personal relationship of love and loyalty to the one who has loved us more than we can begin to imagine. And the test of that love and loyalty remains the simple, profound, dangerous and difficult command: love one another.

Thank you, Lord, for the love you have shown us, and for showing us how to love.

16 Your hearts will rejoice
John 16:12–22

Like Paul in Romans 8, Jesus in this passage uses the imagery of giving birth to express what is going to happen, and he invites his followers to prepare themselves for a sorrow and a subsequent lasting joy that is modelled on the sorrow and joy of a woman going into labour.

Giving birth is terrifying. It involves sharp pain, convulsions, breathing difficulties, a form of agony that men can only watch with awe. But most women giving birth go through it with eager expectation. Their hearts are already set on the new life that's waiting to come into the world. Within minutes, or even moments, of the birth (assuming they and the child are reasonably healthy), they are deeply content. There may be days and weeks of pain to come as the body recovers from its ordeal. But new life has come, and with it new joy.

Jesus' disciples are about to be plunged into a short, sharp and intensely painful period that will be like a moment of birth. Jesus will be taken away; but they will see him again. 'Not long from now, you won't see me any more. Then again not long after that, you will see me!' His death and resurrection are the necessary events that will lead to his going to the Father and his sending of the Spirit. These are extraordinary, cataclysmic events, the like of which the world has never seen before. The disciples can hardly prepare properly for them, but Jesus wants to warn them anyway.

It's all happening because, with Jesus' death and resurrection, a new world – *the* new world – is indeed being born. That is what John wants us to grasp. It's a matter of seeing that when we find ourselves at the foot of the cross, and then when we find ourselves after that with Mary Magdalene in the Easter garden, we shouldn't miss the significance of these events. They are not merely strange, shocking and even unique. They are the visible sign that God's new world really is coming to birth.

It's hardly surprising, then, that Jesus has another warning as well. There are all sorts of things he would love to talk to them about which they aren't ready for. That's why part of the job of the Spirit, the 'helper', will be to remind them of what Jesus has already said to them. The Spirit will also guide them, nudging their minds and imaginations into ways of knowing and things to know that Jesus would like to have said but couldn't at the time.

Lord, may I always rejoice, even when the journey is scary and painful.

17 That they may be one
John 17:20–6

Imagine some great figure of the past, someone you admire. Shakespeare, perhaps. George Washington, possibly. Now imagine that the historians have just found a letter from that person. And imagine that it was talking about... you. How would you feel?

That is how you should feel as you read verse 20. Jesus is talking about *you*. And me. 'The people who will come to believe in me because of their word', that is, through the word of his followers, who announced the message around the world. Those who heard them passed it on. The Church is never more than one generation away from extinction; all it would take is for a single generation not to hand the word on. But it's never happened. I am writing this book, and you are reading it as a result. It's awesome, when you come to think about it.

But what is Jesus praying for, as he thinks about you and me? He is praying that we may be, just as the old words from the Nicene Creed say, 'one, holy and universal', founded on the teaching of the followers, the 'apostles', the ones who were with him on that occasion. In particular, he longed that we should all be one. United.

This unity isn't to be just a formal arrangement. It is based on, and must mirror, nothing less than the unity between the Father and the Son. Just as the Father is in the Son, and the Son in the Father, so we too are to live within that unity and be united. And, in case we might miss the point, the result of this will be that the world will see and know that this kind of human community can only come from the action of the creator God.

Unity is vital. Often we sense it, like hearing soft music through the partition walls we set up around ourselves. Sometimes we experience it, when for a moment we meet Christians from a totally different background and discover that, despite the traditions that keep us apart, we know a unity of love and devotion that cannot be broken. But just as often, alas, we sense and experience that Jesus' prayer for us has not yet been fully answered.

As in any human relationship, unity cannot be forced. There can be no bullying, no manipulation. But in a divided world, where the divisions have often run down so-called 'religious' lines, there is no excuse for Christians not to work afresh for unity in every generation.

Lord, help us constantly to look for ways of healing the divisions that exist among your children.

18 Jesus is arrested
Luke 22:39–53

One person's downfall can take the others with them. That is what Jesus is most anxious to avoid. The disciples don't understand what he is doing or saying, but with hindsight we can see it. He knows not only that he will be arrested, tried and killed, but also that this is his God-given vocation. And he knows, too, that he must go alone into the hour and power of darkness.

When rebel leaders were rounded up, their associates were frequently captured, tortured and killed along with them. It is vital that this shouldn't happen to Peter and the rest. Jesus will fall, but he mustn't drag them down with him; his vocation is to give his life for the sheep, not to have them killed as well. In any case, they are the ones who will carry his mission forward in the days to come; he has prayed for Peter particularly (Luke 22:32), and it is vital that he and the others stay out of the process that will shortly engulf him.

That's why he tells them to pray 'that you won't come into the trial'. What 'trial' is he talking about? At one level, it's the trial that Jesus knows will await him once he's arrested. But this trial will be only the human and earthly version of the greater 'trial' that is coming on Jesus, on Israel, on the whole world. 'Your moment has come at last,' he says to the arresting party, 'and so has the power of darkness.' Like many Jews of his day, Jesus believes that Israel's history, and with it world history, will pass into a moment of great terror and darkness, and that the coming kingdom and all that it means will emerge the other side. This will be the 'trial', the 'test', the 'great tribulation'. Unlike any other leaders of the day, Jesus believes that it is his appointed task to go into that darkness all by himself, to carry the fate of Israel and the world through to the other side. He will face The Trial, in both senses, alone.

And in the middle of it, the disciples still don't understand what Jesus' kingdom is all about. Their attempts at defending him miss the point just as much as the swords and clubs of the guardsmen. He is neither a revolutionary fighter nor a military Messiah. But the time for explanations has passed. The hour of darkness has come, and nobody will see clearly again until the new dawn in three days' time.

Lord, our words cannot express our thanks for the love and care you showed your disciples – then and now.

19 Peter denies Jesus
Luke 22:54–71

It's a scene worth stepping into for a few moments, as we ponder what is at stake and what it all means. Think of the fireside, that chilly April night. Loyalty has taken Peter this far, but as the night wears on, tiredness saps his resolve. It's a familiar problem. We sign on to follow Jesus, and we really mean it. We start work on our vocation, and we have every intention of accomplishing it. Beginnings are always exciting, if daunting; the midday heat or the midnight weariness can drain away our intentions, our energy, our enthusiasm. Few, if any, Christians will look down on Peter and despise him. Most, if not all, of us will think: yes, that's what it's like. That's what happens.

Now see the guardroom where Jesus is blindfolded. Some of the guards are brutal and rough, ready for any sport that comes along. Others are simply doing a job, but are unable to stand back when an ugly mood takes over. Their colleagues would think them weak, and might make them the next target for their fun. One of the things that makes a bully all the more violent is the sight of weakness; he covers up his own inner fears by mocking others.

Finally, and tragically, step into the courtroom. The council members have real power, if only as puppets of Rome. They have inherited a thousand-year tradition of believing in the God of justice, and they boast of how their nation can bring that justice to God's world. But their overmastering aim here is to get rid of Jesus at all costs. For the moment everything else is on hold. One statement from him will do, however cryptic it may be, as long as they can twist it and spin it to frame a charge.

Someone asked me today what it means to say that Jesus died for the sins of the world. I gave a rather rambling but I hope adequate answer. Luke is answering that question all through this passage. Peter's weakness, the guards' bullying, the court's perversion of justice: all this and much more put Jesus on the cross. It wasn't just a theological transaction; it was real sin, the dehumanised humanity that has lost its way and spat in God's face. 'And they said many other scandalous things to him.' Yes, and we've all done so. As Luke leads our eyes to the foot of the cross, he means us to feel not just sorrow and pity, but also shame.

Lord, we acknowledge and repent of the sinfulness we share with those who sinned against you as they engineered your death.

20 Jesus before Caiaphas
Matthew 26:57–68

The gulf between them is so great, it is as though Jesus and Caiaphas are speaking two different languages. Caiaphas knows that Jesus has been leading a kingdom-of-God movement and that he has done some strange things, not least in Jerusalem itself. It seems that he has been laying claim to some kind of authority over the Temple. But Caiaphas lives in a world where he, as high priest, has supreme authority over the Temple.

Jesus, however, lives in a different world. He has been going around Galilee and Judaea doing and saying things whose clear implication is that God is doing a new thing; a new thing, moreover, that will upstage the Temple itself. Wherever he is, folk discover that it is like being in the Temple for a great festival. People get healed, people are celebrating, people even find forgiveness of sins, find the love and presence of God, which they've assumed they could only find in the Temple or by studying Torah. They don't have to go and get it. It is coming to meet them and embrace them.

Realising the radical difference between his world and that of Caiaphas, and the impossibility of explaining what he is doing and saying in words that Caiaphas would understand, Jesus remains silent. Until, that is, the high priest, anxious to secure some kind of quasi-legal conviction that he can take to the Roman governor the next day, puts him on oath. Then, and only then, Jesus speaks; but he speaks in his own language, the language he has learned and lived for many years: the language of biblical prophecy.

The two languages belong in worlds that are not only incompatible and mutually incomprehensible; they are bound to meet in head-on collision. God will vindicate one or the other.

Underneath the highly charged meeting of high priest and Messiah, the dark question remains. How do you speak God's truth into a situation where lies and distortion, injustice and ambition, have created a world in which words mean different things? Those who have tried to speak the truth in dangerous situations will know that people seem almost bound to misunderstand them. How can Christians remain loyal to Jesus, knowing when to keep silent and when to speak in such a way that true wisdom may be heard?

Lord, give us the wisdom to discern between truth and falsehood, and to uphold your truth whenever it is challenged.

21 My kingdom is not from this world
John 18:33–40

'Are you the King of the Jews?'

The idea is, of course, so laughable that Pilate knows, within his own frame of reference, what the answer is. He sees before him a poor man from the wrong part of the country. He has a small band of followers and they've all run away. Of course he's not the king. But... maybe he thinks he is. Maybe he's really deluded. Better ask him and find out.

Jesus' answer is both apparently incriminating and deeply revealing. His kingdom (yes, he agrees he has a kingdom; Pilate seizes on this) doesn't come from this world. Please note, he doesn't say, as some translations have put it, 'My kingdom is not *of* this world.' That would imply that his 'kingdom' is altogether other-worldly, a spiritual or heavenly reality that has nothing to do with the present world at all. That is not the point. Jesus, after all, taught his disciples to pray that God's kingdom would come 'as in heaven, so on earth' (Matthew 6:10).

No: the point is that Jesus' kingdom does not come *from* 'this world'. Of course it doesn't. 'The world' in John's Gospel is the source of evil and rebellion against God. Jesus is denying that his kingdom has a this-worldly *origin* or *quality*. He is not denying that it has a this-worldly *destination*. His kingdom doesn't come from this world, but it is for this world. That is the crucial distinction.

In particular, as he points out, if his kingdom were of the normal type, his followers would fight to stop him being handed over. They nearly did, of course, and he had to restrain them (John 18:10–11). Peter needed to learn the lesson Jesus is now teaching Pilate. Only with the resurrection would Peter understand.

Jesus is, in fact, speaking and bringing the truth. Jesus has come to give evidence about this truth. He is himself the truth. The truth that belongs with Passover. The truth that says one man dies and the others go free. Pilate doesn't see it. Even cunning Caiaphas probably doesn't appreciate the irony of the point (see John 11:50). But John wants us to see it. This is what the cross will mean. This is what truth is and does. Truth is what Jesus is; and Jesus is dying for Israel and for the world.

And for you and me.

Lord, give us the courage to speak truth to power, no matter the consequences.

22 Jesus before Herod
Luke 23:6–12

Herod has been in the background throughout Luke's Gospel. Only Luke tells us that he wanted to hunt Jesus down and kill him much earlier, during Jesus' Galilean ministry (Luke 13:31); only Luke now gives us this scene where they meet at last, the present and precarious 'king of the Jews' face to face with the real and coming King. Herod has longed for this moment. He sees Jesus as a combination of John the Baptist, who fascinated him with his talk but frightened him with his warnings, and the kind of circus artiste who can do magic stunts to order.

Jesus disappoints him. He says nothing and does no miracles. We might have expected, like Moses at the court of Pharaoh, that the leader of the new exodus would either threaten Herod with God's judgement or perform remarkable feats to demonstrate his claims, but Jesus does neither. He isn't that sort of prophet, and he isn't that sort of king. Luke, for whom Jesus is certainly both a true prophet and the true King of the Jews, places this meeting in a sequence of scenes designed to reveal the truth of this kingship and the falsehood of all other types. At this moment, the truth is more eloquently stated by silence.

Why, then, does Pilate say that Jesus is innocent of the charges laid against him? Why does Herod noticeably not accede to the chief priests' accusations? Partly, it seems, because it is obvious that Jesus is not leading the sort of revolution normally spearheaded by would-be 'kings of the Jews'. His few close followers were only lightly armed, and have in any case run away. Jesus makes no threats, offers no resistance and says hardly anything. They can see that the main reason he is before them is because the chief priests and their associates want to get rid of him – and both Herod and Pilate dislike them and try to do them down, as part of the power struggles that dribble on throughout this period.

Once again, Jesus is caught at the point where competing interests and agendas met. Not only the sins, but also the petty aspirations of the world conspire to put him on the cross.

Lord, we pray you will forgive not only our sins but also the petty aspirations that blind us to the truth about ourselves and what is going on around us.

23 Pilate pressured by the crowds
Luke 23:13–26

Barabbas is not a common criminal. Luke informs us that he was thrown into prison for his part in a violent rebellion that took place in Jerusalem. This is all we know about this particular rebellion, since the non-Christian historian Josephus doesn't mention another uprising at this time. We can assume that such events were a regular occurrence, and that in the ancient world (as, alas, in the modern) the Middle East would be a place where political and social frustration would regularly spill over into violence, sometimes focused on particular targets, sometimes mindless and born of the apparent hopelessness of the cause.

Luke describes the event in such a way that we can hardly miss the point. Barabbas is guilty of some of the crimes of which Jesus, though innocent, is charged: stirring up the people, leading a rebellion. We don't know whether he sees himself, or whether his followers see him, as a possible 'king of the Jews', but that is not unlikely. One of them is to die, and it turns out to be Jesus. Jesus ends up dying the death appropriate for the violent rebel. He predicted that he would be 'reckoned with the lawless' (Luke 22:37), and it has happened all too soon.

Luke's readers are by now used to seeing Jesus in company with tax-collectors and sinners. We have been told that this was the appropriate and necessary focus of his ministry, embodying the outstretched love of God to all in need, going in search of lost sheep wherever they might be found. We were not, perhaps, quite prepared for it to end like this. It is one thing for Jesus to go in to eat with a man who is a sinner (Luke 19:7). It is a considerable step beyond that for him to go off and die the death of the violent rebel.

But this is in fact the climax and focus of the whole Gospel. This is the point for which Luke has been preparing us all along. All sinners, all rebels, all the human race are invited to see themselves in the figure of Barabbas, and as we do so, we discover in this story that Jesus comes to take our place, under condemnation for sins and wickednesses great and small. In the strange justice of God, which overrules the unjust 'justice' of Rome and every human system, God's mercy reaches out where human mercy could not, not only sharing, but in this case substituting for, the sinner's fate.

Lord, we thank you that there is nothing that sinful humans can do to thwart or overcome your mercy.

24 Here's the man!

John 19:1–7

When we looked at the opening of John's Gospel, we saw that the long and carefully crafted Prologue, telling the story of creation and new creation, was designed to lead the eye up to verse 14. This is the equivalent, within John 1, of Genesis 1:26–8. 'The Word became flesh, and lived among us.' The one who was with God, the one who *was* God, alongside the Father and reflecting his character and love, became a human being.

Now at last we find ourselves on a Friday morning, the sixth day of the week, looking at the Roman governor and his peculiar new prisoner. He lets the soldiers dress him up as a king – of sorts: the crown of thorns and the slapping about the face tell us what they thought of such a claim. And Pilate says the words that still haunt us: 'Look! Here's the man!'

Here's the man! Here is the true image of the true God. Here is the one who has brought God's wisdom into the world. Here is the living embodiment of God. Here is the king. Here is the true the emperor-of-all, placed within the emperor's world so that people could see who is their true master. And all his rebel subjects can do is mock and slap and scream for his blood. He's made himself God's Son, they say!

Well, John's reader knows by now that Jesus has indeed behaved as the one who, as of right, reflects God into the world. All this is part of what it means to be God's image, planted in territory that belongs to God but is in rebellion against him. 'He was in the world' (John 1:10). Now we have learned what John means by 'the world'; that little sentence says it all.

It says, in particular, that when the living, loving God comes in person, in the person of his own Son, to live among us rebels, in the world he made and still loves, the appropriate form for him to take is not the superhero, sweeping through the rebel state with horses and chariots. The appropriate form for him to take is the form Jesus has now taken. The King of the Jews, crowned with thorns. The innocent king, the true man, the one who has told the truth and is accused of blasphemy. 'Here's the man!'

This is what it means that Jesus, the eternal Word, took our flesh. Look at this man, and you'll see your living, loving, bruised and bleeding God.

We give thanks, O Lord, for the man who bore our sins and carried our sorrows.

25 The King of the Jews
John 19:16–24

'JESUS OF NAZARETH, THE KING OF THE JEWS'

The notice is full of irony. The chief priests are furious with Pilate. He doesn't believe Jesus is the King of the Jews any more than they do, and they don't want him making fun of them in this way. Pilate, of course, is getting his own back. It's a calculated snub. But clearly, what John is telling us is that Jesus is now announced as Israel's Messiah to all the world. This is what he said would happen. The world doesn't at the moment know that what it needs, to rescue it from its desperate plight, is the Messiah promised by the one God to Israel. But this is what John believes. Israel's Messiah, after all, will rule from sea to sea, from one end of the world to the other. All nations will do him homage (Psalm 72).

But how can this happen if the Messiah is being executed as a common criminal, or a revolutionary? John's answer is unambiguous: it is precisely *through* his execution that it will now happen. As the King, he is also fulfilling the extraordinary biblical prophecies about the suffering righteous one, through whose tribulation and death evil would be exhausted and the kingdom of God be born on earth.

One of the most popular of these biblical prophecies among the early Christians was Psalm 22. That is the psalm from which, according to Matthew 27:46 and Mark 15:34, Jesus himself quoted, or perhaps we should say screamed out, at the moment of his greatest agony: 'My God, my God, why did you abandon me?' As that psalm continues its awful litany of suffering, one of the many horrors it describes is the moment when the sufferer is not only stripped naked but also suffers the added indignity of seeing people gambling for his clothes.

John doesn't need to do more than give the briefest description of the gambling at the foot of the cross and to draw our attention to the psalm in question. He leaves us to think through the implication. Jesus is the fulfilment of prophecy and sacred song. He is the righteous sufferer. He is the true King. He is the one through whose shameful death the weight of Israel's sin, and behind that the sin of the whole world, is being dealt with. The King of the Jews is God's chosen representative, not merely to rule the world but also to redeem it.

Lord, you are our redeemer as well as our ruler. Take away our sins so that our hearts may be open to your righteous reign.

26 The death of Jesus
John 19:25–30

The moving scene between Jesus, his mother and 'the disciple he specially loved' has been the subject of much painting and meditation. Many churches have Mary and John (let's call him 'John' for the sake of discussion, though we may never know for certain that it was him) painted at the foot of the cross, on either side.

But this moment – the last time we meet Jesus' mother in the Gospel story – is full of pathos all of its own. Think back to that story, early in the Gospel, when Mary pointed out to Jesus that the wine had run out (John 2:3–4). She didn't understand then that his time hadn't yet come, but she knew that the way to get things done was for people to do whatever he said. She doesn't understand now that his time has come, that his calling to turn the water of human life into the rich wine of God's love is now at last being fulfilled. We assume that she quickly came to believe all this through Jesus' resurrection; and we assume it the more readily because of what happens here. John takes her to his own home and welcomes her as though she were his own mother.

But the story of the water and the wine has more resonance with this scene than simply Jesus' comment to Mary. Here is Jesus, thirsty, and they give him the low-grade sour wine that the soldiers use. He gave others the best wine, so good that people remarked on it. He himself, at his moment of agony, has the cheap stuff that the lower ranks in the army drink when on duty.

Jesus drinks the bitter wine and then gives one last cry. 'It's finished!' 'It's all done!' 'It's complete!' He has finished the work that the Father gave him to do (John 17:4). He has loved 'right through to the end' his own who were in the world (John 13:1). He has accomplished the full and final task.

The word that I've translated 'It's all done!' is actually a single word in the original language. It's the word that people would write on a bill after it has been paid. The bill is dealt with. It's finished. The price has been paid. Yes, says John: Jesus' work is now complete, in that sense as in every other. It is upon this finished, complete work that his people from that day to this can stake their lives.

Help us, Lord, to be like Mary and like John, staying loyal to you to the end and showing our loyalty by loving one another.

27 The empty tomb
John 20:1–10

Mary Magdalene doesn't feature in John's Gospel until her appearance, with the other Marys, at the foot of the cross (John 19:25). John has told us nothing of her history; the little we know, we know from the other Gospels. But her place here is spectacular. She is the first apostle, the apostle to the apostles: the first to bring the news that the tomb is empty. And in the next section, a greater privilege yet: the first to see, to meet, to speak with the risen Master himself.

For the moment, the empty tomb is simply another twist of the knife. Chaos upon chaos. Someone's taken him away. No faith, no hope, no 'maybe, after all…' Just a cruel trick. Some gardener, some labourer, some soldier, someone's servant. But we must find out. It's urgent. She runs back into the city, back to Peter in his hiding place, back to the young lad she stood with by the cross, the one Jesus specially loved.

They run, too. The younger man gets there first. Sure enough, the tomb is open and empty. And here's a curious thing: there are the linen cloths lying there. Someone has not only taken the body away; they have first gone to the trouble of *unwrapping* it. Why on earth would they do that?

Peter, out of breath, arrives at the tomb a few moments later. He acts in character: no waiting, no shall-we-shan't-we. In he goes.

Then comes the moment. The younger man, the beloved disciple, goes into the tomb after Peter. And something quite new surges up inside him, a wild delight at God's creative power. He remembers the moment ever afterwards. A different sensation. A bit like falling in love; a bit like sunrise; a bit like the sound of rain at the end of a long drought.

A bit like faith. Oh, he had faith before. He believed that Jesus was the Messiah. He believed that God had sent him, that he was God's man for God's people. But this is different. 'He saw, *and he believed.*' He believes that God has said 'Yes' to Jesus, to all that he has been and done. He believes that Jesus has gone on, through death and out into a new world, a new creation, a new life beyond, where death itself has been defeated and life, sheer life, life in all its fullness, can begin at last.

Thank you, O Lord, for the joy of Jesus' resurrection and for the hope it gives us of new life in the new world that you have promised.

28 Mary Magdalene and the risen Jesus
John 20:11–18

Where did the angels come from? They weren't there a few moments before, when Peter and John were inside the tomb. Or maybe they were. Maybe sometimes you can only see angels through tears. Whatever. When people are afraid, angels tend to tell them not to be. When people are in tears, angels ask why.

Now, as you stand with Mary and ponder her answer, and the answers the question would receive today from around the world, turn around and see the strange figure who's standing there. Who is he? What's he doing? Who do you think he is? Mary's intuitive guess, that he must be the gardener, is wrong at one level and right, deeply right, at another. This is the new creation. Jesus is the beginning of it. Remember Pilate: 'Here's the man!' Here he is: the new Adam, the gardener, charged with bringing the chaos of God's creation into new order, into flower, into fruitfulness. He has come to uproot the thorns and thistles and replace them with blossoms and harvests.

As we stand there and listen, we hear him call Mary's name. It is greeting, consolation, gentle rebuke ('Come on! Don't you know me?') and invitation, all rolled into one. Of course we know him. Of course we don't know him. He is the same. He is different. He is alive, with a new sort of life, the like of which we've never seen before.

A puzzling feature of the passage is Jesus' warning to Mary in verse 17. 'Don't cling to me'; or, as some translations say, 'Don't touch me.' This is a way of telling Mary that the new relationship with him is not going to be like the old one. He won't be going around Galilee and Judaea any more, walking the lanes with them, sharing regular meals. They will see him now and then, but soon it will be time for him to go to the Father. 'Don't cling to me' is a way of saying, 'Don't try to keep me, to possess me.' Strange words for a strange moment.

Mary is not upset by this. She has business in hand. Once again she is the apostle to the apostles. 'I've seen the master,' and he 'said these things to her'. Nothing like first-hand evidence. And it still counts today. If someone in the first century wanted to invent a story about people seeing Jesus, they wouldn't dream of giving the star part to a woman. Let alone Mary Magdalene.

Lord, we give thanks for the witness of Mary Magdalene, and share in her joy and devotion to the risen Jesus.

29 Jesus revealed at Emmaus
Luke 24:28–35

Jesus has gone through death and out the other side into a new world, a world of new and deathless creation, still physical only somehow transformed.

Luke has, of course, told the story in such a way as to help us live in it ourselves. We, too, are invited to listen to the exposition of the Bible, to have our hearts burning within us as fresh truth comes out of the old pages and sets us on fire. In this passage, Luke emphasises what the Church all too easily forgets: that the careful study of the Bible is meant to bring together head and heart, understanding and excited application. This will happen as we learn to think through the story of God and the world, of Israel and Jesus, not in the way our various cultures try to make us think, but in the way that God himself has sketched out.

Only when we see the Old Testament as reaching its natural climax in Jesus will we have understood it. Equally, we will only understand Jesus himself when we see him as the one to whom Scripture points, not in isolated prooftexts but in the entire flow of the story. And, when we grasp this, we, like the two on the road to Emmaus (who, in the light of John 19:25, may well have been Clopas, or Cleopas, and Mary his wife), will find our hearts burning within us.

So, too, we are invited to know Jesus in the breaking of the bread. The way Luke has described the simple mealtime takes our minds back to the upper room, and to many other meals that Jesus shared with his followers. Cleopas and Mary, not being members of the Twelve, were not present at the Last Supper, but what Jesus did then was (apart from the special words) typical, most likely, of the way he had always broken bread with them.

But Luke also intends that his readers should see this simple meal pointing forward to the breaking of bread which will quickly become the central symbolic action of Jesus' people. Though Jesus is no longer physically present, they will discover him living with and in them through this meal (Acts 2:42). Scripture and sacrament, word and meal, are joined tightly together, here as elsewhere. Take Scripture away and the sacrament becomes a piece of magic. Take the sacrament away and Scripture becomes an intellectual or emotional exercise, detached from real life. Put them together and you have the centre of Christian living as Luke understands it.

Lord, we thank you for revealing yourself to us in the breaking of bread.

30 Jesus and Thomas
John 20:24–31

With this story of Thomas, what John set out to tell us in his Gospel, from those unforgettable opening lines onwards, has been completed. The story has taken its time. We have met many interesting characters and watched them interact with Jesus. Some have misunderstood him. Some have been downright hostile. Some have come to believe in him. We now have another such character.

'My Lord,' says Thomas, 'and my God!' He is the first person in this book to look at Jesus of Nazareth and address the word 'God' directly to him. Yet this is what John has been working round to from the beginning. 'In the beginning was the Word...and the Word was God' (John 1:1). 'Nobody has ever seen God. The only-begotten God, who is intimately close to the father – he has brought him to light' (John 1:18). What does that mean? What does it look like when it's actually happening?

Well, says John, it looks like this... and off we go, through Galilee and Jerusalem, moments of glory and doom woven together until they meet on the cross. Now, a week after Easter, it looks like this: a muddled, dogged disciple, standing on his rights not to believe anything until he's got solid evidence, confronted by a smiling Jesus who has just walked, as he did the previous week, through a locked door. This is what it looks like.

And of course it baffled Thomas just as it baffles us. What sort of a person – what sort of an *object* – are we dealing with here? The whole point of the story is that it's the same Jesus. The marks of the nails in his hands. The wound in his side. This isn't a ghost. Nor is it someone else pretending to be Jesus. This is him. This is the body that the grave-cloths couldn't contain any longer.

Thomas just happened to be the one who was somewhere else on the first Easter day. He sees the others excited, elated, unable to contain their joy. He's not going to be taken in.

Fair enough. At the end, Jesus issues a gentle rebuke to Thomas for needing to see before he would believe; but we notice that the beloved disciple describes his own arrival at faith in the same way: 'He saw, and he believed' (John 20:8). This isn't, then, so much a rebuke to Thomas; it's more an encouragement to people of subsequent generations. We are all 'blessed' when, without having seen the risen Lord for ourselves, we nevertheless believe in him.

We thank you, our Lord and our God, for being with us and for us through Jesus.

31 Breakfast on the shore
John 21:9–14

'None of the disciples dared ask him, "Who are you?" They knew it was the master.'

That is a very, very strange way to put it. It belongs with the other exceedingly strange things that are said in the resurrection accounts. They knew it was him... yet they wanted to ask, and were afraid to. Why did they want to ask? They had been with him night and day for two or three years, and they wanted to ask who he was?

And yet. The sentence only makes sense if Jesus is, as well as the same, somehow different. No source mentions what he is wearing. No source describes his face. Somehow he has passed through death and into a strange new world where nobody has ever been before and nobody has yet been since – though we are firmly and securely promised that we shall join him there eventually. His body is no longer subject to decay or death. What might that be like?

We have no means of knowing. We are in the same position that someone in the sixteenth century would have been in if they'd been shown a computer logging on to the internet. They didn't have electricity in those days, let alone microchips! The difference between our present body and Jesus' risen body is like that, only more so. This is a whole new world. It isn't magic. It isn't ghostly. It's real, but it's different. God help us if we ever imagine that our normal everyday world is the sum total of all that there is. What a dull, flat, boring idea.

We must always be ready to be surprised by God. They were, that spring morning, the third time they saw him after his resurrection. They were surprised by the huge catch. They were surprised by Jesus himself. And they were surprised, we may suppose, at themselves. Who were they? What were they doing? What was to happen next?

Lord, the life you now live is far beyond our understanding, but we thank you for your promise that one day you will share it with us.

November

THE CHURCH IS BORN

1 Here comes the sequel!
Acts 1:1–5

At one level, the book of Acts is of course the story of the early church. But Luke, as we shall see, also wants us to read it as a book about Jesus. It is as though we are reading a play in which Jesus is the principal actor – and in whose action *we ourselves are called to continue.* We need to refresh our minds as to how the opening scenes worked so that we can play our parts properly.

As we do so, Luke is keen that we latch on to two things that are fundamental to his whole book. First, it is all based on the resurrection of Jesus. In the last chapter of his Gospel, Luke described some of the scenes in which Jesus met his followers after being raised from the dead: it really was him, in a transformed body that could eat and drink as well as walk and talk, but which seemed to have… some different properties. His body could, for instance, appear and disappear, and come and go through locked doors. To us, that sounds as if he was a ghost, someone less than properly embodied. What Luke is saying, rather, is that Jesus is *more* than ordinarily embodied, not less. His transformed body is now the beginning of God's new creation; and in God's new creation, as we know from passages like Revelation 21 and Ephesians 1, heaven and earth will come together in a new way. Jesus' risen body is the beginning of that.

The second thing Luke wants us to latch on to is the presence and power of the Holy Spirit. Jesus, Luke says, pointed back to the beginning of his own kingdom-work, the time when John the Baptist summoned all Israel to a baptism of repentance and renewal. It's going to be like that, he says, only much more so. Instead of being plunged into water, you'll be plunged into the Holy Spirit. They will experience a renewal that will form them as the restored humanity, celebrating the fact that God is becoming King of the whole world, *and knowing that as a reality inside their own selves.* That is the very heart of the spirituality, and indeed the theology, of The Acts of the Apostles. God is at work to do a new thing in the whole world. And it catches up, within its powerful movement, every child, woman and man who comes within its orbit.

Lord, we thank you for baptising us in your Spirit, and we pray for your guidance as we read about the beginnings of your Church.

2 When, what and how?
Acts 1:6–8

The apostles are very puzzled. They believe that God has appointed Jesus to be the true King of Israel, and they have imagined that he will be king in some quite ordinary sense, which is why some of them asked if they could have the top jobs in his government. They weren't expecting that Jesus would die a violent death. His crucifixion made it look as though they were wrong: he wasn't the Messiah, they weren't heading for the top jobs. And then he rose from the dead. What does it mean? Does it mean that their dreams that he will 'restore the kingdom to Israel' are now back on track?

Well, it does and it doesn't. Like everything else, the dream of the kingdom has been transformed through Jesus' death and resurrection. At this point, many people reading Acts have assumed that Jesus is simply saying, 'No, this isn't the time. All of those things will happen a long way off in the future.' And, actually, there is a sense in which all that is indeed true. There is a 'still-future' dimension to everything that happens in this book. But wait a minute. Is that really what Jesus' answer means? I don't think it is. Jesus does indeed warn them that they won't be given a timetable. But what he goes on to say hints at something different. 'You will receive power… Then you will be my witnesses in Jerusalem…and to the very ends of the earth.'

'My witnesses'? What does that mean? Quite simply this: Jesus is indeed being enthroned as Israel's Messiah and therefore King of the whole world. In the world of the first century, when someone was enthroned as king, that new authority would take effect through heralds going off throughout the territory in question with the news, 'We have a king!' *And that is what Jesus is telling them they must now do.* You're asking when the kingdom will come about? Well, in one sense it has already happened, Jesus is saying, because in my own death and resurrection I have already been exalted as Israel's representative. In another sense it is yet to happen, because we still await the time when the whole world is visibly and clearly living under God's just and healing rule. But we are now living in between those two points, *and you must be my witnesses from here to the ends of the world.* The apostles are to go out as heralds of the one who has *already* been appointed and enthroned.

Send us out, O Lord, as witnesses to your kingdom rule – yesterday, today and forever.

3 Ascension!

Acts 1:9–14

In the Bible, heaven and earth are the two halves of God's created world. Talking about heaven and earth is a way, in the Bible, of talking about the fact that everything in our world has another dimension, another sort of reality that goes with it. You could think of earth as the 'inner' reality, the dense material of the world where we live at the moment, and heaven as the 'outer' reality, the side of our reality that is open to all kinds of other things, to meanings and possibilities that our 'inner' reality, our busy little world of space, time and matter, sometimes seems to exclude.

If these illustrations don't help, leave them to one side and concentrate on the reality. The reality is this: 'heaven' in the Bible is God's space, and 'earth' is our space. God's plan, as we see again and again in the Bible, is for 'a new heaven and a new earth' (Revelation 21:1), and for them to be joined together in that renewal once and for all.

Part of the point about Jesus' resurrection is that it was the beginning of precisely that astonishing and world-shattering renewal. And once we grasp that 'heaven' and 'earth' mean what they mean in the Bible, and that 'heaven' is not a location within our own cosmos of space, time and matter, situated somewhere up in the sky, then we are ready to understand the ascension, described here quite simply and briefly by Luke.

That is the point of the event and its explanation as we find them in verses 9–11. Jesus is 'lifted up', indicating to the disciples not that he is heading out somewhere beyond the moon, beyond Mars or wherever, but that he is going into 'God's space', God's dimension. The cloud, as so often in the Bible, is the sign of God's presence – think of the pillar of cloud and fire as the children of Israel wandered through the desert (Exodus 13:21), or the cloud and smoke that filled the Temple when God became suddenly present in a new way (2 Chronicles 5:13–14).

Jesus has gone into God's dimension of reality; but he'll be back on the day when that dimension and our present one are brought together once and for all. That promise hangs in the air over the whole of Christian history from that day to this.

Lord, hasten the day when you will be with us again in the new heaven-and-earth reality you have promised us.

4 Here comes the power
Acts 2:1–4

The gift of the Spirit is the direct result of the ascension of Jesus. Because he is the Lord of all, his energy, the power to be and do something quite new, is available through the Spirit to all who follow him.

The wind and the fire are wild, untameable forces, and the experience of the wind rushing through the house with a great roar and the fire coming to rest on each person present must have been both terrifying and exhilarating. Of course, there are many times later in this book, as there are many times in the life of the Church, when the Spirit works softly and secretly, quietly transforming people's lives and situations without any big noise or fuss. People sometimes suppose that this is the norm, and that the noise, the force and the fire are the exception – just as some have supposed, within Pentecostal and similar circles, that without the noise and the fire, and particularly the speaking in tongues, something is seriously lacking or deficient. We should beware of drawing either conclusion. Luke clearly intends to describe something new, something that launched a great movement, as a fleet of ships is launched by the strong wind that drives them out to sea or a forest fire is started by a few small flames. He intends to explain how it was that a small group of frightened, puzzled and largely uneducated men and women could so quickly become, as they undoubtedly did, a force to be reckoned with right across the known world.

People sometimes feel guilty if they think they haven't had such wonderful experiences as the apostles had on the first Pentecost. Or they feel jealous of those who seem to have had things like this happen to them. But we need to remember that God moves mysteriously among his people, dealing with each individual in a different way. Some people are allowed remarkable experiences, perhaps (we can't always tell) because they are going to have to go into difficult situations and need to know very directly just how dramatically powerful and life-transforming God can be. Other people have to work in quiet and patient ways and not rely on a sudden burst of extra power to fix all the problems which in fact need a much more steady, and perhaps much deeper, work.

There is no room for pride or jealousy in a well-ordered fellowship, where everybody is as delighted with the gifts given to others as with those given to themselves.

Lord, open our hearts to the gift of your Spirit, guiding and directing us today and every day.

5 New words for new news
Acts 2:5–13

One of the great themes of Acts is the outworking of God's promise to extend his kingdom; his saving, sovereign rule; not only in Israel but *through* Israel to the rest of the world. Part of Luke's aim, in other words, is to show how God is going to fulfil what he said to Abraham in Genesis 12:3: 'In you, and in your family, all the families of the earth will be blessed.' Now this promise to Abraham comes directly after the dramatic chapter in Genesis in which the people of Babel are building a tower, thinking arrogantly to make a name for themselves. God's response, as always, to human pride and arrogance is to overturn the project, which he accomplishes by confusing their languages so that they cannot work together on creating a human society that would have no need of the creator God.

Now, with the day of Pentecost, this curse is overturned; in other words, God is dramatically signalling that his promises to Abraham are being fulfilled, and the whole human race is going to be addressed with the good news of what has happened in and through Jesus. Granted, all the people present are Jewish or at least proselytes (Gentiles who have converted to Judaism), since the reason they are in Jerusalem is to attend the Jewish festival. But they have come from countries all over, each of which would have its own native language and local dialects. Luke gives the list of where they come from in a great sprawling sweep, covering tens of thousands of square miles. The point is not to give an exact list of precisely where everyone has come from in the crowded city of Jerusalem that day, but to splash across the page the sense of a great polyglot company all hearing words spoken in their own language.

Hardly surprisingly, to some it sounds simply like the slurred and babbling speech of people who have had too much to drink. Again and again in Acts we find opposition, incredulity, scoffing and sneering at what the apostles say and do, at the same time as great success and conviction. And again and again in the work of the Church, to this day, there are always plenty who declare that we are talking incomprehensible nonsense. Part of the challenge of this passage is the question: have our churches today got enough energy, enough Spirit-driven new life, to make onlookers pass any comment at all?

Lord, please renew your Church in the power of your Spirit, that it may continue to fulfil its vocation to spread your word throughout the world.

6 It's all coming true at last!
Acts 2:14–21

'In the last days...'

What does that mean to Peter and his audience? It is a general term for the time to come, the time when God's promises will be fulfilled. But, though Peter declares that these are 'the last days' of which the prophet Joel has spoken, they are not 'the last day' itself. There remains another 'day' (not necessarily a period of twenty-four hours), which the prophets referred to as 'the day of the Lord'. The early Christians believe, in other words, that they are living in a period of time between the moment when 'the last days' have been launched and the moment when even those 'last days' will come to an end on 'the day of the Lord'.

Part of the point of 'the last days' is that they are the time of new creation – and the new creation will start with God's own people! This is where the quotation from Joel functions as a direct explanation of the otherwise bizarre behaviour of the apostles, shouting out in several different languages the powerful things that God has done. Peter connects it directly with the promise of Joel that God would pour out his Spirit in a new way. Up to this moment, God has acted by his Spirit among his people, but it's always been by inspiring one person here, one or two there. Now, in a sudden burst of fresh divine energy released through the death and resurrection of Jesus, God's Spirit has been poured out upon a lot of people all at once. Male and female, young and old, are all marked out, side by side, as the nucleus of God's true people.

This work of God is wonderfully inclusive, because there is no category of people left out. But it is wonderfully focused, because it happens to 'everyone who calls on the name of the Lord'. Here, once more, 'the Lord', which in Joel meant Israel's God, Yahweh, now seems to mean Jesus himself. And with this Luke introduces a vital and complex theme in his work: 'salvation'. All who call on the Lord's name will be *saved*.

Peter will now go on to encourage his hearers to call 'on the name of the Lord', and so to know that salvation as a present reality as well as a future hope. If these really are 'the last days', then salvation has already begun. Anyone who knows they need rescuing, whatever from, can call 'on the name of the Lord' and discover how it can happen.

We thank you, Lord, for the salvation you offer all the world through Jesus.

7 The new family
Acts 2:42–7

Luke's book has got off to a flying start, with the extraordinary conversation between the risen Jesus and the apostles and then the spectacular events of the day of Pentecost. Peter's address to the puzzled crowds, the first public statement of the good news about Jesus and about God's rescue operation through him, is dramatic. And now, at the end of that first Pentecost, we pause for breath, look around and see where we've got to. Luke is careful to point out the landmarks. In fact, Acts 2:42 is often regarded as laying down the four marks of the Church. The apostles' teaching, the common life of those who believe, the breaking of bread and the prayers. These four go together. You can't separate them, or leave one out, without damage to the whole thing.

This shared life quickly developed in one particular direction, which is both fascinating and controversial. The earliest Christians lived *as a single family*. We are 'family'! We are brothers and sisters! Our baptism, our shared faith, our fellowship at the bread-breaking, all point in this direction. And they had a word for this way of ordering their life, a word we have often taken to refer to feelings inside us but which, for them, was primarily about what you do with your possessions when you're part of this big, extended family. The word is 'love', *agapē* in Greek.

The challenge remains for every generation in the Church, especially now that Jesus' followers number several million all around the world. Many Christians give themselves tirelessly to the work of making this sharing of resources a reality in all the complexities of our world.

When Jesus' followers behave like this, they sometimes find, to their surprise, that they have a new spring in their step. There is an attractiveness about a life in which we stop clinging to everything we can get and start sharing it, celebrating God's generosity by being generous ourselves. And that attractiveness is one of the things that draws other people in. They were praising God, says Luke, and stood in favour with the people; and day by day the Lord was adding to their number those who were being rescued. Where the Church today finds itself stagnant and shrinking, it's time to read Acts 2:42–7 again, get down on our knees and ask what isn't happening that should be happening. The gospel hasn't changed. God's power hasn't diminished. People still need rescuing. What are we doing about it?

Lord, help us to recapture and sustain the joyful generosity toward one another that was there when your Church began.

8 The clash of loyalties
Acts 4:13–22

There are more ways of learning things than studying them in books. Book-learning, in fact, is often a poor substitute for first-hand experience if you want to really get inside a subject. And that is what is so striking about Peter and John.

The authorities are no doubt used to rounding up troublemakers and teaching them a lesson. Normally such people wouldn't be able to string together more than a few sentences once they are put on the spot. But with Peter and John it is different. Clearly, they haven't been to rabbinical school to study the Scriptures. They are 'untrained, ordinary men'. What's more, they have come out with a shrewd use of a psalm, such as you might expect only if someone had learned about various types of biblical interpretation. But they haven't. What on earth is going on?

Peter and John have a secret – a secret that enables them to run rings round the book-learning of the authorities. They were with Jesus night and day. They know how he read the Scriptures, in his fresh, creative way, drawing out their inner message and finding his own vocation in the middle of it. Now that he has died and then astonishingly been raised and then exalted into the heavenly realm, all Peter and John have to do to explain what they are about is to develop the lines of thought they heard him use over and over again. This doesn't just give them boldness in the sense of courage to stand up and say what they think. Sometimes people can be bold even when they're muddled. It gives them something more: a clarity, a sharp edge. And the authorities know it.

They are therefore at a loss. And so, in what must be an embarrassing climbdown, all they can do is to tell Peter and John not to speak any more in the name of Jesus. They must know, in issuing this order, that they are trying to shut a door when a howling gale is already blowing through it. But Peter's answer to them is more than merely pragmatic. It is theological, and forms the basis of all Christian resistance to the powers of this world from that day to this. We could paraphrase it like this: 'You're the judges around here? Very well, give me your legal judgement on this one! If we're standing here in God's presence, should we obey God, or should we obey you?'

Lord, give us the wisdom and courage to obey you at all times, even if that should lead to conflict with human pressure and authority.

9 The words of this life
Acts 5:17–26

One of the fascinating things about Acts is that nobody knows what to call the new movement. It isn't called 'Christianity' for quite some time; indeed, it's only in chapter 11 that anyone calls the followers of Jesus 'Christians', that is, 'Messiah-people'. Even so, there is still a bewildering variety of names given not just to the apostles but also to the movement itself. Later on we find it referred to as 'the Way'. Here, for the only time, but significantly, it is referred to as 'this Life'. 'Go and take your stand in the Temple,' says the angel, 'and speak *all the words of this Life* to the people.' It's a strange way to put it but we can see what is meant. What the apostles are to do is quite simply to *live* in a wholly new way. Nobody has lived like this before; that, indeed, is one of the extraordinary challenges that impinges on people as the gospel sets off. This is 'a way of life', as we say, that people haven't ever tried.

But of course it isn't just a way of conducting your personal day-to-day living, though it is that – a way that involves living as 'family' with all those who share your belief; a way that involves a radically new attitude to property and particularly to the sacred symbol of the holy land; a way that means that the centre of your life before God comes when you break bread in individual houses. It is all of that, but it is also much more. It is 'a way of Life' in the sense that Life itself has come to life in quite a new way; a force of Life has broken through the normally absolute barrier of death and has burst into the present world of decay and corruption as a new principle. And it is this Life, of course, that is carrying the apostles along with it.

And this Life has to be spoken as well as lived. 'Go...and speak all *the words* of this Life to the people.' Without the words to guide it, faith wanders in the dark and can easily fall off a cliff. The angel doesn't just get the apostles out of prison; they are given specific instructions for an urgent continuing task: 'Go...and speak all the words of this Life to the people.' We don't even know, yet, what to call it, but you've got to get on and speak it.

Lord, we thank you for the words of this Life that we have heard and believed, and we pray that we will live up to them.

10 Stephen tells the story
Acts 7:1–16

Stephen is accused of speaking against the Temple and the law; of saying that Jesus would destroy the Temple and change the customs Moses gave. How is he to respond?

He could simply wave the charges away. They are obviously false. He hasn't been saying that at all. Or he could avoid them and use the opportunity to speak about Jesus himself, about his cruel death and astonishing resurrection, about the future hope of the renewal of all things that is now coming true. Instead, he goes for the big picture. What you need, he says, is to rework your run-up. Tell the story again from the very beginning and get it right this time. Pace out the whole journey, from Abraham onwards, so that you arrive at the present moment from the right angle.

This explains why much of the speech doesn't seem to be a direct answer to the charges made against Stephen. What we have to do is to listen carefully, see the way he is telling the whole story and note which points he wants to highlight. Instead of a head-on rebuttal of the charges, he has chosen a kind of outflanking movement. Tell the story *this* way, he is saying, and you will see what I am saying about Jesus and how it relates to everything else that matters.

Are there already some in Stephen's audience who see where this is going? One of the great arts of Christian theology is to know how to tell the story: the story of the Old Testament, the story of Jesus as both the climax of the Old Testament and the foundation of all that was to come (not, in other words, a random collection of useful preaching material with some extraordinary and 'saving' events tacked on the end), and the story of the Church from the first days until now.

Sometimes we, too, have to take a long walk back and have another run at things to make sure we get everything in the proper rhythm, and draw out the lessons we need for our own day. Sometimes a story is the only way of telling the truth.

Lord, save us from the temptation to be satisfied with quick and superficial an-
swers, and give us the patience to stand back and take the time to absorb the
longer story.

11 Philip and the Ethiopian
Acts 8:26–40

The question the Ethiopian has run into is one that many discuss in our own day. Who was the prophet Isaiah writing about when he described the one 'led like a sheep to the slaughter' (see Isaiah 53:7–8)?

Now at this point it is important to stress how the early church read the prophets. It wasn't just a matter of discovering strange passages here and there and lining them up with Jesus in some arbitrary fashion. As we saw in Stephen's speech and will see again in Paul's great address in chapter 13, they were aware of the Hebrew Scriptures primarily as a great *narrative*. This story stretched forward from Abraham through Moses, David and the prophets, and on toward the present day. And the question was not only whether there are passages here that give a foretaste of what was to come, but more particularly, how does this story reach its climax?

Isaiah wasn't simply looking through a long-range prophetic telescope, seeing Jesus a few hundred years away and describing him in cryptic poetry. Rather, he was meditating deeply on the fate of Israel in exile, and on the promises and purposes of God that remained constant despite Israel's failure to be the light to the nations. Gradually a picture took shape in his praying, meditating mind: the figure of a Servant, one who would complete Israel's task, who would come to where Israel was, to do for Israel and for the whole world what neither could do for themselves, to bear in his own body the shame and reproach of the nations and of God's people, and to die under the weight of the world's wickedness. Only so, he perceived, could the promises be fulfilled.

No wonder the Ethiopian is excited when Philip explains how Jesus was the one through whom the slow and winding story of God's people had reached its destination, and with it the moment of redemption for the whole world! When you tell the story of Israel like that, with Jesus at its climax, it opens up to include everybody, including people like him, doubly excluded as both a Gentile and a eunuch, and now wonderfully welcomed. No wonder he wants to share in the death and resurrection of this Jesus by being baptised. No wonder he goes on his way celebrating, and to become, if later tradition is to be believed, the first evangelist in his own native country.

Lord, we thank you for the witness of the unnamed man of Ethiopia, for his example of faith and for his life that mattered so much to you.

12 The conversion of Saul
Acts 9:1–9

Saul's world has been turned upside down. Years later he will write of seeing 'the glory of God in the face of Jesus the Messiah' (2 Corinthians 4:6) – a seeing, like Stephen's in his death, that involved the coming together of heaven and earth. 'I'm an apostle, aren't I?' he wrote to the Corinthians (1 Corinthians 9:1). 'I've seen Jesus our Lord, haven't I?'

This 'seeing' overturns everything Paul has been taught. The Law and the Prophets have been torn to pieces and put back together in a totally new way. It is a new world; it is the old world made explicit. It shows him that the God he has been right to serve, the God of Abraham, Isaac and Jacob, has done what he always said he would, but done it in a shocking way. The God who has always promised to come and rescue his people has done so in person. *In the person of Jesus.*

Everything that Saul of Tarsus says and does from this moment on, and particularly everything he writes, flows from that sudden seeing of Jesus. We can imagine the recesses of his mind darting to and fro, from passage to passage of Scripture; from the recent memory of Stephen, dying under a hail of rocks and with a prayer to Jesus on his lips; to his parents, his teachers, his fellow students, his family; and back again to the stories of Abraham and Isaac, of Moses and the burning bush, to the prophecies of Isaiah and Daniel, to the Psalms. Surely it couldn't mean – surely it doesn't mean – supposing it really does mean…

And Saul sinks to the ground, blinded by the light, with the words ringing in his head. 'I am Jesus…and you are persecuting me.' *Me?* Somehow, these men and women Saul has been dragging off to prison are Jesus' people, his own extended self. It's all too much. They lead him by the hand and bring him to Damascus. It is three days before he can do anything except simultaneously recoil from the horror of what has happened and gasp at its glory.

We call this event a 'conversion', but it's more like a volcanic eruption, thunderstorm and tidal wave all together. If the death and resurrection of Jesus is the hinge on which the door of history swung open, the conversion of Saul of Tarsus is the moment when all the ancient promises of God gathered themselves up and came hurtling through that door and out into the wide world beyond.

Lord, we give thanks that Saul became Paul, and for all that he accomplished in your service.

13 Peter's vision
Acts 10:1–16

Luke's narrative now turns to the conversion of the Gentiles, and he makes it clear that God is preparing the way most carefully, step by step, for this to happen. Peter has found his way to Joppa, about thirty miles down the coast from Caesarea. He is staying by the sea and has leisure to pause at midday to pray. Then comes his vision – a large vessel, like a sail or sheet, full of every sort of creature you might want to eat and a large number you decidedly wouldn't. Especially if you were a devout Jew.

At this point we must remind ourselves of one of the basic points about the Jewish food laws. It wasn't just that the Jews weren't allowed to eat pork. There was a whole range of meat that was forbidden; they are listed (for example) in Leviticus 11. And these food laws served to mark out the Jewish people from their non-Jewish neighbours, a rule reinforced by the prohibition on Jews eating with non-Jews, sharing table fellowship. The reasoning was clear: the people you sit down and eat with are 'family', but the Jewish 'family' has been called by God to be separate, to bear witness to his special love and grace to the world, and must not therefore compromise with the world. All of this we must keep in mind as we join Peter on the roof and watch this great sail descending from heaven – with unclean food in it.

'Get up, Peter!' says a voice. 'Kill and eat!'

Peter is horrified. 'Certainly not! I've never done that before and I'm not going to start now! It's unclean!'

Then comes the response that echoes through the centuries, and still challenges all kinds of prejudice.

'What God has made clean, you must not call unclean.'

Peter doesn't know, of course, what is about to happen, and hence what this vision is supposed to mean. We know, because Luke has told us at the start of this passage. But as the story progresses we must make sure we are standing in the shoes of a first-century Jewish fisherman, feeling his way toward some astonishing and revolutionary understandings.

Save us, Lord, from looking for interpretations of your word that support and justify our prejudices.

14 Peter's rescue
Acts 12:5–19

Rhoda takes the prize for being, unwittingly, the comic star turn in this story; but it is the church at prayer that ought to raise a smile at the same time. Here is the church praying fervently for Peter. This is the church, remember, that has seen God at work in remarkable ways and which, after all, is celebrating at Passover time the resurrection of Jesus himself. They tell the story of how all of them were let out of prison, back in chapter 5. And yet. Here is Peter, released astonishingly in answer to their prayers. Here is Rhoda, so excited at hearing his voice that she forgets to open the door, and skitters in to say, 'It's Peter! It's Peter!' And here they are, so full of faith that they tell her she's mad.

I find all this strangely comforting: partly because Luke is allowing us to see the early church for a moment not as a bunch of great heroes and heroines, but as the same kind of muddled, half-believing sort of people as most Christians we all know. And partly I find it comforting because it would be easy for sceptical thinkers to dismiss the story of Peter's release from jail as a pious legend – except for the fact that nobody constructing a legend out of thin air would have made up this ridiculous little story. It has the ring of truth, at the very moment that it is telling us something truly extraordinary and heaven-on-earthish.

But of course the main point of the story, which Luke gets across nicely not least by means of this splendid little comic scene, is the vindication of Peter, as the chief representative (for the moment) of the family of the true King, and the frustration and disappointment of the official king. The end of the passage conveys a sense of the sulky grumpiness of a ruler who hasn't got his way: Herod looks for Peter, condemns the guards, then flounces off and leaves Judaea, goes down to Caesarea and doesn't come back. That's got rid of him, then, the young church might think; and they would be right, as the next passage shows. In other words, as the first half of the book comes to its close, the believers in Jerusalem have been announcing Jesus as the rightful Messiah, King of the Jews. The present king of the Jews takes umbrage and tries to stop it; but the grace of God and the prayers of the church have prevailed, and we can take it that the true King is vindicated against the sham.

Lord, we believe; please help us overcome our unbelief!

15 A light to the Gentiles
Acts 13:44–52

At the heart of this passage stands one of the great biblical witnesses to the turnaround that is taking place in the first generation of Christian faith. As so often, it is from the central section of the book of Isaiah, the passage that speaks of God's word doing new things, working through the strange ministry of the Servant (Isaiah 49:6).

The point is that *within* the hope of Israel there always lay the promise that when God did for Israel what Israel longed for him to do, then the Gentiles would come into the picture. Abraham had been called so that in him all the families of the earth might be blessed. Israel at Sinai was called to be a nation of priests. And Isaiah specifically said that the work of the Servant, the one who embodies Israel, will not be merely to restore the tribes of Israel, but also to be a light to the nations.

It is at this point where, without too much reflection, we can see why many of the Jews who hear this message in the first century reject it angrily. It must sound to them like a compromise. All these years they have been maintaining their Jewish distinctness, keeping themselves clean from the impure, pagan lifestyle of the wider world. They have suffered many things – mockery, social ostracism, sometimes physical abuse or even death – to be true to this heritage. And now – all these pagans surrounding them are going to come flooding in to *their* world, without so much as a by-your-leave? This is blasphemous nonsense! And the 'righteous indignation' that wells up in them, deeply understandable as it is – and corresponding exactly to the reaction of the young Saul of Tarsus only a few years before – is, again, this thing called 'zeal'.

And it is this 'zeal', in Antioch as in so many other places later on, that leads to the trouble that causes Paul and Barnabas to leave town in a hurry. Jesus spoke of apostles wiping the dust off their feet when a town refused their message of peace (Luke 10:11). That is what they do now, faced with leading local people coming out in support of those of the synagogue community who have been stirred up to anger. At the end of this first major missionary visit we have three distinct groups: the angry and aggressive people who don't want to know; the joyful, Spirit-filled local people who have believed the message; and the two apostles, escaping persecution and scurrying on to the next town.

Lord, give us zeal to defend your word, but without bitterness or malicious anger.

16 The judgement of James
Acts 15:12–21

James's speech in this important chapter sums up so much of the theology of Acts, and it does so by citing a biblical passage that speaks of the time when the house of David has been re-established and the Gentiles come flocking in to share in the blessings that follow (Amos 9:11–12). James draws the conclusion that the Gentiles are indeed welcome as they are, with faith in Jesus as their only badge of membership.

It is important to consider the impact that the decision will have on the Church as it spreads throughout the larger world, not least where it will be living side by side with substantial Jewish communities who will be perplexed by it. What is it, this body that looks very Jewish from one angle but very unJewish from other angles? And so James and the others work out the double principle of *no needful circumcision* on the one hand and *no needless offence* on the other.

No needful circumcision. The Gentiles who have believed in Jesus do not have to be circumcised; that is, they do not have to become Jewish in order to become Christians. They are not second-class citizens. But *no needless offence.* Since the Christians claim that in Jesus as Messiah the Law and the Prophets have been fulfilled, and because this claim is always going to be at best puzzling and at worst offensive, the Gentile Christians are not to offer needless slaps in the face to their as-yet-unbelieving Jewish neighbours. It would therefore be a great help if they would observe the most obvious point: to keep well away from pagan temples. This would be the most obvious and (to Jews) offensive form of continuing pagan behaviour for any Christian to indulge in. In fact, all this looks strongly like a way of saying something to the Gentile Christians out in the wider world while really saying something to the Pharisees back home: 'Look, it's all right; admitting these Gentiles who have believed won't mean a total collapse into idolatry and immorality.'

What impresses me is the realism with which the question is addressed, rather than the brittle absolutism that so many might prefer. And if anyone thinks that this is some kind of a compromise, it is not only a compromise that stands here in Scripture itself; it is also one that James himself argues on the basis of Scripture. Let the reader understand.

Lord, give us the wisdom to hold fast to the fundamental principles of the faith that all believers hold in common, and to reject all forms of idolatry.

17 A huge row
Acts 15:36–41

There is no point beating about the bush. This is a shameful episode, and the fact that it stands in Scripture should not make us afraid to say so. When Paul writes, as he often does in his letters, about the dangers of anger, he must many times look back on this incident and hang his head in shame.

Part of the trouble is, as usual in this kind of thing, that both men are, in a sense, in the right. We can all too easily imagine the scene. Barnabas apparently wobbled in his commitment to what Paul sees as a fundamental principle. Paul was shocked; and even though they've clearly made up and went together to Jerusalem and won a great victory for the point at issue, there may be not just a shadow, but a dark cloud, in the back of Paul's mind as he thinks ahead to the problems that might await them in Galatia. Will Barnabas wobble again – on this issue, or perhaps on some other? Will he be able to trust him?

For Barnabas himself there would be anger as well. Paul, after all, was his protégé. He introduced him to the Jerusalem apostles when they were all suspicious of him. He fetched him from obscurity in Tarsus and gave him the chance to become a famous preacher and teacher in Antioch. He took the lead in their first missionary expedition, and if Paul more or less took over as the chief speaker after that there is still a sense that Barnabas is a senior figure.

I doubt if there is a church leader anywhere who does not look at this scene and say, 'There but for the grace of God go I.' At the same time, we should note that something fresh comes out of it all. Two missionary journeys instead of one. The God who makes human wrath to serve his praise has done it again (Psalm 76:10). That doesn't excuse sinful human wrath, of course. It simply shows once again what the gospel message itself massively demonstrates: that God can take human folly and sin and bring great good from it.

That is a humbling lesson for the Church to learn in each generation. Luke could quite easily have found a less embarrassing way of explaining the new missionary pairings. I have a hunch that he tells this shocking little story at least partly because he wants this lesson to be taken to heart.

Lord, please help me to see when my burning conviction that I am right risks burning those I believe to be wrong.

18 Earthquake and salvation
Acts 16:25–34

In traditional versions of the New Testament, the panic-stricken Philippian jailer cries out, 'Sirs, what must I do to be saved?' Many preachers have since asked the same question on behalf of their audience, so that they can be ready with Paul's answer about believing in Jesus. In doing so they invest the jailer's remarks with all the theological freight of a much later generation of conscience-stricken Westerners. In a long line from Augustine to Luther and beyond, they came with a strong sense that there is a heaven and a hell, that some will go to the former ('saved') and some to the latter ('not saved').

But of course the Philippian jailer knows none of this. In his pagan world there are all kinds of theories about the afterlife, but none of them is anything like so clear, or so precise, as the medieval heaven-and-hell scenario. In any case, it's midnight; there has just been an earthquake; the prison he is in charge of has burst open; he is going to be held responsible for escaped prisoners, which will probably mean torture and death; he is on the point of committing suicide – and is he about to ask these strange visitors for a detailed exposition of justification by grace through faith?

No, of course not. In any case, as we have seen, 'salvation' in the ancient world doesn't mean 'going to heaven when you die', and that is by no means how the New Testament writers use it. Jesus himself frequently speaks of someone being 'saved' when he means 'healed'. So 'saved' means, simply, 'rescued', 'delivered' – from whatever problem or disaster might be threatening.

Having made that clear, the confident appeal of Paul and Silas, that the jailer should 'believe in the Lord Jesus' so that he and his household may be saved, does of course stand as a classic summary of what the Christian message is all about. It is about recognising, acknowledging and hailing *Jesus Christ as Lord*. As Paul later writes to the Romans (10:9), 'If you profess with your mouth that Jesus is Lord, and believe in your heart that God raised him from the dead, you will be saved.' Everything else is contained within that – all the volumes of systematic and pastoral theology, all the worship and prayers and devotion and dogma. The phrase 'Jesus is Lord' is what, from the earliest times, people have said as they come for baptism, as the jailer and his household promptly do.

Lord of all, we thank you for rescuing us from the power of sin and saving us from death.

19 Paul among the philosophers
Acts 17:22–34

One of the philosophical options available to serious first-century pagans is what became known as the Academic, or the view taken by the 'Academy' founded by Plato himself. According to the Academic point of view, there is simply not enough evidence for us to tell whether the gods exist or not, and, if they do, what if anything they want from us. This can breed a shoulder-shrugging couldn't-care-less attitude; or it might produce a kind of humility, an openness, a readiness for something new. It is the second attitude that Paul assumes motivated whoever put up the altar 'to an unknown god'. In fact, he begins and ends the address with the question of ignorance and what God is doing about it.

So Paul agrees with the Academy that it is indeed impossible, granted what is available to them, to know very much about the true God. Ah, but, he says, God himself has been aware of this difficulty, and has now brought this time of 'ignorance' to an end. And he goes on to show how this God not only *can* be known, in a way that Greek philosophy never bargained for, but actually *wants* to be known. And he brings the address to a close with a flourish by telling the story of the future hope: God is going to hold a great assize and put the whole world right!

As the speech turns the corner into the home straight, Paul insists that he and his hearers are living at a new moment in the history of the world. Something new has happened! Now there is something to say, particular news about particular events and a particular man, which provides just the sort of new evidence that the genuinely open-minded agnostic should be prepared to take into account. This God, declares Paul, has set a time when he is going to do what the Jewish tradition has always said he would do; indeed, what he must do if he is the good and wise creator: he will set the world right, will call it to account, will in other words *judge* it in the full biblical sense.

Paul leaves them with a double challenge. First, repent: turn from your old ways, particularly from your idolatry. Second: turn to the living God, grope for him and find him. Think hard about the unknown God, and leave behind the distant signposts of philosophies, poets and the religious rubbish that humans manufacture. There is a living God, and he is now calling everyone everywhere to repent and believe.

Thank you, O Lord, that through Jesus we can know you, the only true God.

20 A year in Corinth
Acts 18:1–11

In Corinth, Paul is back to the normal procedure: debate in the synagogue, and then, if they reject the message, turning to Gentiles. But here it is with a difference. In the Galatian cities on his first journey, and then in Philippi, Thessalonica and even Beroea, his visits were cut short by angry reaction, often initiated by 'zealous' Jews who resented both his message and its simultaneous claim to be both the fulfilment of the ancient Scriptures and freely available to all without distinction, Jew and Gentile alike. But in Corinth he stays longer than a few days, or even a few weeks. He stays for a year and a half – the longest time he has been in any one place for quite some while, probably since the time back in Syrian Antioch in 11:26.

One reason for this is that Paul has met a Jewish couple who run a business in the same line of work that Paul himself practises, namely tentmaking. Some may be surprised to think of Paul as a manual worker, but he wouldn't see anything strange in it. It is commonplace among Jewish teachers for rabbis to have a trade by which to support themselves and their families. It looks as though Aquila and Priscilla have set up a business in Corinth, in which Paul is, in effect, taken on as a partner or even as a hired worker.

Another reason why Paul stays so long is the remarkable vision he has one night. Whereas the last vision he had was of someone telling him to go somewhere he hadn't expected (Acts 16:9), this one is telling him to stay put. And the Lord, speaking to him personally and not through an angel or a figure like a 'man from Macedonia', gives him an interesting reason: 'There are many of my people in this city.' In other words, evangelism is only just beginning here. I am at work here, and you must trust me and stick it out.

Presumably Paul needs that encouragement. Visions, both in the New Testament and in much later experience, are not normally granted just for the sake of it. One of the many lessons Acts teaches quietly as it goes along is that you tend to get the guidance you need when you need it, not before, and not in too much detail. Enough to know that the Lord Jesus has many people in this city, and that he wants you, Paul, to stay here and work with them.

Lord, help us to discern when it is right to stay put and when it is right to move on.

21 'Great is Ephesian Artemis!'
Acts 19:23–41

Artemis (her Roman name is Diana) was the most powerful divinity in Ephesus, and had been for a long time. The temple of Artemis was massive, and her cult – run entirely by female officials – was the religious centre of the whole area. Images of Artemis, large and small, dominated the city. And, as in Philippi and elsewhere, the message of Jesus the Messiah was having its impact on business. No wonder Demetrius and his friends were alarmed.

This rushing together of the economic, religious and cultural impact of the gospel is one of the major issues that Christians are having to grapple with once more in our time. Many of us in the West have lived quite comfortably with all these things in separate compartments, and everything clinically wrapped so that nothing can leak from one compartment to another. We are inclined to look at the riot in Ephesus, shudder and thank God that we don't do things like that any more. But we should think again about the way wickedness gets a grip on a society, somewhere below its polite exterior, and about the way in which, sooner or later, someone needs to take their courage in one hand and their Bible in the other, throw to the winds any caution about their own prospects and say what needs to be said.

Luke ends the story with the town clerk in Ephesus giving his verdict: Demetrius and his friends are welcome to bring charges against Paul and his companions if they have done something wrong, but there is no sign that they have. Pagans would often accuse Jews of blaspheming the local gods and goddesses or robbing their temples, but nobody is suggesting Paul did either of those. He is innocent until proven guilty.

There are all kinds of lessons here for the Church in later days. Have we learned the lesson of being so definite in our witness to the powerful name of Jesus that people will indeed find their vested interests radically challenged, while being so innocent in our actual behaviour that there will be nothing to accuse us of? There is a fine line to be trodden between a quiet, ineffective 'preaching' of a 'gospel' that will make no impact on real life on the one hand, and a noisy, obstreperous, personally and socially offensive proclamation on the other.

Lord, let us not forget or shy away from the challenge the gospel poses to all forms of idolatry and superstition in our own day.

22 Watch out for yourselves
Acts 20:28–38

Paul is mainly a townsman, and his imagery is normally drawn from the urban world where most of his ministry is spent. Here, for a change, he draws on the pastoral image of sheep and their shepherd. And it is of sheep that he now thinks, sheep whose shepherd he has been, sheep that will now need feeding, leading, caring for and protecting: 'Watch out for yourselves...and for the whole flock.'

The task before the shepherd is a solemn one. God gave his own dear Son to die a shameful, sacrificial death in order to purchase this flock. This is perhaps the most direct, certainly the most striking, statement of the meaning of Jesus' crucifixion to be found anywhere in Acts, and it opens up vistas both of the love of God and of the responsibility of the shepherd. The shepherds are therefore to keep watch, because the wolves are prowling around, ready to come and attack.

More worrying still, some of the sheep, and even some of the shepherds, may turn out to be wolves in disguise. And the attack will then take the form, not of direct contradiction or a clash of powers, but of distorting the truth. The greatest heresies do not come about by straightforward denial; most of the Church will see that for what it is. They happen when an element, which may even be important but isn't central, looms so large that people can't help talking about it, fixating on it, debating different views of it as though this is the only thing that matters. Something like that happened in the Middle Ages with the theory of purgatory (life after death is important, but not like that); in the twentieth century with calculations regarding the 'rapture' (the second coming is important, but not like that); in the twenty-first century with...

And when you can fill in that blank, humbly and looking at yourself hard in the mirror as you think about it, you will know something about the calling of the shepherd in today's Church. 'Therefore keep watch,' Paul insists. Be alert. Stay awake. 'I commit you to God, and to the word of his grace.' God and his grace will see you through. Your part is not to fall asleep.

Lord, help us to stay alert to the dangers of teachers who distort, detract and distract us from the eternal truths of the gospel.

23 Riot in the Temple
Acts 21:27–36

In Jerusalem at that time it wasn't difficult to whip up a crowd and get them excited at the thought of catching a traitor. Forget the purification, the shaved head, the vow: here is the man who is teaching everywhere that Judaism is finished, that our people, our law, our Temple are all a waste of time!

The miracle is that Paul survives. If a crowd is intent on killing someone, they can often succeed before the time it would take for an officer upstairs in the fort to notice and hurry down to intervene. By this time, they have dragged Paul out of the Temple gate and, says Luke, 'the gates were shut', a sentence heavy with meaning, rather like John's comment that when Judas went out, 'it was night' (John 13:30).

The tribune, faced with the riot and a battered victim, tries to find out what the problem is, but since the charges are inaccurate, it's hardly surprising he can't make head or tail of them. So, having secured Paul with a chain, he tries to bring him up into the barracks. The chief priests have not so far been involved in Paul's case, though they soon will be. Paul is handed over to Roman custody by sheer force of mob violence.

The one note of clarity in the whole scene is the point Luke is making yet again. The mob is trying to kill Paul because of false charges to do with his disloyalty to the Jewish law and customs. And the Roman soldier rescues him. Luke is not, as some have supposed, trying to suck up to Rome, saying that Romans always do the right thing. No: Luke is trying to establish a pattern. Give this man a chance and he will show you his innocence. Let cool-headed justice prevail over hot-tempered mobs, and Paul will be vindicated. Yes, wherever he goes there is a riot. But that is because he is being loyal to the true, if extraordinary and dangerous, purposes of the God of Abraham, Isaac and Jacob, the creator God who will one day call the whole world to account. God can and will use Roman justice, for all its glaring faults, to show in advance that Paul has done nothing worthy of death. Learn to hear the story in these terms, and to wrestle with today's complex problems of faith, politics, justice and loyalty with new courage and hope.

Help us, O Lord, to work out how best to respond to the ignorance, misunder-standings and injustices that result in violence committed in the name of God and nation.

24 A defence of the hope
Acts 24:10–21

It would be easy, reading through Acts, to get a little weary by this time, and to think, 'Here he goes again – not guilty about the Temple – believing in the prophets – resurrection – yes, we've heard all this before.' Well, we have and we haven't. This is where, quite carefully, Luke turns the kaleidoscope of the various things Paul has been saying and brings them all together in a new, striking and clear form.

First, Paul provides a refutation of the main, central charge against him: that he has been causing a disturbance in or trying to defile the Temple. But before he goes on to the positive explanation of what precisely he was doing in the Temple, he wants to explain the framework. He does indeed plead guilty to the charge of being part of the sect of the Nazoreans, though he doesn't call it that, preferring the ancient phrase 'the Way'. And he admits that the non-believing Jews see 'the Way' as a 'sect' in the sense of a dangerous faction – but he doesn't accept that. 'The Way' isn't just a silly option, a strange, distorted group within Judaism. This is the main line: 'I do worship the God of my ancestors according to the Way which they call a "sect." I believe everything which is written in the law and the prophets.'

In other words, Paul is claiming the moral, theological and biblical high ground. For him, Jesus is the way, indeed the Way, by which the one true God has fulfilled all that the Scriptures said. Paul, in other words, is claiming to be a loyal and faithful Jew. That is his boast throughout, that Jesus has not made him stop being true to his ancestral faith, but that Jesus has revealed who the God of Abraham has been all along. For Paul, the knowledge of God in the face of Jesus the Messiah means not that he is abandoning the faith of his ancestors but that he is penetrating to its very heart.

In particular, Paul believes in the mainstream, standard hope of Israel, as expressed in the Psalms and the Prophets, and growing directly out of the belief of ancient Judaism that Abraham's God is 'the judge of all the earth' (Genesis 18:25) who will judge justly and overturn corruption, injustice, decay and death itself. That is the great hope of Israel. According to Israel's classic poetry, it is the great hope of the whole creation (Psalm 96:10–13; 98:7–9).

Lord, we join together in hope for the time when you will judge the earth and put everything right at last!

25 'To Caesar you shall go'

Acts 25:1–12

Once more, Paul is brought before a Roman tribunal. Jewish leaders have come from Jerusalem, surrounding Paul and throwing all kinds of accusations at him.

Does Paul know what is likely to happen next? He's had two years to think and pray about it. It is highly likely that he has thought through all the different possible scenarios. He knows well enough that he is in a strong position, since however much Festus wants to please his new province, he wouldn't want to do anything, or be seen to do anything, to effect injustice on a Roman citizen. Festus could of course simply acquit and release him, in which case he would still be at serious risk from plots against his life as soon as he were out of the security of Roman custody. Assuming he's unlikely to do that, Paul has him in something of a cleft stick. But he knows how to break the stalemate.

Paul knows his rights. He is standing at Caesar's tribunal, before Caesar's delegated officer. He insists not only on justice, but also on properly constituted officials doing their properly authorised job. And so, with all other cards in his hand exhausted, he finally plays his ace of trumps: 'I appeal to Caesar.'

The 'appeal', of course, is not like an 'appeal' today, when a verdict has already been reached, a sentence already imposed and the convicted person appeals against one or both. The case against Paul has still not been tried and has still not reached a verdict, far less a sentence. What Paul is appealing for is for the case to be tried elsewhere, in the highest court in the Empire. This is his right as a citizen. Paul has been promised by Jesus through a special vision (Acts 23:11), that he will get to Rome. What Luke is now telling us is that Paul himself has had to take responsibility, at one level, for making this happen.

This is an important point about the interaction between God's purposes and our praying. Sometimes, when we pray and wait for God to act, part of the answer is that God is indeed going to act, but that he will do so through our taking proper human responsibility in the matter. It's hard to tell in advance what the answer will be. Discerning and discovering the answer is a major element in the discernment to which all Christians, and especially all Christian leaders, are called.

Lord, let us not pray in words alone, but help us back up our words with action.

26 Paul before Agrippa
Acts 26:1–11

At the heart of his defence before Agrippa, Paul is saying that though there was an obvious break between Saul of Tarsus prior to his conversion and Paul the apostle afterwards, there is a strong line of continuity making a bridge between the two. This is where the language of 'conversion' may be misleading, because, as Paul himself would put it, at no point has he wavered in his belief that the God of Abraham, Isaac and Jacob was and is the true God, the one and only creator God. He hasn't changed Gods. From his point of view, he hasn't even, really, changed religions. Rather, he has followed the one God, the creator, Abraham's God, down the line he has always promised to lead his people, the line that will lead to resurrection. And the main break that has occurred is that he has become convinced that resurrection has already occurred, in one single case, while everyone else (apart from those on the Way) is still expecting it as a solely future event.

His message about resurrection – (a) that it is what we were all waiting for, and (b) that it has happened, to our enormous surprise, in Jesus – is at the heart of his claim that this changes everything at the same moment as fulfilling everything.

It is all too easy to present conversion, our own or Paul's, as a black-and-white change from one religion (or no religion at all) to another. But what Paul believed as a zealous Jew and what he now believes as a zealous Christian are both alike grounded in God the creator. In the same way – this is a different point, but an important one – the human lives people lead, whether they realise it or not and whether they live by faith or not, are in fact rooted in God the creator. When they come, if they do, to faith in Jesus Christ, this is not a turning away from the God who has actually been the source of everything they are and have all along. To learn from Paul the deeper meaning of conversion may be delicate and difficult, but it would be worthwhile to try.

Lord, as we look back on our lives and how we have changed, we thank you that you were always there for us back then, just as you are now and always will be.

27 'Paul, you're mad!'
Acts 26:24–32

Paul's address has just reached its peak, but the newly arrived Roman governor has had quite enough. Some translations say Festus 'exclaimed', which sounds like someone saying, testily, 'Really, Paul, I think that's a bit over the top.' But the Greek says he shouts at the top of his voice – an embarrassing thing to do, perhaps, in front of his distinguished guests, but then this Roman official, who certainly has never dreamed of anything remotely like this in his life before, is bound to find Paul's explosive material too, well, explosive. 'PAUL, YOU'RE OUT OF YOUR MIND! YOU'VE DONE TOO MUCH STUDYING!' (Always a good move for those who don't like what the scholar is saying.) And the speech, and the meeting, is over.

But not before Paul has made a final appeal, direct and also embarrassing in the way such appeals are, to Agrippa. Paul asks him a simple question: Agrippa, you are a loyal Jew, aren't you? You do believe the prophets, don't you? Of course you do!

Agrippa knows there is no way he can simply avoid the question, with a sudden hush coming over the gathering and everyone craning their heads to see what answer the king will make to this extraordinary mad-or-perhaps-not-mad scholar who has had the temerity to put him on the spot. Agrippa sees well enough, of course, where it's going. It's either got to be, 'No, I don't believe them,' in which case he has well and truly lost his street credibility, for ever, with a good swathe of his own people. Or it's going to be, 'Yes, I do believe them,' in which case Paul will clinch the point and say, 'So you do believe in resurrection! So why can't you believe in Jesus?'

It's a bold move, but Agrippa isn't having it. 'You reckon you're going to make *me* a Christian, then…and pretty quick, too, by the sound of it!' He's off the hook, but he's a bit embarrassed as well, because (I think) he sort of believes the prophets, even though the life he's led has been a clever riding of both horses, the Jewish one and the pagan one, and he doesn't really want to give either of them up. There may just be a wistfulness about his response. 'In another life, if I hadn't bought so heavily into this thing, and that thing, and the other thing… then maybe it might have all made sense. I can see where you're coming from. But… not today, thank you.'

Lord, save me from allowing what I believe to be determined by the need to keep favour with other people.

28 The storm and the angel
Acts 27:13–32

The whole point of the voyage is to get a good price for the cargo at the other end. But when the ship is in danger, you throw the cargo overboard. At this point a reader with an alert biblical memory may be thinking, where have I heard something like this before? And the answer (which Luke certainly intends us to pick up) is: Yes! Jonah! He was running away to Tarshish to avoid having to go and preach to the great imperial city of Nineveh. When the great storm came, the sailors did what Paul's sailors did: they threw the cargo into the sea (Jonah 1:4–5). At that point Jonah was in the hold, fast asleep, but they woke him up, asked him what was going on and ended up throwing him overboard, which quelled the storm.

And, of course, part of Luke's point is precisely that Paul is *not* Jonah. He is not running away; he is being faithful to his calling to preach in the great imperial capital to which he is bound; and he is certainly not going to be thrown overboard. Instead, in a dramatic reversal, he tells the ship's company to cheer up. He has had a vision. An angel has stood beside him during the night, telling Paul that he must indeed stand before Caesar. That's what this voyage is all about. And all the rest of them will be safe along with him.

Paul's vision is the turning point in the story. Up to now they have been going down into the darkness; now things are still bad, but there is a light shining. Paul has to go, one more time, through the process he describes in 2 Corinthians: 'we recommend ourselves as God's servants: with much patience, with sufferings, difficulties, hardships…as dying, and look – we are alive' (2 Corinthians 6:4, 9). Paul's own understanding of the cross helps us to see what Luke is saying throughout this tale.

There are many Christians who have been taught that once they have faith everything ought to flow smoothly. Acts replies: you have not yet considered what it means to take up the cross. The idea of the Church as a little ship has probably not been invented at this stage, but Luke is there already. The storms do not mean that the journey is futile. They merely mean that Jesus is claiming the world as his own, and that the powers of the world will do their best to resist.

Lord, be with us to guide and reassure us when our journey becomes dark, frightening and unpredictable.

29 Shipwreck
Acts 27:33–44

I always get cross when I read verse 42. For goodness' sake, I want to say to the soldiers, you've all been through so much together. How can you now, when rescue is within reach, turn round and kill these prisoners in cold blood? Part of the answer is, of course, that they are Roman soldiers. That's what Roman soldiers would do, kill people in cold blood. If they didn't, and if the prisoners got away, it would be their turn to be killed instead. That's how the system worked. No sentimentality allowed.

It is only the centurion, who has realised that he has one of the most unusual prisoners he's ever met in his care, who saves the day. He has treated Paul kindly right from the start, and has not regretted it, even though he didn't take his advice at Fair Havens. And now he sees a larger vision. He does the wrong thing, which is also the right thing.

This final twist, just when we are heaving a sigh of relief and thinking all is going to be well, reminds us yet again of the fragility of the whole project. It is, of course, the same risk as that of incarnation itself. What if Jesus had died of influenza in his teens? What if he'd been kicked by a camel and never recovered? Ridiculous? No; that's the risk God takes in everything he does, the risk of creation itself, the risk of making a world that is other than himself, the risk of deciding to rescue it by *becoming himself* as a human being.

And if we say that the risk isn't really that great because God remains in control, I think Luke would say emphatically that that is both thoroughly true and thoroughly misleading. The apparent clash of overruling providence and utter human wickedness is worked out, not through everything being cheerfully determined in advance. Nor is it worked out through a dark, unrelieved, groping around in which we have no certain hope, no security, no assurance, no strong sense of God's living and rescuing presence with us. That, too, is well and truly ruled out by Luke's whole narrative.

Somehow, the answer to the puzzle of divine sovereignty and human responsibility is not to be found in a formula, but in flesh and blood. In Jesus' flesh and Jesus' blood. And in our flesh and our blood. Maybe all true doctrines are, in the last analysis, like that.

Thank you, Lord, for becoming one of us in this risky, sometimes dangerous and shocking world, and for showing us that, whatever may happen, salvation and joy await us.

30 The end is where we start from
Acts 28:23–31

This final scene in Acts shows us Paul arriving at the gates of 'the very ends of the earth', as in the programme set out in Acts 1:8. The agenda set for the young church by its Lord has, in principle, been accomplished.

Here in Rome are Paul's kinsfolk according to the flesh, doing their best to sing the songs of the God of Israel in a strange land. They have known persecution and danger, and there is a longing for God's justice to come. How can they be at home in this new world? Paul knows the answer, but they cannot hear it. He spends all day in yet another of those lengthy Bible expositions. And in and through it all the question of God's kingdom, highlighted in the first chapter, comes back into its own. This is, after all, the point of Paul's message: that Israel's God, the creator, the God of Abraham, has, in the Messiah, Jesus, claimed his throne as Lord of the world.

'Kingdom of God' is always a political – no, a revolutionary – concept in first-century Judaism. If you believe that Jesus is risen, ascended and glorified, you have no choice. Jesus is not a distant divine being to whom one might fly off in an escapist spirituality. If he is the Messiah, he is the world's true King. And that is how Luke wants us to end our reflection. We may think of Paul as the central character, the hero, of Acts. But the real hero of the whole book is, of course, the Jesus who was enthroned as the world's Lord at the beginning, and is now proclaimed, at the end, openly and unhindered. And here, for once, Luke gives a full 'Pauline' title to Jesus: 'the Lord Jesus the Messiah'. King of the Jews; Lord of the world.

Jesus of Nazareth, Messiah and Lord: through his servants, through their journeys and their trials, through their pains and their puzzles, still reaching out into the future, out beyond Rome and the first century. Luke has brought them all before us, drawing us in, reminding us once more that this is a drama in which we too have been called to belong. The journey is ours, the trials are ours, the sovereign presence of Jesus is ours, the story is ours to pick up and carry on. Luke's writing, like Paul's journey, has reached its end, but in his end is our beginning.

Lord, help us to see how we can play our part as servants of King Jesus in the great drama of salvation that he has set in motion.

December

EARLY CHRISTIAN WISDOM

1 Prayer, sonship and the sovereignty of God
Romans 8:26–30

How many names can you think of for God? It may sound an odd question. God's proper name in the Old Testament is of course Yahweh; but he is referred to in a great many other ways as well. Here in Romans, God has been referred to as the one who raised Jesus from the dead (4:24; 8:11). Now, in this passage, we have an equally powerful but more mysterious title: 'the Searcher of Hearts'.

The word 'searcher' comes from a root that suggests someone lighting a torch and going slowly round a large, dark room, looking for something in particular. Or perhaps he is searching in the dark by listening. What is he wanting to find, and what happens when he finds it? No doubt God, in searching the dark spaces of our hearts, comes across all sorts of things we would just as soon remain hidden. But the thing he is wanting to find above all else is the sound of the Spirit's groaning.

Paul's understanding of the Spirit is new and striking at this point. When we are struggling to pray, and have no idea even what to pray for, at that very moment the Spirit is most obviously at work. The Spirit calls out of us not articulate speech but a groaning that cannot at the moment come into words. This is prayer beyond prayer, beyond human sight or knowing.

But not beyond the Searcher of Hearts. As part of Paul's picture, not just of the world or of the Church, but of God, we discover that the transcendent creator is continually in communion with the Spirit who dwells in the hearts of his people. God understands what the Spirit is saying, even though we do not. God hears and answers the prayer which we only know as painful groanings. There is a challenge here to every church and to every Christian: to be willing to shoulder the task of prayer of this kind, prayer in which we are caught up in the loving, groaning, redeeming dialogue between the Father and the Spirit.

To be sure, there are plenty of things in the world for which we can and must pray articulately. But there are plenty of others where all we can do is be still in God's presence and allow the Spirit to groan, and the Searcher of Hearts to seek for that groaning and to recognise it as what it is: suffering according to the pattern of the Messiah.

Lord, Searcher of Hearts, be with us through your Spirit and plead for us in groanings too deep for words.

2 The living sacrifice
Romans 12:1–5

Paul's clear instruction at the opening of this chapter is that Christians should refuse to let 'the present age' squeeze them into its mould, to dictate how we should think and indeed *what* we should think, Instead, we are to be transformed. Christians, in other words, are called to be counter-cultural – not in all respects, as though every single aspect of human society and culture were automatically and completely bad, but at least in being prepared to think through each aspect of life. We must be ready to challenge those parts where the present age shouts, or perhaps whispers seductively, that it would be easier and better to do things *that* way.

The key to it all is the transforming of the *mind*. Many Christians never come to terms with this. They hope they will be able to live up to something like Christian standards while still thinking the way the rest of the world thinks. It can't be done. Having the mind renewed by the persuasion of the Spirit is the vital start of that true human living that is God's loving will for all his children.

This, after all, is a way of growing up to maturity. People sometimes suggest that living a Christian life means a kind of immaturity, since you are guided not by thinking things through for yourself but by rules and regulations derived from elsewhere. That isn't Paul's vision of Christian living. Of course, there are plenty of firm boundaries. But at the centre of genuine Christianity is a mind awake, alert, not content to take a few guidelines off the peg but determined to understand *why* human life is meant to be lived in one way rather than another.

For Paul, the mind and the body are closely interconnected, and must work as a coherent team. Having one's mind renewed and offering to God one's body are all part of the same complete event. Here Paul uses a vivid idea: one's whole self (that's what Paul means by 'body') must be laid on the altar like a sacrifice in the Temple. Christian living never begins with a set of rules, though it contains them as it goes forward. It begins in the glad offering of one's whole self to God. Within that, it involves the renewal of the mind so that we are enabled both to think straight, instead of the twisted thinking that the world would force upon us, and to act accordingly.

Merciful Lord, I offer myself to you as a living sacrifice and pray that you will transform all I am and all I do by the renewing of my mind.

3 The character of love

1 Corinthians 13

When people say, as they sometimes do, that Paul must have been a very difficult person to have around, this passage is one I often quote in reply.

But what does Paul mean here by 'love'? The very word 'love' causes us all sorts of problems in the English language. Our vocabulary has become impoverished. Where Greek has four words, we have at most two – 'love' and 'affection'. All right, there are related ones like 'fondness' and 'compassion', but none of them comes near what Paul is talking about. The older word 'charity' has come to be associated so closely with the splendid work of organising and administering relief for those in need that it has ceased to be useful as a translation here.

No: what Paul has in mind is something that, though like our other loves in some ways, goes as far beyond them as sunlight goes beyond candles or electric light. Look closely at the type of person he describes in verses 4–7. Perhaps the best thing to do with a passage like this is to take it slowly, a line at a time, and to reflect on at least three things: first, ways in which we see this quality in Jesus himself; second, ways in which we see it in ourselves; and third, ways in which it would work out in practice.

Such an exercise should never be undertaken simply in order to feel either good about oneself or frustrated at one's lack of moral growth. It should always be done in prayer; and at the third stage, as we ask for grace to envisage situations where we could behave differently, we should try to imagine what doing that would feel like, what steps we would have to take to make it happen. Then, when we're faced with the relevant situation, we will at least have a choice we have already thought about, instead of behaving as creatures of habit.

And, of course, the ultimate aim is for *this* way of life, peculiar though it seems and almost unbelievable at points, to become the engrained way we habitually behave. Some people have taken steps along that road ahead of us. When we meet them it's like hearing gentle music or seeing a beautiful sunrise. But this life is within reach of each one of us, because it is the life of Jesus, the life inspired by the Spirit, the life that is our birthright within the Messiah's body.

Lord, thank you for showing me what love means; please help me to absorb and reflect it more and more each day.

4 The transformed resurrection body
1 Corinthians 15:35–49

We may as well go to the heart of the passage, to the verse that has puzzled people many times in the past, and still does. In verse 44 Paul contrasts the two types of bodies: the present one and the resurrection one. The words he uses are technical and tricky. Many versions translate these words as 'physical body' and 'spiritual body', but this is highly misleading. If you go that route, you may well end up saying, as many have done, that Paul is making a contrast simply between what we call a 'body', that is a physical object, and what we might call a ghost, a 'spiritual' object in the sense of 'non-physical'. But that is exactly what he is *not* saying.

The contrast he's making is between a body *animated by* one type of life and a body animated by another type. The present body is animated by the normal life all humans share. But the body that we shall be given in the resurrection is to be animated by God's own Spirit. The contrast between the two bodies in themselves is stated in verses 42 and 43. It is the contrast between corruption (our present bodies fall sick, bits wear out, we decay, die and return to dust) and incorruption (the new body won't do any of those things).

We can now stand back from the detail in the middle of the passage and see how the whole argument works. The first paragraph (verses 35–8) introduces the idea of the seed that is sown looking like one thing and comes up looking quite different. The point Paul is making is simply that we understand the principle of transformation, of a new body in continuity with the old yet somehow different. And he emphasises particularly that this happens through the action of God: 'God then gives it a body.' That's the first thing to grasp: the resurrection is the work of God the creator, and it will involve transformation.

As with Jesus' resurrection, so with ours: this will not be a strange distortion of our original humanity, but will be the very thing we were made for in the first place. That is the hope set before us; and it is all based, of course, on the fact that Jesus himself, the Messiah, already possesses the new type of body. He is 'the man from heaven'; and, as we have borne the image of the old, corruptible humanity (see Genesis 5:3), so we shall bear the image of Jesus himself (see Romans 8:29).

Thank you, O Lord, for inviting us to share in your victory over death.

374

5 New creation, new ministry
2 Corinthians 5:16 – 6:2

Paul is appealing to the believers in Corinth to see the world with the new eyes of the gospel, instead of expecting everything to conform to the fashions of the world they have been used to. He begins by describing the view from where he now is. He is on the threshold of the new creation itself, and everything looks different because everything is different. When he looks at people – other Christians, himself, anyone – he sees them in a new way. When he looks at the Messiah, he sees him, too, in a new way; there was a time when all his dreams of a Messiah were concentrated on a Messiah who would conquer the enemies of God and establish a 'merely human' kingdom. All such dreams must come to dust; that's what the Messiah's death and resurrection have taught him. The way to the true kingdom is *through* death, and out the other side into God's new world.

So: put together what he's learned about other people and what he's learned about the Messiah, and what do we get? Verse 17, one of his great summaries of what Christianity is all about. In the Greek language he is using, he says it even more briefly: 'If anyone in Messiah, new creation!' The 'new creation' in question refers both to the person concerned and to the world they enter, the world that has now been reconciled to the creator.

The next verses (18 and 19) explore this theme of reconciliation, emphasising that what has happened in and through the Messiah is not a matter of God claiming a world that didn't belong to him, or making a new one out of nothing, but of God *reconciling* to himself his own world, after the long years of corruption and decay. And this, once more, explains what Paul is up to. If God was doing all this in the Messiah, that work now needs to be put into effect, to be implemented. And that's where Paul and the other apostles come in. 'God was reconciling the world to himself in the Messiah… *and entrusting us with the message of reconciliation.'*

This new world has a new King, and the King has ambassadors. Paul is going into all the world with a message from its Sovereign, a message inviting anyone and everyone to be reconciled to the God who made them, loves them and has provided the means of reconciliation for them to come back to know and love him in return.

We thank you, O Lord, for coming to us in Jesus and reconciling us to you through his death and resurrection.

6 Fruit of the Spirit
Galatians 5:22–6

If Paul is famous for his contrast of 'flesh' and 'spirit', he is also famous for the key words he uses that go with them both. He speaks of the *works* of the 'flesh' (verse 19) but the *fruit* of the 'Spirit'. Underneath the two lists – the works of the flesh and the fruit of the Spirit – there lies Paul's whole vision of what happens to someone when they come into the community of the Messiah's people. There are various stages to be observed.

People start off in the condition he calls 'flesh'. They are born into human families, with ethnic and territorial identities. They discover within themselves all kinds of desires, which, if allowed full rein, will produce the 'works' listed in verses 19–21. A society in which most people behave in such a way is unlikely to be a happy or thriving place. What is more, when God finally establishes his kingdom, people like that will have no place in it. That's not the state of affairs that God wishes to create.

But then, through the announcement of the gospel of Jesus, God's Spirit goes to work and people are renewed. The first sign of that renewal is their faith in Jesus as the risen Lord. But their membership in the Messiah's people involves them in a movement through death to new life. What is left behind in this death, this co-crucifixion with the Messiah, is precisely the life in which 'the flesh' determines who a person is.

Instead, they begin to 'bear fruit'. The nine qualities Paul lists in verses 22–3 are not things that, if we try hard enough, we could simply do without help, without the Spirit. The point of all of them is that when the Spirit is at work they will begin to happen.

Not, of course, that this process bypasses our thinking and willing. We have to set our minds and intentions to do them; it isn't a matter of just relaxing and doing what comes naturally. Otherwise Paul wouldn't need to urge the Galatians to 'line up with the spirit', that is, to see the effect the Spirit wants to produce, and through our own moral effort to let the life of the Spirit have its complete way.

But the point is that when these qualities appear, with all their quiet joy, all their rich contribution, they come like the fruit in an orchard. They will truly be part of who we will have become.

Lord, cultivate in us the fruits of your Spirit, so that they become a natural part of who we are.

7 God's love, God's power – in us
Ephesians 3:14–21

Paul is praying here for young Christians. He prays that they may discover the heart of what it means to be a Christian. For Paul, this means knowing God as the all-loving, all-powerful Father; it means putting down roots into that love. It means having that love turn into a well-directed and effective energy in one's life. And it means the deep and powerful knowing and loving into which the Christian is invited to enter; or the knowing and loving that should enter into the Christian.

At the heart of all this is a phrase that has become popular in the language of Christian experience: 'that the Messiah may make his home in your hearts, through faith'. People talk easily, perhaps too easily, about 'inviting Jesus into your heart'. The danger here is that it's easy for people, particularly when they are soaked in the culture of individualism, to imagine that being a Christian consists simply in being able to feel that Jesus has taken up residence within. In fact, Paul speaks far more often of Christians being 'in Christ' than of Christ being 'in Christians'. It's important to see our individual experience within the larger picture of our membership in God's family.

But, of course, when that's been made clear, then it is also important that the living Lord should make his home within each Christian. That is what strengthens and renews us. That, as verse 17 implies, is what enables us to put down roots into God's love and to be built up as a secure, unmoveable house. That, as Paul says in the climax of the prayer in verses 18 and 19, will expand our mental and spiritual vision of the whole range of divine truth. Everything that might be offered in the fancy religions of Paul's day and ours, all is ours in the King and in his love. Having him, we are filled with all the fullness of God.

Once all this is in place, the results will start to emerge. Verses 20 and 21 are often used as a benediction in church services, and it's easy to see why. As we draw to the end of a time of prayer, the overarching aim should be to give God the glory. But if it's the true God we've been worshipping, we should be filled with a sense of new possibilities: of new tasks and new energy to accomplish them.

Lord, we know you can do far more than we can ask or imagine, through the power of your Spirit working in us. To you be glory in King Jesus!

8 The mind of the Messiah

Philippians 2:5–11

The poem Paul places here, whether he wrote it himself or was quoting an even earlier Christian writer, is a very early statement of Christian faith in who Jesus was and what he accomplished.

Let's clear one misunderstanding out of the way. In verse 7 Paul says that Jesus 'emptied himself'. People have sometimes thought that this means that Jesus, having been divine up to that point, somehow stopped being divine when he became human, and then went back to being divine again. This is, in fact, completely untrue to what Paul has in mind. The point of verse 6 is that Jesus was indeed already equal with God; Paul is saying that Jesus already existed even before he became a human being. But the decision to become human and to go all the way along the road of obedience to the divine plan was not a decision to stop being divine. It was a decision about *what it really meant to be divine.*

Jesus retained his equality with God; the point of the cross, for Paul, is that 'God was reconciling the world to himself in the Messiah' (2 Corinthians 5:19). The point of verses 6 and 7 is that Jesus didn't regard this equality as something to take advantage of. Rather, the eternal son of God, the one who became human in and as Jesus of Nazareth, regarded his equality with God as committing him to the course he took: of becoming human, of dying under the weight of the world's evil. This is what it meant to be equal with God. As you look at the incarnate Son of God dying on the cross, the most powerful thought you should think is: this is the true meaning of who God is. He is the God of self-giving love.

Here is the very heart of the Christian vision of God himself: that within the Jewish vision of one God, the creator and sustainer of the universe, we are to see different self-expressions – so different, yet so intimately related, that they can be called 'Father' and 'Son'.

Jesus' progression through incarnation to death must therefore be seen, not as something that required him to stop being God for a while, but as the perfect self-expression of the true God. And the true God is known most clearly when he abandons his rights for the sake of the world. Yes, says Paul; and that's 'the mind of Christ', the pattern of thinking that belongs to you because you belong to the Messiah.

Lord Jesus, we bow before you and honour your name, to the glory of God the Father!

9 In praise of Jesus Christ
Colossians 1:15–20

Christianity isn't simply about a particular way of being religious. Christianity is about Jesus Christ; and this poem, one of the very earliest Christian poems ever written, tells us why. There are three things in particular that the poem tells us.

First, it tells us that it's by looking at Jesus that we discover who God is. He is 'the image of God, the invisible one'. If there is somebody sitting in the next room, I can't see them because there's a wall in the way. But if there is a mirror out in the hallway, I may be able to look out of my door and see, in the mirror, the mirror-image of the person in the next room. In the same way, Jesus is the mirror-image of the God who is there but who we normally can't see.

Second, Jesus holds together the old world and the new, creation and new creation. Jesus Christ, says the poem boldly, is the one through whom and for whom the whole creation was made in the first place. This isn't just a remarkable thing to say about an individual of recent history. It is also a remarkable thing to say about the 'natural' world. It was his idea. When the lavish beauty of the world makes you catch your breath, remember that it is like that because of Jesus.

But the world is also full of ugliness and evil, summed up in death itself. Yes, that's true too; but that wasn't the original intention, and the living God has now acted to heal the world of the wickedness and corruption that have so radically infected it. And he's done so through the same one through whom it was made in the first place. This is the point of the balance in the poem. The Jesus through whom the world was made is the same Jesus through whom the world has now been redeemed. He is the firstborn of all creation, *and* the firstborn from the dead.

Third, Jesus is therefore the blueprint for the genuine humanness that is on offer through the gospel. As the head of the body, the Church; as the first to rise again from the dead; as the one through whose cruel death God has dealt with our sins and brought us peace and reconciliation; and, above all, as the one through whom the new creation has now begun; in all these ways, Jesus is himself the one in whom we are called to discover what true humanness means in practice.

We thank and praise you, O Lord, for creating and redeeming our world through Jesus.

10 Children of light
1 Thessalonians 5:1–11

Christians are daytime people, even though the rest of the world is still in the night. You are children of the day, says Paul, children of light. God's new world has broken in upon the sad, sleepy, drunken and deadly old world. That's the meaning of the resurrection of Jesus, and the gift of the Spirit – the life of the new world breaking in to the old. Stay awake, then, because this is God's new reality, and it will shortly dawn upon the whole world.

You must not be like those who say, 'Peace and security, peace and security. Everything's all right. Nothing's going to happen.' No, says Paul, everything's not all right. Sudden disaster is on the way. Who is he talking about? Anybody who imagines that God's new world will never break in. The slogan 'peace and security' was one of the comforting phrases that the Roman Empire put out to reassure its inhabitants around the Mediterranean that the famous 'Roman peace' would hold without problems. That is what Paul is attacking. Don't trust the imperial propaganda, he says. The world will soon plunge into convulsions. Within twenty years of this letter, the warning came true.

That is why Paul adds one last piece of advice. The dawn is breaking, the birth-pangs are coming upon the world, the robbers might break in at any time and the Empire itself is under threat – so you need to put on your armour! Verse 8 is a shorter version of the fuller paragraph in Ephesians 6:10–20; here he mentions only the two main defensive pieces of armour: the breastplate and the helmet. Faith and love are the breastplate, to ward off frontal attacks. The hope of salvation is the helmet, protecting the head itself. Underneath it all we find God's action in Jesus the Messiah. In verse 10 we hear again the basic Christian creed: he died for us and rose again. That is the main defence against all that the dark world can throw at the children of light.

We, like the Thessalonians, need to remind one another of this as we face a world where sudden convulsions still occur; the world into which, one day, the final dawn will break. As children of the new day, we already belong to the Messiah. Here is Paul's main message: hold fast in faith to the gospel message, and you will find in it all the comfort and strength you need.

Lord, may we hold fast in faith and hope to your promise that one day your glorious light will dawn upon our world.

11 The coming of Jesus
2 Thessalonians 1:7–12

This passage is about God's justice, not his vengeance. Some translations of verse 8 use the word 'vengeance', but today this suggests quite the wrong idea. God is not a petty tyrant who throws his political opponents into jail simply for being on the wrong side. God is the living and loving creator, who must either judge the world or stand accused of injustice.

Paul's vision of the moment when God finally puts the world to rights is coloured by several biblical passages. There are, in Scripture, many moments of judgement, which are at the same time moments of deliverance for those who have clung to the God of justice and mercy. Into this biblical picture comes the stunning news that the judgement will be in the hands of Jesus himself. This is one among many indications that Paul sees Jesus as Messiah, the one through whom God's justice would be brought to the nations (see, for example, Isaiah 11:1–10). But of course, for Paul, Jesus is principally the crucified one, the one in whom God's love and mercy have been lavished on an undeserving world.

Because in Jesus and his gospel the living God has been unveiled, those who cling to wickedness and injustice can be described as 'those who don't know God and those who don't obey the gospel of our Lord Jesus'. Evidence of people like that is all around in Thessalonica, not only in the idols but also in the behaviour of people on the street; and, in particular, in violent opposition to the gospel. The small group of believers who have been grasped by the message Paul has brought them will one day be amazed at the way in which the standards of their culture will be reversed.

Christians, however, cannot be complacent as they contemplate the final judgement. When that day comes, they must not appear as people who began to believe but never got around to working out what it might mean in practice. They must be people who have lived up to their initial 'call'. In describing how this works out, Paul sounds almost like the Jesus of John's Gospel: 'so that the name of our Lord Jesus may be glorified in you, and you in him' is full of echoes of Jesus' great prayer in John 17. This glorifying of Jesus' name requires Christian moral effort, but underneath that as well is the mystery of God's grace.

O Lord, please guide us as we work out how to love mercy and act justly, even as we eagerly look for the day when your justice is revealed to all the world.

12 Godliness and contentment
1 Timothy 6:6–10

It is hardly an exaggeration to say that this famous passage is an indictment of modern Western culture. Never before in history has there been such a restless pursuit of riches. Never before has the love of money been elevated to the highest good, so that if someone were to ask you, 'Why did you do that?' and you were to respond, 'Because I could make more money that way,' that would be the end of the conversation. Never before have so many people tripped over one another in their eagerness to get rich and thereby impaled themselves on the consequences of their own greed.

The greatest irony of it all is that it's done in the name of contentment – or, which is more or less the same thing, happiness. Many people give lip service to the maxim that 'money can't buy you happiness', but most give life-service to the hope that it just might, after all. The pursuit of happiness and the idea that this is a basic human right is all very well, but when it's taken to mean the unfettered pursuit of wealth it turns into a basic human wrong. And yet every advertisement, every other television programme, is designed, in subtle and not-so-subtle ways, to make us say, 'If only I had just a bit more money, then I would be content.'

The point is that the present world, the created order in which we live, is full of all kinds of good things. We should enjoy them in their appropriate ways and, by thanking God for them, maintain the careful balance of neither worshipping the created world nor imagining that it's evil. But when money comes into the equation, everything looks different. Money is not, as it stands, God's creation, but a human invention to make the exchange of goods easier and more flexible. The further it becomes removed from the goods themselves and the more it becomes a 'good' in itself, the closer we come to idolatry. A society that values wealth for its own sake has forgotten something vital about being human. Money itself isn't evil; but, as verse 10 famously puts it, loving money is not only evil, it's the root of all evils.

It's a sorry picture. But in the background stands Paul saying, 'There is a different way.' We don't have to live like that. What's more, the Church is called to model the different way. Do we have the courage to try?

Lord, help me to resist the craving for more money, and to be content with living my life in loving service to you.

13 Continue in the Scriptures!
2 Timothy 3:10–17

Many people who open the Bible for the first time feel perplexed. To begin with, it looks like a jumble of old bits and pieces, a ragbag of poetry, history, folk tales, ethical instruction and some strange stories about some even stranger people. Reading it can seem like wandering through old courtyards where somebody once lived. But then, just when you're tempted to put the whole thing aside as interesting perhaps but not really relevant, you sense movement and life. Something is stirring there. There's an energy, as though someone's left a light on or music playing. Maybe it's inhabited, after all. It seems to have a life.

The early Christians believed that the reason the Scriptures were alive was because God had 'breathed' them in the first place, and the warmth and life of that creative breath was still present and powerful. The 'breath' of God, or Spirit, who caused Scripture to be written, who spoke through the different writers in so many ways, is as powerful today as ever, and that power can transform lives.

The Spirit speaking through Scripture can make us wise – can help us think in new patterns, see things we haven't seen before, understand ourselves and other people and God and the world. If we let Scripture have its way with us, all this is within reach; because, of course, Scripture not only unveils the living God we know in Jesus Christ, but, through our reading and pondering, it also works this knowledge of God deep into our consciousness and even subconsciousness.

Paul spells out how this might work. Scripture is useful for teaching; well, of course. For rebuke; that's a bit different. It means, clearly, that as we read Scripture it will from time to time inform us that something we've been doing is out of line with God's will. Sometimes this will lie plainly on the surface of the text; other times we will begin to hear the voice of God telling us that this story applies to *this* area of our lives, or perhaps *that* one. When that happens we do well to pay attention.

This negative possibility is quickly balanced by the positive: reading the Bible will transform you, will improve you, in the sense of somebody making improvements to a house. And it will train you 'in righteousness', all with the aim of helping you to become complete, richly human beings, reflecting God's image in all its many-sided splendour.

Lord, help me to hear your voice speaking through the Scriptures, and to attune myself to all you have to tell me.

14 God's kindness and generosity – and ours
Titus 3:1–8

This is the one place in all Paul's letters where he talks about 'new birth'. This is familiar to us from the third chapter of John's Gospel, but, apart from the present passage, it hardly occurs at all in other early Christian writings. The main thing Paul says about it here is that it's God's free gift, and it involves being made clean. The reference to 'washing' is almost certainly intended as a reference to baptism itself.

Up to this point Paul has spoken of the 'appearing' of God's salvation in terms of the future arriving in the present. This time, however, he wants to highlight *the effect on us* of the 'appearing' of God's kindness and goodness. It isn't just that we've glimpsed the future and discovered that it's full of God's grace. We are invited to look at our own selves and to take stock of the radical change that God has accomplished. What we see, in a life transformed by the gospel, is the direct result of God's lavish, generous love. *And that's why he wants us to be generous, kind and gentle in turn.*

That's the point of verse 2. It's not just that God has decided to set up some new rules for the sake of it, and one of them happens to be that Christians should be nice to people. The reason for the early Christian rule of life is always more deep-rooted than that. The reason we are summoned to avoid speaking evil of people and so on is that we are ourselves the creatures of God's generous love, and if we aren't showing that same forgiving love, we have obviously forgotten the path by which we've come.

This works at two different levels. At the first, our obligation to be kind and gentle to others is simply our response to God's love. But, at the second level, we discover with a shock that when we are kind and gentle to people, *this itself is part of the 'appearing' of God's kindness and loving goodness.* God wants to continue the work of self-revelation he began in and through Jesus, and one of the primary ways he does this is through his followers, when they act in such a way that people will realise who God is. The creator of the world is a lavish host, who has sent out a worldwide invitation to his party. We, as his messengers, must live in such a way that people will want to turn up.

Lord, may your kindness and loving goodness shine through me and all that I do in your name.

15 Paul's appeal to Philemon
Philemon 8–14

Persuasion, particularly the persuasion that comes genuinely 'in the Messiah', is a remarkable thing. Of course, it can be misrepresented: as manipulation, as bullying, as 'unfair pressure'. All those things do exist, and they're ugly. But that is not Paul's way. His style throughout this letter is one of gentle, almost playful, Christian persuasion. He knows Philemon well enough to adopt the right tone. What he's going to ask is very, very difficult, but he is reasonably sure that Philemon will take the point and act on it. But, just to be sure, he takes it step by step.

First, he builds a secure foundation: the relationship that he and Philemon have. Then he names the person at the centre of the problem. Then, quickly, he makes it clear that when Philemon is confronted with Onesimus himself, he is actually looking at… Paul! This is the heart of his strategy in this delicate and highly skilful piece of writing.

Paul, of course, has a status in the church that would enable him, if the worst came to the worst, to give commands. But that's not the best way to do things except in an emergency. Much better that Philemon is helped to think through the issues and come to the right decision for himself. So, having established that he and Philemon are bonded together with several strands of love, partnership, affection and respect, Paul goes on to show that he and Onesimus have established a similar bond. Onesimus is his 'child'; he has become a Christian through Paul's teaching and love. And, like a fond parent sending a son or daughter off into the wider world for the first time, when Paul sends Onesimus to Colossae, he is sending his very heart.

That is why, when Philemon discovers that Onesimus, his own runaway slave, has returned, Paul doesn't want him just to see Onesimus standing there. He wants him to see Paul himself. That is the foundation for the appeal Paul makes as the letter reaches its climax.

What we are watching here is a living example of the Christian practice of reconciliation. This letter shows how costly it is, but also how explosive. Where in your world does reconciliation need to happen today? What social barriers stand in its way? How can people who believe in Jesus make it happen?

Lord, help us to see where the healing art of reconciliation needs to be practised in our world today, and help us play our part in making it happen.

16 The Messiah and his brothers and sisters
Hebrews 2:10–18

The author of Hebrews describes Jesus as the older brother of a large family – a brother who comes to find us where we are and helps us out of the mess we are in.

In sketching this picture, the author adds three more elements that give it its special colour. First, he sees Jesus as the pioneer. Imagine an explorer cutting his way deep into the jungle. Nobody has been this way before. Yet on he goes, forging his way through impossible terrain, until he reaches the goal. Once he's done that, others can follow.

The second element is that Jesus has done all this specifically through his death. The writer quotes from Psalm 22:22: 'I will announce your name to my brothers and sisters.' You might think that is simply a quotation to back up the point about Jesus bringing his siblings to a knowledge of God. But go back to Psalm 22 and read the first twenty-one verses. You will find that they describe, in horrendous detail, the suffering and death of the one who truly trusts in God and yet finds that he himself seems to be God-forsaken. 'My God, my God, why did you forsake me?' asks the psalmist.

Next, the writer picks up another biblical theme: the exodus from Egypt. Israel had been enslaved to Pharaoh, and God went and rescued them. Now, declares this letter, Jesus has set the slaves free – those who were enslaved under the fear of death. It's interesting that we are still no nearer to getting rid of this fear than our ancestors were. But God promised Abraham that he would have a great, worldwide family (Genesis 15:5); and it's this family that Jesus is concerned with, rescuing them from their slavery and pioneering the way to God's future world.

This leads to the third element. In suffering and dying on behalf of his people, Jesus has become the true high priest who makes atonement for their sins. A true high priest, as set out in the Old Testament, should be on the one hand someone who is able to act as God's representative to his people, embodying God's mercy and reliability, and on the other hand someone who can fully sympathise with those to whom he ministers. He is no distant older brother, unable to cross the gulf to rescue his siblings. He shared in flesh and blood, and even death itself. There is nothing we face with which Jesus cannot sympathise.

We thank you, Lord, for sharing our flesh and blood, and for going before us as our faithful and sympathetic high priest.

17 Christian suffering is God's discipline
Hebrews 12:4–11

If we are genuinely God's children, we should expect that God will treat us as a wise parent does, bringing us up with appropriate discipline. Here the writer traces the roots of this notion in the biblical book of Proverbs, quoting in verses 5–6 from Proverbs 3:11–12. He might have chosen several other passages from the same book, or similar ones from the Psalms, such as Psalm 94:12–13.

It may come as a shock to some Christians to discover that there lies ahead of them a life in which God, precisely because he is treating us as sons and daughters, will refuse to spoil us or ignore us, will refuse to let us get away for ever with rebellion or folly, with sin or stupidity. He has his ways of alerting his children to the fact that they should either pause and think again, or turn round and go in the opposite direction, or get down on their knees and repent.

The truth of verse 11 is offered so that we can cling to it when things are difficult. There is much sorrow in an ordinary human life; sorrow which was, of course, shared by the Man of Sorrows as he identified completely with us. It is possible, even for Christians, to see it all as meaningless, to fret and fume as though everything has gone wrong. Well, things do go wrong, and we mustn't make the mistake of blaming God for everything ('Why did you do this to me?') as though there were no evil forces out there – and even 'in here', within one's own only partly redeemed human heart – which still have the power to create havoc.

But again and again, when we find ourselves thwarted or disappointed, opposed or vilified, we may in faith be able to hear the gentle and wise voice of the Father, urging us to follow him more closely, to trust him more fully, to love him more deeply. Suffering can be the trowel that digs deeply in the soil of our lives, so that the plant of peaceful righteousness – a life of settled commitment to live as God's new covenant people – may have its roots deep in the love of God.

Teach us, O Lord, as your disciples, to respect and not reject your discipline!

18 Faith and works
James 2:14–26

James is very concerned about a problem that is already arising in the earliest church, and which is with us to this day. He has already begun to address it in the previous chapter, when he spoke about being 'people who do the word, not merely people who hear it' (James 1:22). He has heard people talking about 'faith', not meaning a rich, lively trust in the loving, living God, but rather a shell, an empty affirmation.

We can see this clearly in verse 19. James goes back to one of the most basic points of ancient Judaism, the confession that 'God is one'. That was, and still is, at the heart of Jewish daily prayer: 'Hear, O Israel: the Lord our God, the Lord is One; and you shall love the Lord your God with all your heart, and mind, and soul and strength' (Deuteronomy 6:4–5). It was at that point that Jesus himself added what James has earlier called 'the royal law': 'You shall love your neighbour as yourself' (James 2:8).

But simply saying 'God is one' doesn't get you very far if it doesn't make a difference in your life. So it becomes clear that what James means by 'faith' in this passage is not what Paul and others developed as a full, Jesus-shaped meaning; it is the basic *ancient Jewish* meaning, the confession of God as 'one'. This, he says, needs to translate into Jesus-shaped action if it is to make any significant difference. At this point, he is actually on the same page as Paul, who in his fiercest letter about faith and works defines 'what matters' as 'faith, working through love' (Galatians 5:6).

The same point emerges in the earlier illustration James uses, in verses 15 and 16. Actually, this isn't just an 'illustration', because one of the key 'works' that James expects followers of Jesus to be doing is caring for the poor. But this is how it works: there is no point in saying to someone without clothes or food, 'Be warm, be full!' Those words won't do anything to help. They need to be translated into action. The 'faith' that isn't enough is a mere verbal formula. It won't do simply to tick the box saying, 'I believe in one God,' and hope that will do. It won't. Without a radical change of life, that 'faith' is worthless.

Translating belief into action, even when it seems impossible or downright dangerous. That is the faith that matters. That is the faith that justifies. That is the faith that saves.

Lord, may our faith be true and meaningful, showing itself in action.

19 Genuine faith and sure hope
1 Peter 1:1–9

The opening three paragraphs of this wonderful letter are like the width, the height and the depth of a building within which everything that follows will take its place.

To begin with, the width. This is what Christians are: chosen, set aside, sanctified for obedience. It is easy to forget our basic identity as Christians, and it is therefore important to be reminded of it on a regular basis. So who are we? We are people who, by the mercy of God, have been chosen for a particular purpose. All Christians live a strange double life: Peter addresses his audience as 'foreigners' because they now have a dual citizenship. They are simultaneously inhabitants of this or that actual country and citizens of God's new world which, as he will shortly say, is waiting to be unveiled.

This is God's purpose: to set people aside from other uses so that they can be signposts to this new reality. They are therefore to be 'holy', both in the technical sense that God has set them apart for this purpose and in the practical sense that their actual lives have been transformed. The way they behave now reflects God's desire for his human creatures. That – however daunting and unlikely it seems – is who we are as Christians.

But what about the vertical dimension of this building into which we are invited? The best way of talking specifically about God and what he's done is by praise, not simply description; and praise is what Peter now offers. May God be blessed, he says, because of his mercy. The height of this building is the mercy of God. God has, in his mercy, created a whole new world. At the moment it is being kept safe, out of sight, behind the thin invisible curtain that separates our world (earth) from God's world (heaven). But one day the curtain will be drawn back, and then the 'incorruptible inheritance' will be merged with our earthly reality, transforming it and soaking it through with God's presence, love and mercy.

Finally, the depth. Quite a bit of this letter is concerned with the suffering of the early Christians. Here Peter states the theme he will develop: that this suffering is the means by which the quality of the Christians' faith can shine out all the more, and when Jesus is finally revealed this will result in an explosion of praise. Meanwhile, they are to live their lives with love for Jesus in their hearts and 'a glorified joy' welling up within them.

We praise you, O Lord, because of your abundant mercy!

20 Confirm your call!
2 Peter 1:1–11

All too often, people think that 'religion', or even 'Christian faith', is about what God wants from us – good behaviour, renunciation of things we like, a gritted-teeth morality of forcing ourselves to behave unnaturally. This is a total caricature. Here, in this breathtaking paragraph from verses 3 to 11, we see the truth.

First, God has already given us everything we need: a starter kit, if you like, for all that we need to become. There is indeed quite a lot in this letter about the moral effort we have to make. But Peter is quite clear: it all comes from God in the first place.

Second, he wants nothing less for us than that we should come to share his own very nature. Some Christians have felt uneasy about this idea, as though the humility to which we are so often exhorted ought to stop us short from thinking of actually sharing God's very being or nature. Others, though (particularly in the Eastern Christian traditions), have seen this as central to what it means to be a Christian. After all, if we say that the Holy Spirit is fully divine, and if we say that the Holy Spirit comes to live within us and transform us from within, what is that but to say that the divine nature is already dwelling within us, leading us forward until we are suffused with God's own presence and power?

Third, God has indeed called and chosen those who find themselves following Jesus. Peter urges his readers to 'confirm' this call and choice. He doesn't mean that they can make *God* more sure of it; rather, they can make themselves more sure. This leads directly to the fourth point: God has already set up his 'kingdom', his sovereign rule over earth as well as heaven. When the 'coming age' has fully and finally arrived, those who in the present time follow Jesus will find that they are welcomed into that ultimate heaven-and-earth reality.

All this is just the outer framework for this remarkable passage, but it is all the more important because it shows that whatever *we* do by way of obedience and allegiance to God and the gospel, it all takes place within the grace of God, by means of the promise of God, through the power of God and leading to the kingdom of God.

Gracious Lord, we thank you for giving us all we need to lead us to your kingdom.

21 The Word of Life
1 John 1:1–4

The secret at the heart of the early Christian movement was that the age to come had already been revealed. The future had burst into the present, even though the present time wasn't ready for it. The word for that future was Life, life as it was meant to be, life in its full, vibrant meaning. Life itself had come to life, had taken the form of a human being, coming into the present from God's future.

The very idea of God's new life becoming a person and stepping forward out of the future into the present is so enormous, so breathtaking, that a tone of wonder, of hushed awe and reverence, becomes appropriate. That is what we find in these opening verses. 'That which was from the beginning...' pause and think about that for a moment '...which we have heard, which we have seen with our eyes, which we have gazed at...' pause again: your own eyes? You didn't just glimpse it, you gazed at it? Yes, says John: we heard, saw and touched this from-the-beginning Life. We knew him. We were his friends.

And we still *are* his friends. Those who have seen this life and have been captured by its beauty and promise find that they have come to belong to a new kind of family, a 'fellowship' as we sometimes say. Indeed, John sees God's own life as already a shared fellowship: the fellowship between Father and Son. The earliest Christians quickly seized upon the words 'Father' and 'Son' as the simplest and clearest way of saying the unsayable at this point: that there is a common life, a deep sharing of inner reality, between God and Jesus.

But it doesn't stop there. This deep sharing of inner reality, this 'fellowship' between Father and Son, has been extended. It extended to all those who came to know, love and trust Jesus while he was alive. And now this sharing, this 'fellowship', is open to others too, to others who didn't have the chance to meet Jesus during his period of public display. This 'sharing' can be, and is being, extended to anyone and everyone who hears the announcement about Jesus. They can come into 'fellowship' with those who *did* see, hear and touch him. And they, in turn, are in 'fellowship' with the Father and the Son, with the two who are themselves the very bedrock and model for what 'fellowship', in this fullest sense, really means.

Lord, we thank you for revealing in Jesus what it means to share in the fellow-ship of the Father and the Son.

22 God's love
1 John 4:7–21

'Nobody has ever seen God. If we love one another, God abides in us and his love is completed in us.'

Stand that statement in parallel with the concluding verse in the Prologue to John's Gospel: 'Nobody has ever seen God. The only-begotten God, who is intimately close to the father – he has brought him to light' (John 1:18). The meaning of that statement is striking: we don't really know who 'God' is – until we look at Jesus. Now we see the meaning of our present statement in 1 John 4:12: people don't really know who 'God' is – until they see it revealed in the life of Christians. Until, that is, 'his love is completed in us'. What God launched decisively in Jesus, he wants to complete in and through us. Love is that important.

That's why, at the end of this passage, John comes back to the same point. If you say you love God, but don't love your brother or sister (he means a fellow member of the Christian community), you are quite simply telling lies. The same door that opens to let out your love to God is the door that opens to let out love to your neighbour. If you're not doing the latter, you're not doing the former. It's as simple – and as devastating – as that.

We may well find this daunting. Who can live up to it? But in verses 17 and 18 John moves into almost lyrical mode as he talks not about the fear that we should have of being found out, but of the boldness and confidence that we shall have on the day of judgement. He does not say, as we might expect, that we have this boldness and confidence because we look away from ourselves and simply trust in God's all-powerful love. No. He says that 'just as he is, so are we within this world'. What does he mean? He means, it seems, that if God revealed himself in the world by turning his love into flesh and blood, when we do the same we should realise that we are 'completing' God's love. What will be operating through us will be the true love of the true God.

When that happens, there is no need to fear any longer. Love that has been made complete leaves no room for fear. Once you learn to give yourself to others as God gave himself to us, there is nothing to be afraid of any more, just a completed circle of love.

Lord, help us to reflect and complete the love you have given us in Jesus.

23 Don't be deceived!

2 John 7–13

Today, 'love' is regularly supposed to mean 'tolerance'. You should never insist on anything, but always 'love' the other person who does things differently. You should never say that anything is actually wrong: that's 'unloving' to the person who is not only doing it but also claiming that it's the right thing to do.

But, as with protest movements, this passion for 'tolerance' only extends so far. Such a position is in fact extremely 'intolerant' of people who take a more definite stance – which includes the mainstream adherents of many traditional faiths. Underneath the nice language this view is just as 'arrogant', just as 'intolerant', as those it opposes. If anything, more so, because it effortlessly claims the high moral ground without taking seriously the claims of other world views.

We need to bear all this in mind when reading a passage like this, because our modern cult of 'tolerance' is bound to react sharply against what John has to say in this letter. Here, when he gets down to business, he is about as 'intolerant' as it's possible to be. Don't be taken in by the Deceiver, the Antimessiah! Don't be hoodwinked by those who follow him! Watch out for yourselves too; if you're not careful, all the work of building up the church might go to waste.

As in the longer letter, 1 John, the critical question here is about Jesus the Messiah actually coming 'in the flesh' (see 1 John 4:9). This was such a scandalous idea in the ancient world, as it has been in the modern world, that people will do anything to avoid having to believe it or live by it.

No doubt this challenge is too hard for some. And, yes, it is difficult to know where to draw the line today. It's quite unlikely that we will be faced with people teaching what John's opponents were teaching. There may well be other issues which, when we understand what's at stake, function as flashpoints. And, yes, it is always tempting to draw the line just a bit more tightly than one should, boosting one's own sense of rightness at the cost of someone who, in their own way, may be moving closer to the light. But just because that danger exists, that doesn't mean that these verses have nothing to say to us.

Lord, help us to understand when our love for others means confronting and combatting evil when we see it.

24 Hospitality for God's people
3 John 1–8

As in his previous letter, John is delighted to know that someone is 'walking in the truth'. We can take it that this involves not just correct doctrine and proper outward behaviour, but also love for God and for one's fellow believers which, for John, is the sign that the truth of the gospel has really been grasped.

It is this love that must then flow out into hospitality to fellow believers. This is even more important in the early church, where all that most people know about this new movement is that it is bizarre, crazy and socially undesirable. If that is the probable context, we can understand that travelling missionaries would be very much dependent on local groups of believers for board and lodging.

But Gaius, it seems, has gone out of his way to be generous. Those from John's church who visited Gaius have come back with a glowing report, and part of the reason for this letter seems to be to thank him. This is love in action, as John was urging in 1 John 3:18: not in word only, but in deed and in truth. In fact, 'love' for the early Christians is not primarily something you do with your heart and emotions. It is something you do with your whole life, not least your money and your home.

Truth, as always in John, is not simply a fact or a quality. It is an energy, the living and dynamic quality that transforms people, communities and ultimately the world. We are privileged to be caught up in the work of Truth, turning our misguided and often wicked world into a place where once again the creator God is honoured and glorified. And this collaboration in the work of the Truth comes right down to the practical details of a meal, a bed for the night and a good start in the morning.

That, indeed, is perhaps the main lesson of these verses. If I were to turn up unexpectedly on the doorstep of a close family member, I would expect them to welcome me. At the heart of the New Testament vision of the Church is that sense of *family*, of being brothers and sisters. I have sometimes been privileged to see this sense coming alive in local churches, even in our cynical Western world where the Church so often reflects the hyper-individualism of our culture. When it happens, it is a lovely thing. It's like being back with John, Gaius and the rest, trusting in the Truth.

Lord, help us to look for opportunities to show love and generous hospitality to others.

25 Rescued by God's power
Judah 17–25

After all the warnings and denunciations in the first part of this letter comes the word we need to hear: the word of strengthening, of promise, of holiness. Judah puts his ideas together in quick succession.

First, 'build yourselves up in your most holy faith'. This is the 'faith' for which he said, in verse 3, that they were to struggle hard. 'The faith', meaning both a body of teaching and a heart-level commitment to it, is the firm ground on which we stand, and we must learn to stand tall at that point.

Second, 'pray in the holy spirit'. Prayer remains a mystery, but it is the mystery to which we are totally committed as Christians. One of the most important works of the Spirit is to call out prayer from the depths of our hearts, even if it may be a prayer of lament on the one hand and a prayer for protection on the other. It is God's lament we share as we look in sorrow at human wickedness and arrogance invading the Church itself. It is God's protecting power and love we draw down as we pray by his Spirit in the midst of turmoil.

Third, 'keep yourselves in the love of God'. This sounds strange: surely it's God's job to keep us in his love? But, granted that, it is also our job not to wander away. The good shepherd doesn't keep us locked up. He wants us to learn to follow him because we love and trust him. Don't give him more work to do by getting yourself lost somewhere.

Fourth, wait patiently for the mercy leading to God's new age, which will come when Jesus is revealed. All Christian discipleship has this forward look. As we see moral and religious disarray all around us, we long and pray for that 'mercy', for ourselves and for the Church, which will come at the last and, please God, will also come, in a measure, in times of healing and renewal in advance of that day if it is delayed.

Judah then gathers the whole thing up in one of the all-time classic bursts of Christian praise, praise that wells up when the Holy Spirit has flooded the heart with the knowledge of God in Jesus. If the book of Revelation had not been written, this last verse would not have been a bad way to conclude the whole New Testament.

'To the one and only God, our Saviour through Jesus the Messiah our Lord, be glory, majesty, power and authority before all the ages, and now, and to all the ages to come.'

26 Jesus revealed
Revelation 1:9–20

For some people, Jesus is just a faraway figure of first-century fantasy. For others, including some of today's enthusiastic Christians, Jesus is the one with whom we can establish a personal relationship of loving intimacy. John would agree with the second of these, but he would warn against imagining that Jesus is therefore a cosy figure, one who merely makes us feel happy inside. To see Jesus as he is would drive us not to snuggle up to him, but to fall at his feet as though we were dead.

In particular, this vision of Jesus draws together the vision of two characters in one of the most famous biblical visions, that of Daniel 7. There, as the suffering of God's people reaches its height, 'the Ancient of Days' takes his seat in heaven, and 'one like a son of man' (in other words, a human figure, representing God's people and, in a measure, all the human race) is presented before him and enthroned alongside him. Now, in John's vision, these two pictures seem to have merged. When we are looking at Jesus, he is saying, we are looking straight through him at the Father himself.

Hold the picture in your mind, detail by detail. Imagine standing beside a huge waterfall, its noise like sustained thunder, and imagine that noise as a human voice, echoing round the hills and round your head. And then imagine his hand reaching out to touch you… Yes, fear is the natural reaction. But here, as so often, Jesus says, 'Don't be afraid.' It's all right. Yes, you are suffering, and your people are suffering. Yes, the times are strange and hard. But the seven churches – seven is the number of perfection, and the churches listed in verse 11 thus stand for all churches in the world, all places and all times – need to know that Jesus himself is standing in their midst, and that the 'angels' who represent and look after them are held in his right hand.

And the Jesus in question has, as his credentials, the fact that he 'was dead', and is 'alive forever and ever'. Like someone whispering to us that they know the secret way out of the dungeon where we have been imprisoned, he says, 'I've got the keys! The keys of death and Hades – I have them right here! There's nothing more you need worry about.'

To grasp all this requires faith. To live by it will take courage. But it is that faith and that courage that this book is written to evoke.

O Lord, we bow before you in reverence and awe.

27 In the throne room
Revelation 4:1–6

What do you think of when you read about 'a door in heaven'? For many years I imagined that John looked up to the sky and saw, far away, tiny but bright like a distant star, an open door, through which he was then invited to enter into the heavenly world. I now think of it quite differently. 'Heaven' and 'earth', as I have often said, are not, in biblical theology, separated by a great gulf, as they are in much popular imagination. 'Heaven', God's sphere of reality, is right here, close beside us, intersecting with our ordinary reality. It is not so much like a door opening high up in the sky. It is more like a door opening right in front of us where before we could only see this room, this field, this street. Suddenly, there is an opening leading into a different world – and an invitation to 'come up here' and see what's going on.

This is not, as some people have supposed, anything to do with God's people being snatched away to heaven to avoid awful events that are about to take place on earth. It is about a prophet being taken into God's throne room so that he can see behind the scenes and understand both what is going to take place and how it all fits together. What we are witnessing here, then, is not the final stage in God's purposes. This is not a vision of the ultimate 'heaven', seen as the final resting place of God's people. It is, rather, the admission of John into 'heaven' *as it is at the moment*.

I have spoken of this scene so far in terms of God's throne in heaven, and John's appearing before it like an Old Testament prophet. But the idea of a throne room, with someone sitting on the throne surrounded by senior counsellors, would instantly remind John's readers of a very different court: that of Caesar. There are hints of the power struggle (the kingdom of God against the kingdoms of the world) in the opening three chapters. Now, by strong implication, we are being invited to see that the powers of the world are simply parodies, cheap imitations, of the one Power who really and truly rules in heaven and on earth. As John's great vision unfolds, we will see how these human kingdoms have acquired their wicked, cruel power, and how God's radically different sort of power will win the victory over them.

Lord of heaven and earth, we thank you for revealing your power and your glory in Jesus, and for the victory he has already won.

28 The dragon is angry

Revelation 12:7–18

This passage presents us with a puzzle. A decisive victory has been won, but it seems that two quite different groups of people have been involved in winning it. There is 'war...in heaven'; Michael, the great archangel of Daniel 10, summons all his angels to fight against the dragon and his angels. If we are able to give this any meaning in our imaginations, it must be that the moral and political struggles of which we are aware, the battles between good and evil, between justice and injustice, which go on in this life, reflect a more primeval battle that has taken place in the spiritual sphere. Michael has won, and the dragon has lost. This loss means that he is thrown down to the earth, ejected from heaven altogether.

But wait a minute. The song of victory that follows this great event gives credit for the victory, not to Michael, but to God's people on earth. 'They conquered him', says the loud voice from heaven, 'by the blood of the lamb and by the word of their testimony, because they did not love their lives unto death.' So who defeated the dragon? Was it Michael or was it the martyrs?

Well, in a sense it was both. John is positioning his hearers on the map of the great cosmic drama. They are to know and celebrate the great victory that has already been won: 'the accuser' has no place any more in heaven, because the death of Jesus (who claimed in Luke 10:18 that he had seen the satan fall like lightning from heaven) has nullified the charges that the celestial Director of Prosecutions would otherwise bring. But he will do his best, in the time remaining, to attack the woman who has fled to the wilderness, even though, as in Exodus 19:4, God has given her eagle's wings so that she could fly away.

The decisive battle has been won, and the devil knows it; but his basic nature of 'accuser' is now driving him, more and more frantically, to attack, to accuse where it's justified and where it isn't, to drag down, to slander, to vilify, to deny the truth of what the creator God and his Son, the Lamb, have accomplished and are accomplishing. This is the ongoing battle in which all Christians are engaged, whether they know it or not.

We offer you our thanks and praise, O Lord, for mortally wounding the power of evil, and we pray for courage and resilience while the fight goes on.

29 The monster defeated
Revelation 19:11–21

As with all the imagery in Revelation, the military imagery of the present passage is symbolic language, pointing to a reality that lies beyond it. It would be as much a mistake to suppose (as some, sadly, have done) that this passage predicts, and legitimates in advance, an actual military battle between followers of Jesus and followers of other gods as it would be to suppose that the reality which corresponds to the monster that comes up from the sea is an actual physical creature with the heads, horns and so on described in chapter 12. The victory here is a victory *over* all pagan power, which means a *victory over violence itself.*

The symbolism is appropriate because it is taken directly from the passages that speak most powerfully and are most regularly referred to in the New Testament, of the triumph of the Messiah: Isaiah 11, where the Messiah will judge the nations with the sword of his mouth; Psalm 2, where he will rule them with a rod of iron; Isaiah 63, where he will tread the winepress of the wrath of God. As John's readers know well by now, the actual weapons Jesus uses to win the battle are his own blood, his loving self-sacrifice.

The ultimate justice that drives his victorious battle is the justice of God's love, which will not work with anything other than the Word, and will not be dressed in anything other than purity and holiness (note the 'shining, pure linen', matching the bride's dress in verse 8). Love will win the day, because in the person of Jesus it has trampled the grapes of wrath once and for all.

Many in our own day are still oppressed by monstrous forces and the local propaganda machines that promote their cause. Equally, many otherwise well-intentioned people are taken in by the lies and deceits that these systems continue to put out. Revelation 19 stands as a promise to the first and a warning to the second. Once you understand who Jesus was and is, and the significance of the victory he has won in his death, there can be no doubt about the final outcome. Monstrous regimes may come and go. Lies and deceits will continue to be spread. We must be on our guard. But the King of kings and Lord of lords will be victorious. In the meantime, there must be no compromise.

Lord, we thank you for securing the ultimate victory over the monstrous forces of evil that, for the present, continue to deceive and threaten to destroy our world.

30 New heaven, new earth
Revelation 21:1–5

'Look, I am making all things new.'

All things: here we have the new heaven, the new earth, the new Jerusalem and, not least, the new people, people who have woken up to find themselves beyond the reach of death, tears and pain. 'The first things have passed away.'

The word 'dwell' in verse 3 conjures up the idea of God 'dwelling' in the Temple in Jerusalem, revealing his glory in the midst of his people. This is what John's Gospel says about Jesus: the Word became flesh and lived, 'dwelt', pitched his tent, 'tabernacled' in our midst, and we gazed upon his glory. What God did in Jesus he is doing here on a cosmic scale. He is coming to live, for ever, in our midst, a healing, comforting, celebrating presence.

The newness of this vision is not a matter of God throwing away his first creation and, as it were, trying again, having a second shot to see if he can get it right this time. What we have in Revelation 21 and 22 is the *utter transformation* of heaven and earth by means of God abolishing, from within both heaven and earth, everything that has to do both with the as yet incomplete plan for creation and, more particularly, with the horrible, disgusting and tragic effects of human sin. The new world, in other words, will be like the present one in the sense of its being a world full of beauty, power, delight, tenderness and glory, but without all those features, particularly death, tears and everything that causes them, that make the present world what it is.

The centre of the picture, though, is not, or not yet, the new world itself, but the one true God who made the first creation and loved it so much that he sent the Lamb to redeem and renew it. Up to now, 'the one who sat on the throne' has been mentioned only obliquely. Now, at last, for the first time since the opening statement in Revelation 1:8, God himself addresses John, and through him addresses his churches and ours. This personal address by God himself is, it seems, part of the newness, just as God himself 'will wipe away every tear from their eyes', an act of utter gentleness and kindness to be performed not by some junior heavenly official but by God himself. Through this revelation of God's eternal character, most of us, as we contemplate this wonderful prospect, will feel a whole new world opening up before us.

Lord, we long for your new world, when heaven and earth will be joined for ever!

31 'I am coming soon!'
Revelation 22:8–21

Coming soon! That had been the hope of Israel for many a long year, before ever John saw Patmos, indeed before Jesus opened his eyes to the frosty light of a Bethlehem morning. Malachi, four hundred years earlier, had warned the bored and careless priests that 'the Lord whom you seek will suddenly come to his Temple' (Malachi 3:1). He will come! Ezekiel had described the glory of the Lord abandoning the Temple to its fate (Ezekiel 10:18–19; 11:22–3), but Ezekiel had also promised that the Lord would come back once the Temple had been properly restored (43:1–5). At no point in the next four hundred years, however, did anyone report the kind of vision Ezekiel had, or an experience that might correspond to the vision of God's glory in the Temple as in Exodus 40 or Isaiah 6. The Lord had not returned – but he would come. The hope of God's coming back was at the heart of the hope for the restored Temple, which was itself at the heart of the hope for a restored Israel. The hope within the hope within the hope. Surely, he is coming soon!

The early Christians all believed that this promise had been fulfilled – in Jesus. He had come to Jerusalem, to the Temple, as the solemn judge whose coming they had been promised. But they saw the promise fulfilled even more completely when Jesus was 'lifted up' on the cross and then raised from the dead. This was the real 'return of the Lord to Zion'.

And so they were able, without difficulty and from the very beginning, to translate the much older Jewish hope for Yahweh to come back into the sure and certain hope that Jesus would come back. The fusion of identity between Jesus and God, sharing the throne and both able to say, 'I am the Alpha and the Omega' (21:6; 22:13), gave this translation a firm base.

The letter – it always was a letter, as well as a prophecy and a revelation – ends as it should, with a closing greeting: 'The grace of the Lord Jesus be with you all.' But, however conventional, this greeting now carries the freight of the entire book. It is dense with a thousand images of 'grace', pregnant with the power of the word 'Lord' when spoken under the nose of Caesar, sparkling in the still-open invitation to 'you all', and above all delicious with the name, the name that is now exalted high over all, the name of the slaughtered Lamb, the name of the one we love and long to see.

Amen! Come, Lord Jesus!